SLESSOR:
BOMBER CHAMPION

SLESSOR:
BOMBER
CHAMPION

The Life of Marshal of the Royal Air Force
Sir John Slessor, GCB, DSO, MC

Vincent Orange

With a Foreword by
Phillip S. Meilinger

GRUB STREET · LONDON

Published by
Grub Street
4 Rainham Close
London
SW11 6SS

Copyright © 2006 Grub Street
Text copyright © 2006 Vincent Orange

British Library Cataloguing in Publication Data
Orange, Vincent
  Slessor: bomber champion: the life of Marshal of the RAF
  Sir John Slessor, GCB, DSO, MC
  1. Slessor, John Cotesworth, Sir, 1897- 2. Bomber pilots –
  Great Britain – Biography 3. Marshals – Great Britain –
  Biography
  I. Title
  940.5′44941

ISBN-10: 1-904943-57-8

Typeset by Pearl Graphics, Hemel Hempstead

Printed and bound by MPG Ltd, Bodmin, Cornwall

To Tim Cooper and Errol Martyn
who laid me some foundations.

'If it is well and cleverly written,
that is what I wished, if it is
undistinguished and mediocre, that
is all I could achieve.'

CONTENTS

FOREWORD

Jack Slessor is one of the great stars in the Royal Air Force (RAF) firmament. A leading air thinker, operational commander and staff officer between the wars, he led Coastal Command during World War II at the time it achieved victory over the German submarine. Following the war he became the Chief of Air Staff with the rank of Marshal of the Royal Air Force. Yet, as Vincent Orange shows us in this candid, revealing and masterfully written biography, Slessor also had numerous shortcomings of intellect and personality. It was a tribute to his abilities that he was able to overcome these difficulties and rise to the top of his service.

Slessor joined the Royal Flying Corps during the Great War and saw combat aged nineteen. It was a near run thing. Crippled by polio as a child, he was initially rejected for military service, but family connections saw him into uniform and pilot training. After winning his wings he saw action in Africa, England and France, receiving a serious leg wound in the process. Like many of his generation, the experience of the war shaped him profoundly and formed his thinking in ways not always useful. In England during the German bombing raids of 1915, he saw first-hand the near panic that gripped a populace never before exposed to air attack. From this brief encounter he deduced that civilian morale was fragile. If defence against air attack was impossible – and few then thought otherwise – then a vigorous air attack on a nation's "vital centres" would have a devastating effect on an enemy's morale and thus its war-making capability.

Hugh Trenchard, the first head of the RAF and its commander for the decade following the war, believed passionately in the war-winning potential of strategic bombing and its psychological impact. Slessor, who served on Trenchard's staff in the 1920s and admired his superior 'inordinately,' tripped down this same dangerous path. Slessor was a bomber advocate, as the book's subtitle proclaims. This in itself was no reason for condemnation. Rather, Slessor's error – shared by many others – was to elevate a theory of war to doctrine without the proper foundation having first been laid. Flawed doctrine became dogma, and the RAF suffered grievously as a result when the test of war arrived.

Sound military doctrine must be based on three pillars: history, theory and technology. A military planner must look to history to see what has worked and what has not worked – there are certain principles that tend to endure over time. Yet, looking backwards is not enough. A general who looks only to the past will be condemned to fighting the last war. And so, theory must also be used – a planner must look ahead, especially to the technological environment that has become so crucial in modern war – and project what future conflict will look like and how new weapons will transform it. Again, however, there is a danger here. A planner who looks forward too much – who ignores the past – is in danger of building a foundation on quicksand. For airmen, the danger was doubly precarious. Unlike warfare on land and sea that had existed for millennia, air warfare was barely in its infancy; there was little past upon which to base a doctrine of air power employment. Worse, the technology component was similarly precarious because aviation was in its infancy. It *seemed* to hold great promise; but it was just that, promise. For airmen, the result was an intriguing and intellectually pleasing view of war that was imagined rather than real, based on faith rather than on fact and on technologies not yet invented. The doctrine of air power rested uneasily on the single pillar of theory.

Slessor was caught up in this contentious atmosphere. Yet, as Orange points out, he had a brilliant and incisive mind, and although it was untrained (he never attended college) this allowed him to adopt and adapt more quickly than most of his contemporaries to the demands of modern war. In 1931 he was posted to the army's staff college at Camberley where he taught army-air cooperation. Forced to focus on a type of air power other than that of strategic bombing, his intellect allowed him to fashion a doctrine of tactical air employment that was far in advance of anything written in English prior to World War II. When he published his Camberley lectures in 1936 under the title, *Air Power and Armies*, the result was a masterpiece.

After Camberley, Slessor was sent to India where he became heavily engaged in using air power to pacify rebellious natives. In one sense, the concept of air policing was a great success – huge tracts of sparsely populated frontier were controlled by a relatively small and cheap use of air power. The mission of air policing went a great distance towards saving the RAF as a separate service between the wars when the other services, as well as the budget cutters, would have killed the infant air force quickly had they been given the chance. On the other hand, the success of air policing reinforced Slessor's tendency to exaggerate the psychological effects of air attack. Because bands of illiterate natives largely devoid of industrial understanding were awed and cowed by air attack occurring out of the blue, he assumed that civilians everywhere would be similarly shocked. In short, it appeared that the theories of strategic bombing were proven in practice. Events would soon show otherwise.

In 1937 Jack Slessor returned to the Air Staff to work as a planner. Although Trenchard was long retired, his strategic bombing legacy lived on, and Slessor wanted mightily to foster such ideas. But once again his own intelligence forced him to confront reality. He soon realized that the RAF was incapable of carrying out the task of strategic bombing that it claimed was its primary mission. The RAF's bombers were too few, too small, and too inaccurate, and their crews were too ill-trained. It was a bitter pill to swallow after more than a decade of faith. The reality of war against a tenacious foe showed all too quickly that prewar doctrine had glaring deficiencies. (I should also note that it was one of the paradoxes of air power development that the theorists who prophesied unbridled advances in aviation technology failed to anticipate radar – technology that would so call into question their entire corpus of theory.)

While in Whitehall Slessor also recognized the essential need for intelligence on an enemy's economy. If airmen posited that bombing would disrupt or collapse an enemy's economic infrastructure, then they would require detailed intelligence on precisely how that economy worked, and how it could be made to *not* work. Slessor played a role in building the intelligence apparatus essential to modern air warfare.

In the summer or 1941 he was named commander of a bomb group. This seemed an appropriate assignment – where else should a devoted bomber advocate go? But in truth, the posting was unusual. Slessor actually had had very little operational experience with modern aircraft since the Great War. To his credit, he learned quickly and began to display the quick grasp of both small details and broad strategy that marked him apart. It was therefore a bit inexplicable that after less than a year in the post he was given orders for a fighter command! As Orange notes a bit dryly, this was one of the RAF's more self-defeating tendencies – to misuse so grossly the expertise of its personnel. There was no logical reason why Slessor should have gone to a bomber command. There was even less to then move him to fighters just as he was beginning to learn his job. Cooler heads prevailed, and after a brief stop back in Whitehall Jack was instead directed to take over Coastal Command. Of course, Slessor knew next to nothing about this mission either. Yet, this was perhaps Slessor's finest hour.

Once again he was forced to learn his business quickly. He did so, while also becoming a skilled political in-fighter in an arena teeming with inter-service and inter-allied rivalries. Coastal Command had been an unwanted stepchild between the wars. The Royal Navy, and for that matter the US Navy, assumed away the problem of the submariner – despite the fact that German U-boats had nearly brought Britain to its knees in 1917. At the same time the RAF – and the US Army Air Forces – had been reluctant to take on the mission of air control of the sea lanes. When war demonstrated the seriousness of such omissions, the services seemed more intent on bickering amongst themselves than about solving the problems at hand. Although the eventual solution to the submarine crisis was not Slessor's alone, he was adept at implementing a multi-pronged plan that led to success. Long-range aircraft equipped with special radar and weapons closed the mid-Atlantic gap where the U-boats had long enjoyed a sanctuary. In the Bay of Biscay inspired tactics combined with more and better aircraft similarly turned the tide – although as was so often the case during the war, German blunders also played a part in Allied success. In the event, Coastal Command's victory over the U-boats in 1943 was of enormous importance. The American build-up for Overlord could have been severely disrupted had the submarine menace not been effectively countered.

From this success Slessor moved on to become the deputy commander of the Mediterranean Allied Air Forces, another great challenge for which he was seemingly ill-prepared. He excelled there as well. When the war ended, Slessor served as the RAF's personnel chief and then Commandant of the Imperial Defence College before being selected to succeed Arthur Tedder as CAS. It was the pinnacle of his career. During the next three years Slessor saw the outbreak of the Korean War, the expansion of NATO, the hardening of the Cold War and deployment of American atomic bombers to Britain, and the move to a jet-propelled force structure. Upon his retirement in December 1952, Slessor's beloved RAF was in a firm position. Returning to mufti after 35 years, Slessor took a hand at business while also writing about the nuclear balance of terror that dominated the Cold War.

Interlaced with all of these tales of competence and success, Orange also shows the more tendentious and truculent sides of his subject. Jack Slessor was often outspoken about those he met or worked with – superiors, subordinates and colleagues alike. His reputation for making snap judgements on people – denigrating their intelligence, integrity and capabilities – led to charges that he was a snob and back-biter. He picked needless fights with those he should have left alone, men he would have to work with in war. Of these, the most important was Arthur Tedder, an even more illustrious airman who should have been one of Slessor's closest colleagues. (Both men were intelligent, capable and driven. They tended to agree in principle on most major issues, although both would have been loath to admit it.) Slessor was also verbose offering unsolicited advice to all and sundry, at great and tedious length on almost any subject. He was at times embarrassingly ambitious and was altogether too willing to play up to superiors and politicians who he thought might aid his career. As he grew older some of these traits grew more pronounced, and Slessor was wont to pontificate on subjects about which he knew very little.

And yet, despite personality flaws that should have doomed him to obscurity, Slessor's innate intelligence, energy, industriousness and common sense approach to problem-solving repeatedly emerged to counterbalance his weaknesses. There were any number of RAF commanders with more impressive operational credentials, political connections, family backgrounds, and interpersonal skills, but it was

Slessor who rose to the position of CAS.

Like many great men, Jack Slessor was after all a human being with peccadilloes and shortcomings. But these must not obscure the reality. Slessor was a proven air leader in peace and war. In the two decades following the Armistice he had a powerful influence – even if not necessarily by design – on the development of tactical air operations that would prove remarkably prescient. He understood strategic bombing and long-range planning. Although he swallowed too readily the nostrums bandied about between the wars about the physical and psychological effects of bombing, he revised his views in the furnace of war. His memos and studies written on the eve of World War II were marked by bluntness, trenchant logic, acerbic wit, and an increasing reality of what the RAF could expect in the coming battle. When given command, he learned quickly and proved an unusually flexible and resourceful leader. As CAS he shepherded his service through some particularly difficult and dangerous years when the Russian bear was bellowing loudly and the West was not yet sure how much of it was bluff.

Jack Slessor was a great airman and Vincent Orange has done him justice.

Phillip S. Meilinger
Potomac Falls, Virginia

PROLOGUE

BOMBER PILOT, MAY 1916

Jack Slessor, later to earn fame on both sides of the Atlantic as an air power champion and in particular a bomber champion, was not yet 19 when he enjoyed his first experience as a bomber pilot. He later recalled that 'it was a thrill to think that we were to fly the first aeroplanes ever to appear somewhere in the middle of darkest Africa, a place called Darfur that none of us had ever heard of.' A thrill also to take part in a Victorian-style campaign, about which he had read so avidly as a boy: 'a nice old-fashioned little force called the Western Frontier Force', of mounted infantry, mountain guns, a machine-gun battery, five camel companies, Sudanese, Arab and Egyptian infantry – plus something new: 'iron horses' (as the enemy commander called them), two BE 2c two-seater biplanes of 17 Squadron, Royal Flying Corps.

Darfur was a vast Dervish-ruled desert region south-west of Khartoum. Its ruler, Sultan Ali Dinar, had repudiated his allegiance to the British authorities in Khartoum and proclaimed a holy war against them on behalf of Germany's ally, the Sultan of Turkey. Young Slessor, flying one of the biplanes, armed with four 20 pound bombs and a machine-gun, helped to overthrow Ali in April and May 1916. The bombs, he recalled, 'were very good little man-killing bombs, with instantaneous fuses and an excellent shattering effect.' The targets were rebels: some on horseback, some marching along, others sheltering in flimsy huts. On May 23rd, Slessor spotted Ali himself, mounted on a splendid white camel and carrying a large banner. Although one of his bombs killed the camel, Ali escaped but El Fasher, his capital, was captured and Darfur was then absorbed into the Anglo-Egyptian Sudan and officially designated a pacified province. Ali was hunted down by British troops who eventually cornered the fugitive Sultan and shot him dead on November 6th.

Meanwhile, on May 27th, only four days after Slessor killed the camel, he was commended, though not named, in the House of Commons by Sir Reginald Brade, Secretary of the War Office, who said, 'before and during the action, a valuable air reconnaissance was carried out by an officer of the Royal Flying Corps, who succeeded by means of bombs and machine-gun fire in forcing first a large body of hostile cavalry and then a body of some 2,000 infantry to retire in disorder.'

11

W. T. Massey, writing to the *Daily Telegraph* in July, repeated in *The Times* in August, thought that 'the brilliant work of a flight of the Royal Flying Corps during the operations in Darfur will rank as one of the finest efforts of our army airmen in the war.' Unlike Brade, Massey named Slessor for his deeds on May 23rd: after he was wounded, 'he had to steer with his hand instead of his foot on his way back to Hilla, his difficulties being greatly increased by a storm which broke suddenly. He brought the first news of the victory, and it was transmitted to the Sirdar from the aerodrome.' General Sir Reginald Wingate's account of the campaign made two favourable references to Slessor. One praised his bombing 'in the course of a gallant and successful flight.' The other noted that he was 'slightly wounded' while doing so, but nevertheless brought the first news of Ali Dinar's defeat to headquarters.

Slessor enjoyed the campaign hugely, even though he suffered a bullet wound in one of his thighs. 'I saw large numbers of Dervish cavalry going like smoke away from our guns, scattered all over the place', he wrote to his mother. 'I came down and strafed them with a machine-gun and they were a jolly fine sight really, galloping like mad and shooting up at me with a sort of jezails [a long antique rifle] as they galloped.' More than a thousand Dervishes perished, but Slessor was one of only 24 British casualties, killed or wounded. He was consoled by taking possession of the bullet that struck him, keeping it as a conversation piece for the rest of his life. He also enjoyed permission to wear a 'wound stripe' on the sleeve of his khaki tunic: a thin strip of gold braid, he wrote later, 'that was one of the sartorial peculiarities of the 1914-18 war.'

Meanwhile, his mother learned that her son 'had the best little scrap I have ever seen just before I was hit.' He flew over Ali's warriors, 'all bunched together like a footy crowd, blazing away at me. Of course, you couldn't miss them. I got three bombs smack in amongst them, with pretty good effect. They all scattered like rabbits all over the place.' The airmen had been ordered to drop notices calling on armed enemies to surrender and warning peaceable persons to keep away. They were careful to do this on several occasions before opening fire. The use of air power to warn and control opponents of British rule would become an important part of Slessor's thinking, not only between the world wars, but even in the nuclear age with the hope of deterring potential enemies of the NATO allies.

He was, however, far from well at the end of his first bomber sortie. Not surprising really, because a 'native medical officer' had dug the bullet out 'with a razor and a pair of scissors, no chloroform or anything.' But being young, fit and lucky, he survived and was soon well enough to be sent to Khartoum and shipped to Southampton as a cot case. He landed there on July 1st 1916, just in time to hear that a massive offensive had begun on the Somme.

CHAPTER 1

EARLY DAYS

Oxford

John Cotesworth Slessor was born on June 3rd 1897 in Ranikhet, India: a military base in the Himalayan foothills, about 160 miles north-east of Delhi. Jack, as he was usually known, was the eldest of three sons and a daughter of Major Arthur Kerr Slessor (Sherwood Foresters) and his wife, Adelaide Constance Cotesworth[1]. The family was full of soldiers, sailors, clerics and diplomats with strong Indian connections. A long tradition of service to church and state shaped Jack's whole life. His grandfather, the Reverend John Henry Slessor, formerly a fellow of University College, Oxford, and rector for 45 years of Headbourne Worthy, near Winchester, had been born in 1821, only six years after the battle of Waterloo, in which *his* father (Major-General John Slessor, who died in 1850) commanded a battalion. When the reverend died it was said that his passing severed a link 'with a bygone generation and with manners and customs fast fading into the dim past.' He was a 'ripe scholar, in politics a determined Tory, in his younger days a keen sportsman and athlete, a man of cultivated artistic tastes, zealous for his church.' If the last word were replaced by 'the Royal Air Force', these words apply precisely to Jack.

Major Slessor retired from the army in 1903 and settled his branch of the family in Oxford, where he had taken a second class degree in Classical Moderations at Christ Church in 1886 and a third in 'Greats' the following year. He was employed as steward by his old college for the next 25 years, responsible for catering, accommodation and porterage; akin to the manager of a grand hotel. His appointment reflected a tendency in public schools and colleges to appoint military men, in the hope of disciplining large staffs and rooting out such sins as stealing produce and taking bribes from local tradesmen. At the same time, he had to keep the fellows and young gentlemen happy, men who were inclined to complain long, loud and eloquently whenever dinner or the wines were less than perfect. He had a sharp temper, was on top of his job, and stood no nonsense from anyone.

---

[1] Arthur (1863-1931) married Adelaide (1869-1925) on June 10th 1896. After Adelaide's death, he married Susan Margaret Cotesworth (1878-1948) on December 14th 1927.

According to Jack, the Major was 'a good classical scholar, in addition to being a good soldier, an excellent gardener and a sound judge of vintage port.' When the lease fell in of the buildings which then occupied the site on St. Aldate's owned by Christ Church, it was the Major's own idea to clear the site and keep it permanently free from further obstruction. 'The result', recorded *The Times* in a warm obituary, 'has fully justified his foresight and tenacity, though even he, as were certainly his critics, must have been surprised at the full beauty of the aspect revealed by the clearance. Coming into Oxford over Folly Bridge, the visitor now has on his right a clear view of the Meadows across an agreeable walled garden and a collonnade; nearer at hand is a fine memorial gateway; and confronting him is the unbroken southern face of Christ Church, one of the best examples of Tudor architecture in the country.' A memorial service in his honour at Christ Church Cathedral was attended by an impressive gathering of eminent Oxford persons.

According to cousin Priscilla, Jack was 'an enchanting, fiendish little boy with curly hair and round blue eyes, a nanny's terror.' At three, he caught a bad cold. 'I can't do nothing with him', his nanny complained a few days later, 'he's naughtier than ever. Every time I stand him up to dress him, he just falls down.' He had in fact contracted poliomyelitis, which caused him to limp for the rest of his life.

Educated first at the Dragon School, Oxford, and then at a public school – Haileybury, near Hertford, north of London – Jack was 'an idle boy', in his own opinion, 'with a capacity for making friends and getting a good deal out of life, but with a marked distaste for hard work.' He had an uncommon talent for drawing and learned to love cricket, rugby and such rural pleasures as hunting, shooting, fishing, polo, camping and messing about in boats, although 'two gammy legs' (the result of polio as a child) meant 'I could not spare a hand for a spear' in order to enjoy pig-sticking in India, nor could he manage all the strokes needed in polo. He had the happiest memories of being taken out 'to listen to the nightjar on the heath or watch snipe and reed-warblers on the Lea Marshes.'[2]

The Slessors lived in Iffley Road, Oxford, and their garden ran down to the Christ Church cricket ground. 'We looked out onto an expanse of smooth turf and beyond to the trees of Christ Church Meadows – hardly another building in sight.' One summer afternoon, to mark a visit by Australian cricketers, Jack's parents hosted a garden party: 'the ladies with tight waists in long sweeping dresses and floppy picture hats and the men in flannels with straw boaters or panamas.'

Young Jack had vivid memories of the Oxford of his childhood. He recalled that 'a Mr Morris kept a little bicycle shop somewhere near Magdalen... Horse trams still clanked down the High and hansom cabs waited for fares in St Aldate's, their horses wore straw hats in high summer

---

[2] Recollections in Haileybury Archives, 1968. I am grateful to the Archivist, Victoria Sheppard, for my Haileybury references.

and tossed their nose-bags, scattering grain on the cobbles of the cab-stand to the delight of the Oxford sparrows... Winter was fun. There was skating on the flooded meadows downstream of the Barges... members of the Bullingdon [an exclusive dining and sporting club] in mud-splashed pink coats cracking hunting whips in Tom Quad to the disgust of Mr Sidney Owen [an eminent Classical don]; and everywhere young men in shorts and sweaters with great scarfs round their necks walked or bicycled between their colleges and the innumerable playing fields.' Sadly and unlike his father, Slessor would never be among their number. Quite apart from missing the social delights of student life at Oxford, his active mind and ready pen would have benefitted greatly from the discipline of writing numerous essays for dons who (presumably) placed a higher value on chronology and concise argument than Jack ever did.

Haileybury

The child, they say, is father to the man, so we see already four aspects of Slessor's personality that would never change. Firstly, he was devoted to a vast, influential network of family and friends, a network he kept in good repair. Secondly, that network inspired in him a lasting devotion to imperial service, particularly in British India. Thirdly, he admired the masters and boys – past, present, future – of public schools, his own Haileybury above all. Such schools, he believed, produced leaders and fostered a 'selective and controlled nepotism' of which he had good reason to approve. And fourthly, he loved outdoor activities despite his physical handicap, which he stubbornly ignored until near the end of his life.

While camping with a friend near the Thames at Lechlade in Gloucestershire on August 6th 1914, Slessor learned that Great Britain was at war with Imperial Germany: 'I suppose we must have seen something in the papers some weeks before about some unknown potentate who had been murdered at some place of which we had never heard; but the idea of war had never entered our heads... I was foolishly, though perhaps naturally, elated. Born with the army in India of a family with a tradition of military and naval service, educated at a school that had started as the nursery of the men who made British India, I had always taken it for granted – in an age when Kipling was writing *Recessional* and Elgar his *Land of Hope and Glory* – that wider still and wider would our bounds be set. As for war, well, that was something that did happen sometimes; was not my father away fighting a war on the North-West Frontier when I was a baby?' And there was a rousing leaving song to help Jack on his way:

> 'I'm one of the fellows that's leaving –
> I can't stay at school any more;
> But I've hardly a moment for grieving,
> For there's work to be done for the corps.

I pity the chaps – they can't help it perhaps –
Who've never yet shouldered a gun;
It gives you a taste of things to be faced
When schooldays are over and done.'[3]

Like many other boys of his generation, Slessor had a 'boon companion' who was killed during the Great War. Of the 46 boys in his house at Haileybury in 1913, 20 were dead within five years – he knew all their names – but that terrible statistic is easily matched in schools throughout Britain (and elsewhere in Europe). Nowhere else in the countless words Slessor has left us does he write with anything approaching the same passion or clarity as when he describes his friendship with Revere Osler – so named in honour of his direct ancestor, Paul Revere, but always known as Tom or Tommy.

As we know from all the books published about the world wars of the 20th century, two generations of young men lost friends 50 years before their due time, friends who would never grow merely ordinary, let alone old, fat and boring. 'I often think it strange', Slessor wrote in 1968 (when he was 71), 'that the one above all to whose loss I have never been able to reconcile myself is the boy who was my boon companion in the years before the Kaiser's War. I still have only to close my eyes to see him and hear his voice as clearly as if he was in the room with me, though he has been gone these 50 years, killed as a gunner subaltern in the Ypres Salient.'[4] So many boys of Slessor's generation would grow old with a similar ache in the heart, a memory frozen and unfading for an intensity of emotion rarely matched in later life.

---

[3] Composed by G.H. Sunderland Lewis, a master at the school.
[4] Tommy's father, Sir William Osler, a Canadian, was Regius Professor of Medicine at Oxford; his mother American. He was their only child and neither long survived him.

CHAPTER 2

THE GREAT WAR

Zeppelin hunter

One day in May 1915, not yet 18 years old, Jack Slessor visited a room in the War Office, Whitehall, London, seeking a commission in the Royal Flying Corps. His relatives and family friends had unsuccessfully heaved on strings for him and he had himself failed dismally to grasp the workings of a petrol engine in Mr Morris's new garage in Longwall. Undaunted, however, he persisted and was now about to be 'squeezed in through the back door', despite a medical report declaring him permanently unfit – because of his lameness – for any form of military service. One of the officers in the room, Lieutenant-Colonel Willie Warner, happened to be a brother officer of Slessor's uncle. Of this, Slessor later remarked, 'Perhaps that is why ever since I have been convinced that judicious and controlled nepotism is the best method of selection of officers.'

Some five months later, in October 1915, having learned to fly – 'the most glorious sensation I know'[5] – he was a proud young pilot 'sitting at the end of a telephone beside my BE 2c in a canvas hangar on a stubble field at Sutton's Farm [Romford, Essex, later to be Hornchurch, one of the RAF's most famous fighter stations], while a couple of Zeppelins bumbled through the murky darkness overhead.' Warner rang Slessor from the same room where nepotism had triumphed, ordering him to take off and look for those Zeppelins. 'It was pitch black and there was a fog like a blanket', he later wrote to his mother. 'At 9.30 pm, the fog was a bit clearer and I decided to go up. I was carrying four eight-pound powder bombs in a rack under the machine with a patent releasing gear, and six inflammable bombs... I had not been up ten minutes and was about 3,000 feet high, still climbing, when I saw a Zep over Thamesworth somewhere, with the searchlights on him. He looked like the underside of a salmon and I judged he was about 8-9,000 feet up. I climbed up as fast as I could, but lost him after about three minutes and searchlights got off him and I never saw him again.'

---

[5] He was awarded his Aviator's Certificate, No. 1447, by the Royal Aeronautical Club on July 6th 1915.

This was 'the most ambitious raid yet launched against London, and the costliest in casualties': five Zeppelins took part and between them killed 71 Londoners and injured a further 128. The Zeppelin spotted by Slessor was L.15, commanded by *Kapitänleutnant* Joachim Breithaupt, who 'achieved the most competent performance of the night.' He reached central London at 9.25 pm, dropped 30 bombs between the Strand and Limehouse, and flew safely home. But five months later, during another raid on March 31st 1916, L.15 was damaged by ground fire, forced to ditch off Margate, and the crew saved from drowning by a British destroyer. In November, no fewer than 353 gunners were each awarded a gold medal for their joint effort in bringing down the first Zeppelin destroyed over the British Isles.

Having lost his 'salmon' and with it the prospect of his own gold medal and certainly a decoration, Slessor cruised about until 11 pm looking for another target, when he was signalled to land after 90 freezing minutes, mostly at 10,000 feet. He found the mist thicker than ever when he got down to a hundred feet, and all he could see of the flares was an orange haze and the searchlight dazzled him, 'so I landed sort of sideways' and broke the undercarriage. Glad to be alive and undamaged, he ended a letter to his mother on a chirpy note: 'Did you see in the paper this morning that only one aeroplane saw a Zep, but could not overhaul it? Well, that only one was me. Wow! Wow!' Some 40 years later, no longer chirpy, he harshly described his brave and determined effort as 'a very amateur and wholly ineffectual encounter.' True enough, but given his inexperience as a pilot in broad daylight, let alone in a London fog at night, flying a poorly-designed aircraft equipped with inadequate weapons, not even Biggles could have done any better.

On the evening after his 'sideways' landing, Slessor was driven from Farnborough through the East End of London, where several bombs had fallen, in a lorry carrying spares to repair the damage to his aircraft. 'I and my little party were mobbed', he wrote in 1966, 'and had to get a policeman to stand on each running board of the tender to get us through a crowd which it is no exaggeration to describe as panic-stricken.' If so, the crowd had good reason: nearly two hundred Londoners were killed or injured that night; the defences – ground and air – achieved precisely nothing; and Londoners could expect suffering and destruction of property on a similar or greater scale from that night on. In 1939 he recalled Hastings Ismay (Assistant Secretary, Committee of Imperial Defence) saying to him: 'You know, Jack, I really shudder to think of the effect on our easy-going, peaceable people of being subjected to this sort of thing.' Slessor agreed. This 'boyhood experience', as he described it, helped to shape his subsequent enthusiasm for the bomber as a decisive weapon in war.

The Western Front

A few weeks later, young Jack was sent to Egypt and on to Darfur where he was wounded and shipped home. He made a good recovery during July 1916 and was then employed at Northolt, in north-west London, as an instructor. In January 1917 he was awarded a Military Cross for his deeds in Darfur and appointed a Flight Commander in 58 Squadron, forming at Cramlington in Northumberland, but broken up to allow reinforcement of squadrons currently being hammered in France. He recalled 'a riotous farewell guest-night, in which I was impelled backwards through a window by Commander Max Horton from the submarine depot at Blyth.' Horton became head of Western Approaches when Slessor was head of Coastal Command in the next war: 'one of the great figures in naval history, he was enormously powerful and a terrific chap in a guest-night rag in his younger days.' Was there something of Shakespeare's Justice Shallow in Slessor when he reached middle age and wrote his memoirs? He usually sees those acquaintances who later became famous – at least in military circles – as larger-than-life characters, and perhaps places himself closer to them than he actually was.

Lieutenant Slessor joined 5 Squadron at Acq (near Arras) on the First Army front as a Flight Commander in May 1917. During that time, he flew a two-seater biplane: the RE 8, popularly known as the 'Harry Tate', in honour of a famous comedian of the day. 'This is a splendid machine', wrote Major John Chamier, a staff officer with the Third (Army) Wing, early in 1917, but it 'gives very little indication of losing its speed until it suddenly shows an uncontrollable tendency to dive which cannot be corrected in time if you are near the ground.' Not really 'splendid', in that case, one would have thought. The RE 8 'was a bad and dangerous aeroplane', according to a more realistic assessment by Jack Bruce, an excellent historian. Even the official historians (Sir Walter Raleigh and Mr H. A. Jones, who wrote under the sharp eye of Sir Hugh Trenchard – head of the RAF in the 1920s – and were therefore rarely critical of men or machines) recorded that 'The evil reputation of the RE 8 spread throughout the Royal Flying Corps', before hastily claiming that it was greatly improved during 1917.

Hundreds remained in service until the Armistice, all sitting ducks for German fighters and only a little less vulnerable to ground fire. Despite the alleged improvements, 'the RE 8 had to soldier doggedly on, its inadequacies compensated by the determination and gallantry of the men who flew it.' The authorities should never have used this machine, recalled one of its survivors, Oliver Stewart. 'It was not a good flying machine, and its performance was meagre'; in combat, to put it mildly, the RE 8 'was not at its best.' Charles Smart, a pilot in 5 Squadron, thought it 'much too heavy and cumbersome, more like flying a steam roller than an aeroplane. Still, they will do 105 mph, which is quite an advantage over the old BE 2e.' Another member of the squadron with mixed feelings about the 'Harry Tate' was Arthur Sanders, a fellow Old

Haileyburian, who became an Air Chief Marshal. He achieved that very high rank even though his flying career ended in May 1917 when he was so badly wounded during a patrol under Slessor's command that he lost his right arm – but he and Harry got each other home.

The deficiencies of the RE 8 gradually became clear to Slessor, though offset by a young man's delight in battle. For example, in a letter to his mother written on June 5th 1917, he exulted over a recent attack – observed from the cockpit at what he hoped was a safe distance – mounted *against* the British front. 'I think it was the most wonderful sight I ever saw. It started quite late in the evening, just before sunset... And then suddenly, at the exact pre-arranged second, there was a sound like one terrific roll of huge drums, and the barrage started. It really was the most amazing sight, all our side of the line, the dusty khaki-brown country, shell-holed and all ploughed up ... It looked as though the whole country was blowing up... the finest fireworks display I ever saw.'

He ended by telling her about the difference between bombs and shells. 'A bomb makes a most objectionable row coming down, and the worst of it is, unlike a shell, you never can tell where it is coming. You think it is coming right on your head, and then it really falls half a mile away, whereas a shell you can always tell more less whether it is coming direct for you or not.' These are words no mother can have wanted to read, but it may be she preferred to know the worst that might happen to her beloved son, rather than have him pretend he was in no danger. Of those pilots and observers who flew with 5 Squadron during the Great War, 46 were killed and an unknown number wounded in combat or injured while training.

A month later, on July 4th, he told her about 'rather a narrow escape' he had while on patrol. 'We were about 500 yards this side of the line and the Hun was shelling us with field guns, as he does sometimes when one gets too low for Archie.' Suddenly, 'there was a devil of a crash and a flash and the rudder bar gave my foot a sound whack... my first thought was of fire, and the motto is get as low as possible as quickly as possible... Then I looked round and saw the tail plane wobbling about in rather a sickening way, and the bottom of the rudder missing and great gashes in the tail.' A shell had hit the tail skid, but the control wires held and though the rudder jammed, it did so centrally. 'I took a day off after that', he ended, and went with friends into Arras, where we ate all day: 'Top hole strawgogs and rasgogs and omelettes and soles and all sorts of things.' Such stark contrasts were typical of the airman's life: mortal fear one day, blissful ease the next.

Corps squadrons worked closely with ground forces, identifying targets for friendly artillery and attacking enemy artillery. They also fired into trenches and reported the progress, if any, of advancing infantry and tried to cover the retreat of those who survived. Every enemy battery, Slessor later wrote, 'was, so to speak, an old friend, and any new construction, changed position, or fresh track was instantly obvious. Every gun-pit and yard of trench was shown exactly on the maps which were made from and kept up-to-date by the air photography that was also the job of the corps squadrons.' Every enemy battery had a code number, and every stretch of trench a name. The fall of shells was reported by clock code, using Morse, air-to-ground only: gunners could only communicate with airmen by laying out strips of white cloth in an agreed pattern.

Both partners became expert. Slessor prided himself on being able to range two or even three batteries on different targets at the same time. But it did require him to keep his eyes on the ground and rely on his observer to watch the sky – although both men knew how vulnerable they were to any attacker, even if they saw him coming. He and his observer, 2nd Lieutenant Frank Tymms, earned a rare official mention on June 21st when they 'carried out a successful shoot in continuous rain: the following morning these officers took some excellent photographs 4,000 yards behind the enemy's lines and ranged three of our batteries on to three hostile batteries.' On moonlit nights, he took part in 'rather aimless bombing and machine-gunning of billeting zones, approach roads, aerodromes and so on in the enemy back areas.' As for bad weather, Slessor had no recollection of ever seeing a 'met. bloke' anywhere near 5 Squadron, and he depended on such old saws as 'there was a nice red sunset this evening' or 'the swallows are flying nice and high' – both of which, he wryly observed, proved no more unreliable than the allegedly expert forecasts of peacetime. Whenever the weather turned so nasty during a flight that even the gulls were walking, one simply got soaked, came home, and hoped one's photographs were not dud – which they usually were.

Anti-aircraft fire, in Slessor's experience, was 'unpleasant but not very lethal', unless one flew straight and level, at a constant speed and height. He was never shot down – just as well, for 'we had no parachutes in aeroplanes in 1917, so we could not get out and walk if we got into trouble.' He often saw shells in the air on a clear day – friendly and enemy, going and coming – and felt the bump as they passed. He saw one RE 8 blasted apart by a direct hit and was himself twice hit, once by a friendly howitzer shell: 'fortunately not with an instantaneous fuse, for it tore an enormous hole in my starboard upper wing and went on its way without exploding... but the old RE 8 was pretty robust, as wood and canvas aircraft went', and got him home. He eagerly shared his thoughts on combat with readers of his school magazine. 'The English [sic: all his life he found it difficult to remember that not all inhabitants of the British Isles were English] are always ready to take risks which ought never to be taken', he wrote. He believed that their eyesight, 'trained in all sorts of school games, is quicker than the Boche's' and was certain that 'our flying men are the best in the business.'

The country anywhere near the front 'looked from the air rather like a vast plate of dirty porridge – one churned mass of overlapping shell holes, water in the bottoms reflecting the sky... The villages were piles of shattered rubble and the woods dreary cemeteries of dead trees lifting gaunt branches and broken trunks to the sky; but there were green patches of untended grass or root-crops, and here and there a drift of scarlet where the poppies had spread over the untilled land.'

In 1926, years after the war ended, Slessor was provoked into writing an article for the *Royal Artillery Journal* by an army officer who had suggested that field commanders should 'send up staff officers who know the strategical position' to reconnoitre from the air. Recalling his own long hours of staring at the ground from a cockpit, and thinking about what he thought he was seeing, Slessor disagreed entirely. The airman, he wrote, is 'trained to report what he sees. But the moment he tries to draw deductions and to report tactical or strategical situations he, and any other observer whatever his rank or service, becomes a public menace... Even in open moving war the air observer, however skilled he may be, fails to see so much that is so important... that his estimate of the general situation will probably more often than not be so distorted as to be almost unrecognizable.' His experience in Africa, the Western Front and India convinced him that it is not a case of the airman telling the soldier where the enemy is, 'but the other way round – the soldier saying where the enemy shooting at him is, and getting the airman to do something about it.'

German airmen, thought Slessor, lacked the 'flat-out offensive spirit which Trenchard inspired', and were rarely to be seen on the Allied side of the lines, 'whereas our offensive patrols always operated deep into enemy territory.' A shallow opinion if he actually held it in 1917; even more so when he wrote it down in the 1950s and had by then both written and lectured on the use of aircraft during the Great War. Did he not realize that a 'flat-out offensive' with inadequate machines and poorly-trained crews might be a foolish strategy, wasting numerous lives without achieving any significant object? On the other hand, German front-line troops felt neglected by their airmen, and artillery fire was dangerously inaccurate because it was obliged to rely more on inaccurate maps than on accurate aerial observation.

Many junior officers criticized Trenchard's tactics at the time (as well as in their later memoirs) and these criticisms, echoed in the press and in parliament, led to a formal enquiry. Only senior officers were heard; they backed Trenchard; no action was taken. But the official historian managed to slip a carefully-worded criticism past the great man's scrutiny. 'It may be said perhaps with truth that the offensive patrols were too much a matter of routine, that their direction and co-ordination were not always sufficiently characterized by an alert imagination.'

Trenchard commanded a strategic bombing force in the last months of the war, and was widely condemned for his 'apparently haphazard attacks and his reckless disregard' for heavy casualties. He refused to develop and execute any systematic plan of attack: 'a soldier of the old tradition,' in the opinion of Tami Davis Biddle, 'he preferred to command more by instinct than by science and analysis.' On the other hand, he had a gift for generating good publicity by making extravagant claims about the material damage caused by his crews and, even more, by alleging that their bombs were fatally undermining enemy morale. After the war, an investigation into the effect of British bombing was dedicated, as Trenchard wished, more to 'advocacy than accuracy': words which might well serve as a motto for the RAF's bomber champions from that time on. Slessor, an indefatigable writer on some aspects of air power, might usefully have explored these important questions, but he never did. By the 1950s, he had long been heart and soul a devoted admirer of Trenchard, 'the father of the Royal Air Force', who was also his mentor, patron and advocate.

Young Jack fairly admitted, however, that at the time 'he could not have cared less what was happening as long as it didn't happen to me.' A sentiment nicely backed by this doggerel (which he may have composed) entitled 'I've got a motto'. It appears in his log-book and probably went better when sung by a roomful of fully-fuelled aviators than it reads in cold print:

> Push off when the Hun is in sight,
> Look around or you will find
> Every cloud has a Hun behind.
> The scouts [escort fighters] may come,
> Although the chance is a slim one.
> I often say as I look up,
> Perhaps the beggar's a Sopwith Pup,
> It's a small cross, not a black one.
> I was sent up on photography,
> My escort was an old FE.
> Did he come over the lines with me?
> No, not by a damned sight.'

Charles Smart, who had so disliked the RE 8 on first acquaintance, came to love a 'gallant machine' that got him safely through more than 150 hours of war flying and commemorated it in a far better verse than the doggerel quoted above, a verse that Slessor would certainly have applauded (and perhaps did):

Poor as a pilot I may be, yet still I have done my best,
You, too, have done your utmost to hold your own with the rest.
The time that we have spent together, you and I combined,
Up, up in the empty blueness, on the 'platforms of the wind',
Circling, diving, fighting, o'er St. Eloi's broken towers,
Have been dangerous, yet, oh such happy, happy hours.
You may have let me down more than once, perchance your engine is
     over-driven,
The fault may have been mine; let us forgive, and all forgiven.

Say 'Farewell' for I leave for the homeland for a well-earned rest,
While you remain 'out here', awaiting your time to 'go west',
Fare thee well, good steed of fabric, wood, and steel;
Words fail me to express the love for you I feel.

Although Slessor had some bad moments, 'I must confess that I rather
enjoyed the first war. It was interesting. One made a lot of friends, had a
lot of fun, fell in love once or twice and generally behaved in the manner
of most healthy young air force officers.' A particular friend was
Lieutenant-Colonel Herbert Carter, a regular in the King's Own Yorkshire
Light Infantry, who commanded 18 Battalion of the West Yorkshire
Regiment in XIII Corps. Slessor was an usher at his wedding to Hermione
Guinness, but Herbert died in February 1919, while serving with
Denikin's White army, fighting against Bolsheviks in Vladivostock. Four
years later, in May 1923, Slessor did 'the best thing I ever did in my life'
and married Hermione. She had a daughter (Pamela) by Herbert, and they
had two children of their own (Juliet Hermione and John Arthur
Guinness) and remained happily together until Hermione suffered a
stroke so severe in 1968 that it left her paralysed and speechless; she died
in a nursing home in September 1970.

A civilian again

Slessor returned to England in June 1918, to instruct at the Central Flying
School, Upavon, on Salisbury Plain in Wiltshire. By September, he was
Acting Commandant and after the Armistice in November was able to
shoot, fish and hunt to his heart's content until early in the New Year,
when he was sent to close a station at Druid's Lodge, near Salisbury.
There he quarrelled with a senior officer (whose name he never revealed)
and decided to leave the RAF. 'I've been making a lot of enquiries and
investigations into the future prospects of the air force', he told his father
in April 1919, 'and have definitely come to the conclusion that any mortal
thing will be better than staying in it.' General Cecil Lucas, Haig's Adjutant-
General Home Forces, had promised to write to his friend General Sir
Edmund Allenby on Slessor's behalf. He was after a position in the
Sudan, but if that fell through he wanted the Indian Cavalry. 'Anyway, one
way or another, I've definitely chucked the RAF as a future career, and
I'm damned glad now that I've done it. I'm sure it was no good.'

Back to civilian life he went. 'I thoroughly enjoyed myself', he later
recalled, 'spending my war gratuity on riotous living, and at last after four
gay but not very profitable months', he returned to the RAF with a short-
service commission in the rank of Flight Lieutenant – equivalent to
Captain in the army – a lowly rank which he held for seven years, longer
than any other in his entire career. Perhaps Trenchard lured him back? Or
perhaps his family network advised him to return? In either case, one
hopes he really did have some 'riotous living'.

CHAPTER 3

FLYING A DESK IN WHITEHALL

Victorian India

Flight Lieutenant Slessor spent the year 1920 as a Flight Commander at a newly-opened Flying Training School in Netheravon, Wiltshire. Then came a plum posting, for a man of his background and interests. He was sent to Parachinar (now in Pakistan), on the North-West Frontier, in April 1921. It lies at the head of the Kurram valley, about 6,000 feet above sea-level, near the Peiwar Kotal, a pass on an old trade route between India and Afghanistan. The local people were Shia Muslims, 'amiable and relatively peaceful', surrounded on all sides by 'unfriendly and more warlike Sunni tribes.' He was to command a flight in 20 Squadron, equipped with Bristol F.2B Fighter two-seater biplanes, one of the only machines of first-class quality he ever flew, and among the finest employed by any nation during the Great War. Life was just as it had always been for the British in India, and Slessor found it deeply satisfying to immerse himself in the world about which he had read so much, the world which shaped the lives of so many members of his family.

He admired the frontier's irregular militias. Their officers were British Regulars, the NCOs and men all Pathan: 'incredibly tough and hence well up to the fighting weight of the wild tribesmen among whom they lived. Every man a marksman, they moved like mountain goats', he wrote, 'cheerful and immensely likeable rogues and their discipline – though perhaps unorthodox by the standards of Caterham [an army training camp in Surrey] – was excellent.' Unlike regular soldiers, the air force 'was no fun at all' for the Pathans of the Frontier: 'no juicy columns to ambush, no perimeter camps to snipe, no rifles to steal.'

The aeroplane had yet to make important changes to this Victorian world. The RAF, Slessor complained, suffered less from tribal unrest at that time than from the disinterest of the Indian government. As a result of postwar cuts and the army's incompetent administration, the RAF in India was virtually 'non-existent as a fighting force', reported Air Vice-Marshal Sir John Salmond to the Viceroy in August 1922. Here begins and justifies – in Slessor's mind – the intensity of his enthusiasm for independent air power. 'Army officers should not have been surprised when, after this early experience, some of us in the RAF were later a bit touchy about any suggestion that an air force command should ever again come under the control of the army.' The frontier was protected, in theory, by six squadrons (four of Bristols, two of DH 9As, also a first-class two-seater biplane), each with 12 aircraft. In practice, no more than a dozen in total were available on any one day – all battered wartime survivors, and there were very few spare parts for them.

Consequently, little flying was possible, ground training was casual, and stupid behaviour only too common, such as driving a lorry into the Mess by an officer – not Slessor – 'who had looked upon the whisky when it was golden.' In June 1921 Jack wrote to his father about 'a baddish show yesterday' when nine Sepoys of the 29th Punjabis were out, unarmed, exercising 18 mules within a mile of the fort. 'The Wazirs came down and collared the lot. One Sepoy, a Sikh, was left on the road with his throat cut, and the other eight, who were Mussulmans, and all the mules, were taken off into the hills and over the border. They were Khoidad Khel Wazirs, and have been causing a good deal of trouble lately.' Even so, Slessor liked their sense of humour. They had sent a message to the Commanding Officer of a regiment about to leave India, expressing regret because they had only stolen half their rifles and had hoped to collect the rest during the coming six weeks.

On the ground, however, Slessor had a wonderful time. Polo three times a week, tennis, shooting, fishing and sometimes playing cricket: 'I always make a duck', he told Hermione Carter (whom he was now courting), 'but am the only man apparently who is fool enough to stand behind the stumps on this pitch.' At Patiala in the Punjab, 'I had the honour of being bowled by Wilfrid Rhodes, one of the game's immortals', who was still playing for Yorkshire and England when not wintering in India. He bought some beautiful Bokhara rugs cheaply from Afghans, 'who are a lot fairer than uncle Bertie, for instance', and thought Parachinar 'a topping little spot. Ideal, if it wasn't for the dust storms, which one gets two or three times a week.' But he was invalided home in October 1922 with various ailments. 'These silly doctors', he complained to Hermione, 'appear to think I'm a bit touched in the wind. Nothing serious, of course, but these pleurisy whatnots are still in my chest and apparently there is some slight risk that they may turn tubercular unless nipped in the bud... Lord, I shall miss polo.'

Learning staff craft

Slessor was well enough by the end of 1922 to begin learning staff craft. In other words, how to fly a desk in Whitehall. During the next 30 years – including his service as Chief of the Air Staff – more than 21 were spent in staff or teaching appointments. Although he held three important wartime commands (for a total of three years), it was his gradual mastery of staff craft that saw him rise to the top. That said, and bearing in mind his outdoor temperament, Slessor would surely have made a stronger mark away from the desk or lectern had he enjoyed full use of his legs.

Writing in the 1950s, he thought officers should remain on flying duties for at least the first ten years of their service. 'I have known some potentially first-class officers spoiled by being condemned too early to an office stool.' Unless a young man was often in the cockpit he risked losing his enthusiasm for flying. Worse still, if he did well at a desk, the authorities were likely 'to rotate him from one to another until he becomes a sort of goldfish swimming round in a bowl without ever getting out to the open sea.' Wise and poignant words from a man cut off by lameness from enjoying those years of flying fun that consoled so many of his contemporaries as they became senior officers and found less and less time for the cockpit. That lameness, together with his intellectual energy, did indeed ensure that he spent more and more time in the Whitehall 'bowl'.

After a year on staff duties in the Air Ministry, this future 'goldfish' was selected in 1924 for the third course at the Staff College in Andover, Hampshire. This was a sign of high favour. Many of Slessor's fellow-pupils made a mark during the Second World War: among them, Raymond Collishaw, Norman Bottomley, George Pirie, Thomas Elmhirst and Leslie Hollinghurst. The college was then commanded by an Old Haileyburian, Air Vice-Marshal Robert Brooke-Popham. The combination of public school (especially his own) with high rank (especially in the RAF) and a liking for field sports ('Brookham', as he came to be known, was a fine horseman and keen fox-hunter) invariably overwhelmed Slessor's critical capacity. In this instance, when writing his memoirs some 30 years later, he asserted that 'many of us who knew him best' – a group that did *not* include Slessor – 'were disappointed and angry when he was relieved as Supreme Commander Far East shortly after the Japanese declaration of war [*sic*], and felt that the sad history of Singapore might have been different but for that unhappy decision.'

We have here our first example of Slessor taking a wild swing and missing the ball. Historians who have examined the records, unlike Slessor, disagree about Brooke-Popham. John Ferris, for example, concluded that 'the RAF in Malaya failed in every way – to stop invasion, detect the enemy, sink transports at sea, protect British warships and soldiers, or achieve air superiority.' Although Brooke-Popham was not solely responsible for the disaster, he was neither blameless nor was he capable of preventing it, had he remained in command. Slessor had no good reason for leaping so ardently to his defence.

Brooke-Popham was a Camberley man and wanted Andover 'to take on some of the same traditions and gentlemanly pastimes as its sister college, such as riding, hunting, and a dinner club. He also encouraged the "Public School Spirit", levelling, and teamwork that were fostered at Camberley.' His senior assistant was Group Captain Wilfrid Freeman,

who would become one of the RAF's outstanding officers. But neither
then nor later did Slessor see any flaw in a man given to expressing
virulent contempt for many fellow-officers, including several with
excellent records. Slessor would surely have known this, had they been
such close friends as he often claimed. He thought Freeman inspired
affection, 'an affection often tinged with amused indignation at the
outrageous things he was apt to say.'

Freeman might be 'critical but never unkind', Slessor assured his
readers. They would have no means of knowing – in the 1950s or for long
after – what Freeman thought of these air marshals: Sir Douglas (Strath)
Evill 'is, of course, a pathological case'; Sir Bertine Sutton is 'hopelessly
senile'; Sir Arthur Barratt 'was incredibly stupid 25 years ago'; and Sir
Frederick Bowhill 'requires no comment from me'. As for Lord (Sholto)
Douglas, 'socially and morally he is beneath contempt' and Sir William
Welsh 'is doing very well there [the United States] – the first job he has
been able to hold down in six years.' Slessor might not have brushed aside
his supposed friend's nastiness so lightly had he known that Freeman
regarded *him* as both 'a snob' (presumably of the social kind) and 'an
intellectual snob'; and readily revealed in the highest quarters what he
regarded as flaws in Slessor's conduct and personality.

It was at Andover, under the inspiration of Brooke-Popham and
Freeman that 'we had to feel our way towards a doctrine of air warfare...
based on the supremacy of the offensive', which Slessor believed had
been vindicated by the end of the Second World War. In addition to
instruction in basic office routines, Slessor and his fellow-students were
left in no doubt as to the wisdom of accepting and regurgitating the
opinions of the directing staff, shaped by Trenchard. These opinions
emphasized the need for incessant offensive and minimized the resources
devoted to home defence; they declared as 'an accepted doctrine' that a
well-drilled formation of day bombers would always get through to its
targets, even if unescorted by fighters; and that those targets should be
'vital centres' rather than enemy aircraft or airfields. Slessor imbibed all
this without reserve and made it his own thought.

'Doctrine is the enemy of history', wrote Noble Frankland. He
recalled a conversation about 1950 with Sir Ralph Cochrane (an
intelligent air marshal, close to both Tedder and Slessor) who regarded
doctrine as revealed truth. He believed the account by Raleigh and Jones
of the Great War in the Air, closely monitored by Trenchard, set an ideal
pattern for all future studies of air power. That is, a detailed, fact-filled
account of events – carefully concealing the muddle, mistakes and malice
that always happens under the fearful stress of wartime and thereby
preventing readers from drawing useful lessons, or at least consolation, if
war should ever return. Still worse, however, was the determination to
resist ideas that did not emerge from Trenchard's cloudy mind. The
influence of doctrine, wrote Air Vice-Marshal Tony Mason, 'became so

pervasive that alternative interpretations of facts, or facts which did not fit the doctrine, were either seriously undervalued or overlooked. Yet the doctrine was enunciated by intelligent senior officers, most of whom had been competent combat pilots and commanders.' Mason had no doubt that the elevation of doctrine owed a great deal to the overwhelming desire to preserve the RAF as Britain's third service.

Slessor later insisted – with surprising and repeated vehemence – that he was not influenced by a famous Italian analysis, *Il Dominio dell'Aria*, published by Giulio Douhet in 1921 (and available in an English translation as *The Command of the Air* as early as 1923). 'We were not (strange as it may seem) nurtured on the pure milk of Douhet. I had never heard of him in those days and even now [the 1950s] I have never read him.' This is an interesting admission from an officer with a reputation as an air power theorist. He evidently saw no need to look beyond Trenchard, whereas his broader-minded American contemporaries studied Douhet and all other theorists. 'Many of [Douhet's] ideas and predictions were wrong', wrote Phillip Meilinger, 'but echoes of his basic concepts are still heard more than 60 years after his death.' The Coalition victory in the 1991 Gulf War 'is an example of what Douhet predicted air power could accomplish. Specifically, his formula for victory – gaining command of the air, neutralizing an enemy's strategic "vital centres", and maintaining the defensive on the ground while taking the offensive in the air – underpinned Coalition strategy.' Slessor's arrogant disdain for such an influential writer clearly reveals his own limitations.

Squadron Commander

From April 1925 to September 1928, Slessor – now promoted to the rank of Squadron Leader, equivalent to Major in the army – commanded 4 (army co-operation) Squadron at Farnborough, Hampshire, which allegedly trained with the army's Second Division at Aldershot. These were grand years of 'pleasant, easy-going, somehow agreeably amateur soldiering', hugely enjoyable for a man devoted to field sports, parades, tattoos, plenty of undemanding flying and ample leave; a man not yet at all concerned about the total lack of realistic joint service training. As he later admitted, we were preparing for the last war, 'and the first whiff of Hitler's grapeshot blew all our elaborately practised technique – and the specialist aircraft designed for it – into limbo.'

An ambitious officer, even when having fun, kept a close eye on Trenchard. During 1925 therefore, Slessor – now married and with a stepdaughter, a daughter and a son (born that year) to care for – made it his business to learn that an inter-service committee was considering what air raid precautions were feasible in Britain to counter the threat of an attack by France's air force, then far stronger than the RAF. The Air Staff – all Trenchard's creatures – reflecting on actual German raids in 1917-1918 and adding the impact of possible French raids, came up with horrifying casualty figures: more than the whole Great War total in only three days! The Air Staff declared that no defence was possible and expected an immediate, complete collapse of civilian morale. Although the War Office answered this nonsense by pointing out that only half the German raiders actually reached London, and the defences accounted for nearly a quarter of them, the Trenchardists were unmoved.

Here begins, in 1925, that absolute belief – based on the shakiest foundations – in the knock-out blow from the air which would dominate air staff thinking and gravely influence government decisions during the 1930s: 'the message brought down by Trenchard from the clouds and engraved on every loyal air force officer's very soul', none more so than Slessor's. He was then a young, junior and inexperienced officer, naturally overwhelmed by the powerful personality of a great man who had noticed him favourably. He was also alert enough to observe that Trenchard did not welcome contradiction. As we shall see, it took the unforgiving experience of high office in wartime to emancipate Slessor from blind adherence to the true faith.

The RAF display at Hendon in July 1926 gave Slessor a rare opportunity to shine as a pilot despite his lameness. The display was watched by more than 100,000 people, among them the King and Queen, several continental royals and a full turn-out of top brass and eminent politicians. 'As an event of the London season', recorded *The Times*, 'the display has now a definite place; but its social aspect must yield to the technical brilliance of the pilots and the manoeuvres executed with such precision and apparent lack of effort.' Slessor competed in the final of the message picking-up event against Cecil Durston and Alec Coryton, all three representing army co-operation squadrons – 4, 13, 16 – and all three flying Bristol Fighters. The event was described in *Flight*: 'Each competitor, after taking off, received instructions by wireless and picked up his message (suspended on a cord between two posts) by means of a hook suspended beneath the machine. He then read out the answer by wireless, after which the ground station instructed him to drop a copy of the message on a certain marked spot. All the wireless messages, both to and from the machines, were broadcast by the loud speakers and were clearly audible.' Durston won, Slessor was second, and all three delighted the enormous crowd.

On the personal front, the decade 1923-32 brought Slessor both joy and tragedy. On the joyful side, were his marriage to Hermione (1923) and the births of his daughter Juliet (1924) and his son John (1925), the marriage of his brother Rodney to the widow of the eighth earl of Jersey (1925), the second marriage of his father (1927), and the marriage of his sister Elspeth – whom he usually called Betty – to Major Cuthbert Fellowes, son of Rear-Admiral Sir Thomas Fellowes (1930). But on the tragic side, his mother died at her home, Newland House in Oxford, in 1925; Rose Delaney, 'valued friend and cook of Squadron Leader and

Mrs Slessor', died suddenly in 1928; his father died of pneumonia in 1931; and his younger brother Anthony, a Lieutenant serving with the 52nd Light Infantry in Mandalay, Burma, lost his life in an accident in December 1932, aged only 28.

Air Ministry plans

Slessor was posted to the plans branch of the Air Ministry's Directorate of Operations and Intelligence in September 1928. Sounds impressive, but the branch consisted of only two officers (Wing Commander Richard Peck and himself) under Air Vice-Marshal Cyril Newall, then Deputy CAS as well as Director of Operations and Intelligence. Slessor spent two years there, working close to Trenchard, a man whom he admired inordinately for the rest of his life.

'This was the decisive period in Slessor's formative years', thought Max Hastings. He was already 'an officer of exceptional ability, charm, and force of personality', but hitherto 'his thinking and most of his experience had centred upon the role of aircraft in direct support of ground forces.' He now became a Trenchardist, devoted to that formidable man's theories of strategic air power as a war-winning weapon. In Slessor's opinion, Trenchard 'created and preserved the service that saved England [*sic*] in 1940... if the RAF had been split up again between two older services after the first war, it would have suffered the fate of the Tank Corps – and we should have lost the Battle of Britain.' There is a fair point here: the British army, having invented the tank, did in fact go to war in 1939 without a single armoured division.

Trenchard

During the South African Wars (1899-1902), Hugh Montague Trenchard had shown himself to be a dashing cavalry officer, fearless in combat, impatient of all orders except his own, and respectful only to those senior officers whom he admired. As well as boundless energy, he had a mighty foghorn voice that earned him the nickname 'Boom'. An indifferent pilot and dangerous tutor, he wisely stayed out of the cockpit from 1914 onwards. If the RAF had not been created in the heat of battle in 1918 out of the fear of defeat, it would never have emerged out of the chill of calculation once the war to end all wars had ended. He deserves great credit for protecting the infant from army and navy predators until it was sturdy enough to survive without help.

Slessor believed that Trenchard was 'one of the few really great men of our time', although he admitted that he could be 'unpredictable, temperamental, often difficult to deal with, sometimes inclined to be egocentric... unduly secretive... and his method of approach to a problem was sometimes a little tortuous and difficult to understand. Sometimes he observed to a fault Lord Fisher's maxim: "Never Explain".' In later life, when no longer in office, he was inclined to press his opinions 'without sufficient regard for the squalid realities of life.' As, for example, over the bombing of Germany early in the war, 'when our resources were still totally inadequate.' If the British army can fairly be accused of living in the past during the 1930s, the Air Staff created by Trenchard can be accused of living in the future. Only in the 1950s did the theories about strategic bombing advanced so confidently by Trenchard and his successors in the 1920s and 1930s catch up with reality.

Slessor attempted to excuse Trenchard's foolishness at that time on the grounds that his successors had not kept him informed. But many sources of information remained open to Trenchard, had he wished to study them, rather than repeat fixed opinions. Moreover, as Slessor knew, Trenchard despised Sir Edward Ellington (CAS from May 1933 to August 1937) and Sir Cyril Newall (CAS from September 1937 to October 1940) and was unlikely to listen to either man. 'Boom could have been more helpful to us', Slessor admitted, 'and, I hesitate to say, less of a nuisance, if Trenchard had really known the facts.' Even Slessor did not attempt to gloss over his mentor's crowning foolishness: in 1948 Trenchard got cross with Slessor 'for refusing to agree that it would be a good idea to send an armoured division down the autobahn during the Berlin blockade.'

Although Slessor played no part in the Battle of Britain, for some reason he was invited to speak on BBC Radio about it on September 16th 1956. He did so, briefly, and then launched into fulsome praise of his old patron, who had died seven months earlier, on February 10th. Slessor thought we owed it to Trenchard, 'more than to any other single man – that we live as a great nation to tell the tale of those glorious summer days and grim autumn nights of 1940.' Had it not been for Trenchard's 'vision, faith and iron determination,' so Slessor believed, 'the RAF would probably not have existed in 1940 as an autonomous service... Trenchard, almost alone, saved the infant RAF from being dismembered [after the Great War] and returned to the two older services.' According to Slessor, 'to the end of his days he was passionately interested in, and devoted to, the RAF and – while he never butted in – he was always a ready and wise counsellor to those who succeeded him in office.' This is simply not true. He 'butted in', as we shall see, often to decisive effect, as every CAS who succeeded him – up to and including Slessor himself – well knew.

A decade later, in 1966, Slessor was invited to contribute an 'afterword' to an account by an American airman of the *first* Battle of Britain. He thought the author had been 'rather less than fair' to Trenchard and rallied yet again to his defence. Trenchard 'was very inarticulate... he was almost physically incapable of expressing his thoughts on paper... His closest friends (or worst enemies) could hardly accuse him of being an intellectual type of officer. But he had a flair, an instinct, for getting at the really essential core of a problem.' Had it not been for him, Slessor again insisted, the RAF would have lost its independence in the early 1920s 'and that might well have resulted in our defeat in World War II.'

Slessor then defended Trenchard and the 'Air Enthusiasts' – including himself – for their belief in strategic bombing. 'Where we were very wrong in 1939 (as I am on record as frankly admitting [in his memoirs, *The Central Blue*] was in a gross under-estimate of the weight of explosive and the technical efficiency of the means of delivery necessary to achieve decisive results; and in an almost equally serious under-estimate of the capacity of civilian populations to stand up to the scale of attack available before the advent of nuclear explosive.' Slessor also admitted failure to make adequate provision for fighters or appreciate 'the enormous, revolutionary implications of radar.' These may be thought fundamental – even damning – failures, springing from a preference for theorizing in Whitehall over practical testing in the real world. Even so, Slessor argued – following Trenchard – that a greater concentration on strategic bombing would probably have brought victory in Europe before June 1944, even as early as the end of 1943. Both men were victims of what Tami Davis Biddle called 'the tension between imagined possibilities and technical realities.'

Air Vice-Marshal Edgar Kingston-McCloughry (a prolific writer on air power matters whom we shall meet again later) was quoted by Major Fredette on the inter-war years, saying 'the Air Force High Command, which at that time was not provided with many particularly intelligent personalities, badly over-stated their claims... based partly on faulty deductions from the First World War, that the morale of the civil population would not be able to withstand the strain of air bombardments. The Air Force High Command over-assessed the material damage that could be inflicted... at that time; and they scarcely appreciated the measures to which an enemy is prepared to resort in order to continue the struggle... Nor did they appreciate the difficulties of selecting the best targets, and of accurate bombing, as well as counter-measures.'

Air control

Trenchard's handwriting was illegible, he was also inarticulate, so Peck and Slessor became his 'English merchants', interpreting his mumbles and setting them down on paper in readable form. Air control was an important issue between the two world wars. Could airmen maintain order throughout Britain's African and Asian empire more effectively – and more cheaply – than soldiers? 'Impressed by Trenchard's claims as to the cost-effectiveness of the air force compared with surface forces,' wrote Christina Goulter, 'the government granted the RAF an Empire-policing role. The results were even more impressive than the air force heads had thought possible; in every instance, RAF squadrons were able to quash uprisings at a tenth of the cost and time taken by land operations. The doctrine seemed vindicated, and the RAF's future secured. But what the air staff failed to appreciate, or preferred to forget, was that in this capacity the RAF was operating against populations who had no previous experience of aircraft, and certainly no anti-aircraft defences other than rifles.'

There can be no doubt that air control caused less damage and loss of life than ground control, and thereby helped to prolong the Empire's death throes, but the damage and losses were far heavier than Slessor admitted. 'The attack with bombs', wrote Wing Commander John Chamier in 1921, 'must be relentless and unremitting and carried on continuously by day and night, on houses, inhabitants, crops and cattle.' Thanks to the aeroplane and the bomb, Slessor argued, Britain was able 'to enforce submission upon people without killing them.' Air control was criticized for being indiscriminate, but in his opinion it was 'surprisingly accurate.' He rejected charges of brutality or of targeting women and children and claimed that 'there is no evidence that air action created special resentment or rancour – indeed the reverse was the truth.'

Either Slessor did not know, or preferred to forget, that 'air action' often caused significant losses to humans, animals and crops. Operations increased in size, as Roger Beaumont found, 'to levels high in bomb tonnage even when compared to early World War II and recent limited war. During March and September 1932, a single village on the North-West Frontier received 213 tons of 20-250 pound bombs. In August-October 1935, the Mohmands [of the North-West Frontier] received almost 180 tons', and suffered 87 casualties including children. In other operations, reports were 'heavily edited by the Air Council to remove all references to details regarding casualties, including the bombing of animals belonging to the tribes. Given the unavailability of figures, for whatever reason, one can only guess at the numbers killed in air policing in various operations from 1919 to 1939. The Aden operations summary, for example, shows an estimate of 170 killed.' Given that operations in Iraq and India were often larger, 'air policing appears to have been less a minor chapter in the history of air warfare than one might conclude at first glance.' David Killingray agreed, finding the same pattern in a thoroughly-documented study. 'Air policing which involved bombing and machine-gunning people and cattle was generally acceptable in official quarters,' he wrote, 'for use in what was termed "uncivilized warfare", in operations against Kurds, Afridis, Somalis and Sudanese, but not in "civilized warfare", as for example in Ireland in 1919-21.'

Slessor's opinion that air control actually saved lives was vehemently backed by Kingston-McCloughry and more calmly by Portal and other officers, but Arthur Harris (later head of Bomber Command) expressed himself in his usual brutally honest way in March 1924: 'Where the Arab and Kurd had just begun to realize that if they could stand a little noise, they could stand bombing, and still argue; they now know what real bombing means, in casualties and damage; they now know that within 45 minutes a full-sized village can be practically wiped out and a third of its inhabitants killed or injured by four or five machines which offer them no real target, no opportunity for glory as warriors, no effective means of escape.'

These words being somewhat robust even for Trenchard's taste, he instructed John Salmond (head of the RAF in Iraq) to ensure that details of bomb tonnage dropped and casualties inflicted were not reported to the Air Ministry. It may therefore be that Slessor remained ignorant of the real effects of air control. However, his claim that the bomber was 'a precise instrument' was 'demonstrably fabulous', as David Omissi has shown time and time again. 'Slessor even admitted' in May 1931, wrote Omissi, 'that the bombers sometimes attacked the wrong targets altogether, but he regarded such episodes as "regrettable accidents" that would happen "whatever the form of force employed". Air force bombing was no more precise than Air Ministry propaganda, and the "surgical strike" was no less a myth over the frontier in the 1920s and 1930s than it was over Libya in 1986.' Nowhere did Slessor mention the fact that the RAF regularly dropped delayed-action bombs, timed to explode after nightfall when villagers thought they might return safely to their homes – and children might safely play with what they thought were 'duds'. He did, however, complain to Liddell Hart in November 1937 that throughout his time at Camberley (1931-4), he was never permitted by the Commandant – Major-General John Dill – to offer students the RAF case for air control on the North-West Frontier.

The relative success of air control 'seduced Trenchard and his successors', wrote Hastings, 'into ignoring the need to prepare for possible conflict with nations as technically advanced as Britain.' The RAF failed to make adequate progress before 1939 in precisely those fields which the offensive doctrine most required. Namely: accurate navigation (in daylight or darkness) in large, properly-heated and fully-armed aircraft capable of carrying heavy loads of efficient bombs (high explosive or incendiary) a long way and dropping them accurately on well-chosen targets. Although Trenchard retired at the end of 1929, the doctrine lived on. The RAF must be primarily an offensive bomber force, he insisted, hitting targets of strategic importance, rather than a defensive fighter force, successfully resisting attempts by enemy bombers to hit British targets.

These opinions were carefully articulated, confidently asserted, insufficiently tested. In March 1930, for example, Slessor composed a memorandum opining that 'we shall very likely always have to have single-seat fighters for our one specialized problem, the defence of London... the sole reason for their existence.' He had not yet learned that there were other vulnerable ports in Britain, not to mention aircraft factories, airfields and centres of heavy industry outside London. The Germans may possibly need them to protect the Ruhr, but 'I believe that very soon the single-seat fighter will die in France.'

As for civilian morale, he remembered only too clearly his single experience of panic after his Zeppelin adventure in 1915. Should there ever be another aerial attack, he sneered, 'your toothpick worker will go to ground again even if he has not already left the area, which is more likely.' His opinions, as Neville Jones observed, 'were in accord with air staff thought, and for this reason were seldom called into question by serving air force officers.' Too many of those officers rising to the top in the 1930s were 'Whitehall Warriors'. Like Slessor, more comfortable in offices or at the podium than in cockpits or hangars; least of all in factories, even those where aircraft were built. Little attention was paid to co-operation with either the army or the navy, or to practising realistic aerial combat, or to the creation of a fleet of adequate transport aircraft.

CHAPTER 4

THE NEXT WAR LOOMS

Camberley

Jack Slessor nearly died of blood poisoning in March 1930, having scraped a foot while walking round the horse-racing course at Aintree, Liverpool. Awarded a long sick leave, he and his wife wandered round Europe. They lingered in Venice, of course, but also visited the Dalmatian coast, 'putting in at places like Split and Zara, which I was to know so well 14 years later when supporting the campaign of Tito's partisans against the Germans.' Back in England, he returned to the Air Ministry, where he was told to write a manual on co-operation with the army. At the end of that year, he spent one term as a student and then four years as an instructor at the Army Staff College in Camberley, Surrey, a few miles north of Farnborough.

In May 1931, Slessor published what Neville Jones has called 'Perhaps the clearest and most convincing statement of the doctrine of the strategic offensive as a means of securing Britain from air attack.' In order to 'afford us any sort of protection [in those pre-radar days] against air forces that could now be directed against us,' wrote Slessor, 'we should require a force of fighters immeasurably greater than we can afford in peace. And even then we should not be secure. So the policy is to provide the essential minimum of fighters for close defence in co-operation with the ground anti-aircraft defences, and to concentrate the bulk of our resources on the maintenance of a formidable striking force of bombers.' The argument is persuasive, but the 'striking force' actually provided during the coming decade was very far from 'formidable'.

These were undemanding years in what Slessor recalled as 'a fool's paradise', one with ample time for the fox-hunting, shooting and fishing that he wrote about so lovingly in his memoirs. 'It was pleasant to relax in the friendly dusk, hat tipped back, coat open and pipe lit, to chew the cud of memory – that big double where many others swerved for the gate, that time when one was a bit clever and cut a corner and came well up with the hounds.'

Each summer he would take a party of students to visit old battlefields on the Western Front. They wandered hither and yon, chatting amiably about strategy and tactics, enjoying plenty of leisurely meals and hot baths. One year they went to Germany, where they noticed nothing amiss, even though the Nazis were already rampaging there. It was such an idle life that Slessor contemplated retiring from the RAF – in his mid-thirties – to set up as a gentleman farmer, even though he was promoted to the rank of Wing Commander (Lieutenant-Colonel) on New Year's Day, 1932.

Looking back on these years, he thought it would be fair to say that at Camberley 'we were pretty good at teaching the student *how* to do things; we were not so successful in teaching them to think *what* to do.' In other words, as several senior RAF officers would complain during the coming war, too many soldiers depended on orders; they lacked initiative. At Anzio [in January 1944], for example, 'if we had there matched our enemy in this particular quality of tactical flexibility and instantaneous exploitation of opportunity, the subsequent history of the campaign in Italy might have been very different.' That may be so, but we shall see – in the appropriate place – that Slessor's typically sweeping opinion is not supported by historians who have actually studied what happened during and after the Anzio landings.

Air power and armies

Slessor did, however, find time for some serious study at Camberley. By the end of 1934, he had written a number of lectures that he revised for publication by Oxford University Press in 1936 under the title *Air Power and Armies*. These lectures, all bearing the mark of Trenchard and heavily dependent on Jones's official air history (which Trenchard closely supervised) founded his reputation as one of the RAF's foremost thinkers. 'The writer's strong point is not lucidity of style', complained *Flight*'s reviewer, F. A. de Vere Robertson, 'and the book does not make easy reading. It is, however, so full of ideas that a careful perusal is well repaid. It should certainly be studied at the RAF Staff College at Andover.' In fact, it was not, perhaps because it had too much to say about air support for ground forces.

He emphasized that the aeroplane was not a battlefield weapon and would best be employed in isolating that 'field' and preventing the enemy from bringing up reinforcements and supplies. Yet he also advocated close air support to meet a crisis, which must bring the aeroplane onto the battlefield. 'In the intervals between battles', Robertson understood Slessor to advocate attacks on sources of military production, attacks that may very well bring about victory in the long run, but at the risk of defeat in the short run. Robertson ended his review by quoting Slessor: 'No attitude could be more vain or irritating in its effects than to claim that the next great war – if and when it comes – will be decided in the air, and in the air alone.'

The book was also thoughtfully reviewed by the military

correspondent of *The Times*: 'a most valuable and illuminating book which fills a big gap in the literature of air warfare.' Like Robertson, he drew attention to Slessor's opinion that another war would not be decided by air power alone, but went on to quote Slessor's hope that 'the days of National Armies on the traditional, early 20th century, man-power and shell-power model are inevitably numbered... Can it really be supposed that we shall ever see in the face of air action the millions of men, the thousands of tons of ammunition, the network of trenches stretching halfway across Europe, and the vast organizations at the bases and on the lines of communication that turned northern France into a passable imitation of Epsom Downs on Derby Day?' The analogy is singularly ill-chosen, but this hope – an inspiration for all air enthusiasts in these years – would soon be destroyed.

Slessor set out what he regarded as principles by which air warfare could assist the army in any future war. War, he argued, is intended to defeat a nation by destroying its army, but implicit in his work is the idea that an army is best defeated by destroying the nation's 'vital centres'. These are neither identified nor ranked in order of importance or vulnerability, nor did Slessor consider that the enemy might have arranged to defend them with ground guns and aircraft, nor did he propose measures to defend Britain's 'vital centres', if the enemy were to devise his own plans for winning a war.

Should war break out, the RAF must win air superiority, using heavy bombers to destroy enemy centres – and, incidentally, to shatter civilian morale: we should not be distracted by 'ethical considerations'. Bombers would usually defend themselves, but they might be escorted by two-seater fighters. At the same time, enemy air bases must also be attacked, to ensure air superiority. These essential tasks meant that aircraft would only rarely be active over the actual battlefield. A point difficult to explain to soldiers, Slessor tolerantly admitted, but they must nevertheless be made to understand – he neglected to explain how – that the best way to protect them might well be to bomb an oil refinery a thousand miles away. The closest aircraft should come to the battlefield would be to attack transports carrying troops and supplies of food, water, weapons and ammunition by road or rail.

'In air operations against production', he opined, 'the weight of attack will inevitably fall upon a vitally important, and not by nature very amenable, section of the community – the industrial workers, whose morale and sticking power cannot be expected to equal that of the disciplined soldier.' Unfortunately Slessor knew nothing whatever about British 'industrial workers', and still less about those of Germany. He may have visited an aircraft factory, but not any other kind. Trenchard was no less ignorant, and yet both men – together with many other RAF officers – believed they knew all about the shaky morale of skilled craftsmen and the labouring poor.

Phillip Meilinger has called *Air Power and Armies* 'perhaps the best treatise on air power theory written in English before the Second World War.' It is certainly a valuable work, but I. B. Holley, Jr. was 'left aghast at the extent to which unchallenged assumptions permeated RAF official thinking, given that the very survival of the nation almost certainly hinged on the soundness of its air power.' Assumptions typical of theorizing academics should have had no standing, among allegedly practical airmen, without rigorous testing.

Slessor was certain that air power would play a vital, perhaps even a dominant, role as the third revolution in warfare, following the invention of gunpowder and the machine-gun. These permitted heavier casualties, but the air 'may stop men or their supplies arriving at the battlefield at all.' Aircraft, he thought, should 'assist and co-operate with the army in the defeat of the enemy's army, and of such air forces as may be co-operating with it.' This was interdiction (interrupting communications and supply lines) rather than attempting 'strategic' strikes on allegedly vital targets. Ground operations would fail without air superiority – and that superiority must be maintained by constant effort. The focus must therefore be on combat in the sky. Only after victory in that combat could a strategic offensive begin.

As Meilinger observed, Slessor did not then discuss the details of such an offensive. Somewhere in all his words is a major role for fighters, rather than bombers, but there is no analysis of the design or development of either type. Here we see a weakness in all this theorizing. Slessor did not know, in the mid-1930s, either what fighters could do to each other or to bombers, or what bombers could actually do to factories, or what damage those factories could sustain and remain in operation, or how quickly they could be repaired or whether they could be dispersed to other locations. Nor was he informed about the capacity of workers either to survive or return to work, with or without government pressure. Did he expect dispersal of industrial plant? Effective anti-aircraft and/or fighter defence of important targets? Did he expect bombing attacks to be made in daylight or darkness? Slessor thought ground fire would be ineffective against attacking aircraft. As Meilinger notes, this was 'a gross miscalculation as the war would soon demonstrate. In addition, like most airmen of his time, he thought escort fighters were theoretically desirable but technically impracticable – another error proven by the war.'

On the other hand, Slessor was well ahead of his time in advocating unified command of air operations. The ablest British and American air leaders would work hard to win this vital point during the coming war. He deplored the division of British air assets in France during the Great War between eight different senior commanders. 'Air assets should be commanded and directed by an airman who was equal in authority to the ground commander. These two individuals and their staffs were to collaborate in the design and implementation of the theatre commander's overall plan.' Their headquarters should be close together, and he even suggested that the theatre commander might, one day, be an airman.

Those historians who wade through 'his fairly convoluted prose' find much to admire, but this may not be the book Slessor really wanted to write, in Meilinger's opinion. At heart, Slessor believed in the heavy bomber and would have argued its case, 'but his army audience would have none of it. He was therefore compelled to write a book that assumed a land campaign', that strongly advocated tactical aviation, and never went on to produce a companion volume on strategic air power.

Slessor's detailed analysis of the Battle of Amiens (August 8th-11th 1918) appealed much more to soldier-students than speculations about what bombers might do in a future war. During his analysis, he criticized the performance of 48 Squadron's unnamed commanding officer. That officer was, in fact, Sir Keith Park, later to earn great fame for his conduct during the Battle of Britain and in Malta. Although Slessor's strictures were aimed mainly at the overall direction of the air assets available, he clearly implied that Park had failed to make the best use of admittedly meagre resources. No other criticism is recorded of 48 Squadron's performance around Amiens and Park, having put his case to Slessor, asked him to amend his text. Slessor refused and Park never forgave him. This is one reason why relations between the two were so poor when they were obliged to serve together in 1944.

Back to India: the Quetta earthquake

Slessor returned to the North-West Frontier in February 1935 to command 3 (Indian) Wing at Quetta, capital of Baluchistan (now part of Pakistan), some 320 miles south-west of Parachinar. He had two squadrons – 5 and 20 – equipped with Westland Wapiti two-seater biplanes, an improved version of the faithful de Havilland DH 9A. Quetta was one of British India's largest military bases and the city, of some 65,000 people, lay to the south. A massive earthquake struck at about 3 am on the morning of May 3rd 1935. It lasted for only a minute and yet it caused more local devastation in that time than Slessor saw even in Germany at the end of the Second World War.

The Slessors, a cousin, and two guests were all injured by collapsing walls and ceilings. 'There were moments under that hot and dusty pile of bricks when I thought – well, this is it – until I saw a tiny gleam from a hurricane lamp and knew that where light could get in, air could, so I was not going to be suffocated after all, as so many of my poor airmen were.' About 30,000 Indians were killed or injured; RAF and family losses were 55 dead and 137 injured. Slessor had his head wound bandaged and went to see what had become of his men, their families, homes, aircraft and equipment.

His most useful action was to signal all stations in India, urging them to fly to Quetta every dose of anti-tetanus serum they could lay their hands on. The impact of the earthquake was so local that at 8.30 am a party from the Quetta Staff College arrived to hear Slessor lecture. Out of the first car stepped a certain Colonel Bernard Law Montgomery, later to become both famous and infamous. He and his party promptly helped in the grim task of digging out the injured and dead and seeing to rapid burials because of the extreme heat.

Hermione thought the earthquake only lasted about twenty seconds and was astounded at the death and destruction caused in that short time. She admired 'the marvellous bravery of the Indian – over all he lost, his wife, his family and all his relations probably, as well as his home and his possessions.' Wives were ordered to stay in their quarters, but 'for the first time in my life' she disobeyed her husband and went to work in the British Military Hospital. Then word came that someone was needed who could ride to go to outlying villages, so off she went to places where she had to be a doctor, as well as a nurse, to set splints and deal with major wounds.

One light moment came in these hateful days when *The Times* noticed Slessor's 38th birthday on June 3rd 1935, saying, 'the anniversary finds him in the midst of a very trying ordeal as a result of the devastation caused by the earthquake. He is known to a large number of army officers because much of his 20 years' service has been on army co-operation duties and he has had three years as a Camberley instructor.'

All senior officers in India, from Edgar Ludlow-Hewitt down, wrote warmly to Slessor at this time, commending his prompt, sensible actions as well as commiserating with the injuries he and Hermione suffered. The Viceroy himself commended Slessor and his men on July 7th for overcoming a 'nerve-shattering experience... The speed with which you got your damaged aircraft into action again was remarkable and proved of the greatest value. The Government of India is truly grateful for the splendid service which the aircraft in Quetta gave in reporting the condition of outlying districts immediately after the earthquake, in flying emergency requirements to Quetta, and in evacuating casualties.'

Two years later, in June 1937, Slessor was Guest of Honour at a 'Quetta Earthquake' reunion dinner in London arranged by members of 31 Squadron. Those present included 26 NCOs and airmen – a rare bridging of the gap between officers and men in those stiffly formal days.

Waziristan: a Gentleman's War

Slessor was granted a month's sick leave in England and Scotland. Ludlow-Hewitt had wanted him to have two months: 'I consider it entirely unnecessary', Slessor told him on June 14th, 'I have never felt better in my life.' But Ludlow-Hewitt insisted on one month and Slessor returned to duty in September with the Air Staff in Delhi, where he tried hard to understand the 'mysterious workings' of the Indian Government, until his Wing was reformed at Miram Shah. Officially, British forces were preparing to deal with either 'the minor danger' (war against Afghanistan) or 'the major danger' (war against the Soviet Union). Neither, in fact, was taken seriously. Slessor tried to take a realistic approach to training and operations in small war situations against opponents who were (in those days) lightly armed and without support from outside their tribal areas. Although a rebel 'was quite happy to lie behind his rock and shoot at unprotected infantry sweating up a slope towards him, he had very little taste for bombs and machine-gun fire from above and behind him.' As for the risk of accidentally hitting some of those sweating infantrymen, Slessor thought it better 'to lose six men from splinters and pull it off, than lose 60 men from enemy rifle fire and fail.' He also made the point that soldiers had never hesitated to shell hostile villages, whereas airmen were strictly forbidden to bomb them.

Slessor was made a Companion of the Distinguished Service Order (an award that embarrassed him at the time, and even more so during and after the Second World War) for his part in suppressing an uprising in and about the Khaisora valley in Waziristan. That operation began in December 1936 and was, he thought, 'one of the last of the "gentleman's wars"'. It was all great fun, 'sitting on a rock watching some action through my field-glasses', while overhead my Wapitis 'bumbled and circled, occasionally slanting downwards beyond some ridge with a rattle of machine-gun fire and the crumph of bombs.' Then it was back to camp for dinner and drinks with 'the knot of healthy-looking chaps in the haze of tobacco smoke', all dressed in picturesque garments, for the nights were bitterly cold.

Slessor was convinced that in 'low-intensity operations', soldiers and airmen must work closely together: the soldier, under fire, must tell the airman as accurately as possible where he – and the enemy – were. As Richard P. Hallion writes, 'he organized what he termed the "Vickers-Bomb-Lewis" method of ground attack: a two-seat aircraft such as the Hawker Audax and Hardy, or the Westland Wapiti, would dive on enemy troops, strafing with its forward-firing Vickers gun, release its bombs, and during the vulnerable pull off the target, the rear gunner would spray the enemy with fire from his Lewis gun.' In addition, he recommended dividing maps into lettered grids, and arranging for aircraft to be in orbit near the battle area and ready to be called into action at need: this 'cab rank' system proved most effective, some years later, in Italy and after the Allied landings in Normandy.

News came of the abdication of King Edward VIII, which distressed some British officers, but not their Indian troops: 'few of them really understood what it was all about – they knew there was a new King-Emperor and that was enough for them.' As it was for Slessor himself. India was an integral part of the British Empire and would remain so for the foreseeable future. He stayed on the ground throughout the campaign, riding a horse as far forward as he could in order to keep in close touch with the army commander, so that he could order his aircraft to attack particular targets with minimum delay. 'Thus I have two tenuous claims to distinction: one that I was the first man to intercept (albeit quite ineffectively) an enemy aircraft over England; the other that I am the only air force commander to have gone to war on a horse!' A third claim is the fact that he is one of the few airmen to be awarded a gold medal. Not, alas, for chasing that Zeppelin, but awarded by the Royal United Services Institution in 1936 for an essay on the changes brought to warfare by the invention of an internal combustion engine.

Given his lack of interest in machinery this was indeed a well-earned prize. Moreover, he later noted that the War Office 'did their damnedest – unsuccessfully – to get this [essay] modified before publication.' One sees why: he recommended a major re-organization of the British army, at home and abroad, to take account of mechanization (tanks and other armoured vehicles) and suggested that aircraft could carry out many of its traditional policing roles throughout the empire more cheaply and efficiently. He did not mince his words. Indian infantry, he declared, was every bit as good as British infantry for frontier warfare. 'Today it seems to be the fashionable belief that the British soldier, and to some extent his Indian comrade, cannot go to war on the frontier without every sot of luxury, with the result that a frontier valley during an operation looks like a cross between Piccadilly Circus on boat-race night and Epsom Downs on Derby Day!'

Off duty, Slessor showed his usual zest for shooting, hunting, fishing and keeping close to his family network, titled persons and senior officers, all described in his memoirs as absolutely splendid characters. Like many Victorians, he grew to love India and wrote a novel (never published) set in the 1930s and entitled *Name on a Bullet: A Story of the North-West Frontier*. Very few things in his life meant more to him than 'a way of life that has gone for ever – a way of life familiar to thousands of British men and women in the years before the dissolution of the Indian Empire, but very different from anything that survives today. It was not especially heroic or particularly glamorous; but it was not ignoble, its rewards were not material gain and its ideals were loyalty and service to the Empire.' Very few of those Britons were brutal imperialists or race-conscious blimps; neither were they supermen. 'They included the usual proportion of fools – and some knaves. But their record stands up well to comparison with any other cross-section of our people; and they left behind them a tradition which is still a proud heritage of the Armed Forces of India and Pakistan.' There is, of course, much truth in this summary, but for many Britons – the Slessors among them – India did offer far greater opportunities for 'material gain', as well as the satisfaction of duty done, than employment at home.

CHAPTER 5

PLANNING FOR WAR

Bombing

Slessor returned to England in May 1937, a newly-promoted Group Captain (Colonel) to be Deputy Director of Plans in the Air Ministry[6]. He and his wife enjoyed a leisurely journey via Singapore, Hong Kong, China, Japan, Korea, Canada and the United States, arriving home aboard the *Queen Mary*. He turned 40 on June 3rd that year and until he died – 42 years later – would never again be so free, either of heavy responsibilities or acute anxiety about Britain's future, about her so-called 'special relationship' with the United States, and about the menace posed by powerful men in the Kremlin, whose likely conduct was so difficult to predict.

While in Singapore, Slessor recalled, 'we spent some pleasant days at Seletar with the Tedders – he was then commanding the RAF Far East.' This is the first of only six references in the 637 pages of his memoirs to Marshal of the Royal Air Force Lord Tedder of Glenguin (CAS from January 1st 1946 to December 31st 1949), a man with whom he would be in frequent touch for five years, 1946-1950. Exceptionally for Slessor, no comment follows along the lines of 'he became this or that and is a great friend of mine.' For his part, the 688 pages of Tedder's memoirs are entirely silent on Slessor. Clearly, there was no love lost between them, although they actually found a great deal of important common ground during the years when their careers intertwined.

En route to Hong Kong, Slessor had composed and sent to Tedder what he himself called 'an uninformed, uninspired and unofficial view' entitled *The Problems of Command in the Far East*. He assured Tedder 'that I am merely an unofficial nobody, out to learn, so that you will not find yourself committed to any strange views', but he was keen 'to get an idea of the atmosphere and point of view of the chaps on the spot', before taking up a position on the Air Staff when he reached England. Tedder did not reply. The paper was indeed 'uninformed', given Slessor's complete

---

[6] He was actually Director: RAF nomenclature in those days had its curiosities. He officially became Director nearly two years later, with Group Captain Hugh Fraser and Wing Commander Conrad Collier as his deputies.

ignorance of the Far East, and Tedder – a far more senior officer, as well as a former staff college lecturer – did not care to be preached at by 'an unofficial nobody'. Nor did he care to be addressed as 'one of the chaps on the spot'. Slessor had not intended to annoy Tedder, but countless colleagues and subordinates – even those who admired his many virtues – would be exasperated by Slessor's readiness to comment at inordinate length on matters about which he knew little. In later years, Tedder was mistaken in thinking Slessor unsuitable for the RAF's highest office, and Slessor was equally mistaken in regarding Tedder as a lightweight, advanced beyond his merits. Professionally, both became exceptional officers, usually in agreement on issues that mattered – personnel, material, relations with other services and allies – but personally the more they saw of each other, the less they liked what they saw.

In May 1937, Slessor noted 'a kind of holiday spirit at the time of the Coronation [of King George VI] which temporarily clouded the sense of urgency proper to the real situation in Europe.' Nevertheless, he expected to have ample time for field sports and one new interest: sailing. But the holiday spirit soon dispersed and Slessor found himself virtually imprisoned in Whitehall. 'The paramount fact' in 1937, he thought, 'was the phenomenal growth of the German air force... it had already surpassed the RAF in first-line strength and reserves.' This was not a 'fact' that would have been confirmed by careful scrutiny of the available evidence. Even less tenable was Slessor's amazing belief that the Luftwaffe was already capable of knocking out Britain from German bases. The Joint Planning Committee estimated that in April 1938 a prolonged attack on the scale of at least 400 tons of bombs every day could be mounted. Although Slessor later admitted this was impossible, it was at the time a grotesque exaggeration.

Two years later, there were no more than 500 Messerschmitt Bf 109 single-engined fighters in service and, as was the the case in all air forces, the transition from biplane to monoplane was marked by numerous accidents as pilots struggled to master its alarming differences, especially in speed. The three bombers in production – Dornier Do 17, Heinkel He 111 and Junkers Ju 86 – were light, twin-engined machines lacking the speed, range, defensive armament and bomb-carrying capacity to serve effectively as strategic bombers. Launched from German bases, they could barely reach London. The Bf 109 lacked the range and the Bf 110 lacked the agility to offer protection all the way out and all the way home. At the end of 1938, the Luftwaffe could muster no more than 1,900 bombers and fighters; even in May 1940 it had only 3,900 for all theatres and no air force can get anything like its full strength into the air at one time. Moreover, Slessor and his colleagues did not realize that the Luftwaffe faced exactly the same problems as the RAF in these years. Crew training (air and ground) took time. The production, provision of spares, and essential maintenance of radically new types of aircraft also took time. And the acquisition of the skills and equipment needed to find targets, hit them hard and cope with the certain dangers of flak, defending fighters and bad weather was a slow, painful process.

Slessor was directly responsible to the CAS (Cyril Newall, from September 1st 1937) for Air Staff policy. He was also a member of the Joint Planning Committee, set up to advise the Chiefs of Staff on current and future strategic problems. Writing in the 1950s about his efforts during the late 1930s, he admitted a share of blame for mistakes made, but he was not slow to excuse them. Being the man he was, and writing when he was, Slessor backed Churchill's version of events, apparently unaware that it was self-serving, and yet he was close enough to the great man during and after the war to observe the feet of clay as well as the brilliance.

It is a great pity that Slessor began his memoirs, *Central Blue*, as early as 1953, when he was only 56. Had he waited another decade, he might have produced a major work, more worthy of his powerful mind and great energy. Also, as anyone who reads his papers in Britain's National Archives will soon find, he had many trenchant comments to make about persons and policies that find no place in his memoirs, long as they are. It is significant that when the book was published, in May 1956, it received only a short review (mostly quotations from his text) in *The Times*, in those years a newspaper of the highest reputation. It gave more respectful attention in later years to his views on defence options in the age of atomic weapons.

By 1963, he was long out of office and would have had time for calm reflection, detailed research and broad reading; time for discussing key issues with men concerned in attempting to resolve them; and – not least – time for careful composition. *Central Blue* contains information and opinions of permanent interest, but these have to be winkled out of an immensely long text that continually rambles back and forth from one subject to another. That text is bloated by potted accounts and sweeping judgements about great events that he played no part in shaping. On the other hand, it is only fair to note here that a distinguished air power historian, Phillip Meilinger, regards *Central Blue* as 'exceptionally well written, insightful and detailed.' Slessor's memoirs will always remain a valuable source for the period as well as for his career, but he had the mind of a lawyer (rather than an historian) and was too concerned to justify his own actions and those of the Air Staff, and too ready with criticism of other services.

His job from 1937 onwards, he wrote, was 'routine preparation of major war plans to meet possible contingencies in all parts of the world.' Sounds impressive, but plans concocted in a Whitehall office without any first-hand experience of what was being done in aircraft factories or in front-line squadrons were unlikely to be realistic. What reliable information did Slessor have access to about the aviation industry or the air forces of other countries? He was too junior (a newly-appointed Group Captain) to be privy to military or political thinking at the highest level.

Much of his time in 1937-8 was actually taken up in numerous exasperating discussions with Indian authorities apparently unaware of military dangers in Europe and overly concerned about their own frontiers.

Assertion becomes doctrine

The basic weakness of Air Staff cogitation in Slessor's day was that plans were not made with the potential enemy in mind, but in accordance with Trenchard's assertions translated into a doctrine that every RAF officer was required to believe and preach. Slessor's own basic weakness was the fact that he had gone straight from school into the army. Three years at university would have helped to broaden his mind and improve his capacity to assess – and answer back to – such powerful personalities as Trenchard, John Salmond and Churchill. Portal and Tedder were two officers who managed this admittedly difficult feat, which is why they are regarded as commanders of the highest category and Slessor is not. His family background encouraged uncritical loyalty to senior officers. When he went to Plans in 1937, he was rising 40 and had never served on either a bomber or fighter station in Britain. He readily confessed that he was quite ignorant about machinery. He never piloted a modern aircraft, and he had no knowledge of the aeronautical revolution of the mid-1930s. He was an able theorist, good at paper work and at arguing around a table, but he knew nothing about the actual condition of the operational or training commands. Like all other Trenchardists, the practical challenges posed by the Axis Powers and by Japan found him wanting.

Slessor would often protest that he and his colleagues had only the experience of World War I to guide them, but they refused to learn anything from either the Spanish Civil War or the outbreak of fighting between Japan and China. 'I think we may be getting exaggerated ideas from the results of low-flying attacks in Spain and China', he wrote in December 1937. 'We must remember those campaigns have mainly been directed against semi-organized and semi-disciplined troops', which would not be the case in the event of war between Britain and Germany. But German commanders welcomed the opportunity of training and fighting in 'a European Aldershot' to gain priceless experience in solving supply problems as well as coping with actual combat. In accordance with its War Manual, the British Air Staff did not intend to offer 'any organized close support by aircraft at all', and bombers would get through to their targets without escort fighters. Air Vice-Marshal Arthur Capel, Commandant of the School of Army Co-Operation at Old Sarum, Wiltshire, from 1936-8, recalled in April 1977 that there was very little instruction in close support tactics during those years. Nor did he recall any pressure being brought to bear either by the War Office or the Air Ministry to provide such instruction.

Other serious errors were made by Air Staff planners during these years, especially in over-rating the impact of bombing on shaky Germans and under-rating the bomber strength needed to have any significant effect on the war-waging power of a major industrial nation. In *Air Power and Armies*, Slessor had written that 'ethical considerations' must be set aside when attempting to destroy an enemy's vital centres, and recognised that 'expediency too often governs military policy and actions in war.' Yet he had a hand in composing this opinion expressed by the Air Staff in January 1938: 'A direct attack upon an enemy civilian population... is a course of action which no British Air Staff would recommend and which no British Cabinet would sanction.' The Air Staff went on to assert that factories could be legitimately destroyed, including the 'workers' inside them, while sparing the 'civilians' living beside them – who were, of course, the same workers or their families and friends at home. Slessor shared Trenchard's delusions about the ability of bombers to influence the course of a war, even when those bombers were small, lightly-loaded, short in range, few in number, and flown by crews inadequately trained and equipped. He was no less remiss in his knowledge of fighters, either as escorts or opponents.

As early as September 1916, Trenchard had decreed that 'The aeroplane is not a defence against the aeroplane', but 'as a weapon of attack, cannot be too highly estimated.' This opinion became 'the core of RAF strategic thinking' throughout the inter-war years. A natural outcome of this belief was a neglect of air defence. Nowhere was the dogma that 'the bomber will always get through' supported more staunchly than in the RAF, which was determined that its own bombers *would* always get through. It required something in the nature of a miracle to bend RAF thinking to the notion that the bomber must not get through, and could be prevented from doing so.

That miracle was the discovery in 1935, and subsequent development, of what we now know as radar: a means of locating aircraft in the sky, at ever-increasing distances and heights. But if methods of air defence were improving in Britain, might they not also be improving in Germany? 'To admit that there was a defence against the bomber', wrote Richard Overy, 'was to question the whole basis upon which an independent air force had been built.' Not a question Slessor welcomed. It was an 'article of faith' with the Air Staff that the counter-offensive was vital, and he admitted to placing too much faith in that doctrine and too little faith in the efficiency of a fighter defence before the advent of the eight-gun monoplane and radar, about which he was then ignorant – which is surprising for a man apparently at the centre of RAF planning.

Chamberlain's government, 'in one of its few far-sighted moves', forced 'an unwilling RAF' to invest in an air defence system. Sir Warren Fisher (Permanent Secretary of the Treasury and Head of the Civil Service) complained bitterly to Chamberlain in October 1938 about Air Staff resistance to creating such a system. Its representative, he said, gave way reluctantly 'with a shrug of his shoulders.' In that year, the Air Staff was arguing 'that the Spitfire and the Hurricane did not represent a satisfactory solution to Britain's air-defence problems.' There exists, for example, a note penned on June 17th 1938 by a Whitehall Warrior who cannot have had recent cockpit experience claiming that 'the speed of modern bombers is so great that it is only worthwhile to attack them under conditions which allow no relative motion between the fighter and its target. The fixed-gun fighter with guns firing ahead can only realize these conditions by attacking the bomber from dead astern.' Mercifully, this nonsense did not kill either the Hurricane or the Spitfire.

Slessor accepted as 'legitimate criticism' of the Air Staff that insufficient attention was paid to the technical difficulties of bombing. These included navigation (very poor in daylight, hardly practised at all in darkness), the design, explosive force and accurate dropping of bombs, the distance to likely targets (which required a careful balance between bomb weight and fuel weight, if the bomber was to have a chance of getting safely home) and – by no means least – the effect on men and materials of weather conditions that were often severe at bombing altitude over the North Sea and north-west Europe.

Slessor tells us frequently that the only experience the planners had was gained during the Great War, but planners must look ahead, and press for realistic and repeated practical exercises with the aircraft available at the time, or expected to become available shortly. He is surely right, however, in arguing that whatever errors of judgement were made by the Air Staff, the main responsibility for Britain's parlous state on the eve of war lay with the government: 'with its complete lack of any sense of urgency, its unrealistic attitude towards foreign affairs, and its insistence on economy and non-interference with the normal processes of industry, regardless of the international situation at the time.'

'Our belief in the bomber, in fact, was intuitive', Slessor admitted, 'a matter of faith.' But faith without works is generally held to earn few rewards. The faith was uncritically imbibed from the incoherent mumblings of Trenchard, a man who had even less first-hand knowledge than his adoring disciples of the actual performance of aeroplanes and their systems. 'We in plans were too optimistic on many counts – on the ability of the offensive to reduce the enemy air attack at its source; on our ability to bomb unescorted by day or to find and hit targets at night; on the bombing accuracy to be expected; on the effects of a hit by the small bombs of the day, and on the numbers required to ensure a hit; and on the results both moral and material to be expected from the bombing of industrial objectives. We attached insufficient importance to things which afterwards became a commonplace, like bombing and navigational aids, signals equipment, D/F [Direction Finding] homing beacons and blind landing systems. We had no Bomber Development Unit until 1939', and trials were few and inadequate. It is a shattering self-indictment, amply confirmed in many subsequent studies, by one of the RAF's outstanding bomber champions. At the time, however, the situation seemed not so bad. Slessor went shooting regularly during these critical years, and even took time out to go hunting in Ireland.

Bomber Command's paper tigers

An 'astonishing aspect' of the Air Staff's fixation on the knock-out blow is the fact that only in the spring of 1938 did the RAF even begin to make realistic plans for the use of bombers. Until then, 'pious intention' prevailed over 'military possibility'. There were no units trained in reconnaissance to help bomber commanders answer an ancient, but elementary, question: 'What hazards lie ahead?' There was no organization charged to interpret photographs and thus answer an equally elementary question: 'What damage was done by our last raid?' Even the simplest navigational techniques were largely unknown. In the two years before the outbreak of war, for example, there were no fewer than 478 forced landings caused by RAF pilots getting lost during short flights in daylight over familiar territory. How such innocents would cope with raids over unfamiliar territory, opposed by ground fire and enemy fighters, was a question not even posed, let alone answered. The answer, of course, is that they suffered. In the autumn of 1940, Bomber Command lost in accidents six times as many aircraft as were destroyed by the enemy. Even a year later, in October 1941, when the assigned targets were Stuttgart and Karlsruhe, bombers were reported wandering over 27 other cities. Very little was done to ensure accurate bombing from high levels, and as for the bombs themselves, the Air Staff had rejected in 1935 a proposal that the standard 500-pound bomb be replaced by bombs weighing 1,000 and 2,000 pounds.

As late as October 1938, the RAF had precisely nine squadrons of Armstrong Whitworth Whitley twin-engined bombers – somewhat less useless than its Bristol Blenheims, Fairey Battles, Handley Page Harrows and Vickers Wellesleys. The Blenheim was quite fast, and had some value for short-range reconnaissance, but none whatever as a strategic bomber. The Battle was a single-engined machine weighed down with a crew of three. Virtually unarmed or armoured, and able to carry a very light bomb load not very far, it was an unqualified disaster, yet more than 2,000 were built. Fortunately for their crews, neither the Harrow nor the Wellesley was sent across the Channel.

Although the Vickers-Armstrong Wellington, Bomber Command's first efficient weapon, was coming into service during 1938, the general standard of navigation remained poor, even in daylight, and all the essential equipment – radios, bomb-aiming and release gear, cameras, defensive guns, cabin heating and even the actual bombs – was inadequate. So also was training in the use of that equipment. To this shameful catalogue one must add the crassness of Air Vice-Marshal

Richard Peirse (occupying the position of Deputy CAS, no less) who suggested that good bombing results might nevertheless be obtained if crews would deliberately slow down over their targets. Newall, fortunately, ruled that it was not 'practical politics' to expect a pilot to do this.

In Malcolm Smith's words, the Whitley's first flight in March 1936 had been 'a memorable fiasco... the aircraft was inherently unstable and could not fly straight; the nose turret would not move in flight because of wind pressure; nobody could see out of the mid-upper turret; the tail guns would only fire in a certain position; the aircraft crashed on landing.' Later Whitleys performed rather better – especially as target tugs – but the fact that this inadequate machine, available in such small numbers, was Bomber Command's principal weapon for several years is a sufficient indictment of Trenchardist theorizing. Did Slessor, or any of his Whitehall colleagues, ever climb aboard a Whitley or go for even a short daytime flight in one? Moreover, even 'a fully-equipped and operationally-experienced Bomber Command' was 'brought to the very edge of defeat over Berlin', during the winter of 1943-4 by efficient ground and air defences.

No-one doubts the bravery, determination and skill of its crews, but the command was not saved by its own efforts, despite the assertions of Slessor and other bomber champions. It was spared to make an important contribution to victory in the last 15 months of the European War by a combination of long-range American fighters (especially the P-51 Mustang), ranging freely over every corner of the Reich to eliminate the Luftwaffe's day fighter defenders, and by the Allied landings in Normandy, which soon eliminated the early warning system of its night fighter defenders.

Expansion schemes

Slessor was involved in several expansion schemes. There were eight of them between 1934 and 1939. All had a dual purpose: to enable Britain to overtake Germany's supposed lead in air power, and to deter Germany from using that air power against Britain. He helped to prepare a paper for the new CAS, Cyril Newall, on September 3rd 1937 that he thought 'pretty strong meat'. We were weak in the air, he wrote, and would remain so for the next two years. Bomber Command was 'almost totally unfitted for war.' A few weeks later, on October 12th, the Secretary of State for Air submitted 'Scheme J' (based on Slessor's paper) to Cabinet. It was the first to be based on 'a calculated estimate of minimum strategic requirements, as opposed to the previous basis of "visible deterrents" or shots at "parity"' with a newly-formed Luftwaffe that was already widely feared even though very little was yet known about its equipment, strength, level of training or quality of leadership.' But the scheme was rejected on financial – not military – grounds.

Roy Fedden, a great engine designer with the Bristol Aeroplane Company, visited Germany in late 1937 and on his return advocated a single controller of aircraft production in the Air Ministry. Someone, he wrote, who would 'cut out once and for all the soul-destroying procrastination and pin-pricking with which the whole organization is at present hidebound.' One sympathizes with Fedden's exasperation, but when the crisis became grave, Britain's aircraft industry showed that it had the skills and initiative needed to overcome bureaucratic hurdles and would quickly out-produce Germany with aircraft of steadily improving quality. In 1940 and 1941, the RAF received over 35,000 aircraft; the Luftwaffe just 22,000. The rate of expansion is astounding. For example, the RAF took into service some 900 aircraft in 1935; over 20,000 larger and more complicated machines in 1941; and over 26,000 that were still larger and even more difficult to build in 1944.

In March 1938, as Germany occupied Austria, Slessor told Newall that Britain might be at war later in the year and should therefore get existing forces ready (rather than expand further) and build up a war-training organization. His advice was rejected. Newall believed, as he told the Secretary of State in April, that without rapid expansion, 'we must accept a position of permanent inferiority to Germany in the air', and would therefore be obliged to yield to German demands. 'Scheme L', which reached the Cabinet in April 1938, aimed at a large expansion of first-line strength.

Meanwhile, Slessor and two of his colleagues were pondering the design of 'an ideal bomber'. It should have a still-air range of 2,000 miles and a minimum bomb load of 2,000 pounds. They were mistaken about the weight and number of bombs required to cause serious damage; mistaken also in believing the bomber could defend itself; and they overlooked the significance of self-sealing fuel tanks and protective armour for crew and engines. They also passed lightly over problems of navigation and bomb-aiming. Such ignorance, though alarming, is hardly surprising. Slessor's previous experience consisted of office work in the Air Ministry, lecturing at Staff College, and petty operations in India. He knew nothing about the revolution, during those very years, in aircraft design and construction.

Then came the Munich crises in September and early October. These provoked 'Scheme M', intended for completion in March 1942. It provided for 1,360 genuine 'heavy' bombers (with four engines), but emphasized the need for fighters, hitherto insufficiently valued. This was the last of the pre-war expansion schemes, and placed a 'new emphasis' – not before time – in the words of Sir Kingsley Wood, Secretary of State for Air, on 'strengthening our fighter force, that force which is designed to meet the invading bomber in the air.' Sir Thomas Inskip, appointed Minister for the Co-ordination of Defence in March 1936, had begun the critical shift in two reports (December 1937 and February 1938) 'from a belief in a costly bomber offensive as the core of British defence policy to a stress upon the importance of cheaper fighter defence.' Inskip was therefore bitterly criticized then and later by Slessor and his colleagues, but his broad grasp of the issues, laced with common sense, helped him to outface his critics.

The main reason why the Air Staff did not get the bomber force it demanded so vociferously was, as Malcolm Smith has said, 'to a large extent, its own fault.' Slessor and his fellow planners drew 'apocalyptic pictures of what the next war would be like', but only succeeded in convincing senior government ministers and civil servants that appeasement was preferable to another war. A policy based on the air deterrent would have failed as dismally as appeasement did, for Hitler would not have backed down over the Rhineland, Austria, or Czechoslovakia, and if the RAF had launched its bombers, their weakness would have been at once revealed. 'Left to their own devices', concluded Smith, 'the Air Staff would not even have prepared adequately for the Battle of Britain.'

Intelligence

Slessor had access to what he believed to be 'an efficient but grossly understaffed' branch of Air Intelligence dealing with possible targets. Its status can best be judged from the fact that it was commanded by a retired Squadron Leader. Edgar Kingston-McCloughry – then a Wing Commander – recalled a visit by a German air mission under Erhard Milch (Goering's deputy) and Ernst Udet (head of technical development) to Cranwell in early 1938. After a long boozy evening, Milch invited Kingston-McCloughry to visit the Luftwaffe College, 'but such was Whitehall in those years that approval was given only subject to my paying all my own expenses.' Kingston-McCloughry was severely critical, in later years, of Britain's fragmented intelligence organization and its ignorance of German industry. In general, he thought, 'the various planning and operational staffs accepted only that intelligence which suited their own ideas, often without question.' They fell into the ancient trap of agreeing with their own assumptions.

Slessor and his colleagues faced real difficulties in attempting to assess the German threat. Secrecy and deliberate deception concealed war preparations, confusion was caused by the inevitable mixture of good, bad, and indifferent information coming from many sources, and there were bureaucratic inefficiencies in the analysis and dissemination of intelligence. There was no co-ordinating authority charged to give systematic scrutiny of the material collected by a plethora of agencies that were rivals rather than allies.

Sir Robert Vansittart, Permanent Under-Secretary of State at the Foreign Office, was one of very few men in Whitehall in the 1930s capable of identifying the German menace and making a rational estimate of its growth and power. He and other mandarins regarded the Air Ministry as an incompetent institution and created his own intelligence service. Vansittart castigated the Air Staff for tenaciously sticking to a conviction that Luftwaffe expansion must mirror that of the RAF. The Air Staff, unfortunately, rejected Foreign Office criticism, and claimed sole rights to interpret information about the Luftwaffe. But the 'excessive rigidity' of Newall, Slessor and their colleagues was merely what Wesley Wark called 'a hedgehog response'. As Air Marshal Sir Victor Goddard (then head of the European Section of Air Intelligence) recalled, 'What passes for "intelligence of the enemy's intentions" is more usually propaganda for a change of government policy: honest propaganda, maybe, but based on ideas more than on facts.'

British intelligence agencies in the 1930s were short of staff, funds, equipment and prestige. There were far too many of them, they refused to co-operate with each other, and they had little influence on decision-makers, civilian or military. Squadron Leader Frederick Winterbotham, a member of the Secret Intelligence Service and head of the Air Department of MI6, visited Germany on several occasions in the 1930s. He gathered important information about aviation personalities and hardware, but found it difficult to get that information through to British political or military leaders. 'The air force chiefs', he later recalled, 'no doubt under pressure from their political overlords, seemed unable until almost too late to take action on the information which I had obtained with such care.' Slessor, however, thought highly of Winterbotham, 'who had wormed himself into the confidence of the highest German leaders, from Hitler downwards, for some years on end.'

The intelligence gathered or received by the Air Staff remained patchy until the outbreak of war. By then, the Air Intelligence Branch had a staff of some 40 officers, half of them 'retreads' (retired officers now re-employed) and many had been army officers in their fully-active days. Despite Slessor's opinion that it was 'efficient', it included several incompetents, as a result of hiring retired officers whose qualifications were limited to a knowledge of languages. Nothing was learned to challenge the Air Staff's belief that the Luftwaffe would be capable of an immediate knock-out blow. There was no continuous, systematic study of Germany's actual capabilities for an air offensive against British targets.

Ever since 1936, analysts had pictured German power as already massive and growing by the day. 'Part of the problem', thought Williamson Murray, 'was that strategic analysis was largely done by each service and its intelligence branch separately and then amalgamated rather than re-thought.' The result was 'an aggregation of worst case assessments as each service took counsel of its own fears and preoccupations', encouraging the government in its determination to appease Mussolini and Hitler. The Air Staff believed that the whole strength of the Luftwaffe might be hurled at Britain on day one of a new war: 'only airmen from island powers', remarked Murray, 'could cast theories in which the entire ground situation would be ignored.'

The RAF's intelligence officers lacked technical details of German bombers, but they had access to full information about British bombers and realistic estimates could have been made by simple analogy to calculate what weight of bombs a twin-engined aircraft (no four-engined bombers were yet in service) could carry to a British target from bases in north-west Germany, allowing for the weight of its crew, fuel, defensive weapons, ammunition and armour. The location and approximate size of all major aircraft factories was known, probable production rates could be deduced, and the scale of the threat sensibly assessed.

Even more reprehensible than their failure to test such alarming notions is the fact that the head of the European Section of Air Intelligence was 'discouraged' from expressing his objections to them. As Wark observed, 'air warfare on the scale imagined was a technological fantasy', well beyond the capabilities (though not the dreams) of any air force in the world. Moreover, the Luftwaffe was neither equipped nor trained for attacking the British Isles. Slessor should have known this at the time; he certainly did so in the 1950s, but here as elsewhere his memoirs are disappointingly superficial.

In October 1937, Lord Swinton (Secretary of State for Air) had circulated an Air Staff note to the Cabinet which estimated that by December 1939 Germany would have a total first-line strength of 3,240 aircraft to set against the RAF's total of 1,736. Britain, he concluded, was today 'in a position of grave inferiority to Germany in effective air strength'; a position that must worsen, at current production rates, during the next two years. Another note, of May 1938, revealed that those 3,240 German aircraft would be faced by no more than 2,373 British aircraft – but not until 1940. Five months later, Sir Kingsley Wood (who had replaced Swinton) informed the Cabinet that the latest forecast was even more alarming. By August 1939, he said, the RAF might have 3,392 aircraft (including reserves), but the Luftwaffe might then have as many as 7,030. Actually, when war began, Germany's air strength was nothing like as great: 3,541 first-line aircraft, including obsolete types, of which 2,893 were serviceable.

A famous American airman, Charles Lindbergh dined at Slessor's flat in Ebury Street, SW1, on September 22nd 1938. Lindbergh had made the first non-stop transatlantic solo flight, from New York to Paris, in May 1927 and was thereafter a global celebrity. He visited Germany five times in 30 months from July 1936 and was always royally received, for he admired Adolf Hitler and shared his hatred of non-whites and Jews. Slessor was presumably unaware of these opinions at the time, for he described Lindbergh as 'a man of outstanding character' and 'he struck us [Ronald Melville, Newall's Private Secretary, was also present] as being entirely sympathetic to the British, so much so that one occasionally forgot that one was not speaking to an Englishman. He has an enormous admiration for the Germans and likes them personally, though he says of course, that there is much in their policy and methods which he cannot forgive.' Slessor and Melville, polite hosts, did not press him on this point.

Lindbergh was convinced that Britain must avoid war at almost any cost. 'His whole attitude was that Germany was immensely formidable in almost every way both in her spirit, her national organization and particularly her air force which, he says, is incomparably the strongest in the world, and stronger than that of France, the United Kingdom and the United States of America put together. He said he thought that Germany was today as supreme in the air as Britain had ever been at sea and its bombers could easily flatten London, Paris and Prague.' But Lindbergh also thought that an attack on London would bring the US into the war. Slessor wondered if Lindbergh under-rated 'the economic factor' in Germany's capacity for waging war and suspected that he had been subjected to carefully-managed propaganda, designed to impress him – and through him, the British and French. Melville took a copy of these notes back to the Air Ministry for Newall to see. Lindbergh's opinions, widely reported on both sides of the Atlantic, played a part in encouraging isolationists in the US and appeasers in Britain.

An Air Targets Intelligence report of September 8th had described the Ruhr as the 'greatest and most centralized industrial area in the world', containing more than half of Germany's industrial population and producing most of her steel, heavy engineering and basic chemicals. If that area were to be 'paralysed', Germany could hardly wage a major war. Air Marshal Sir Edgar Ludlow-Hewitt (head of Bomber Command) was impressed and from a list of possible targets chose 26 coking plants and 19 electricity generating stations. These targets, he informed the Air Staff, could be 'reduced below the critical minimum' by some 3,000 sorties at a cost of precisely 176 bombers.

The Air Staff – becoming more sensible by the month – wisely disagreed and invited Slessor to prepare a plan of 'broader scope'. This he did during January 1939. Although 'we have located no key industrial group', he wrote, 'there is a key service, power, which is mainly electricity, the dislocation of which would bring about a very important reduction of all German War Industry.' By then, however, Ludlow-Hewitt had had second thoughts – as well he might, given the feeble state of his command and growing doubts about the quality of the information gathered by Air Targets Intelligence and used by Slessor. No plan to attack German oil resources was even considered until July 1939. 'It was no secret', as Neville Jones wrote, 'that Germany was heavily dependent upon imported oil or that the industry established by the Nazi government to produce synthetic oil from coal (though technically very successful) had failed to supply more than a fraction of the country's normal consumption.' An oil plan was drafted, but by then – on the very eve of war – the Air Staff was becoming acutely aware of the gulf between lucid plans and effective action.

Meanwhile, in December 1938, Slessor had decided that 'Germany's belt is already about as tight as she can bear, and that in making such stupendous efforts to achieve an initial advantage in military strength, she has used up all her hidden resources. Everything she has is in the shop window, and this is not really at all a satisfactory basis on which to commence a war.' He had no sure grounds for such a confident assertion. Victor Goddard, a more cautious and better informed officer, argued that it seemed more likely that the Luftwaffe would be employed in the east, at first, but even if the German drive were westward, the Luftwaffe would be employed on close ground support. Sir Kenneth Strong supports Goddard. He recalled that when he was Assistant Military Attaché in Berlin before the war, his reports consistently stated that the Luftwaffe was being trained and equipped to support the army. The Air Staff rejected them.

Slessor wrote to his sister, Elspeth (known as Betty) Fellowes, on January 25th 1939. The letter reveals how mistaken a man allegedly 'in the know' could be either about the unaided capacity of 'this Empire' to defeat Germany or about the prospect of war at that date. He urged Betty to do all she could 'to counter this ridiculous wave of defeatism and gloom that seems to be sweeping over this country. Say as much as you like to the effect that you have a brother who is really in the know, and who assures you that Germany hasn't a *hope* in the long run against this Empire. And that, though we may have a bloody time if it comes to war (which I don't believe it will) it is fantastic to suppose that a lot of perverted gangsters can knock us out. But that a hell of a lot depends on the morale and the guts of the ordinary civilian, male and female. If a lot of Spaniards in Barcelona can stick it, good Lord, we can stick it and a lot more. Remember that Germany is spending *millions* sterling a year on propaganda in foreign countries, including this country... Some day, we'll be looking back on all this as a silly nightmare – don't make any mistake.' It is a surprisingly simple-minded letter, for a man in Slessor's position, but his grasp of world affairs would improve dramatically during the next two years. Before then, however, in March 1939, he experienced the great joy of appointment as Air Aide-de-Camp to the King. Clearly, whether war came or not, he had a bright personal future ahead.

CHAPTER 6

WAGING WAR

Attack in the west

Staff talks with the French about how best to counter the German threat did not begin until March 29th 1939. Neither Slessor nor his colleagues foresaw an attack either on the Scandinavian countries or on France through the 'impenetrable' Ardennes (nor, for that matter, a Japanese advance down the Malay Peninsula to the 'impregnable' base at Singapore). He noted that the French were determined to remain on the defensive, and informed Newall that neither Britain nor France could do anything practical to help Poland, should there be a German invasion.

At staff talks in April he declared that Bomber Command was 'an increasingly formidable force for counter-offensive action against an enemy in war', capable of answering various challenges. An 'Advanced Air Striking Force' (AASF) would be based in France, though not merely to collaborate with French and British armies there. Slessor made it clear that neither the command nor the AASF could be placed under the orders of 'the French generalissimo' because they had 'a far wider sphere of responsibility' than any troops in France.

In August 1939, as an outbreak of war became imminent, the Joint Planners were replaced by permanent military representatives to the Supreme War Council, and Air Vice-Marshal Strath Evill relieved Slessor, who had now been promoted to the rank of Air Commodore (Brigadier-General) from September 1st, as the RAF representative in further talks with the French.

In a note to Newall, written four days after the outbreak of war on September 1st 1939, he urged an immediate all-out attack on Germany. 'Although our numerical inferiority in the air is a most important factor, it should not be allowed to obscure other potent considerations. We are now at war with a nation which possesses an impressive façade of armed might, but which, behind that façade, is politically rotten, weak in financial and economic resources, and already heavily engaged on another front [in Poland]. The lessons of history prove that victory does not always go to the big battalions. At present we have the initiative. If we seize it now, we may gain important results: if we lose it by waiting we shall probably lose more than we gain.' Little was even attempted during the next nine months, which is perhaps just as well. When the Battle of Britain began, Bomber Command attacked German airfields, but in 1,097 sorties – at a cost of 61 aircraft – it destroyed only five Luftwaffe aircraft and damaged 12.

After the war, he would do his best to gloss over such ill-informed assessments, but his memoirs would have greater value if he had been more concerned in the 1950s to inform his readers, and less concerned to justify his own conduct and that of his fellow Whitehall Warriors in the 1930s. During the early years of the war, his grasp of air power was insufficient to enable him to understand 'the great part waiting for it in the Middle East [under the inspired direction of Tedder and Coningham] and other overseas theatres.' Like many other senior officers, he would learn a great deal by 1945 that was not in the Trenchard doctrine. Norman Bottomley, for example, was Senior Air Staff Officer at Bomber Command Headquarters in 1939 and absolutely convinced that the unescorted British bomber would get through to its target in daylight. 'In our Service', he proclaimed, 'it is the equivalent of the old "Thin Red Line" or the "Shoulder to Shoulder" of Cromwell's Ironsides.' Years of bitter experience taught him the error of his ways, but at the time he was 'loyally reflecting RAF doctrine, utterly discredited before the end of 1939, that in daylight bombers flying in tight formation could ward off fighters.'

The RAF went to war in 1939 shackled 'to a doctrine as dangerous as those which had possessed the French and Germans in 1914.' What this meant, John Terraine concluded, was that 'the RAF was virtually irrelevant to the decisive Battle of France in 1940; it badly lacked anti-U-boat capacity until 1942; it lacked a realistic army co-operation system until that year; it failed to reach a sensible balance between the demands of the Strategic Air Offensive (prescribed by doctrine) and the Battle of the Atlantic (the lynchpin of agreed Allied strategy). Above all, except in the Middle East under Tedder, it failed to grasp the fact that when critical land operations are in progress, army co-operation is not simply a specialized activity of part of an air force, it is the function of the entire force, with all its available strength.' Although Slessor's grasp of air power improved greatly under the stress of events after 1939, he never ceased to be a bomber champion and a doughty champion of those responsible for the RAF's pre-war failings.

Agitation with the Admiralty

'Most Naval officers are men whose training and service at sea,' wrote Slessor in the 1950s, 'combines with their breeding and tradition to make the very best type of Englishman.' This is a revealing comment, both in tone and content, disarming with praise those whom he so often criticized. To judge from his own career and expressed interests, the cream of the crop were in fact soldiers and airmen, not sailors. When

Slessor returned to the RAF in February 1920, relations with the Royal Navy – especially in the higher ranks – were already tense; they got much worse during the 1920s and 1930s; were never better than wary even in wartime; and became tense again for the rest of Slessor's life. The comment also reveals, perhaps inadvertently, that he was at heart less a Briton than an 'Englishman' – and a home counties rural Englishman at that: a man for whom 'breeding and tradition' were fostered at certain schools, enhanced by a delight in horses (either for polo or the hunt), shooting and sailing, and brought to an honourable climax in years of public or uniformed service. They were not toothpick workers.

Until July 1937, the Admiralty was chiefly concerned, Slessor thought, with wresting control of the Fleet Air Arm from the RAF. It was then that Sir Thomas Inskip, Minister for the Co-ordination of Defence, ruled in favour of the Admiralty. His decision was deeply offensive to Slessor (and many other airmen), as he told Richard Peck in August. 'It was a most amazing decision made in the most amazing way. Our side of the story was practically unheard, and a snap decision was made by the Cabinet on Inskip's advice, two days before the recess.' From a national point of view, he thought the decision 'thoroughly bad', but from an RAF viewpoint he welcomed it, as long as the Admiralty did not go on to press for control of shore-based squadrons and flying-boats. The Admiralty, he lamented, 'have such a terrific pull in society, in Parliament, and in the press, and they use it quite unscrupulously.'

Despite the RAF's 'rhetoric and vitriol', Inskip was right. 'The FAA was mismanaged and deficient... the RAF had neglected its naval air assets', and nothing Slessor wrote then or later alters those facts. Apart from quarrelling with each other, did Slessor and his equivalents in the other services give serious thought to the type of aircraft the navy would need if war came? Did they ever meet to discuss them? Did they have any interest in, let alone knowledge of, American or Japanese naval aircraft, which were distinctly superior to any machines in British service at that time?

In Slessor's opinion – fully justified when war came – the Admiralty thought far too much about possible fleet actions and far too little about submarines and aircraft. These errors were as grave as the Air Staff's 'over-estimate of our capacity to bomb unescorted by day or our neglect of the technique of bombing.' The Admiralty was equally at fault in assuming that war at sea required the maritime airman to be a naval officer. Slessor recalled that one of Coastal Command's most effective squadrons in the coming war would be 311 (Czechoslovakian) Squadron, many of whose crews had never even seen the sea before fleeing to Britain. Sailors – British or American – were notorious for firing at friendly aircraft from start to finish of the war, but Slessor knew of only two cases when aircraft attacked friendly shipping.[7]

---

[7] One was a Coastal Command B-24 Liberator, which damaged a French submarine caught surfacing in a forbidden area on October 10th 1943.

As for the Government's decision to give up access to ports in western Ireland, it proved to be a calamitous one, as Slessor learned in 1943, when he became head of Coastal Command. 'I was foolish enough to feel that, if we secured the goodwill of the Irish Government', access to the ports would be permitted should war break out. He was mistaken, and rightly considered Eire's indefensible action would cost many seamen their lives during the Battle of the Atlantic.

At this point in his memoirs, Slessor once more abandons chronology to have his say about the aircraft carrier – an important element in his later air power thinking. He never ceased to echo Trenchard's dismissive opinion and regarded the carrier era 'with resignation as an appallingly expensive but short phase in the development of warfare, through which we have to pass.' He spoke of the 'absurdity of packing an aerodrome into a steel hull that can be sent to the bottom by one guided bomb with an atomic warhead.' For all his agitation, the many advantages of a properly-protected aircraft carrier have ensured its survival as a major weapon in helping to prevent crises escalating out of control.

Agitation with the War Office

Slessor shared Liddell Hart's opinion 'of the deadening influence on the pre-war army of the Cavalry Club and the age limits for retirement (imagine keeping a Lieutenant-General in active employment to the age of 67!)' The picture of the War Office on the outbreak of the Second World War that emerges from Liddell Hart's *Memoirs* 'is really horrifying', Slessor thought. 'It is itself a sufficient explanation of the disasters that befell the British army in the earlier stages' of that war. 'The attitude of the General Staff to the realities of what was then modern war – for example, to the AA defence of this country in 1937-38 – surely casts some light on the occasional [*sic*] failures of the Air Staff to be as co-operative with them as we might have been.' In Slessor's opinion, Liddell Hart revealed a sound grasp of 'modern strategic and tactical realities – including the implications of air power – tragically lacking in the General Staff of that day.' In his gold medal essay published by the Royal United Services Institute in 1936, Slessor had advocated a re-organization of the army and a composition of the Field Force on similar lines to those advocated by Liddell Hart to Leslie Hore-Belisha, Secretary of State for War. Unfortunately, the Powers-That-Were in this country, unlike those abroad, took little more notice of his voluminous writings than they did of the much less distinguished ones of a mere wing commander – which was precisely nil; the history of the Second World War would make less tragic reading if they had.

However, Slessor admitted to Trenchard in June 1937 that his essay was not 'an honest expression of opinion.' Britain could no longer afford to intervene on land in a European war: 'Our wealth and our overseas trade are such vitally important weapons in our armoury that we should not weaken them by spending millions more than we need on an army of a nature which is not really vital to our existence as an Empire.' The conclusion, which he did not draw, was that Hitler, Mussolini and Japan's rulers would be deterred from wrecking that empire by a combination of British air and sea power. As he wrote in February 1938, one of the army's main tasks was 'to act as a goalkeeper for the navy and the air force, not only at home but abroad.' Not an opinion that endeared him to soldiers, then or later.

Slessor ended his review by reflecting on those ghastly 18 months before war broke out in September 1939. 'I often find it difficult to bring myself to read about that period – it brings back too sharply the awful feeling of frustration and fear that constantly obsessed the mind of anyone who saw at first hand the weakness and ineptitude – more, the idiocy – of what passed for government policy in those days.' True enough, but there was also 'idiocy' in the Air Ministry.

From the moment Hitler seized the rest of Czechoslovakia in March 1939, the dispatch of a British army to the continent became a certainty, despite Air Staff resistance. With that army went protection. The Air Staff was obliged to assign four fighter squadrons to this duty, and earmark six more for probable attachment. The shortage of fighters was obvious, but the Air Staff 'still pinned its faith to bombers and recoiled from any step likely to hold up the bomber programme.'

Close air support and interdiction of ground forces had always been at the bottom of RAF priorities. An Air Staff memorandum of November 1939 declared, even after Germany's conquest of Poland, that 'The two functions of bomber aircraft in support of the army are to isolate the battlefield from reinforcement and supply, to block or delay the movement of reserves, and generally to create disorganization and confusion behind the enemy front... But neither in attack nor defence should bombers be used on the battlefield itself.' In accordance with that absurd doctrine, Bomber Command – weak as it was – did not even try to attack German forces after their invasion of western Europe on May 10th 1940.

Cyril Newall

Cyril Newall had been appointed CAS in September 1937, much to the surprise and disappointment of Hugh Dowding and Edgar Ludlow-Hewitt, both of whom were his superiors in every respect. He succeeded Edward Ellington – another surprise choice – who never flew in combat and saw active service only as a soldier. Although 'Uncle Ted' was apparently a kind-hearted, fair-minded chap, Trenchard, John Salmond and Wilfrid Freeman openly despised him, and in 1975 Slessor would tell the head of the Air Historical Branch that he had been 'a disaster'. Ellington was ineffective in dealing with other service chiefs and had to be carried by his civil servants. Newall certainly inherited a shaky throne, but he too proved incapable of handling a demanding task. Trenchard,

Salmond and Freeman soon became as bitterly opposed to 'poor old Cyril' as they had been to 'Uncle Ted'.

Dowding's personal grief at being overlooked for the RAF's highest office turned out to be a national blessing because he had all the qualities needed at Bentley Priory, to command an air defence system, and none of the smooth amiability and bureaucratic skills essential in Whitehall. Even so, it was Newall who advised Dowding in July 1938 that he must leave Fighter Command in July 1939. The ever-escalating crisis with Germany and Italy (to say nothing of Japan) makes that decision seem unwise, but it is the subsequent dithering in the Air Ministry, resulting in brief extensions of his tenure, tardily notified, that many historians have condemned. Dowding was to have been replaced by one Christopher Courtney, an officer without air defence experience. By the grace of God, who arranged a serious but not fatal aircraft accident for Courtney, that change did not take place.

On March 31st 1940, the day before Dowding expected to leave Bentley Priory, he was invited by Newall to stay on for a further 15 weeks, until July 14th. Newall wrote again, on July 5th, to ask him to remain in office until the end of October. In view of Britain's desperate situation, Fighter Command's key role in remedying it, and his own conviction that he was still the right man for the job, Dowding asked to remain until April 24th 1942, his 60th birthday, unless the war ended before then or he wished to leave. Both Newall and Sir Archibald Sinclair (Secretary of State for Air) apologized for past discourtesy, and on August 13th Newall informed Dowding that he was to remain head of Fighter Command indefinitely. Dowding remained in office until November 25th, when defeat in the day battle over Britain had been avoided, at least until good weather returned with the spring of 1941. As for Courtney, he gave excellent service as head of supply and organization in the Air Ministry for the rest of the war and had nothing whatever to do with the operation of aeroplanes of any kind.

Ludlow-Hewitt had shared Trenchard's 'mystical faith' in the bomber since 1918, but reality broke in soon after he was appointed head of Bomber Command in 1937. He became aware that 'no hard thinking had ever been done about how bombers were to find their targets; how they were to aim their bombs; how the bombs were to destroy large structures; above all, perhaps, how a credible offensive was to be mounted with the very small force at Bomber Command's disposal.' After a generation in which belief in the 'self-defending bomber formation' lay at the heart of RAF policy, Ludlow-Hewitt now realized that fighter escorts would be essential even for bombers that were sensibly designed, adequately equipped, large enough to carry destructive bomb loads and flown by properly-trained crews, including navigators. He made these points – bluntly, in detail, and often – to Newall and his Air Staff. Sadly, as little men do, they took more notice of the acid tone than the constructive content. Consequently, Ludlow-

Hewitt was sacked in April 1940 and replaced by Charles (known to his friends as Peter) Portal, a devout Trenchardist.

Instead of spending time with Dowding and Ludlow-Hewitt, his principal commanders, Newall stuck to his Whitehall desk, vainly resisting the government's growing emphasis on ordering fighters (of exciting performance and armament), rather than bombers (that were poorly designed – with the exception of the Wellington – and capable of carrying only small bomb loads not very far). He learned nothing from the Luftwaffe's conduct of operations during the Spanish Civil War, and even asserted that its adroit support of ground forces was a gross misuse of air power. He therefore resisted demands for similar support of British and French soldiers in the event of, and then in the face of, the German invasion of France. As late as April 1939, Hastings Ismay wondered if the Air Staff 'would prefer their forces under Beelzebub rather than anyone connected with the army.'

Amazing as it may seem for a man in his position, Newall quite failed to realise his short-range, lightly-loaded bombers might cause some significant damage to German tagets only if they operated from French bases. When German forces occupied the Channel coast, and the Luftwaffe prepared to attack targets in southern England, he still thought it best to employ bombers against what he called 'strategic' targets far behind the front line. Sholto Douglas (then working closely with him) thought he was 'an absolute bag of nerves' by 1940. 'He worked at his desk at the Air Ministry during the day, and had a cell underground where he used to work and sleep at nights. He never left the place.'

And yet this man, in Slessor's considered opinion, was 'perhaps the most publicly under-rated among our leaders in Hitler's war.' Together with Wilfrid Freeman, according to Slessor, Newall created 'the structure of air power that was to prove such a decisive contribution to victory.' He was a keen fisherman and whipper-in of hounds – so Slessor tells us – and 'although he would be the last man to claim great intellectual qualities, he was sound, level-headed and decisive... I have seldom met a man who was so good for one's morale as Newall; when times were at their worst I would walk out of his office feeling as though I'd just had a stiff whisky and soda.' Newall, Slessor repeated, was 'the prime architect of the wartime air force.' His opinion, unsupported by specific examples of Newall's professional merits, is not echoed by other contemporaries or by subsequent historians. 'No single, clear and concise rationale underlay the development of British air power in the rearmament period', wrote Malcolm Smith. 'What emerged was a mixture of dogma, opportunism and pragmatism, a "monstrous birth" exploited temporarily by the diplomats but shunned by the British policy makers as a real instrument of war... It is indeed a real measure of the failure of integration in the administration of British defence, the lack of cohesion between defence services, Treasury and Foreign Office that the RAF went to war and won its most famous victory with a policy that made nonsense of everything the Air Staff had been teaching for the last 20 years.'

Newall, like Slessor, was a strictly orthodox disciple of Trenchard, convinced that a powerful bomber force would probably deter an aggressor. If not, it would certainly wreck his economy very quickly, and no effective fighter defence was possible. A persuasive theory, but in practice little attention was paid to the meaning of 'powerful', and an effective fighter defence – based on radar and fast, heavily-armed monoplanes – was then being developed in Fighter Command. Meanwhile, in Bomber Command Ludlow-Hewitt was informing the Air Staff that a Trenchardist 'knock-out blow' lay far in the future. Tragically, Newall and his principal advisers were insufficiently impressed. Newall was ignorant of modern bomber or fighter issues and lacked the staff college experience – either as pupil or teacher – that might have broadened his mind.

On the other hand, it was during Newall's watch that the decision to order Hurricane and Spitfire fighters was taken, and to construct 'shadow' factories, where aircraft were produced in quantity at a time of urgent need. He rejected the prevailing opinion that if war came there would be no special demand for an aircraft repair organization, and that organization played a vital part in boosting aircraft supply to the RAF during and after the Battle of Britain. He also did more in May and June 1940 than some admirers of Dowding admit to resist Churchill's readiness to send British fighters to assist the French in an obviously lost cause.

Slessor must surely have known that strenuous efforts were being made from May 1940 onwards to get rid of Newall. He must also have known what unsavoury parts were played in this intrigue by his heroes – Trenchard and Salmond – backed by Lord Beaverbrook, a man whom he despised even though he had the ear of another hero, Winston Churchill, who became Prime Minister on the 10th of that month. A memorandum composed by Wing Commander Edgar Kingston-McCloughry (a member of the Air Ministry's Directorate of War Organization) and circulated anonymously, castigated Newall as 'a weak link in the nation's defence'. That memorandum also condemned 11 other senior officers, often in extravagant terms, and Kingston-McCloughry's bitterness was certainly exacerbated by not being promoted to the rank of Group Captain as quickly as he thought proper.

An official historian, Noble Frankland, 'enjoyed a close and lively friendship' with Kingston-McCloughry, and regarded him as 'a man of great ability, deep insights and ideas which were much in advance of his time', but he had a 'passion for intrigue or, as he would have put it, constructive criticism.' Merciless attention was drawn to Newall's 'inadequate mental ability, limited practical experience, weakness of character and personality, and lack of judgement and foresight.' Whatever his merits as a diligent office manager, it was clear by mid-1940 that Newall was unable to galvanize the Air Ministry, regarded by Churchill as 'a most cumbersome and ill-working administrative machine' into the alertness required in wartime.

Beaverbrook (appointed Minister of Aircraft Production by Churchill in May) eagerly backed the campaign against Newall, partly because he loved nothing better than wheeling and dealing behind the scenes, partly because he agreed with Kingston-McCloughry, and not least because Newall opposed many of the sweeping and sometimes ill-advised actions of the new ministry. By September, 'The Beaver' was receiving influential support from Trenchard and Salmond (Director of Armament Production in that ministry). They agreed about Newall's general weakness, but they also had two particular fears. Firstly, that he would prove unable to resist growing pressure for the creation of an army air corps to give direct support to ground forces. And secondly, that he no longer believed absolutely in the bomber doctrine.

Unlike Trenchard and Salmond – Bourbons both, in their mental rigidity – Newall had come to realize that his bomber force was quite incapable, at least in the near future, of causing serious injury to Germany and would be more usefully employed helping Fighter Command to prevent an invasion of Britain. Trenchard, whose knowledge of the performance of British bombers was nil, most improperly went over Newall's head on September 25th and wrote directly to Churchill, urging that Bomber Command be used solely against 'strategic' targets in Germany. Churchill agreed on October 2nd that Newall must go, and Portal succeeded him on the 25th.

Despite his best efforts, Newall proved to be an inadequate head of the RAF, and Slessor's fulsome praise – written long after the war – does him no credit as a would-be historian, although it certainly earns him great credit as a loyal friend to a conscientious officer. Newall was promoted to five-star rank (Marshal of the Royal Air Force) and appointed to the Order of Merit, yet so little real value was placed on his long experience at a high level and his relative youth – he was only 54 – that he was sent to New Zealand, as Governor-General, in January 1941. He idled away the rest of the war there, and received a barony on his return to England in June 1946. He took no further part in public affairs, wrote no memoirs, made no speeches of consequence, and died in November 1963.

As for Kingston-McCloughry, he was promoted to Group Captain (in strict accordance with his place on the Air Force List) in December 1940 and sent 'to fill a particularly important post in South Africa', as Sinclair put it, presumably without blushing. But he had earned qualified forgiveness by 1943 and returned to England to fill a genuinely important post in 1944. Although he reached Air-Vice Marshal rank in 1947, he was the only officer of his promotion block still in that rank in 1953. He is not mentioned in Slessor's memoirs.

CHAPTER 7

REALITY BREAKING IN

The Norwegian Campaign

Slessor wrote a paper on the strategy of 1940 during January of that year. He seriously suggested that Britain encourage Finland in her fight against the Soviet Union. In February he advised the War Cabinet that Britain must consider whether 'the onus for the overrunning of Finland by Russia *and of Sweden by Germany* [emphasis his] may not, in the eyes of the world, rest upon us.' He went on to say that we could not help Finland 'too openly', but it might be wise to supply war materials or raise volunteers to go there. If a regular force were sent, 'it must stay and stand its chances... It would blacken the face [*sic*] of Great Britain if the British troops sent to help Finland withdrew as soon as their communications were threatened and left the Finnish army and nation to a fate that we are unwilling to allow even one division of ours to share.' Others were also prepared to risk adding the Soviet Union to Britain's enemies at that time, but Slessor is supposed – not least by himself – to have a sure strategic grasp.

He also advocated an alliance with Turkey, which he described as 'the northern bastion of the Allied position in the Middle East, and it is literally vital that she should not fail us. She will not do so unless we fail her.' Wrong again, though less culpably. In June 1939 he told Newall that 'it has often been said that a judiciously spent million would have kept Turkey out of the German camp in 1914. I wonder how many hundred million pounds and how many thousand lives the failure to produce that million cost us?' However, no amount of persuasion, financial or otherwise, sufficed to bring Turkey into the Allied camp until Hitler was almost beaten.

Slessor wisely argued against mounting a campaign in Scandinavia: 'a proposal that we should invade Norway in order to persuade Sweden to send assistance to Finland and allow the passage of Allied detachments.' Unethical, he thought, and would have 'a disastrous effect' upon opinion in the US and the British Dominions; worse still, neither Britain nor France had the strength to bring it off successfully. Unfortunately, thanks to Churchill – then First Lord of the Admiralty – an Anglo-French force was sent to Norway.

The Germans had occupied Denmark and invaded Norway in early April. It was a campaign that should have enthralled Slessor – at least in retrospect, when writing his memoirs more than a dozen years later – for its wonderful illustration of air power in action. As Adam R.A. Claasen says, 'it was the first time that paratroops were used in war; objectives were secured solely by air power; large quantities of men, equipment, and supplies were delivered to the forefront of battle by air; and the Luftwaffe engaged in large-scale operations over the sea.' The Allied reaction to the occupation and invasion revealed the ineptitude of pre-war planning. For example, as Meilinger says, 'it was not thought that air units would even be necessary for the initial stages of the operation – an incredible oversight. Indeed, one historian [John Terraine] has stated that the joint planning staff "displayed an amateurishness and feebleness which to this day can make the reader alternatively blush and shiver."'

Also, as Kingston-McCloughry recalled, many of the best staff officers were already war weary from the stress of writing papers and making all too many paper plans. 'The first pressure of events proved how inadequate was this part of our High Command for the rough-and-tumble day-to-day problems of modern war... The Whitehall organization was in no shape to conduct operations. The Joint Planning Staff, tooled up for longer-term affairs, tried unsuccessfully to do the work of a theatre commander's staff.' The result was 'one of the biggest fiascos in our history', despite a long tradition of inter-service campaigns.

Slessor spoke out boldly against actions which he thought 'lunacy' or 'crazy' as well as merely impossible to execute with the available resources, but his was not a position of authority. On April 17th, for example, he wrote to Air Marshal Sir Philip Joubert de la Ferté (who had been put in charge of the 'Special Planning Staff' for the assault on Trondheim 'that regarded as a military operation in a purely professional sense, this operation is utterly fantastic' and likely to fail, so 'for pity's sake keep your stakes as low as you can. Don't push in three battleships if you can do with one; and don't push in more destroyers or troopships than you can possibly avoid – especially the former. Don't let's kid ourselves that the capture of Trondheim is going to win this war. And – let us remember – that after Trondheim we've got to go on fighting a long war – possibly with Italy as an enemy.'

Perhaps he was wise, as an English patriot, devout airman and senior planner, to pass swiftly over a string of events that cost many good men their lives or freedom for no useful purpose even though it offered excellent material for military historians (as well as air power enthusiasts) to consider. As Meilinger says, 'For two decades the RAF had maintained that for technical reasons of weight and performance, carrier-based aircraft were inherently inferior to land-based aircraft. Although the Luftwaffe did indeed make short work of the FAA's Swordfish and Skuas, the lesson here is simply that modern aircraft are superior to obsolete ones.' Another lesson that Slessor might well have considered here is the fact that 'modern warfare would be joint warfare... The arrival of air power, necessary for both land and sea operations, helped make joint planning and command an absolute necessity.'

Hitler's main reasons for seizing Denmark and Norway (and squeezing Sweden into benevolent neutrality) were to exploit them as bases for combined air-sea operations. At first, these operations were intended to conquer Britain directly. Later, when that ambition was set aside (until after the Soviet Union fell into his hands) they were intended to conquer her indirectly – by means of a 'Battle of the Atlantic' that would starve Britain into surrender by cutting off vital imports of food, war materials and oil. Excellent intentions, from an air theorist's viewpoint, greatly helped along both by the initial disasters of Franco-British reaction, and later by years of British failure to make life even moderately hazardous for German air and naval forces in Scandinavia. And yet, the alert air theorist would conclude, Hitler's spectacular Norwegian Campaign proved to be a sterile achievement. As Slessor would gradually realize – though not from any study of the Norwegian test case – there is a gulf between what aircraft may do in theory and what they will do in practice. They were not, by themselves, a war-winning weapon. They achieved most when working under leaders who understood the value of partnership with soldiers and sailors, at the behest of an overall commander who – unlike Hitler – fostered co-operation, rather than competition.

The invasion of Western Europe
The German conquest of France and the Low Countries in May 1940 revealed how 'pathetically misplaced' the Air Staff's faith in the 'strategic' bomber had been. As John Terraine says, what the RAF needed was 'twice as many Hurricanes and Spitfires and a good close-support bomber.' The Hawker Henley would have filled the latter role admirably. First flown in 1937, it was a sturdy single-engined two-seater, able to carry a useful bomb load far and fast, but only 200 were built and all were used merely as target tugs.

Unfortunately, the RAF's higher direction resolutely opposed close co-operation with ground forces, and soldiers had little respect for its plans. Portal, head of Bomber Command from April 1940, was as 'bitter a foe' of such co-operation as Trenchardist doctrine required. He believed that 'the bombing of objectives in Germany was likely not only to damage the German war machine in general, but to force the Germans to withdraw fighters and flak from the front to the rear, and to divert their bombing offensive to objectives in England.' He grossly exaggerated the impact his tiny force of light and medium bombers was capable of achieving, and was quite wrong about the effect even much stronger forces would have on the enemy. Bomber Command's gallant efforts against marshalling yards, blast furnaces and oil targets achieved nothing. 'The assault on the Ruhr', described by Denis Richards, an official historian, as the 'most cherished of all Air Staff projects, was a failure. The conception had been admirable, the timing doubtful; the available means utterly inadequate.'

On the afternoon of May 19th 1940, Slessor attended a meeting of the War Cabinet in Whitehall at which Churchill dictated specific orders for the conduct of military operations in France. 'There was an astonishing scene', he wrote on the 24th. 'Everybody in the room recognized that in point of fact this order was not one which could possibly be carried out – and in any event it was to say the least of it dangerous for the War Cabinet (or rather the Prime Minister) to try and command the BEF [British Expeditionary Force] from London, in ignorance of the real situation and regardless of the fact that the BEF was under the orders of the French.' General Sir Edmund Ironside, head of the British army, failed to stand up to Churchill and agreed to cross to France with this order; Slessor was to go with him, to see that the airmen played their part.

Off they sailed to Boulogne and were then driven to General Lord Gort's headquarters, where Slessor learned that the situation was worsening by the hour and the British intended to escape the Germans from Ostend, Nieuport and Dunkirk. He had with him a sketch showing the ranges of fighters based in south-east England and urged a glum Gort to get to Calais if he could because those three ports were too far east for effective fighter cover, but Slessor now began to fear a total defeat. Ironside was at a loss, so Slessor took his car and was driven some 18 miles – in three hours, through streams of refugees – to the headquarters of General Billotte in Béthune. 'I was extremely shocked at the whole atmosphere at that headquarters. They were completely defeated. They were merely sitting around saying "c'est fini", issuing no orders and simply wandering about listlessly while orderlies packed up gear.' Slessor realized nothing useful could be done. He found 'an excellent British military police corporal on a motorbike, and we went through ten miles of refugees and defeated troops like a hot knife through butter.' Back in Calais, they spent a miserable night, being 'well and truly bombed' and flew to London next morning.

When writing his memoirs in the 1950s, Slessor described Gort as 'a splendid soldier and a great English gentlemen... never wavered in my admiration of him... if ever there was a gallant officer, he was one.' But intellectual capacity and physical energy are more useful to a general, especially one in command of a beaten army, than the qualities of a gallant English gentleman, whatever they may be. Slessor's shallow assessment is typical of his attitude to senior officers – an assessment based on a slight personal knowledge and no discernable postwar study of their performance as commanders.

May 1940, Slessor later reflected, was a critical month. In his opinion

– more wildly sweeping even than usual – Hitler should have held the British and French forces in northern France and mounted an invasion of England. 'But, as before [in 1914], the glittering prize of Paris was too much for the Germans, and they lost the war.' They could have 'effected a lodgement with armoured divisions, and it is difficult to see how that could have failed to be decisive at that time, when our army was virtually disarmed.'

Most historians, however, find it even more difficult to see how the Germans could have safely embarked their heavy equipment (and horses, upon which they relied to supplement their motor transport); then crossed the Channel in a variety of vessels, none of them purpose-built for such a hazardous venture; then got ashore, unloaded their tanks, guns, ammunition, food, medical supplies and horses without too many disasters; and then, not least, sailed their empty vessels back to French or Dutch ports to do it all again, time after time. They were to manage all this in the face of Britain's overwhelming superiority at sea and the capacity of her air force to at least match the Luftwaffe in the decisive areas. As Alan J. Levine writes, 'an invasion in June or July was never a possibility... the Germans found virtually no seaworthy craft in the Channel ports, and this alone makes nonsense of the idea of an early pursuit of the British across the Channel. Barges and other craft for the invasion had to be tediously brought from Germany to the Channel ports, which had been heavily damaged by British demolition parties.' These facts were no secret in the 1950s, when Slessor was writing.

The apparent miracle of Dunkirk followed and a wave of relief swept over Whitehall. It soon subsided, however, and Churchill turned on the Joint Planning Committee. He condemned 'the dead weight of inertia and delay which has so far led us to being forestalled on every occasion by the enemy.' In August he therefore ordered it to work under his personal direction, and not that of the Chiefs of Staff. Slessor bridled (silently, at the time), for he had helped to prepare so many plans. When writing his memoirs, he suggested that Churchill, 'by a long chalk the greatest Englishman that ever lived' might possibly have been ill-advised in this instance.

Meanwhile, Slessor had welcomed the creation of a Ministry of Aircraft Production in May, but some 15 years later denied that Beaverbrook's appointment as Minister came just in time to save Britain from the inefficient Air Ministry. Once again, he presumed to criticize Churchill – this time for describing the state of aircraft production in June as 'muddle and scandal'. Slessor would rightly praise Wilfrid Freeman for his splendid achievements in the new ministry. He claimed to know Freeman well, and was therefore probably aware that he greatly valued the work done during two critical years (1938-1940) by his right-hand man, Arthur Tedder. 'I knew and trusted Tedder', Freeman told Roderic Owen in 1951: 'I did not feel like taking on the job unless I could have him.' Slessor could not, however, bring himself even to name, let alone give due credit to, a man he had come to despise.

On September 22nd 1940, Slessor wrote to Newall, suggesting that he ask the Prime Minister to 'restrain the Noble Lords of Aircraft Production' from publicly congratulating the industry for keeping up production in spite of bombing raids. 'If there is one thing that might lose us this war', he argued, 'it is concentrated and intelligent attack on the aircraft industry. The enemy has not yet done that, but let us thank God and keep quiet about it.' He quite understood the need to keep up the morale of workers, but this could better be done by personal messages through factory managers. If Newall said anything it had no effect, so Slessor wrote to Major-General Hastings Ismay (head of Churchill's Defence Office) a week later, on the 29th. It seems 'stark lunacy' to advertise the fact that the air industry has not yet been harmed by German bombers. 'Are we quite mad, Pug [Ismay's nickname]? Or do you think I am making an undue fuss about this?' He was not, but for Beaverbrook positive press headlines – in his own or other newspapers – always had the highest priority.

During the rest of 1940, Slessor toiled away at plans to increase Britain's air strength. He did not think a great army would be needed to liberate the continent because aerial attack, plus economic blockade, would jointly so ruin Germany that an occupation force would suffice. As usual, his confidence in his strategic judgement was utterly misplaced. There would be aerial attacks, by night and day, on a greater scale than he or anyone else could imagine in 1940, and yet a massive and costly landing was found necessary in 1944 that might well have failed had not the Reich been so severely wounded by the Red Army. That army suffered immense casualties during the last weeks of the war before subduing Berlin – a city that had by then been so heavily hammered by British and American bombers that its occupation, according to bomber champions on both sides of the Atlantic, should have been an easy matter.

Meeting Americans

Slessor came into serious contact with Americans for the first time in July 1940 when he met Colonel William J. Donovan – head of the Office of Strategic Services, precursor of the Central Intelligence Agency – who was sent to England by President Roosevelt to see if Britain could survive German attack. Donovan reported favourably, but other American officers did not, so in November 1940 Portal (now CAS) sent Slessor to Washington to set out the RAF's actual situation and explain what it needed. Talks had begun in July between Henry Morganthau (Secretary of the Treasury), William S. Knudsen (of General Motors, brought into the government to run the aircraft programme), General Henry H. Arnold (head of the US Army Air Corps) and Sir Henry Self, an Air Ministry official responsible for Britain's dealings with the US Government on matters of aircraft production. These talks persuaded Morris Wilson (Beaverbrook's representative in Washington) to believe that Britain would soon receive plenty of aircraft.

Slessor, who shared Portal's opinion that Wilson was too optimistic, left England with John Orme, an Air Staff civilian who became a close friend. He flew to New York aboard a Pan American Boeing flying-boat, disguised as a civilian and carrying a false passport, arriving on November 8th. He took with him an outline plan he had drawn up on RAF expansion and soon learned – as would many Britons after him – that the woolly words of Whitehall cut no ice in hard-headed Washington. Morgenthau demanded specific details – of production, pilot training, combat losses – which Slessor did not have. In December, Frank Knox (Secretary of the Navy) and Henry Stimson (Secretary of the Army) sent for him and expressed their displeasure at how little specific information he was able or willing to convey. Mightily embarrassed, he signalled Portal to say that while he did not mind being made to look a fool, he was certain that the government would get little help from Americans unless it trusted them.

Portal sympathised: he had recommended to Sinclair (Secretary of State for Air) on October 24th that Slessor 'should know before he leaves London whether or not he can speak on a basis of complete frankness as regards strategy, training and production, on all of which he will undoubtedly be questioned.' But Portal, newly appointed to his high office, did not yet carry much clout with Churchill or Beaverbrook, Minister of Aircraft Production. Sinclair informed Churchill on November 8th that Slessor's instructions were 'to describe the use which we intended to make of the aircraft due to reach us from America between now and June 1941 and to show how these imported aircraft, with our own production, "married up" with the flow of pilots and other personnel over the period.' A fair outline, but the detail was too sketchy for ·Washington's taste. Churchill, however, was unrepentant. He told Portal that he agreed with Beaverbrook's desire 'to keep our secrets from falling into dangerous hands.' The Prime Minister also told Portal that Slessor's telegrams were far too long, but brevity was never among our bomber champion's virtues.

Slessor's task was to help emphasize the need for increased production in the US of bombers, fighters and trainers for the RAF. As he later wrote, 'The US aircraft industry was then a huge unco-ordinated mass, with no-one to settle priorities or exercise any control; but its potential capacity, and the speed with which it subsequently proved it could work... was vastly in excess of anything that any of us thought possible at that time.' He also did his best to open American eyes to the difference between peacetime training and wartime operations. Aircraft would have to be flown even in bad weather, often from rough airfields; they would be lost or damaged at an appalling rate; experienced pilots would have to be replaced by novices; and there would be nothing like enough spare parts. It was now that Slessor got to know some of the top American airmen – 'Hap' Arnold, Carl Spaatz, Ira Eaker, Haywood Hansell, Hoyt Vandenberg and others – who listened to him and would become important partners and friends during the rest of the war.

He later wrote that he particularly liked Arnold: 'transparently honest', he thought; 'terrifically energetic, given to unorthodox methods and, though shrewd and without many illusions, always with something of a schoolboy naivete about him... No-one could accuse him of being brilliantly clever, but he was wise, and had the big man's flair for putting his finger on the really important point.' Slessor thought the organization at Air Force Headquarters in Washington was chaotic, and he was unimpressed by some of Arnold's assistants. But Vandenberg and Hansell, he thought, were clearly first-class.

Ordering American aircraft was all very well, but how were they to cross the Atlantic? Many could be shipped, despite the U-boat danger and a shortage of suitable shipping space, but others must be flown across. This required experienced pilots (in short supply) and some means of returning them to the United States and Canada for further delivery flights. 'The present system whereby we bribe a few American pilots to fly machines over', wrote Slessor, 'will not touch the fringe of the problem when we begin to get deliveries in really big numbers. Ultimately, we shall need something of the order of at least a thousand pilots on this job, and that, as far as I know, is a commitment which we have never faced in our calculations.' He was right and Portal was reluctantly forced to agree that here was another unforeseen crisis. Solving it was made even more difficult by Beaverbrook's antics as Minister of Aircraft Production and controller of the ferrying organization. Eventually Churchill reined in his old crony: 'you must try to help other people and other interests.' 'The Beaver' thereupon submitted another resignation (his 14th or thereabouts) and this time it was accepted, on May 1st 1941, to the great relief of many harassed men in Whitehall and elsewhere.

Slessor wrote a letter to his wife Hermione on December 4th 1940 in which we see that his understanding of Britain's military situation had greatly matured since writing to his sister Betty in January 1939. 'We must rely on US collaboration to win this war', he told Hermione. 'This is a grand country, and they are on the whole a grand people... I am astonished at the almost complete pro-British feeling here... And there is genuine and universal admiration for the British and the way they are taking it. The RAF stocks are as high as they could be.'

He greatly admired Frank Knox, 'a heady old buccaneer [who] would have the US in the war tomorrow, if he had his way.' He told Slessor about his recent meeting with Joseph P. Kennedy, Roosevelt's ambassador in Britain: 'by God, I could hardly hold myself in', said Knox. 'When he'd left I rang up the President and said: "See here, Mr President, if that God-damned yeller son of a bitch Kennedy ever comes near the navy department again I'll throw the bugger into the Potomac."' Slessor was both thrilled and horrified at this glimpse of a world so different from his own dear Whitehall, where it was usual to conceal equally bitter hatreds with civil words. Knox, he thought, was 'a much better man' than Harold R. Stark, Chief of Naval Operations, who was 'a nice old woman, but some of the Admirals are good.' He later flew to Buffalo on Lake Erie with Colonel Carl Spaatz, 'and had rather fun. But my hat, they do put back some liquor in this country.' Another eye-opener for a man more accustomed, in his official life, to tiny dry sherries – and not much more off duty.

Bill Donovan, he told Hermione, 'has been inexpressibly kind to me, and through him I have met a mass of people that otherwise I never should have met. I have stayed with him twice in New York, and he really is the nicest and kindest person I've ever met... He is a sort of unofficial emissary of Roosevelt and Knox – a sort of person behind the throne in this country, knows everything and everyone. I think he is certain to be in the government soon – either that or Ambassador to London in succession to that swine Kennedy, who is actively working against us in this country.' 'Wild Bill', as he is often known, never became a member of the US government or an ambassador, but his influence on US foreign and military policy was long-lasting. As R. Harris Smith has said, 'However indirectly, many of our latter-day Cold War successes, disasters, and entrapments can ultimately be traced back to him.'

During December 1940, while visiting Hollywood, Slessor wrote an article for *Fortune* magazine entitled *Some Aspects of British Air Strategy*. He was described as 'a high-ranking officer of the RAF who under the rules of the service must speak anonymously.' He began by observing that the three services were essentially interdependent and that 'air strategy is only one component of British imperial strategy, which is fundamentally a strategy of sea power. Great Britain is the centre of a maritime empire and British air strategy must always be governed by that fact.' He went on to praise the efforts of Fighter Command during the summer of 1940 and then turned to the work of Bomber Command. Its operations, he wrote, were not reprisals but 'based on a carefully-considered plan for breaking down the enemy resistance by carrying the economic war to the source of German military power.' Slessor did not pretend that civilians were not suffering, 'if there is such a thing as a civilian in totalitarian Germany today', but 'mere indiscriminate frightfulness as such has never formed part of the British conception of air strategy, not merely because it is barbarous, but because it is senseless, uneconomic and relatively ineffective.'

Hollywood, of course, helped Slessor to forget the war – at least while he was there – and inspired him to write at even greater length than usual to his wife on December 28th. He had been taken to a restaurant where Dorothy Lamour sat at a nearby table, with Spencer Tracy and James Cagney, and all three spoke to him. Other film stars passed back and forth, smiling and posing, while photographers scurried about, snapping away with flashbulbs. He had drinks with the two greatest stars of those days – Vivienne Leigh and Laurence Olivier, who assured Slessor that he was returning to Britain to join the RAF. In fact he joined the Royal Navy, much to Slessor's grief. On another occasion, he was taken to a boxing arena, where various celebrities were invited to take a bow, including 'a distinguished RAF officer', and received the loudest round of applause in his whole life. On Christmas Day he lunched with Barbara Hutton, the Woolworth's heiress, 'who I think is a pet'; later he spent time with the producer and director Cecil B. DeMille and was permitted to watch another director, King Vidor, at work.

The combination of Dowding and Beaverbrook brought him sadly back to earth and the real world of Washington. Sir Hugh Dowding (recently removed from Fighter Command) was persuaded by Churchill and Beaverbrook to go to the United States on an ill-defined mission to look into the purchase or production for Britain of American aircraft or engines. A delicate task, it required diplomatic and commercial skills that he conspicuously lacked. His presence in Washington greatly displeased many members of the Air Staff and Slessor in particular, who had several times been bruised by Dowding's blunt words, spoken or written. Rightly fearing that Dowding would speak candidly to American press and radio reporters, he suggested that the British Embassy provide him with a minder. Slessor also feared, as did Dowding's other Whitehall foes, that he might return, like Banquo's ghost, to haunt them. As it happened, Dowding hated the job and did little to resist Slessor's determination to have him recalled. 'How much easier life would be', Slessor sighed, 'if one only had to fight the Germans!'

The RAF wished to acquire 26,000 aircraft from the US by June 1942. Not enough, thought Slessor, but even that figure was unlikely to be achieved at current rates of production. Harry Hopkins (Roosevelt's most trusted aide) warned him that even when the President approved a programme, delays were likely regarding the supply of materials or manpower. There was also an ever-strengthening feeling that the needs of the US air force should come before those of Britain.

Portal told Slessor early in December that he was to remain in the US as his representative at the first of many Anglo-American staff talks. On January 8th 1941 Hastings Ismay had lunch with General Raymond E. Lee, US Military Attaché and head of intelligence in London. He told Lee that Slessor was the ablest of the British delegates 'and unless something unfortunate happens to him will certainly be Air Chief Marshal some day.' Two days later, as Ismay may have known, Slessor learned of his promotion to Air Vice-Marshal (Major-General). It was work in which he excelled, then and later, made all the sweeter by this significant promotion. His colleagues arrived two weeks later. Chairman of the British delegation was Rear-Admiral Roger Bellairs and Slessor formed a sub-committee with Captain Dewitt Ramsey (US Navy) and Colonel Joseph T. McNarney (USAAF) to consider how best to supply the RAF and build up American air power at the same time. Arnold agreed to defer the full equipment of his own units, as long as the US remained out of the war, in favour of strengthening the RAF. Arnold's decision greatly relieved Slessor, although he was well aware that continuing British resistance to Germany helped to keep the US safe. He reported to Portal on February 1st 1941 that Arnold and Spaatz thought 'we should not accumulate more [aircraft] than we really need, while the US Air Corps, which at present has virtually no modern combat planes, continues to be starved for aircraft.' Slessor agreed with them and underlined the fact that 'they have literally no – repeat no – bomber or fighter squadrons equipped with aircraft operationally fit for use in first-class warfare.'

The talks went on until the end of March, and the British delegation vainly urged the Americans not to concentrate their fleet at Pearl Harbor, far from anywhere, but send a strong force to Singapore, which was better placed to defend American interests in the Philippines, as well as British and European colonies. Had that been done, Slessor often reflected in later years, the course of history in the Far East would have been greatly changed for the better. However, the US Chiefs of Staff did accept a recommendation that if war broke out with Germany and Japan, Germany should be the priority target. Military missions were created in London and Washington to keep contacts alive, and Arthur Harris (later of Bomber Command fame) was appointed first head of the Air Mission in Washington. Slessor returned to England in April 1941, having made his first important mark in high-level matters on both sides of the Atlantic.

On the way home, he composed some 'secret and strictly personal' notes for Portal on his impressions of the US after five months there. 'There is no doubt', he thought, 'that the combination of the US and the British Empire will be absolutely unbeatable. They have a colossal material potential and splendid personnel.' However, at present 'their system of supreme direction and co-ordination of defence matters is almost unbelievably inefficient... There is virtually nothing in the way of a War Cabinet system as we know it in this country', and 'the army and navy really seem to hate each other more than they do the Germans.' Admiral Richmond Kelly Turner was a man of ability and personality, but 'completely lacking in any sense of co-operation or sense of humility; it never occurs to him that he can be wrong... He thinks he knows much better than the Chiefs of Staff how to run the British navy and the RAF in the war' and it would be a good day if he were removed from Washington and given a command at sea.

Morgenthau 'is filled with a genuine desire to help us win the war, but he is completely ignorant about anything to do with defence.' Knox is a man of 'immense energy, drive and courage. He has been almost openly preparing the navy for intervention for some time and is determined to get into the war as soon as he can.' Stimson, however, 'is an old and rather tired man but he is, I think, a really big man and is fired with an almost religious conviction as to the essential need to defeat Hitler.' As for Harry Hopkins, he is 'almost a fanatic on the subject of aid to Britain', but he is sick and, by his own admission, a hopeless administrator: 'his desire to "keep the thing fluid" in respect of the organization of defence is typical of what I think is an ingrained characteristic of this country – the love of doing things "off the record" by personal contacts, by telephone conversations and informal parties, all very exasperating for those of us used to the methodical ways of the British.'

Slessor thought it would be 'difficult to exaggerate the importance of Donovan's influence here... his invaluable experience, his extraordinary grasp of the fundamentals of major strategy and his great influence and prestige with the administration and with the country as a whole' make him a key figure. Slessor regarded Stark as 'largely in the hands of Turner.' Marshall, though, seemed to be a really big man, though one with an impossible job: 'Not only does he have to spend an appalling amount of his time talking to Congressional Committees (a horror which the British officer is mercifully spared), but he is attempting to combine the duties of CIGS, CAS and C-in-C Home Forces, and that in a country where the land and air forces are scattered over an area three times the size of India.'

With regard to the air force, Slessor thought its organization 'hopeless'. 'The have no separate air staff and everything to do with the air arm has to go through all the general staff departments, largely manned by officers whose military experience has brought them in contact with nothing more mechanical than a mule.' As for Arnold, Slessor dismissed him as 'a man of immense energy, but not of really first-class ability or brain, and in any event no-one could possibly hope to run a show properly under the handicaps of this system. [George H.] Brett, as number two, is a weak man with nothing like the ability or personality to hold down his job.' The question of a separate air force was often raised with Slessor and his response was always that it would come, in time, but meanwhile the airmen must set up an air staff within the War Department.

By August, the British Ambassador, Lord Halifax, had had enough of Harris. He complained to Sinclair (and others) that Harris was 'a failure' in Washington: 'unpleasant, domineering, superior'. Freeman promised to suggest a replacement. Slessor, he thought, was suitable, but he had only recently taken up an important position as a Group Commander in Bomber Command. In the event, Harris stayed on in Washington until February 1942 – for Halifax's opinion was not widely shared – and Slessor did not return to Washington. He would have done very well there, but was at the time enjoying a rare escape from Whitehall.

CHAPTER 8

BOMBER COMMANDER

Hapless Hampdens

Air Vice-Marshal Slessor enjoyed an operational command – head of 5 Group, Bomber Command, with headquarters in Grantham, Lincolnshire – from May 1941 to March 1942. The group was equipped with Handley Page Hampdens, a twin-engined machine of little value, used as a night bomber. No fewer than half of those flown on operations (714 out of 1,433) would be lost, and 3,066 crew members were killed, injured or captured. First flown in June 1936, the optimistic makers called it 'a fighting bomber' and for years the Air Staff accepted the claim that a single machine-gun for the pilot, plus three hand-held guns for other crew members gave complete all-round defence without the penalties of heavy turrets. It remained in production until March 1942.

Slessor's last experience of night bombing had been in 1918, 'and I confess to having been over-optimistic to begin with about our capacity to find and hit targets at night.' After 20 months of war, in positions close to the centre of the RAF's war effort, he should have been better informed. However, he gradually learned how essential it was to improve navigation and bombing accuracy by devising a marking technique, using incendiaries and coloured flares. He also hoped that larger and better designed bombers might soon replace the vulnerable Hampdens, but for the moment he and his crews could only talk about these, and look forward to the day – if they lived so long – when self-sealing fuel tanks, protective armour, effective defensive weapons, heavy bombs that exploded with serious force when and where they were supposed to, and radar aids became standard equipment.

Trenchard took it upon himself to send an unsolicited memorandum to the Chiefs of Staff in May 1941. Attacks should be made every night, even if only one bomber could be sent over. Losses would be heavy – perhaps 70 percent in a month, he breezily admitted – but plenty of willing crews were available and top priority must be given to bomber production. 'All the evidence of the first war and of this shows that the German nation is peculiarly susceptible to air bombing', he declared. 'The ordinary people are neither allowed, nor offer, to play their part in rescue or restoration work; virtually imprisoned in their shelters or within the bombed area, they remain passive and easy prey to hysteria and panic without anything to mitigate the inevitable confusion and chaos. There is no joking in the German shelters as in ours, nor the bond which unites the public with ARP [Air Raid Precautions] and military services here of all working together in a common cause to defeat the attacks of the enemy.'

Even by Trenchard's standards, this was absolute poppycock and one wonders who fed it to him. At that time, Bomber Command lacked the capacity to inflict serious – let alone devastating – damage on German targets, quite apart from the fact that about half the bombs dropped were falling in open country. Many of those that did fall on or near a target failed to explode – and all had little explosive power. Portal, however, 'agreed emphatically' with Trenchard's nonsense, and so too did Slessor. There may be some excuse for the long-retired Trenchard, but none at all for such senior serving officers, who were widely regarded even then as outstanding. They had forgotten 'the inherent paradox of offensive air power' discovered by British and German airmen before the end of the Great War. 'Attacks on enemy targets', as Tony Mason summarized it, 'either tactical or strategic, will undoubtedly force him to devote more resources to air defence. But the more successful the policy in forcing the enemy on to the defensive, the more difficult and costly it becomes to inflict proportional damage on the original targets.'

As Terraine has said, 'what grates is the absolute assurance' even in 1941, with which the Air Staff 'announced their certainty that they could produce decisive results single-handed, when the inadequacy of their force was becoming daily more apparent, and they had clear evidence of its weakness in performance... it is the cocksureness that offends.' Slessor shared that cocksureness then, although it is muffled in his memoirs, where he often made the point that he and his colleagues were learning, and years later Bomber Command really would be effective. He does not link that effectiveness to the massive Soviet victories on the eastern front and the destruction by US air power of the Luftwaffe. Without those Soviet and American achievements, British bombers could hardly have made a telling – let alone decisive – contribution to victory despite the amazing courage and determination of their crews and the brilliant devices scientists and engineers provided for them.

Slessor wrote to Freeman on June 1st 1941 about an 'attempt by the army to wreck the air force in order to provide them with a vast fleet of close support aircraft.' They have never accepted that 'this war can ever end without a full-scale land campaign on the continent of Europe... And they are obsessed with the success of the enemy close support, not realizing – or deliberately shutting their eyes to – the fact that the achievements of the Germans in Poland, France, Greece and Crete in the face of either slight or negligible air opposition and AA equipment bear no relation to the possibilities against the German army with its colossal

standard of light AA defence and fighter support.' Slessor was convinced
that the bomber force was at last becoming effective: 'We are getting
evidence that the Boche really is feeling it', but the War Office, backed by
Beaverbrook and Moore-Brabazon were trying to wreck it. 'I think one of
Boom's charges against us – that we never make use of outside assistance
– is really justified. The other services have never hesitated to use every
sort of backstage influence, in Parliament and the Press, in country houses
and dinner parties, to further their own ends, and we think we can support
our case on its own military merits. We can't, however good it may be...
What folly it all is', he ended. 'I am so sorry for CAS having his attention
distracted and his time wasted by this sort of thing at such a time. You
know, we really don't deserve to win this war, and if we're not damned
careful we shall not if we go on like this.'

Slessor wrote to John Baker (Director of Bombing Operations in the
Air Ministry) in August about the slow build-up of his force. His first-line
establishment was only 240 (192 Hampdens, 48 Manchesters) and his
actual strength much less. 'And I feel it's a sorry business to have to admit
that we are not going to get much bigger than that this year.' Baker
explained why. Partly because of the 'ruthless decisions' taken last
autumn during the Battle of Britain to focus on fighter production. 'It is
astonishing what a time lag there is in getting these matters put right.' And
partly, 'though I hate to admit it', a lack of drive in the factories in recent
months in reaction to the heavy pressure put on everyone last year and
also in reaction to news of Hitler's move eastward, against the Soviet
Union. He urged Slessor not to get too downhearted: production would
certainly improve next year.

Slessor was also exasperated by the slow pace of work on runways in
his group. 'When I complain to the works people', he told Sir Oliver
Swann (RAF Liaison Officer in Nottingham) in March 1942, 'I am
invariably told a sad story about the impossibility of getting labour', and
yet he had been observing for the past fortnight a gang of 11 men and a
steam roller widening a little side-road, hardly ever used, east of Welby
village (between Grantham and Sleaford) from about 14 feet to 17 feet.
Last year, 'at great expense in labour, material and interference with
traffic, the streets of Grantham were studded with brick deathtraps
known, I understand, as street shelters. One of these stands outside the
entrance to my headquarters. For the best part of a week now a gang of
nine men have been engaged in knocking a series of square holes in the
walls of this "shelter", each the size of a brick – what for, I have no idea.
Today being Sunday, I need hardly say that no "work" has been done on
this since yesterday midday... I suppose this sort of thing makes sense to
somebody. To me, and many others like me, the mentality which makes it
possible looks uncommonly like losing us the war if we don't look out.'

The Portal plan

In August 1941 Portal told Arthur Tedder (then commanding in Cairo)
that the attack on Germany 'is really beginning to have great results.' In
fact, it was not, and Portal was sadly deceived, by himself or others, if he
really thought that was the case. Bomber Command's failure was
highlighted in that same month by the famous Butt Report: a detailed
analysis of bombing photographs taken by aircraft on operations in June
and July showing that only one in five of the command's aircraft were
dropping bombs as close as five miles from their targets: four out of five
were not doing so well. Portal and other senior airmen already knew these
facts, but fear of criticism from other services and even a public outcry
caused them to deny the undeniable for many months. Churchill followed
the Portal line, assuring President Roosevelt in September that 'we know
our night bomber offensive is having a devastating effect.' We knew
nothing of the sort, but Portal's belief in that offensive was absolute. He
sent a note to the other British Chiefs of Staff on September 30th which
Slessor later read and regarded as 'one of the best I remember.' Portal
advocated a plan 'to shatter German resistance by air and then put in the
army'; he thought 'a combined heavy bomber force rising to a peak of
between 4-6,000 might be necessary'; and victory would be possible in
1944 with the assistance of 'a relatively small land force.'

The other Chiefs backed this proposal during October, even before
Portal spelled out his apocalyptic vision on November 3rd. In 1943 and
1944, he told them, it would be possible to drop one and a quarter million
tons of bombs on Germany: '25 million Germans would be rendered
homeless, 900,000 would be killed and one million seriously injured.' The
strain of the Russian war, the North African campaign, the current air
offensive, and the blockade were all undermining the Nazi state.
'Damaged resources, plant and stock of materials cannot now be
adequately replaced; structural damage can no longer be adequately
repaired; replenishments obtainable from the stocks of occupied countries
are a waning asset. The output of German labour is falling through war
weariness, food difficulties and other domestic problems, while that of
foreign labour – whether in Germany or in the occupied territories – falls
with Germany's diminishing prospects.'

Portal had no reliable evidence to support any of these assertions. In
November 1941, after more than two years of gallant effort, Bomber
Command's attack on Germany had had hardly any effect. This view of
the condition of Germany, which Slessor shared, 'is nothing less than
astonishing. It is a fearful proof of the power of faulty intelligence and
wishful thinking to misguide strategy.' Underlying this wishful thinking
was the Air Staff hope that bombing would save the lives of British
soldiers. 'Do we envisage winning the war in the same way as last time',
asked Slessor, as early as November 1939, 'a series of land battles over a
period of years, a succession of Passchendaeles leading to military

occupation of Germany?' The answer to his question was, in fact, 'yes'. About 125,000 aircrew served in Bomber Command during the European war of whom 73,741 – nearly 60 percent – became casualties: killed, wounded or captured. In the early months of 1943, only 17 percent of crews could be expected to survive 30 operations and Portal wisely insisted that knowledge of such horrifying statistics be confined to 'the smallest number of people.' At least they were not 'slaughtered', as Harris feared, 'in the mud of Flanders.' In neither war did the British army suffer anything like the same rate of loss.

When writing his memoirs in the 1950s, Slessor still believed that a stronger bomber offensive would have permitted Allied soldiers to walk into occupied Europe. Like Portal, Harris and other devout Trenchardists, Slessor refused to accept – then or later – that German ground and air defences were too much for unescorted bombers in daylight or darkness. Churchill doubted the wisdom of betting so heavily on the bomber and, on reflection, Portal's fellow-Chiefs backed off on November 24th. First priority, they decreed, was aid to the Soviet Union; in second place was preparation for the liberation of occupied Europe; and in third aerial bombing.

'Even if all the towns of Germany were rendered largely uninhabitable', Churchill told Portal, 'it does not follow that the military control would be weakened or even that war industry could not be carried on': this very important point was lost on Slessor (as well as Portal and Harris), then and later. Churchill went on to remind Portal of the Air Staff's earlier claims for strategic bombing. 'Before the war we were greatly misled by the pictures [the Air Staff] painted of the destruction that would be wrought by air raids. This is illustrated by the fact that 750,000 beds were actually provided for air raid casualties, never more than 6,000 being required.' Air Staff exaggerations, claimed Churchill, depressed the politicians then in office and played a part in the desertion of Czechoslovakia in 1938. Derek Waldie, however, observed that 'most politicans did not enquire too closely into the facts and figures' in case they found them to be untenable. But responsibility for these facts and figures lay with the Air Staff: 'It was they who saw the next war as an isolated battle of bombers, and they who clung obstinately to this contention even after their own research had thrown serious doubt upon the feasibility and efficiency of strategic bombing.'

It would not be until the early months of 1942, in the fourth year of the war, that the Air Staff accepted the obvious fact that every member of an aircrew must be a specialist. The pilot was now to be assisted by a 'flight engineer'. The new designation of 'navigator' was introduced. Bombs were to be dropped by a 'bombardier'. It was recognized that 'air gunner' and 'wireless operator' were separate duties. These changes, belated though they were, at last permitted crew members to be more thoroughly trained, and greatly improved their performance on operations. It was also officially admitted that the interior of high-flying bombers became bitterly cold at all seasons of the year, and that electrically-heated flying suits might usefully supplement British grit. Not having been designed and tested in peacetime, the suits gave only poor protection, but the fact that they existed at all testifies to a growing awareness of reality in the Air Ministry.

Pathfinders

Given that Bomber Command could only operate at night with any hope of success, various navigational aids were devised to help in finding designated targets. Many of the young men who actually flew in bombers advocated 'the creation of a special force, using the best equipment available and consisting of the most efficient crews, to mark targets and so guide in the main body' of less skilled or experienced crews. They were backed by Group Captain Sidney Bufton, Director of Bombing Operations in the Air Ministry, and a man who had been a squadron commander until November 1941. Bufton, a close friend of Barnes Wallis and Frank Whittle (inventors of the Dambuster bomb and Britain's jet engine) was also a gifted electrical engineer, who had developed a number of aids to help night bombing. He argued the case for an élite force of 'pathfinders' to find and illuminate targets for those following behind. Sadly, Bufton 'ran head-on into one of the RAF's deep prejudices: a strong, irrational distrust and dislike of anything smacking of a corps d'élite.' Chaps with the right stuff in them could surely be expected to press on, without special training, as boldly as their fathers and uncles had done throughout the Great War.

As Terraine has observed, the bomber commanders 'regarded area bombing as an end in itself, and, if vigorously enough pursued, as a means of winning the war.' According to the official historians of the strategic air offensive, however, Bufton 'thought it was only a preparatory phase through which Bomber Command would inevitably have to pass before it could perfect the technique of precise attack.' Certain facts nevertheless got through to Harris and Portal. Notably, that very few crews were dropping bombs anywhere near their targets. A Pathfinder Force was therefore created in August 1942, but significant improvement was slow.

During the autumn of 1941, Slessor had argued strongly against the formation of such a force, but three years later in a letter to 'my dear Sidney' he admitted: 'You have been proved so right by events, but I do sometimes wonder whether my plan of each group having its own Pathfinders would not have worked. I suppose the fact is that one would never have developed the technique or equipment without one central organization. Anyway, it seems a far cry to 1941 with our "starred crews" and beer bottles to put the searchlights off!' Like Harris, he had objected to taking the most skilful and determined crews out of a group, believing the effect on the morale of those left behind would be bad. Bufton's arguments convinced Portal, however, and a Pathfinder Force was created under the command of an exceptional navigator, Donald Bennett. It performed with great skill and courage for the rest of the war.

Nearly half a century later, Bufton reflected on the high commanders he had known. He had no time for Harris, who never led or even flew on a single wartime operation and could not fly any of his command's bombers. He spoke glibly about the loss of hundreds of aircraft, but was silent about the thousands of young lives lost. 'He misused the bomber force in pursuit of his own policy which had no validity, no authority and no future. He played to a gallery of Buckingham Palace and Chequers, and hoped to emerge as some sort of Duke of Wellington who won the war on his own, his way. Unfortunately, he overlooked the fundamental fact that industrial cities are living organisms that quickly recover from attack.' Harry Broadhurst and Basil Embry rated highest with Bufton, closely followed by Portal and Slessor, with Tedder only a little ahead of Harris.[8]

Throughout his time at 5 Group, Slessor got out and about whenever he could, and was often present when crews landed and were interrogated by intelligence officers about what they thought they had seen and done. He was surprised at the absence of German intruders over his airfields when the heavily-laden Hampdens were taking off or expected to return – with crews tired and sometimes injured. Runways were necessarily showing lights, and intruders could have caused severe damage both to aircraft and ground installations.

On December 18th 1941, he sent all captains of aircraft a slogan to keep in mind for the coming year: 'When in doubt – *don't*'. For example, when you are uncertain whether you can land without under- or over-shooting; when you wonder whether your wing-tip will clear the next aircraft on the taxi-track; when you doubt if your under-carriage is down and properly locked; when you think it would be fun to fly low over the airfield – in all these cases don't. Be responsible, and think of the number of aircraft lost and crews killed or injured, in avoidable accidents.'

Slessor strongly objected to restrictions placed by the Air Staff on weather experts changing their forecasts after crews had been briefed. There was no such thing, he fairly observed, as an accurate forecast in north-west Europe at any season of the year, and no honest meteorologist ever claimed otherwise. On at least one occasion, Slessor's reliance on the up-dated opinion of his local expert saved 5 Group from serious loss. This was the infamous raid on Berlin during the night of November 7th-8th 1941. Of 392 bombers sent out on the orders of Sir Richard Peirse (head of Bomber Command), no fewer than 37 were lost and many others damaged. But Slessor diverted his own squadrons to a nearer target and so informed Peirse. Only two of 5 Group's 75 Hampdens were lost that

---

[8] I am grateful to Tony Furse for my copy of this letter.

night. Several aircraft which went to Berlin, despite the predicted dreadful weather, ran out of fuel on the way home because their crews used so much in trying to fly over or round the worst of it. Peirse was cunning, deceitful, and sufficiently ruthless to break Slessor – and would probably have done so, had his own judgement not been immediately questioned after the disaster. He was very properly relieved of his command, but Slessor was well aware that Peirse had friends in high places – powerful enough to get him another command, which they did, in India – and made a brave decision, worthy of a man aspiring to the highest ranks.

Slessor wrote several times to Peirse on the sensitive subject of 'lack of moral fibre' during 1941. He recounted the case of a Pilot Officer observer which seemed 'a perfectly genuine case of hysteria' at the prospect of flying over enemy territory. We should be careful, thought Slessor, 'not to be too humane and "progressive" in our treatment of these cases. I am terribly sorry for these poor devils who can't face it. We all have the utmost admiration for that vast majority of the chaps who go cracking on day after day without batting an eyelid', but we owe it to them not to be too light-handed with the weak minority.

There was still a possibility of invasion in the summer of 1941, and Slessor sent Freeman 'some vapourings of a country cousin' on July 11th. 'It is now getting on for three months since this country was really seriously bombed', he wrote. 'Even if Russia collapses (and I imagine it is very unwise to assume as yet that she will not [the German invasion had begun on June 22nd]), we should have another two months of relative inactivity on this side. In effect, the Almighty has provided us with about five invaluable summer months in which to set our house in order to meet the inevitable blitz that will come with the early autumn.' He feared there was a great deal of slackness everywhere. 'I am told that nothing is being done to build hutted camps outside the munitions towns or western ports, to organize proper transportation services to get workers and dockers to and from their work.' As it happened, Slessor's fears were not realized, for the Soviet Union did not collapse and the Luftwaffe never returned in force, but his urgent energy contrasted sharply with the 'business as usual' attitude of many local authorities and civil servants.

He was particularly concerned about the defence of his bases and to meet this danger the RAF Regiment was being formed. Slessor opposed this decision, believing that the army should be held responsible. Perhaps he was right, in an ideal world, but in the real wartime world – especially overseas – a ground force trained in airfield defence proved invaluable. As late as February 1942, Slessor still feared an invasion. 'I feel sure the main reason for the army not fighting in Malaya', he told Freeman, 'was the Japanese air superiority. If we keep command of the air over the United Kingdom, I'm sure the army will fight; if we lose air superiority we lose the war – let's face it.'

Slessor was much concerned with training during 1941. He argued against Air Staff plans for a massive expansion of front-line numbers (aircraft and crews). Training units, he argued, were under-valued, and overall the plans were unrealistic: 'an opium-smoker's dream', he called them. It would be much better to have a force of 2,400 really good crews under picked junior leaders, than a force of 5,370 crews, of whom '40 percent will be useless and will never catch up, but deteriorate through being kept on the ground, will crash aircraft and get in the way of the chaps who will do the job.'

For such an intelligent, experienced officer, this was a thoughtless assertion. Who was going to select the 'really good crews' he asked for, or identify the 'picked junior leaders' and on what basis? His knowledge of 5 Group was limited, of other groups in Bomber Command nil. The record of its crews during the terrible years ahead of them – a record only too well known when he was writing his memoirs – clearly indicates that not even four percent proved 'useless'. In 1941 many of those selected and trained in peacetime for service in the RAF's most prestigious command had already perished while flying aircraft that they and their commanders knew were little better than death traps. Very few of their successors were found wanting.

The Channel Dash

On New Year's Day, 1942, Slessor learned that he had been made a Companion of the Order of the Bath (CB) and was thus half-way to his longed-for knighthood. In February came the notorious 'Channel Dash'. Two German battle-cruisers, *Scharnhorst* and *Gneisenau*, accompanied by a heavy cruiser, *Prinz Eugen*, six destroyers, mine-sweepers and torpedo-boats, with ample fighter cover for most of their journey, fled from Brest through the Channel to Wilhelmshaven and the Elbe estuary. They achieved this amazing feat despite the fact that both the Royal Navy and the RAF were supposed to be poised to prevent just such a dash succeeding. The fact that all three capital ships reached safety in a severely damaged condition – from mines previously laid probably by Slessor's Hampdens – and that they were no longer a threat to Atlantic convoys did not alter another fact: that they were not intercepted and sunk en route.

Writing more than a decade later, Slessor had nothing to say about the massive public outcry following the successful 'Dash', provoking an immediate judicial inquiry. Instead, he reacted angrily to suggestions that Bomber Command failed to exert itself either fully or skilfully during this crisis. No fewer than 242 bombers were sent to intercept the German ships, he tells us; 79 were from 5 Group and its losses were heavy: nine destroyed, 11 damaged. Slessor blamed bad weather for the fact that not a single hit was even claimed by the handful of bombers that reported sighting the enemy vessels. He did not mention reconnaissance errors, faulty radar reports or the use of unescorted Fairey Swordfish torpedo-armed biplanes in suicidal attempts to hit the ships. Nor did he explain what Stephen Roskill describes as 'the long delay in providing Coastal Command with a properly-trained and well-equipped torpedo striking force'; nor that 'the pre-war preference of the Air Staff for the bomb, as opposed to the torpedo, as the main weapon for use against ships was shown to have been mistaken.'

Slessor had an opportunity to analyze the failures of inter-service co-operation, as well as those of the Royal Navy, all three RAF Commands and the Air Staff. These failures offered Slessor excellent material for drawing out 'lessons to be learned' in the hope of avoiding a repetition of such a fiasco. Two examples: firstly, Coastal Command's poor performance during the 'Dash' provoked an Air Ministry decision to provide it with more and better aircraft, equipment and personnel. This was a decision from which Slessor himself would benefit a year later (when head of Coastal Command). At the time, however, he resisted it. Coastal Command, he assured its then head, Philip Joubert de la Ferté, was 'very well done' in its aircraft allocations, to which Joubert replied: 'If for "done" you read "done down" it would be about right.' Secondly, the fiasco led directly 'to the first major review of anti-shipping tactics since the start of the war. The result was the decision to adopt Strike Wing tactics.' This was another important decision, and one from which both Coastal Command and Slessor personally benefitted greatly. Here, as elsewhere, he shows himself more of a lawyer than an historian, in that he makes a couple of points in defence of Bomber Command and moves swiftly away from shaky ground. Without benefit of hindsight, the German Naval Staff recognized that the 'Dash' was 'a tactical victory, but a strategic defeat.' A standing threat to Atlantic convoys had been abandoned and ships concentrated for defence against a British invasion of Norway which few Germans other than Hitler expected.

A considerate commander

Shortly before he left 5 Group, Slessor took the trouble to write at length to a Wing Commander John Kynoch whom he had sacked as CO of 97 Squadron, demoted to squadron leader, and sent to an Operational Training Unit at Upper Heyford in 7 Group. 'I'm all for a chap stating his case', he wrote, 'and should have been sorry if you had thought you didn't know me well enough to write as you did.' He offered Kynoch two pieces of advice. Firstly, 'You are inclined to be too slow and deliberate by nature and I think probably a bit too easy going with your subordinates.' Secondly, 'If your aircraft are u/s [unserviceable] for lack of some spare, don't let the equipment bloke get away with it, stand over him till he rings up the MU [Maintenance Unit] and send a lorry over if necessary.' He urged the man to accept that he had failed, and not kid himself that he had been done down. 'You've got guts and character, you've got a fine operational background, and I shall be disappointed if you don't turn out a high-class squadron and station commander before this war is over.'

This is a thoughtful, helpful letter and shows Slessor in a good light, although he had already written, at even greater length, to Group Captain Herbert Rowe at Coningsby in Lincolnshire, about Kynoch. He had not trained his squadron properly to master the handling of heavy aircraft. As a result, there had been at least three avoidable Lancaster crashes. Incompetence and/or negligence on this scale should surely have resulted in the sack, rather than demotion.

Slessor's group had been re-equipping, at first with the twin-engined Avro Manchester, and then with its much-praised successor, the four-engined Lancaster. But early in March 1942 he was relieved of his command. He was to succeed Trafford Leigh-Mallory as head of 11 Group, Fighter Command. This is so typical of the RAF's random posting policy, then and later. Having only just got a grip on a demanding assignment with bombers, after years as an office-wallah, Slessor was now to command fighters, about which he knew nothing. He should have been left at 5 Group, where increasing experience would have made him a commander of increasing value. He might well have succeeded Harris as head of Bomber Command, perhaps in April 1944, after the disastrous failure of the so-called 'Battle of Berlin'. He would have proven a more flexible and much more intelligent member of the Allied team to liberate Occupied Europe than Harris. At the last moment, however, Freeman persuaded Portal to agree that Slessor must be 'once more immured within the walls of the Air Ministry in King Charles Street', in a new position: Assistant CAS (Policy), However, the decision to return him to Whitehall was certainly wiser than sending him to Fighter Command.

CHAPTER 9

BACK TO WHITEHALL

A mighty ally in prospect

In April 1942, General George C. Marshall (head of the US Army) and Mr Harry Hopkins (President Roosevelt's must trusted adviser) went to London to propose an invasion of the continent in 1943. As the Air Staff's new policy expert, Slessor thought it a wildly unrealistic proposal, preferring to see a continued build-up of an aerial offensive against Germany that he believed was already causing significant damage. But at least the American proposal showed more willingness to co-operate than anything emerging from Stalin's Kremlin. Slessor shared the fear of many Britons and Americans that Stalin would be defeated or that he would suddenly agree a truce with Hitler. The Soviet Union, as Slessor would learn to his great grief in 1944 (when the Red Army allowed the Germans to destroy Warsaw and kill or use as slaves many of its inhabitants), was not an ally but a co-belligerent.

Slessor planned away busily at the heart of RAF affairs throughout the year, but he was never on close personal terms with Portal. They never lunched or dined together, never shared any 'off duty' breaks. Unless firmly discouraged, Slessor was as eager to express his many opinions in person as on paper, whereas Portal valued silence (when he could get it) and preferred to keep his thoughts to himself. For instance, Slessor did not learn until after the war that Portal always had grave doubts about the American daylight offensive without fighter escorts. He himself, a more faithful Trenchardist, believed bombers could get through to their targets without them.

General Arnold and Rear-Admiral John H. Towers, together with Air Marshal Strath Evill (head of the RAF Delegation in Washington) and Colonel Hoyt S. Vandenberg (head of the Policy Section of the Plans Division) arrived in England on May 24th to discuss the allocation of aircraft from American production to the RAF. Arnold was anxious for action by American aircraft, and concerned to build up his own forces as well as those of the RAF. In Slessor's opinion, he was too optimistic about the likely performance – in the short term – of either American aircraft or their crews. Slessor had written to Evill in Washington on May 1st to ask whether he thought 'Arnold has the slightest idea of what is really involved in raising and training a first-line [American] force of the strength envisaged (16,000) which is more than twice the first-line strength of the British and Dominion air forces after two and a half years of war?' Arnold, in fact, had more than 'the slightest idea' of what was required and Slessor would not be alone, at the end of the war, in expressing astonishment at US achievements in production and training.

Political rather than military considerations made it difficult for the RAF to obtain sufficient Consolidated B-24 Liberators (an excellent four-engined bomber) or Consolidated PBY-5 Catalinas (an almost equally valuable twin-engined patrol-bomber flying-boat). Agreement was reached, because Arnold was 'a very reasonable person', but the RAF got few heavy bombers, apart from the Liberator for service in Coastal Command. It was eventually supplied with a reliable transport aircraft – the Douglas DC-3 Dakota – to fill a yawning gap in its inventory.

Back to Washington

Slessor accompanied Arnold on his return to Washington for further talks, aboard a Boeing 307 Stratoliner (designated C-75 in military service). This was a luxuriously-appointed four-engined aircraft, suitable for carrying distinguished persons. Among them on this flight were Averell Harriman (President Roosevelt's special envoy in London), two important American generals (Dwight D. Eisenhower, Mark W. Clark) and King George VI's cousin, Lord Louis Mountbatten, whom Churchill had appointed Chief of Combined Operations.[9]

The talks went well, but then came news of the fall of Tobruk on June 21st. Arnold rang Slessor to tell him that an agreed programme must be presented at 4 pm that day to the President and Prime Minister Churchill (who had arrived in Washington on the 18th). Arnold and Slessor, together with Hopkins and Harriman, met at the White House at 3 pm and signed an agreement that became known as the Arnold-Towers-Portal agreement (ATP). Dinner at the British Embassy that very hot night was a glum affair. The sudden, unexpected fall of Tobruk exposed Alexandria and Slessor was not alone in rightly supposing that the Royal Navy would be preparing to move part of the fleet to Haifa, the rest south of the Suez Canal, and planning to block the canal. He had rather too much to drink and flared angrily when General Alan Brooke (head of the British Army), snapping out his opinions as if they were holy writ, assured Churchill that all setbacks – not only in the desert campaign – were a result of RAF failures. Then came a signal from an American observer in the Middle East declaring that the RAF's conduct of operations was a prime cause of disaster there. 'Colonel Shrapnel' (as Brooke was known to those unlucky

---

[9] For some reason, Louis Francis Albert Victor Nicholas Mountbatten was known, to himself and friends, as Dickie.

souls who served within range of his daily outbursts) immediately snapped louder than ever – this time in support of the RAF. Slessor was both amused and unimpressed. Outsiders, it seemed, especially Americans, were not to be allowed to voice criticism of British efforts, even in the air.

Tense relations with the army

Relations with the army, Slessor recalled, were poor throughout 1942. Brooke demanded control of aircraft, and even the right to decide which types should be produced. Although the RAF had been an independent service for 24 years, Brooke found it difficult to see airmen as anything other than soldiers in blue uniforms; forming what should be an army corps. 'Portal was wise and very patient', observed Slessor, 'if I had been in his place, I am sure there would have been a rare bust-up.' Only in the desert was there harmony, but Slessor was unable to give credit for this to Tedder, who was largely responsible for that harmony.

The army also demanded airborne forces, even though the RAF had few transport aircraft and no gliders (nor tugs either). Even if they had been available, Slessor believed that 'airborne operations against an enemy unbeaten in the air are a spectacular and expensive form of mass suicide.' In mid-1942, the airborne forces in Britain – some 15,000 men – would have required 760 gliders (plus tugs) to go into action. The resources ultimately devoted to them, he had good grounds for arguing, would have been better used in strengthening both the army and the strategic air offensive.

In March 1946, Slessor recalled how deeply impressed everyone had been by the success of German paratroops in Norway, Holland and Crete – all against negligible air opposition and even so the last of these was horrendously costly. But Churchill decreed on June 22nd 1940, 'off his own bat and without any consultation with anybody about practical possibilities', there should be 5,000 parachute troops in action this day. Slessor found the problem on his desk: how were they to be recruited, trained, dropped or tugged in gliders, which they did not have? 'Then, of course, the enthusiasts rushed in, headed by Louis Strange and hotly followed by a number of others in khaki coats. Everything must take second place to the parachutists – hadn't the PM said so? They must have Stirlings, Wellingtons, Dakotas (we hadn't got any). They must have airfields, our best officers, all the men they wanted. Louis Strange used to get up at seven in the morning so as to be in my office before my PA arrived so as to waylay me when I arrived at 8.30!' In August 1940, he wrote to Strange – then a Squadron Leader at Ringway, Manchester – 'I promise you I am not trying to be the heavy senior officer – I have far too vivid a recollection of the old days when I, as a very young and insignificant Second Lieutenant in the RAF, was under your command at Gosport, to do any such thing', but he had to curb his enthusiasm and point out the practical difficulties. Gradually, however, an airborne force was built up at great expense and achieved little. 'Suppose all that effort had been put into bombers. Should we have ever had to do an opposed landing in Sicily or France? If so, and the weight of those extra bombers had been used behind the beaches or at Arnhem or over the Rhine, would they not have been as effective in ensuring the success of the operation as the airborne troops were?' As it happened, they spent most of their time training or doing nothing.

Slessor still believed that the war could be won by a combination of economic pressure and air bombardment. These together must reduce German strength greatly before the Allies could set armies ashore. 'I did not foresee anything in the nature of Overlord', he bravely confessed, 'but rather major harassing action on the fringes of Europe on our historic model, in the Balkans for instance, and possibly even from Gibraltar through Spain with the help of Spanish guerrillas... until we were in a position, with the help of the French resistance, to get the army into Germany in the face of only sporadic resistance.' An important passage this – entirely at odds with American strategy, though not with Churchill's thinking, and entirely mistaken. Whatever his merits as a bomber champion, Slessor was evidently out of his depth when it came to framing a strategy whereby the western Allies might overcome Germany, and at the same time ensure that the Red Army did not 'liberate' western Europe.

American intentions

Sir Archibald Sinclair (Secretary of State for Air) wrote to Slessor in September 1942 to ask him if he could discover what part the Americans intended to play in the strategic air offensive. Have they yet, he asked, 'dropped a single bomb on Germany, outside the range of our single-seater fighter cover?' Slessor replied on the 25th. Carl Spaatz had invited him to his headquarters to discuss a new plan, AWPD-42, drawn up by Haywood Hansell, which had been approved by the President. By January 1st 1944, there were to be over 2,000 heavy bombers in Britain, 960 mediums, and 1,500 fighters.

Next day, Slessor wrote again to Sinclair. 'They intend to do precision bombing in Germany by daylight. This is the basis of their air policy in this theatre. They believe that with their good defensive armament they can do this when they get sufficient numbers. Their early operations lend some support to this belief – the B-17 [Flying Fortress] has shown that it can defend itself and take an enormous amount of punishment. It has yet to be proved whether it is possible to carry the war into Germany by day. But they believe they will and I personally am inclined to agree with them *once they get really adequate numbers*' [emphasis his]. Neither Slessor nor American airmen had yet realized that day bombers, even in great numbers, needed fighter escort if they were to cause serious damage and avoid heavy losses.

Hansell's plan, Slessor continued, was to destroy the German war economy, 'based on the assumption that we shall continue area bombing by night, aimed at devastation, dislocation of normal life and undermining morale while they single out the vital war industrial targets one by one and destroy them by high altitude precision bombing by day. I have seen this plan – while in some respects academic and unduly optimistic, it is a very impressive bit of work and, always assuming it is possible to bomb Germany by day, I believe it is a war-winner.' The Americans were still feeling their way, and keeping in weekly touch with the British. Slessor thought both Spaatz and Eaker were 'good sound commanders who know their business. Through no fault of their own it is taking longer to get going than they had hoped.' The plan might turn out well, but if not they would then turn to night bombing, which would call for 'a substantial readjustment of American air policy', and might well mean 'a sharp swing away from this theatre towards the Pacific.'

Slessor had been told as early as October 1942 that he was to take over Coastal Command. Once again we see the RAF's random posting policy in action. A man whose strength lay in staff work, Slessor was not at 5 Group in Bomber Command long enough to master that demanding job. Then he was almost sent to command fighters, before common sense intervened to return him to Whitehall. He had hardly warmed his seat before another demanding front-line command was found for him. He knew no more about air war over the sea than he did about handling fighters, which was nothing.

Meanwhile, though, he was sent back to Washington early in November for another month of talks about aircraft allocations. On his return to England in December, he got a friendly note – addressed to 'Dear Jack' – from General Arnold. 'We had a good friendly scrap and they are always good for both sides. As I explained to you over and over during your stay here in Washington, my one desire is to have combat airplanes in the hands of combat personnel in the active theaters with first priority the European theater. I will not permit combat airplanes to sit on the ground. They are going where they can be used to fight the Axis or to train units so they can go to the active theaters for the same purpose.'

These words delighted Slessor, who drafted a 'Note on Air Policy' for Sinclair to send to Churchill. 'The view of the Air Staff is that the Americans and the RAF will be able to bomb Germany in daylight. Given sufficient strength to saturate the defences, they think it quite possible that our losses in the aggregate will be no heavier than by night, and that the results, combined with night attack, should be doubly effective. No-one can say for certain until it has been tried – and tried repeatedly', but not with 'insufficient numbers and with crews inadequately trained.'

Slessor also wrote to Portal in December about Churchill's promise to Stalin, made in August 1942 without consulting his military advisers, to invade the continent in 1943. It could not be done, and the result will be,

Slessor thought, 'either that the Russians will win the war for us and we shall have a correspondingly weak hand at the peace table, or (less likely) Stalin will patch up a peace with Hitler next spring and we and the USA will be left to face another two or three years of possibly inconclusive war.' How can we get out of this 'second front' offer? 'I wonder', Slessor went on, 'first whether we ought not to be as tough with Stalin as he always is with us. I don't believe we need worry unduly about his patching up a peace – unless we sit and do nothing for the next nine months, preparing for a Round Up [an invasion of the continent] that we shall anyway not be strong enough to launch. Nor do I believe it certain that he (realist as he is) really cares whether we invade France or not as long as we keep the Germans engaged and relieve pressure on Russia.' Better than 'a Dieppe on a major scale' would be an all-out bomber offensive together with exploitation of opportunities in the Mediterranean. Slessor also wondered if it might not be possible to persuade Turkey to join the Allies and from bases there destroy the Romanian oilfields. 'We know the importance Stalin attaches to the bomber offensive. Let us tell him that he cannot have it both ways – bomber offensive and Round Up – because there are not the ships.'

Casablanca

Portal decided to take Slessor with him to what turned out to be one of the war's most important meetings in Anfa, a suburb some miles outside Casablanca, on Morocco's north-west coast. They left on the night of January 11th 1943 in a 'crudely-converted Liberator' – no comfortable Stratoliner this time – with Brooke, Mountbatten and Admiral Sir Dudley Pound, head of the Royal Navy. There they were joined by Roosevelt, Churchill, Field Marshal Sir John Dill (who represented British interests in Washington), Tedder, the US Chiefs of Staff and a host of other luminaries.

The Americans still favoured a direct assault across the Channel in 1943 and were wary of an ever-deepening involvement in the Mediterranean. They also thought the British under-rated the war in the Far East and the Pacific. On the morning of the 18th, there was still a wide divergence of opinion between British and American points of view, with Admiral King, Chief of Naval Operations – 'the nigger in the woodpile' as Slessor called him – bitterly opposed to British proposals. Brooke, as usual, was also out of temper. 'Portal asked me as we went to lunch whether I thought the position was as hopeless as it looked.' Slessor thought not, and after a hasty lunch went up to the roof of the hotel, sat in the sun watching the long Atlantic rollers breaking on the beach and scratched out a few notes. Portal read them, altered a word or two and said: 'Let's try it on them.' The deadlock was broken and an agreement about an Anglo-American bomber offensive, to be directed by Portal, was reached by the Combined Chiefs of Staff on January 21st. It was loosely worded, but at least it kept most of the US heavy bombers away from the Far East or the Pacific, although Portal was obliged to yield to demands by both Pound and King for the bombing of heavily-fortified U-boat bases in the Bay of Biscay – bombing that did nothing to impede the U-boat offensive at a heavy cost in British and American crews.

The Combined Chiefs had in mind five competing strategies. King gave priority to Pacific campaigns; Marshall to a landing in Occupied France; Pound to the Atlantic battle against U-boats; Portal and Arnold to the strategic bombing offensive over Germany; and Brooke to the Mediterranean campaign. Competition between these priorities was the 'fundamental factor', argued Noble Frankland, in Allied strategy and 'the key to most of the discontent and frustration' which Brooke so often expressed in his diary. All five were important and at different times one came more to the fore than another, but one could never be given permanent first place. Brooke, however, frequently urged Churchill to do precisely this, quite overlooking the fact that Britain's Prime Minister could not impose his will on the heads of the American armed services – nor was Churchill prepared to prefer Brooke's opinions on all issues to those of Pound, Portal or the Americans.

No individual service strategy argued Frankland, 'such as winning the war by bombing alone, or by producing an astronomical number of army divisions, or by providing every possible means for the destruction of U-boats', could be given exclusive priority. Compromise, which Brooke resisted, was essential. His view of the war was 'narrow and restricted... He regarded air power almost exclusively as an auxiliary to surface military power.' After Dunkirk Brooke had supposed that 'everything was up to the inadequate and ill-equipped army which he commanded', whereas it was up to Fighter Command. Unless the Luftwaffe achieved superiority there could be no invasion. But Brooke regarded the Battle of Britain as 'almost an irrelevant issue and he continued to expect the German invasion after it had been won.'

Brooke never appreciated the potentialities of strategic air power and in his diary he scarcely mentions it, except in the context of a diversion from the tactical army air arm which he wished to create. He often referred to his wish to delay Overlord until German mobile reserves were defeated or committed to other fronts. He did not understand that Anglo-American air power was wearing down German material and moral resources and – before Overlord – was gravely damaging communications by rail, road and waterway in France and Belgium, thereby hampering the movement of German reserves in those countries.

The Italian campaign, urged so vehemently by Brooke, proved to be 'an expensive diversion.' It tied down Allied as well as German reserves and contradicted a cardinal principle of war: bring maximum force to bear at the decisive point. Marshall saw this clearly, but Brooke arrogantly dismissed him as 'a good general at raising armies and at providing the necessary link between the military and political worlds, but his strategical ability does not impress me at all. In fact, in many respects, he is a very dangerous man whilst being a very charming one.'

More than 40 years later, in 1975, Slessor denied that the intention of the Casablanca directive was 'to defeat Germany if possible by strategic bombing alone.' The directive 'merely defined the role of the bomber forces in the programme for victory; it did not say they were to win the war by themselves.' Slessor then attacked the common assertion that the bomber offensive was 'the costliest failure in the history of British arms.' Without it, he argued, the Allied armies could not have landed in France in 1944; could not have stayed there if they had got ashore; and therefore could not have overrun occupied France and Germany 'at a cost in casualties absurdly light compared to the holocausts of human life in France in the First World War.' As he did so often, Slessor damages a fair argument by his careless reference to 'absurdly light' casualties: the Allied victory in Normandy alone was dearly bought – over 200,000 men lost in 80 days – and thousands more suffered death or injury before VE-Day. Nothing 'absurdly light' about these figures.

Here as elsewhere Slessor relies more on memory than research for his statements – unlike John Kenneth Galbraith, who directed the post-war US study of the impact of bombing on the German war economy and became one of the most influential economic gurus of the 20th century. Galbraith upset many pundits, especially in air forces on both sides of the Atlantic, by his finding that 'the attack on transportation, beginning in September 1944, was the most important single cause of Germany's ultimate economic collapse.' Bombing was certainly important, but only late in the day and in combination with all other attacks. The war was won, wrote Galbraith in a review of Goebbels' diaries in 1978, 'by the ground troops east and west and the tactical air forces that cleared the way. The long-range bombers helped principally by disrupting the transportation network, holding defensive forces in the interior and attacking oil supplies. Goebbels saw only the bombed cities. Accordingly, he attaches a wholly disproportionate importance to these attacks in assessing the Allied advantage. Even at this late date, it is possible that some proponents of strategic air power will seize upon his testimony to argue that the bombers won the war. They did not. That they did not careful studies long ago established.'

CHAPTER 10

COASTAL COMMAND AND THE APPALLING GAP

Cinderella was late for the ball

Although Coastal Command was regarded in the 1930s as a Cinderella by the Air Staff (devoted as Slessor and other members were to its allegedly powerful and therefore much-admired bomber and fighter sisters), maritime air power would prove to be an essential weapon throughout the war. The Admiralty as well as the Air Staff had 'gravely underestimated the importance of aircraft for the protection of shipping, especially of convoys against U-boat attack. This was all the more surprising', wrote Sir Maurice Dean (a senior civil servant in the Air Ministry) because the importance of aircraft in this role had been fully demonstrated in the First World War.' And yet in the first major U-boat campaign of the war (1940-1), Coastal Command did help to force the boats away from British coasts. In the second (1942-3), it was 'a decisive factor by closing the mid-Atlantic air gap and by taking a heavy toll of enemy submarines': in all, more than a quarter of the total number destroyed by the Allies.

Between the wars, however, the Air Staff was chiefly concerned with bombers and fighters, and, in Terraine's words, 'directed Coastal Area [later Command] away from its roles of trade defence and anti-submarine warfare into an imperial cruising and prestige function, based on flying boats of little military value.' The navy was no wiser. It was chiefly concerned to recover its carrier-based aircraft (the Fleet Air Arm) 'and the coastal elements of maritime air power were merely a peripheral issue' because the ruling admirals believed that Asdic[10] or Sonar (a system for underwater detection of objects by reflected or emitted sound) had ended the U-boat threat. They therefore felt free to focus attention on what they regarded as proper tasks for seamen – offensive patrols, looking for fleet actions – and put the tiresome duty of guarding convoys out of mind. They also put out of mind the annoying fact that Asdic was 'virtually useless against enemies on the surface.' The navy foresaw a need for

---

[10] A word formed from the initials of the Anti-Submarine Detection Investigation Committee in 1917.

reconnaissance aircraft, to help locate enemy surface vessels, but these would usually be dealt with by the navy's bigger and better warships, though torpedo-armed aircraft would certainly be useful.

An effective coastal air defence force could have been created before 1939, but 'largely due to the policies and attitude of the Air Staff, no such force emerged, leaving the RAF incapable of the effective defence of Britain's trade routes against a German surface naval threat.' The Air Staff claimed to have such a defence force in its bombers, supposed to be capable of decisive destruction. The result was that on the outbreak of war Coastal Command had precisely two squadrons of obsolete torpedo-bombers for the task of coastal defence and for the interception of enemy surface vessels. Evidence 'contradicting the Air Staff was available [from pre-war exercises] but was ignored because it did not fit with their grand strategy. The myth that the massed-bomber force could handle any threatening situation pervaded Air Staff thinking well into the Second World War.'

The twin-engined Avro Anson, the RAF's first monoplane with a retractable undercarriage, typified Coastal Command in the late 1930s: it carried a tiny bombload, 'defended' itself with two machine-guns, was completely unarmoured, and so short of range that it could not get from one side of the North Sea to the other. Despite these gross failings, the Anson was acceptable to the Admiralty (aircraft were of use merely to direct surface vessels at the enemy) and the Air Staff (focussed on a bomber force).

This useless aircraft was to be replaced by two types that proved almost as useless: the Bristol Bolingbroke (a modified Blenheim) and the Blackburn Botha, also a twin-engined machine. Cyril Newall – then CAS – dithered between them. Eventually, and reluctantly, he cancelled them both. Although the useful Beaufort gradually appeared, it became necessary to look abroad for replacements, and as a result of a 'flash of perspicacity' 200 twin-engined Lockheed Hudsons were ordered from the US in June 1938. They proved to be the command's most efficient weapon in the early stages of the war. As for the Sunderland, it was only slowly brought into service, thanks to time and resources being squandered on another disaster, the Saunders-Roe Lerwick, a twin-engined flying-boat. Fortunately, another excellent American machine, the Catalina, would be bought for RAF service, but cancellation of failed types was postponed simply to keep companies in business: a severe indictment of Air Staff policies.

For years after war began, Coastal Command and the Admiralty contended with the Air Staff over the merits of trade defence versus strategic bombing. According to a thorough recent analysis by John Buckley, this was 'a strategic tussle which almost cost Britain and the Allies the war.' As late as March 1943, the U-boat seemed to be winning the Atlantic battle 'as a direct result of the lack of very long range aircraft.'

One battlefield: from the Hebrides to Halifax, from Casablanca to the Caribbean

Although Slessor had no experience of war at sea, he was appointed head of Coastal Command at Northwood, near Watford, about 20 miles north of central London, in February 1943 and promoted again, to the rank of Air Marshal (Lieutenant-General). His predecessor, Philip Joubert de la Ferté, had irritated the Portal-Freeman axis by complaining about his shortage of aircraft, and by criticizing Shorts for producing no more than four Sunderlands a month in Northern Ireland, where the Protestant unions would not permit the hiring of Roman Catholic workers. He also had a gift for public relations, wrote articles, gave interviews, and launched *Coastal Command Review* – all of which displeased Churchill, another gifted publicist. Freeman disliked Joubert personally, doubted his adherence 'to the doctrines of the Air Staff' and had him replaced by a man who was 'one of us'. Slessor regarded him with contempt. 'Joubert', he assured the head of the Air Historical Branch in 1975, 'was always lacking in judgement, and most people who knew him at all well were astonished that he ever got as far as he did.' That opinion is not supported by Terraine and other historians. Unlike Slessor, they have studied what Joubert actually did as head of Coastal Command, and what difficulties he had to overcome – some of them exacerbated by Slessor and his Air Staff colleagues.

Joubert may have been slack doctrinally, but he was a fine practical airman. Slessor would benefit greatly from his 'Planned Flying and Maintenance', a scheme introduced in August 1942. It was a standard peacetime procedure in the United States (overlooked by the RAF) to get the maximum number of safe air hours out of aircraft. The result, of course, was to increase significantly the command's effective strength. As for Joubert's *Review*, it was a welcome sign – as Christina Goulter wrote – 'of a general honesty when dealing with operational problems not seen since the First World War.' Although Slessor despised Joubert, he valued his *Review* – edited by Hector Bolitho – and encouraged its circulation.

Bolitho admired Slessor and thought of becoming his Boswell. Sadly, he dropped that idea, but he did leave us a sketch of our bomber champion at work. 'Sir John Slessor', he recalled in 1955, 'disliked dictating even his briefest memorandum. In the archives of the Air Ministry, and of Coastal Command, there must be thousands of his notes [there are]... This was his way of holding his forces together and of commanding us all. Sometimes one heard a murmur of protest, "My God, another note from the Old Man!" But the protests were superficial, the notes made us all feel that we were in friendly touch with our general. In his manner, Sir John was seldom warmly personal, and he wasted little time on jokes or small talk. But he compensated for this with his refreshing memoranda. They were cast as requests, not orders.' He wrote the summary of each month's operations himself – which neither Joubert nor Sholto Douglas (his successor) cared to do – and Slessor's personal assistant told Bolitho that 'the Chief sometimes sat at his desk until two o'clock in the morning, to keep faith with me, and with the printer. While making history he still cared about the writing of it.'

Slessor's chief assistant was Air Vice-Marshal Albert Durston, 'a real old salt', especially valuable to a commander without sea experience. Air Vice-Marshal Forster Maynard and his deputy, Air Commodore Ivor Lloyd, handled administration, and Air Vice-Marshal Thomas Warne-Browne was chief technical officer. Slessor loved his time in Coastal Command, the pinnacle of his career in many ways, even though he later achieved higher rank and heavier responsibility. 'I have never known a happier headquarters, and no Commander-in-Chief can ever have been better served.' As he had done throughout his brief stint in Bomber Command, Slessor radiated pleasure at escaping from planning duties in Whitehall to face the altogether different challenge of conducting operations. His pleasure was greatly enhanced in June 1943 when news of his knighthood came through: Knight Commander of the Order of the Bath, KCB. He was undeniably now, despite his physical handicap, a match for any member of either his own family, ancient or modern, or that of his wife. Not surprisingly, most of the men and women who saw Sir John regularly at this time responded warmly to his evident joy in his new position and his new title.

Among them was Squadron Leader Mick Ensor, a New Zealand-born pilot in Coastal Command, decorated four times for gallantry before his 23rd birthday. He had arrived at Northwood in January to feed his exceptional operational experience into the planners' deliberations. During the next six months, he saw a lot of Slessor and came to regard him as 'the most approachable very very senior officer I ever knew.' Ensor also admired him for making so light of his lameness. He happened to catch Slessor by himself in a corridor one morning before a formal parade, flexing his leg and grimacing. When he saw an embarrassed Ensor he immediately grinned cheerfully and said: 'Not even a bloody war wound, damn it!' and stomped off to do his stuff, barely leaning on an old stick.

Peyton-Ward

Ensor also got to know the command's key figure, the indefatigable Captain Peyton-Ward, RN. Officially, 'PW' (as he was known to humble and haughty alike) was the Admiralty's representative, but in fact his main concern was the efficient use of aircraft in co-operation with surface vessels against U-boats. He was 'a very gifted ex-submariner, much loathed by the Admiralty', recalled Sir Edward Chilton, one of Coastal Command's outstanding personalities, 'which is why we got him as their liaison officer. He turned out to be first-class for Coastal Command; he understood the German mind, he understood submarines – and we couldn't have got on without him.' Slessor agreed. 'He had an insight into the workings of the air/sea war that must have been unparalleled.' Crews who had sunk a U-boat were summoned to Command HQ, where PW would go through the whole incident with them, getting at what had really happened – as opposed to what they had told senior officers of their squadrons – and extracting practical lessons. PW was the command's representative on a committee assessing the results of attacks on U-boats and strikes against enemy shipping. 'He never seemed to take any leave and, no matter what hour of the day or night, seemed always to be there at his post in the operations room, on the telephone to Admiralty or one of the groups and ready with wise advice and willing help.'

The drill was that each morning PW would obtain from the Admiralty what was currently known about the whereabouts of all U-boats, plus suspected movements and any educated guesses about the intentions of their commander, Grand Admiral Karl Doenitz. In February 1943, the Germans had about 400 U-boats in commission and 433 by May, of which 118 were at sea – the highest figure achieved throughout the war.

Slessor thought Doenitz failed to handle his forces skilfully, but he did not consider – as an air power student should – the refusal of Hermann Goering (commanding the Luftwaffe) to provide wholehearted support for the vital U-boat campaign. Unlike their comrades in other commands, Coastal Command crews were largely spared from start to finish of the war the fear of aerial attack. For this wonderful boon, given that they flew aircraft barely capable of defending themselves – except in the strike wings – they had Goering to thank. His backing for Doenitz in the early war years might have transformed the U-boat from a potential to an actual war winner; it would certainly have multiplied its already serious impact on Britain's ability to keep fighting. As Doenitz sadly remarked after the war, the Germans managed only one combined air, surface ship and U-boat operation in the entire Atlantic battle.

Goering was also Germany's economic overlord in those years, and refused to give high priority to U-boat production, encouraged in this foolish decision by Grand Admiral Erich Raeder, head of the Kriegsmarine and in love with beautiful surface vessels (which were also enormously expensive and alarmingly vulnerable). 'If Goering's megalomania contributed nothing else to the final defeat of his country,' concluded Stephen Roskill, 'his long and stubborn refusal to co-operate with the German navy, and his recurrent strife with Raeder, must have contributed a good deal towards the Allied victory in the Atlantic.' Mercifully for Britain, Hitler chose not to exert his overwhelming personal authority to ensure either effective sea-air co-operation or an adequate supply of U-boats. 'It was hard enough to find a U-boat anyway', remarked Ensor, 'given the limitations of our equipment and flying conditions that were rarely clear. I doubt if we could have done any good at all if there had been more of them and if German aircraft had been systematically pestering us north of Scotland or out in the Bay [of Biscay].'

It is no secret now – but it was when Slessor was writing – that he received a steady stream of accurate information about German intentions, thanks to the work of code-breakers at Bletchley Park in Buckinghamshire who were able to provide the Admiralty with translations of signals passing between Doenitz's headquarters and U-boats at sea. PW had a large softboard map of the Atlantic in his office on which he built a display of the day's situation in a simple but effective way. As Ensor put it, 'even I could tell what was going on.'

In December 1942, the experts at Bletchley Park, after ten months of persistent effort, had at last managed to master the four-wheel key of the Enigma machine – a victory of such significance that 'some historians have seen in it virtually the whole explanation of the victory over the U-boats which soon followed.' Thereafter, Allied naval and air forces received 'immediate operational intelligence about the departure and return of U-boats, the numbers and types of U-boats at sea, the dispositions of their patrol groups and their operational orders.' Not least among the Allies' growing advantages was the Admiralty's decision in June to replace its Atlantic cypher with one that the Germans could not read.

Detailed reports of all U-boat sightings and attacks, however inconclusive, arrived at PW's office within a few days of the event, and PW would reconstruct them – with diagrams – in a standard format. Such reconstructions could not be complete without a direct input from the crews concerned and it fell to Ensor to arrange for them to visit Northwood. He was already well aware that crews were rarely forthcoming, even within their own squadrons, about any dramatic or alarming incidents during operations. This was partly because they naturally feared accusations of line-shooting from other crews, but it was also because they found it difficult to grasp the overall shape of events in which their own part was so fleeting and often bewildering. Fortunately, Slessor and Durston were always ready to talk – easily and informally – to them. These visits by crews to Northwood provided an invaluable link with the tactical level, and whatever they had done – or tried and failed to do – they at least went back to their squadrons feeling that their efforts were understood and appreciated in high places.

Gadgets

Imports to Britain of food, raw materials, munitions and fuel had declined from about 61 million tons in 1940 to about 39 million in 1942. Merchant shipping losses – both Allied and neutral – were running at a disastrous rate. When Slessor took command, losses rose to 403,000 tons in that month, and over half a million in March: well above the rate of new construction, quite apart from the loss of experienced seamen. At the end of 1942, it had to be admitted that only six percent of attacks upon U-boats were resulting in destruction and there was continual argument between squadron crews blaming poor weapons and the Operational

Research Section (ORS) at Command Headquarters blaming poor aiming. Wise men on both sides, however, agreed that the realistic answer lay in practice and yet more practice as well as the development of more efficient weapons.

An ORS had been set up at Northwood in March 1941, when Professor Patrick Blackett was appointed Scientific Adviser to the head of Coastal Command. Linked to that work was a Development Unit, responsible for testing equipment and tactics. Although he moved to the Admiralty in January 1942 as Chief Adviser on Operational Research, systematic study of all major problems was by then safely established. Slessor did not trust Blackett's judgement, then or later. In May 1963, having heard a rumour that Blackett was to be Chief Scientific Adviser at the Ministry of Defence, if the Labour Party won the next election, he wrote to George Brown (Labour's likely Foreign Secretary) to say that he thought Blackett 'totally unsuitable (to say the least of it) for any such post.' Slessor thought him 'emotionally and temperamentally incapable of taking a really objective view of strategic problems... As long as 20 years ago, I resisted (unsuccessfully) in the Cabinet U-boat Committee a suggestion of his to the effect that the Battle of the Atlantic could be quickly won by taking 190 bombers away from Bomber Command and giving them to me; that claim was on the basis of one of the most bogus pseudo-scientific analyses I have ever seen.' Since then, Blackett had further angered Slessor by his criticism of British bombing strategy and suspicion of American 'global ambitions'. Although he was not appointed Chief Scientific Adviser, that influential position went to a man who was almost as unsuitable, in Slessor's opinion: Solly Zuckerman, Tedder's close friend, who held it for 11 years.

A scientific officer – Mr E. C. Baugham – was working on bombing errors that occurred in attacks on U-boats and seeking means of increasing the probability of causing fatal damage. He concluded that the spacing between depth charges should be increased from 50 to a hundred feet, thus doubling the margin for error in release distance, but the change did nothing to solve the problem of late releases resulting in over-shoots – a problem very common with Liberators in the Atlantic. The new depth charge spacing nevertheless went out as a mandatory tactical instruction.

The need for a practical low-level bombsight had been evident for some time, and numerous scientists were giving it their attention. One of them was a regular train-traveller (so the story went) and one day, while watching a long paling fence passing the carriage window, he noticed that it appeared to stop for an instant at a certain point. He quickly realized that the illusion was a result of a special combination of angles and velocities that might be related to the low-level, high-speed bomb-aiming problem with which no current sight could cope. He was right and eventually a handy sight, no bigger than a small football, was produced. The optics consisted of a glass plate about four inches square, facing forward and slight down, mounted on a bracket and gyro-stabilized. Onto this, using the same principle as that for reflector gunsights fitted to fighters, a vertical centreline and about 20 horizontal lines were projected. A control box was provided into which the co-pilot fed the length of the stick of bombs or depth charges, height, and ground speed. The latter was always a guess, but a long stick would compensate for inaccuracy. When the sight was switched on, the glass screen would take up the correct angle and the horizontal lines moved down, like a ladder being moved down outside a window. During a bombing run, the target would first appear to move slower than the lines; then for an instant at the same speed; then faster again. Ensor remembered the device being welcomed by Slessor, who never pretended to understand gadgets. 'He would ask, politely, to have them explained in words of one syllable. Some members of his staff did pretend and got caught out, sooner or later, but Jack was too fly to fall into that trap!'

Another exciting weapon then being developed was the 'High Velocity Aircraft Rocket'. There were two types: one with a 60 pound explosive head that was said to have the power of a six-inch shell, the other with a 25 pound solid head. The latter had a higher velocity with great penetrating power, and if the motor was still burning when it entered the water, it would drive on at a lethal pace for about a hundred feet before failing. The chief weapon, however, was the Mark XI torpex-filled depth-charge, dropped in sticks of four to eight from low levels.

The Bay of Biscay, at that time, was the key area. Because of the high priority accorded to combatting the U-boat menace, Coastal Command got an airborne radar as soon as it was available that would scan all around the aircraft and 'paint' a picture of any objects 'seen' on a circular screen in front of the operator. He was given a wealth of information simply not possible with the earlier fixed-beam radars. The ASV III form of centimetric radar was able to detect with great clarity convoys at 40 miles and surfaced submarines at 12 miles. By September 1942, the Air Staff had at last recognized that defeat in the battle of the Atlantic must be avoided and decreed – over Harris's objections – that 40 H2S sets (the land version) be converted to ASV III (the sea version), and the Americans agreed to install their equivalent apparatus (SCR 517) in all Liberators intended for Coastal Command. In Roskill's opinion, centimetric radar stood out above all other scientific achievements because 'it returned to us the initiative in attack by night or in low visibility.' At first, for surface escorts, soon for Coastal Command, 'a renewal of the Bay Offensive in greatly improved conditions would then be possible.'

Liberator

Slessor's 60 squadrons in February had a total strength of about 850 aircraft and three American squadrons were also under his operational control. Of this large force, 34 squadrons, about 430 aircraft (including

Sunderlands and Catalinas) were employed on strictly anti-submarine duties. In addition, there were 127 torpedo-armed strike aircraft with a hundred long-range, cannon-armed Bristol Beaufighters as escorts. He got his photo-reconnaissance from five squadrons based at Benson, about ten miles south-east of Oxford. Three squadrons of Fleet Air Arm Fairey Swordfish biplanes were attached to his command for short-range strikes against E-boats. He also had two squadrons of Air-Sea Rescue aircraft and a large fleet of fast motor-boats had the duty of trying to save airmen who survived ditching at sea. Last but not least, some 50 aircraft were permanently employed to collect weather information.

Slessor praised the arrival of Very Long Range (VLR) Liberators in numbers just sufficient to have a decisive effect. Nothing else was up to the job. Another big American bomber – the Boeing B-17 Flying Fortress – had neither the range nor the load-carrying capacity for use in war over the ocean and was in any case the USAAF's preferred weapon in the assault on Germany. The Hudson and the Wellington had insufficient range, the Sunderland was too slow, and the Catalina lacked fire-power. Until February, the command had only two squadrons of this essential aircraft, the only type capable of closing the 'Atlantic Gap', that ocean area where U-boats had hitherto sought victims safe from aerial attack. It was 'by far the most complicated and expensive combat aircraft the world had seen', in the words of an aviation historian, Bill Gunston, 'it was built in bigger numbers than any other aircraft in history, and served on every front in World War II and with every Allied nation.'

Ensor would grow to love 'the great ugly beast' and named his even more beloved dog 'Lib' to honour both of them. He flew 47 operations in command of a Liberator, each one lasting on average just over 11 hours. But he was disappointed by the appalling lack of forward and downward vision for its pilots and even more by the fact that he could no longer be his own bomb-aimer. The long flat nose with an astrodome sticking up at the front limited their view of the sea to a sector between the captain's left and the co-pilot's right. Good co-operation between the two reduced the problem, but Ensor was certain that this design flaw cost many sightings and sinkings. He was, however, well aware that 'the big beast had not been designed as a sub-hunter'; so too was Slessor, who also knew that it played a vital part in the Atlantic victory despite its shortcomings.

Until the employment of a handful of Wellingtons equipped with both radar and searchlights in June 1942, there had been no serious aerial threat to U-boats at night. Consequently, they had used the long hours of darkness during previous winters for safe and speedy surface travelling to those sea areas where convoys were likely to be intercepted. By 1943, the much more powerful Liberators were being fitted with searchlights. As soon as radar indicated the presence of a surfaced U-boat, the pilot would close to within about two miles and then switch on the light. The hope was that this sudden, alarming light would panic the German gunners into opening fire too soon, giving away their precise position and expending their loaded ammunition before the Liberator came within dangerous range. The gunners would then be changing clips with dazzled eyes – and ears straining to catch the first note of the dive klaxon.

With or without searchlights, the Liberators performed admirably, denying U-boats freedom of movement on the surface in the vicinity of convoys. They sank, damaged, or at least gave a bad fright to enough boats to make them so cautious that the old, deadly wolf-pack tactics became rare. However, it would be better still if fewer boats even reached the convoy areas, so the navy formed attack groups to operate in the Bay of Biscay. Under Captain F. J. Walker, they proved successful in obliging the Germans to travel submerged – and therefore very slowly – to the convoy areas.

A legacy of ill feeling

In early November 1940, the Admiralty – backed by Lord Beaverbrook (Minister of Aircraft Production), Admiral Sir Roger Keyes (Director of Combined Operations) and a new First Lord, A. V. Alexander (a Labour Party politician) – had made what Slessor thought was 'an extraordinary demand' for control of all maritime aircraft. Eventually, a compromise was reached by which Coastal Command came under the Admiralty's operational control, but the Admiralty delegated that control to the head of Coastal Command. The arguments on both sides had been put so often and so passionately, in public and private, that Slessor inherited 'a legacy of ill feeling' on his arrival at Northwood.

That ill feeling survived the war. Writing to Hilary St. George Saunders (an official RAF historian) on June 22nd 1949, Slessor referred to this 'conspiracy to nobble Coastal Command in the winter of 1940'. Of 'The Beaver' he wrote: his 'crass ignorance of air or sea warfare was only excelled by the unsoundness of his judgement on anything connected with the conduct of the war.' As for Keyes, he was 'a very stupid old blue-water Admiral whose ignorance and fear of Air Power in principle were sharpened by his personal vendetta with his brother-in-law Trenchard.' But Beaverbrook was 'really the villain of the piece. Unlike Alexander, his activities in the matter were unhampered by any sense of responsibility or of decent feeling towards another service.'

The Admiralty, on reflection, backed off from its initial demand, once its staff officers began to ask practical questions. For example, where would it find the necessary airfields? What facilities were available for training an ever-growing number of pilots? Who would provide the essential logistic and maintenance support? Moreover, the Air Staff agreed to transfer more aircraft to Coastal Command and on December 4th 1940 the Cabinet's Defence Committee ruled that operational control should pass to the Admiralty. Slessor regarded this transfer as 'an amiable fiction' because this had been the case, in practice, since the outbreak of war.

Service in Coastal Command, Slessor recalled, 'though less murderously expensive in casualties than some, was exacting, dangerous, and highly skilled, and far too commonly tedious and unrewarding.' It was difficult to keep up morale because public recognition was rare. The Admiralty insisted on secrecy regarding the number of U-boats destroyed from the air, but eagerly published details of any victories by surface vessels. Slessor complained about this in a letter to Sinclair of November 13th 1943. 'There is no doubt in the minds of any of us who have to deal constantly with the Admiralty that it is the settled policy of that department to soft-pedal on the share of the RAF in the war at sea and to glorify that of the navy.' He thought this a serious matter for two reasons. 'Firstly, that if the air force is to have its proper share in winning this war and preventing another, the public must know that the RAF is as vital and valuable a component in victory over the sea as it is now generally recognized to be over the land. And secondly, it is essential to the morale and enthusiasm of the personnel in Coastal Command that the results of their efforts are known, just as the results of the navy's efforts and of those of other RAF commands are known.' He had complained officially in July, but received no answer; nor did this letter make any difference. Years later, in April 1952, Slessor criticized the navy's staff history for attempting to denigrate Coastal Command's achievements.

As for Churchill, in his memoirs so fulsomely praised by Slessor, he said very little about Coastal Command. Its achievements were simply not dramatic enough for his boyish taste. 'The matter is of cardinal importance', argued the official naval historian, 'because it has often been suggested, and in the highest circles, that the strategy of convoy and escort is "defensive" compared with allegedly "offensive" hunting and patrolling.' As Churchill put it, 'I always sought to rupture this defensive obsession by searching for forms of counter-offensive... I could not rest content with the policy of "convoy and blockade."' In fact, as studies of both world wars reveal, the escorted convoy is the most effective means of prosecuting the counter-offensive against both U-boats and surface vessels.

After the war, it was supposed that the so-called 'hunter-killer' groups of aircraft carriers and surface vessels had been the U-boat's deadliest foe. In fact, of the 771 German and Italian boats sunk at sea by Allied action, only 20 were destroyed by hunter-killer groups, as compared to 255 by aircraft alone. A further 17 were sunk by RAF-laid mines and 66 more destroyed by bombing in ports. Slessor constantly pressed for the hunting groups to support Air Vice-Marshal Geoffrey Bromet's 19 Group in the Bay of Biscay offensive, but they did so only rarely and reluctantly.

At the highest level of control on the British side was the Anti-U-boat Sub-Committee of the War Cabinet, usually chaired by Churchill. Admiral Stark and Mr Harriman (Roosevelt's personal representative in Britain) often attended and received all the papers. Slessor worked closely with Rear-Admiral Sir Patrick Brind, Assistant Chief of the Naval Staff (Home). In April, Brind had raised with him the question of a re-organization in the Admiralty of efforts against U-boats. Slessor thought the current system worked well and strongly opposed the notion of a great combined headquarters in which 'two high panjandrums in different coloured coats sit looking at a great chart and moving flags about.' The best way to improve the system, he concluded, was by 'even closer consultation between us on matters of major policy.' Slessor took up the suggestion for a combined anti-submarine headquarters with Sir Stafford Cripps, Minister of Aircraft Production. 'We were too ready,' he argued, when a new situation arose, 'of trying to deal with it by creating yet another staff organization, a lot of people sitting in an office somewhere', when the current system could be made to work. And that needed changes in the Admiralty. Rear-Admiral J. H. Edelsten was 'useless', as Cripps agreed. Pound (First Sea Lord), though himself 'a wise old bird', was not well advised. His staff involved themselves in a mass of operational detail on air matters which they did not understand and listened too readily to 'professors' – 'operational research workers' – who were a tail wagging the Admiralty dog. Find a competent Admiral, Slessor urged: 'I should have a desk in his office and he should have a desk in mine, and we should get on with, hand-in-glove, running the machine as it now exists. And we should both be told that if either of us puts up any plan or paper to anyone or takes any action affecting the U-boat war as a whole without consulting the other, he will get the sack.'

Slessor also worked with Admiral Sir Max Horton at Western Approaches (Derby House, Liverpool) who was responsible for all North Atlantic convoys. Horton was one of the war's great commanders: 'he constantly went to sea in the little ships and flew in the lonely aircraft of Coastal Command, sharing their dangers and discomforts.' Better still, he had a complete understanding of the human and technical problems arising day by day in opposing U-boats. Four years later, in February 1947, Slessor wrote that no-one knew more about the Battle of the Atlantic than Horton. He went on to emphasize 'the association of the airman and the scientist with the sailor': it eventually worked well in wartime and must be kept alive and improved to meet any crises ahead.

Horton was assisted by Leonard Slatter's 15 Group, whose squadrons were based on the west coast of Scotland and in Northern Ireland. Aubrey Ellwood (head of 18 Group) covered the east coast from Rosyth, on the north shore of the Firth of Forth. He was responsible for guarding the northern passage into the Atlantic and movement along the Norwegian coast. At Chatham, on the Medway river in Kent, was 16 Group under Brian Baker, concerned mainly with the Dutch coast and E-boats skulking in Channel waters. Bromet's headquarters were in Plymouth and he had squadrons based in the south-west 'with the most interesting of all responsibilities'; to engage U-boats in transit between their Biscay bases and the open ocean. In Iceland was Kenneth Lloyd, who linked eastward with 15 Group and later westward with the Canadians in Newfoundland

and Labrador to cover the North Atlantic convoys. At Gibraltar, Sturley Simpson covered west African convoys and the southern flank of the Bay offensive. When the Azores were occupied, with Portuguese agreement, Bromet formed 247 Group at Terceira, Baker relieved him in Plymouth, and Frank Hopps took over 16 Group from Baker. Finally there was 17 Group (Operational Training) in Edinburgh under Reggie Smart.

Coastal Command Review became a monthly in September, and Slessor increased its circulation. He regarded it as 'a serious professional review of the previous month's work', a best-seller among all his men. He summarized in his memoirs the account of the year's work that appeared in the issue for December 1943, correcting some figures for U-boats destroyed in the light of postwar evidence.

The Atlantic campaign, waged over a vast area by two services (RAF and Royal Navy) and three nations (Britain, the United States, Canada) took some directing. It was one battlefield, from the Hebrides to Halifax and from Casablanca to the Caribbean. But Coastal Command was even less adequately prepared for war at sea in 1939 than Bomber or Fighter Command, and the Royal Navy was in no better shape. 'One shudders to think what would have happened', Slessor later reflected, if the Germans had built up 'their really decisive arm, the U-boat service' before the war, instead of wasting resources, human and material, on a 'third-rate heavy ship force.' Churchill thought so too. 'It would have been wise for the Germans to stake all upon it', he later wrote. And so did Doenitz. On the very first day of the war, September 1st 1939, he said that the 'only possibility of bringing England to her knees with the forces of our navy lies in attacking her sea communications in the Atlantic... I therefore believe that the U-boat will always be the backbone of warfare against England.' Despite plans to build about 30 U-boats per month from that date on, only 13 were actually commissioned during the first nine months of the war. Worse still, German torpedoes were unreliable (and long remained so), while the Luftwaffe – thanks to Goering – 'devoted only one group of 40 aircraft to the battle, with the result that on any one day, there were on average only three German aircraft over the Atlantic. In 1942, the Allies committed about 500 aircraft to the Battle of the Atlantic, perhaps ten times the German total.'

And yet, until the end of 1942, the 'exchange rate' was still in Germany's favour: eight ships and 45,000 tons of cargo per U-boat lost. By April 1943, the rate had fallen to 28,000 tons, and by the end of May had collapsed to a mere 5,000 tons. It did not recover. German captains became more concerned to locate and avoid powerful enemies than to find and destroy the precious freighters, oil tankers, and troop transports that those enemies now guarded so skilfully. Yet they remained at sea in a successful attempt to keep very large Allied naval and air forces fully occupied, away from Germany. Even in the last two months of the war, U-boats actually sank as many as 44 Allied ships.

CHAPTER 11

THE GAP CLOSED

Admiral Ernest J. King, USN

The Atlantic, as Slessor wrote, was 'one battlefield' and the enemy was under the control of one man, Doenitz, who moved his forces wherever he thought best. To counter him, Slessor thought the Allies should also have a unified command. Robert Lovett, US Under-Secretary of State for Air, agreed in May 1943 that all anti-submarine operations in the Atlantic ought to be under a single commander, but Slessor was rightly convinced that Admiral King would never agree to a British officer moving American squadrons from, say, the Caribbean to Iceland. Relations with the US Navy were never close, and for this King was largely responsible. He was a man unable to accept that he might be mistaken on any issue, and absolutely certain that the US Navy was superior to all others. He became a master of operating great carrier task forces in the Pacific, but he never understood anti-submarine warfare and detested the idea of independent air forces. King has been lauded by Samuel Eliot Morison, an offical US naval historian, as 'undoubtedly the best naval strategist and organizer in our history.' Although (or perhaps because) his father was Scottish, he became notorious not only for his dislike of all things British, but all civilians and all other services. Americans, Canadians and Britons alike found him difficult to argue with, for he was a man of 'Olympian simplicity' and very great force of personality. His only weaknesses were 'other men's wives, alcohol, and intolerance.' It was one of his own daughters who said: 'He is the most even-tempered man in the navy. He is always in a rage.' As the historian Marc Milner wrote, King was 'a notoriously obstinate and prickly character and a great burden on his peers'; his 'anglophobia proved a serious impediment to the Allied campaign in the Atlantic.' It is easy, especially for non-American historians, to make of King an easy target, and yet he agreed to allow the US Navy to escort vital oil tanker convoys between the Dutch West Indies and Britain, and he allocated an American Support Group – one escort carrier, five destroyers – to operate under British control in the north Atlantic. He was not, in short, always in a rage – at least, not against the British.

After Pearl Harbor, the Americans suffered unnecessarily heavy losses to U-boats along the east coast as a result of poor equipment, even poorer relations between the navy and the army, and civilian reluctance to accept that 'business as usual' must be interrupted. 'The violence of inter-Service rivalry in the United States in those days had to be seen to be believed', recalled Slessor, 'and was an appreciable handicap to their war effort.' King contemptuously rejected Arnold's proposal to create a Coastal Command along British lines, but Stimson and Marshall insisted in August 1943 on the formation of a command something like that of the British under the direction of the Navy Department. An army air force Anti-Submarine Command was then set up in New York in October, but there was still no effective co-operation between the services. Slessor thought Arnold at fault here. He had a long-standing agreement that air operations were his responsibility even if they involved flying over the sea. He should have stuck to that principle and given his personal attention to the work of the Anti-Submarine Command. He was not, however, really interested. The strategic bomber offensive was his main concern, as the Pacific was King's.

Anglo-American air co-operation over the Atlantic in the years 1942-43 was, in Buckley's words, 'a catalogue of mistrust and suspicion that did nothing to enhance the ideal of Allied friendship. The most logical procedures were passed over simply because they would have required the Allies – and indeed the two American services – to co-operate fully with each other, and this was anathema to the powers and personalities involved.' It proved quite impossible to achieve a centralized command structure for all the forces involved in the Atlantic campaign. The issue was debated at Casablanca in January 1943. Discussions were held between British, American and Canadian representatives from February onwards. The Canadians wanted operational control because most of the forces deployed in the western Atlantic were Canadian. Buckley points out that 'in addition, pressure was growing from the eastern side of the Atlantic for the Americans to sort out the command muddle across the width of the ocean, but more particularly in the west, where nine different commands existed to control the American and Canadian forces.'

One ray of light was the Atlantic Convoy Conference, which met under King as chairman on March 1st 1943. His intention was to ensure that American forces did not fall under British or Canadian command. In fact, as Albert Durston (Slessor's representative at the conference) observed, King was mistaken in believing that Allied forces could not work together: two squadrons of the USAAF had actually been operating under British control for some time. However, several improvements in organization were approved, and a few more Liberators were found to help cover the air gap.

'On the eastern side of the ocean there was effective unified control of air operations in support of convoys by Coastal Command and the

Admiralty; on the other side, there were six different authorities concerned – Canadian Eastern Air Command, which had many pre-occupations other than with the maritime war, and five American commands, three naval and two army air force.' The situation was so obviously inefficient that something was actually done about it. Britain and Canada assumed responsibility, with some American help, for the security of convoys on either side of an agreed 'Chop Line' (Change of Operational Control). Direction and control remained at Northwood and in Whitehall. The Canadians re-organized their Eastern Air Command at Halifax along lines similar to an RAF Group. An Area Combined Headquarters was set up at St. John's, Newfoundland, in which the top airman and seaman were jointly responsible for covering all shipping within their range. They had operational control of all anti-submarine aircraft – British, American or Canadian – based on Canadian soil.

Another important result of this conference was concerned with the notorious Atlantic 'gap': an area several hundred miles wide in the north-east of the ocean in which ships were beyond the range of shore-based air cover either from Canada or Iceland, and therefore particularly vulnerable to U-boat attack. In February 1943, there was not a single Liberator based west of Iceland and too few east of it. The essential aircraft, crews, and equipment had long been available, but not concentrated where they could be most effective because King insisted on US aircraft guarding the eastern coast of North America and the approaches to Gibraltar. The USAAF had 72 Liberators and the US Navy 48: 'a total of nearly three times my strength,' fumed Slessor, 'all in an area where for some months past there had been virtually no threat to the US coastal convoys moving between one US frontier and another.' With great persistence, in the face of King's dogged resistance, Slessor managed to extract some American support, but not enough.

'Eventually I could stand it no longer, and with the approval of the Chiefs of Staff, flew to Washington to see if I could not loosen this log-jam by personal intervention with King.' He called at Halifax and Ottawa en route to discuss the problem with the Canadians and reached Washington on June 24th. Some progress was made. Noticing that the ogre was wearing a new uniform, Slessor congratulated him on choosing air force blue. He was rewarded with a grimace that might have been an attempt at a smile. On leaving King, Slessor had a meeting in the White House with Hopkins and 'over the usual stiff whiskies, held forth at some length.' Hopkins, impressed, led him into Roosevelt's presence. 'A couple of his martinis on top of Harry's whisky wafted me up to heights of unsuspected eloquence on the Battle of the Atlantic and what we could do to the U-boats if only we had enough VLR aircraft.' King's reluctance to help was fuelled, Slessor discovered, by 'misleading information from some relatively junior officers on Stark's staff in London, who knew equally little about the problem and did not take the trouble to visit my headquarters to find out.'

All this war-losing nonsense should be contrasted with the relative harmony achieved in the Mediterranean – later in England and north-west Europe as well – under Eisenhower, ably seconded by Tedder and Spaatz, in spite of the antics of Montgomery, Patton, Brooke and others. What a desperate situation would have arisen in both theatres with an American of King's stamp in Ike's place! 'Coalition operations are difficult enough', wrote Richard Cousens, 'without the corrosive effect of doctrinal sniping.' Eisenhower led one of history's most successful coalitions, but even for him it was difficult to get 'a degree of co-operation that ensures seamless and successful combined operations... Ultimately, the cohesion of any coalition hinges on a single, intangible characteristic – trust. It is trust – not doctrine or technology or equipment – that binds a successful coalition and enables effective multinational operations.'[11]

The Bay of Biscay

The Bay of Biscay, Slessor told the Combined Chiefs of Staff in April 1943, was 'the trunk of the Atlantic U-boat menace, the roots being in the Biscay ports and the branches spreading far and wide, to the North Atlantic convoys, to the Caribbean, to the eastern seaboard of North America.' Five out of every six boats passed through the Bay, within range of aircraft based in England and Gibraltar. Successes were achieved, because Slessor did what he could to strengthen Bromet's Group, and many boats that were not destroyed or damaged were obliged to transit that sea area submerged (travelling at no more than three knots), rather than the 17 they could reach on the surface.

Slessor identified four phases in the Biscay battle. At first, U-boats dived when sighting an enemy aircraft. Then, secondly, they remained on the surface, using heavy guns and cannon to fight back – a tactic which alarmed many in Whitehall, but not Slessor. 'I knew that a U-boat was at best a poor AA firing platform even in a calm sea, and was confident that my crews would not be deterred by casualties.' He did, however, take the precaution of providing additional forward-firing armament in all his anti-submarine aircraft. In the third phase, beginning in June, the Germans sent their boats through in groups of five or more. This helped them to spot attackers sooner, and reduced the number of transits. It was a tactic that worked well in June, when only two were sunk, but in July 11 were destroyed. The fourth phase began in August, when boats remained submerged in daylight and attempted to cross the Bay only in darkness and steering close to the Spanish coast. They were helped by the fact that

---

[11] Cousens, of the Centre for Defence and International Security Studies, Henley-on-Thames, had in mind the move in November 2004 of the Black Watch to closer support of American troops around Baghdad, but his argument applies as well to earlier coalitions.

many radar 'blips' obtained by searching aircraft turned out to be Spanish trawlers. 'The Germans realized our radar would lead us to the trawlers just as much as to their submarines,' explained Wing Commander Arthur Clouston, CO of 224 Squadron, based at St. Eval in Cornwall. 'Formations of eight or ten Junkers Ju 88s would fly out from their bases in occupied France and wait for us high up in the sun, above the trawlers. It happened so often that we could not help thinking there was a liaison between some of those neutral ships and the enemy aircraft.'

Not until mid-June was it found possible to spare a surface hunting group from duty in the North Atlantic to assist in the Biscay battle. Five ships, under Captain Walker, supported 19 Group aircraft in sinking three U-boats in July. But the ships were withdrawn at the end of August, and the Admiralty refused to detach any destroyers from Scapa Flow for service in Biscay. The combined efforts of airmen and seamen could have inflicted far heavier losses on the Germans. Even so, Slessor attributed much of the success that was achieved to errors made by Doenitz: he seemed to lack a cool, determined brain, he was for ever changing tactics, he unwisely boasted – in a memorable but unwise image – that 'the aircraft can no more eliminate the U-boats than a crow can fight a mole', and, like most Nazi leaders, fell back too readily in bad times on frantic exhortation to do or die. U-boats, argued Slessor, should not have been asked to remain on the surface and fight back. They should have been allowed the time needed to run submerged through the Bay. This would have reduced their effective patrol time, but they would at least have had a good chance of reaching their patrol areas safely.

Although Slessor urged a strong Bay offensive, he did not want it to be at the expense of Bomber Command. But suddenly at the end of March and 'out of the blue, without consulting me', the Admiralty demanded the immediate transfer by the Air Ministry of 190 aircraft to support the bay offensive. They cited the 'independent' opinion of Admiral Harold Stark (Chief of Operations, US Navy) and his staff in London. Professor Patrick Blackett also backed the demand, much to Slessor's anger – which time did nothing to heal. Blackett, he recalled, 'was currently making mathematical deductions based on arbitrary estimates, after spending some time in the more practical-minded Operational Research Section at Northwood.' The aircraft demanded could only come from Bomber Command and, as Slessor observed, Blackett was 'intellectually and temperamentally opposed to the bomber offensive.' Slessor at once informed Dudley Pound (First Sea Lord) that he could not accept 'slide-rule strategy of the worst kind.' The transfer of bombers from Harris's command, where they were becoming skilled in attacking land targets, would not help Slessor in warfare over the sea. 'What I wanted was aircraft of the right type, with the right sort of radar equipment, and with crews trained in the right way – and I wanted them quickly.'

He got them, though not quickly. By the time Slessor left Coastal

Command, the Bay offensive was virtually over. But no more than 50 U-boats had been destroyed and another 56 damaged out of a total of 2,425 which had passed in and out of their Bay bases, at a heavy cost of 350 aircraft. Until April 1943, Coastal Command had very little success partly because it lacked – as Slessor said – the right aircraft, equipment and crew training, but mostly because U-boats crossed the Bay on the surface at night at top speed. At the end of that month, fortunately, Doenitz ordered his captains to cross in daylight and fight it out with aircraft: an order Slessor would have loved to give them himself. The odds were in his favour. A Liberator, by far his most expensive weapon, cost no more than £60,000 and carried a crew of ten, whereas a U-boat cost over £200,000 and had a crew of 50. 'The habit of fighting back', Slessor wrote to his crews, 'may cost us a few more aircraft; but if persisted in (which is at least open to doubt), it will undoubtedly mean more U-boats killed. It is up to us to take the fullest advantage of the good opportunities offered, before the buzz goes round in the Bay ports that fighting back is an expensive and unprofitable pastime.'

For three months, despite heavy losses, Doenitz stubbornly insisted on these disastrous tactics. 'Such a rich harvest was then reaped by Coastal Command', recorded Stephen Roskill, 'that the percentage of U-boats sunk on passage increased ten-fold compared with the preceding period, and at a far lower cost in aircraft losses.' As soon as Doenitz saw sense, Slessor's aircraft found victories very hard to come by. Had it not been for that grave error, the results of the Bay offensive would have been poor. On the other hand, that offensive undoubtedly placed a severe strain on the U-boats which evaded aircraft. 'The War Diary of the U-boat Command makes it plain that the delays caused to boats on passage, and the wear and tear on the nerves of their crews, materially reduced the efficiency of boats starting out on long ocean patrols.'

The Strike Wings

By 1943, German merchant shipping was highly organized to import iron ore from Sweden, maintain war supplies to Norway, and conduct 'a traffic with the Far East in articles of very high value to the Axis war effort.' Coastal Command operated over two widely-separated areas in disrupting these routes: the North Sea and the Bay of Biscay. Aubrey Ellwood (18 Group) was responsible for attacking merchantmen and their well-armed escorts moving along the Norwegian coast. That coast was so frequently and irregularly indented that it offered numerous hiding places. Brian Baker (succeeded by Frank Hopps at 16 Group) had the task of disrupting traffic on the Frisian coast, despite the opposition of both flak ships and fighters. Although the Germans seized many merchant ships after their conquest of western Europe in 1940, their total stock was inadequate, and they were also short of locomotives and waggons. Consequently, attacks on shipping were not only serious in themselves, recorded Slessor, 'but combined with action against enemy rail and inland water communications to put a serious strain on their transportation system as a whole.'

In early 1943, the Germans based a flotilla of torpedo-boats (later reinforced with heavier destroyers) in French ports to protect small, fast blockade runners, skilfully handled, but few in number. They were difficult to intercept either on their outward or homeward voyages, especially in the light of the command's concentration on combating U-boats, and the shortage of both aircraft and surface vessels. Few 19 Group aircraft possessed a bomb-sight suitable for attacking them because their main purpose was to hit U-boats with depth charges from very low levels, using sights designed for this purpose. Nevertheless, a blockade runner was sunk on her run home in January, with a cargo of rubber, vegetable oil, fats, quinine bark, tin, tea, rice and wolfram: 'the rubber alone', Slessor claimed, 'would have been enough to supply four armoured divisions for a year.' By the end of April, five more had been sunk. From this time on, very few blockade runners avoided destruction, thanks to closer co-operation between Allied surface vessels and aircraft.

Slessor was eager to emphasize his new command's share 'in our offensive strategy at sea, the maritime blockade of Germany.' The Third Reich's resources in iron ore, nickel and molybdenum were negligible and consequently her capacity to manufacture modern weapons for her armed services depended upon imports. The conquest of France and good relations with Spain enabled her to acquire, via land routes, substantial amounts of low-grade iron, but high-grade Swedish ores remained essential to German factories and most of these ores came by sea from Norwegian ports. Fish and timber were other precious imports. Clearly, Allied hopes of winning the European war would be improved by interrupting and ultimately ending this traffic.

Official historians, whether of Britain's economic, operational or intelligence efforts in the Second World War, have failed to give proper weight to Coastal Command's anti-shipping campaign. Slessor was better placed than most to remedy this failing, and his personal contribution to the success of the Strike Wings – though only for a brief period – was significant. Nevertheless, he chose to devote most of his numerous writings to four subjects that were worked over, time and time again. One was reflections on his planning days before or during the war. A second was explaining the value of strategic bombing. Thirdly came expression of fears that Soviet aggression might overwhelm the West, with or without nuclear weapons. And finally he was deeply concerned to enhance the RAF's role as Britain's major weapon against opposition from other services, especially the Royal Navy.

Slessor found space to discuss the U-boat war in his very long memoirs, but wrote less than was needed about the anti-shipping campaign. In fact, that campaign gradually became a highlight of Coastal

Command's 'Constant Endeavour' (its grim motto) during Slessor's year as head. The Strike Wings earned a very important victory during and after 1943, when the bravery and skills of crews were at last given a fair chance in more and better aircraft, equipped with more and better weapons, radio and radar aids, precise intelligence information, reliable weather forecasts, and a means of estimating accurately the speed of enemy vessels. There was also valuable help from experience gained in Mediterranean waters under the direction of Tedder and his senior colleagues – both in reports detailing effective methods and, in some cases, by the transfer of seasoned crews to England.

The Strike Wings are of 'historical importance' because they represented from April 1943 onwards a joint enterprise by Bomber, Fighter and Coastal Commands. Slessor's words at that time 'merit preservation for posterity', thought Stephen Roskill, because he stated unequivocally that 'The Royal Air Force shares with the Royal Navy the responsibility for sea communications within range of shore-based aircraft.' Roskill was then moved to wonder how many of the disasters suffered during 42 months of war 'could have been avoided had such a simple truth been accepted by both services in 1939.'

In early August 1943, however, Slessor doubted the value of attacks along the Dutch coast. Perhaps the powerful – but scarce – Beaufighters could be more usefully employed elsewhere? The suggestion produced 'a flurry of activity', resolved at a meeting of interested parties convened in the Air Ministry later that month. These parties included representatives from three RAF commands (Bomber, Fighter, Coastal), the Ministry of Economic Warfare, the Admiralty and the Nore Command, responsible for naval operations in Dutch waters. Compelling arguments in favour of continuance were made and Slessor was persuaded. He now agitated, with no immediate success, for twin-engined de Havilland Mosquitos – another powerful but scarce aircraft – to be employed on anti-shipping strikes. They could carry 86 pound rockets, which had the impact – if all were fired together – of a broadside from a large cruiser.

At the same time, Slessor was vigorously encouraging both Operational Research and the Development Unit. 'We used to exchange ideas', he later recalled, 'think aloud, clear our minds on the operational requirements and the practical scientific possibilities of meeting them, and were sometimes able to decide there and then [during meetings in his headquarters] on some tactical method to be tried out or some technical strategem to be examined... I was frequently surprised at the ability of ORS to tell me, not only what I did not know, but what would never otherwise have occurred to me that I ought to know about an operational or administrative problem, and the constant scientific analysis of past results was of utmost help in planning future operations.'

Slessor had several squadrons equipped with the Mark XIV bomb-sight by the end of 1943. Some of them were able to carry rockets and all were assisted by the formidable Beaufighter, armed with torpedoes, rockets and heavy cannon. Hawker Typhoons of Fighter Command joined in at times to provide escort and photo-reconnaissance. These aircraft – formed into what became famous in their day as the Strike Wings – were sometimes assisted by surface vessels and sank many blockade runners. Each strike, wrote Slessor, 'was a carefully-planned, highly-organized and hard-fought action involving up to 30 or more aircraft, each of which had its own particular role in the attack.' The torpedo aircraft went straight for the merchant ships, while their escorts hit the warships protecting them with bombs, cannon-fire, and rockets. At Slessor's insistence and despite strong competition for their services, 'three Beaufighter strike wings were built up – a formidable offensive force.'

Were these wings, in blunt economic terms, 'cost effective'? Between April 1940 and May 1945, mines dropped by Bomber and Coastal Command during nearly 20,000 sorties, at a cost of 450 aircraft, sank 638 vessels in the Channel and North Sea. Direct attacks during nearly 38,000 sorties, at a cost of 857 aircraft, sank 366 vessels. These are appallingly heavy casualties on both sides: an average of 22 aircraft and 17 ships down in every month for five years. They reveal that this aspect of the war at sea was no mere sideshow in comparison with the better known campaign against U-boats. It would seem, however, that mining was far more 'cost effective' than direct attack because it took only 31 sorties by minelayers to sink a vessel whereas strike aircraft flew nearly 104 sorties to sink one. On the other hand, Slessor was familiar with arguments used to justify strategic bombing – that it obliged the enemy to divert men and materials from operational areas to protect vital targets – and the same arguments more than justified the efforts of his Strike Wings.

Roy Conyers Nesbit, who served in such wings, argued that 'it would have been far more advantageous for the Allied war effort if resources had been diverted from Bomber Command to Coastal Command.' He agreed with Blackett (Director of Operational Research at the Admiralty) that 'if the Allied air effort had been used more intelligently, the war could have been over half a year or even a year earlier.' Nesbit thought Coastal's commanders, including Slessor, were 'lamentably slow in recognizing the correct anti-shipping tactics for their strike aircraft. Indeed, it is doubtful if these tactics would have been developed at all without the impetus from pilots at squadron and flight commander level, who had to devise the methods by bitter experience in a hail of enemy fire.' But, in Goulter's words, 'the vast majority of the Air Staff' – under Tedder no less than under Slessor – 'still equated air power with strategic bombing.' The anti-shipping campaign 'was treated largely as a wartime expedient, and it was not long before strategic bombing doctrine re-asserted its total command over Air Ministry thinking. The rhetoric by the end of the 1940s was again Trenchardian: any deviation from the "primary role" of bombing land objectives could not be justified.'

North Atlantic victory

For all that Churchill proclaimed a 'Battle of the Atlantic', long after it was actually in full swing, he remained far more concerned to increase the strength of Bomber Command, and regarded Coastal Command as merely a defensive necessity. That battle, he later wrote, 'was the dominating factor all through the war. Never for one moment could we forget that everything happening elsewhere, on land, at sea, or in the air, depended ultimately on its outcome.' Yet at the time he vehemently resisted the use of Liberators in that command and even objected to its possession of Wellingtons and Whitleys. Harris, of course, also objected. Among his more infamous mouthings was the opinion, expressed to Churchill on June 17th 1942, that the proper use of air power would ensure a 'speedy and complete' victory over Germany 'in a matter of months'; as for Coastal Command, it was 'merely an obstacle to victory'. Fortunately, wiser heads prevailed and Slessor did get just enough VLR aircraft to close the deadly gap in air cover over the North Atlantic.

Reality had broken in by the end of 1942, when shipping losses reached catastrophic proportions. Unless Doenitz was defeated, the Allies would find it impossible to build up sufficient strength in men and weapons to mount a successful liberation of Occupied Europe, and, as Terraine put it, 'there would be no massive demonstration of strategic air power, because there would be no oil.' U-boats had sunk no fewer than 141 British and American tankers during the first six months of 1942. Clearly, it was here that the war – so far as the western Allies were concerned – was being won and lost.

The U-boats, wrote Jean Kessler, 'were never so close to breaking the line of communications between the old and the new worlds as they were in the first few days of March 1943.' Roskill had already written that even a dozen years later 'one can sense the relief which the dawning realization that the crisis of crises had come, and had been successfully surmounted, brought in London.' It was a month of terrible storms and terrible shipping losses, despite all that brave, skilful and determined airmen and seamen could do. Doenitz's men – no less brave, skilful and determined – sank 120 ships during March, many of them while sailing in convoys.

If the U-boat overcame the convoy system, there would be no Overlord and no bomber victory either. The Third Reich would be destroyed – but mainly by the Red Army which would then, presumably, pursue the Germans as far as the Atlantic coast, imposing its own version of 'liberation' on non-Germans. From April, however, the tide turned against the Germans, for many reasons: 'decryption of German signals, centimetric radar, escort carrier support groups, but most of all the closure of the North Atlantic "black hole" by the use of long-range four-engined aircraft, at last available in sufficient numbers. Doenitz was obliged to admit in May that: 'We are facing the greatest crisis of the U-boat war because the enemy, with new detection systems, is making combat impossible and is inflicting heavy losses on us.'

Doenitz's defeat was a turning-point in the war, 'far more significant than the battles of El Alamein', John Terraine argued. 'Britain would not starve; British industry would not wither for lack of raw materials; Bomber Command's offensive would not halt for want of oil; armoured forces could be built up with the certainty of useful action.' In other words, 'Overlord would happen.' Between January and March 1944, 105 convoys of 3,360 merchant vessels crossed the northern ocean, and only three ships were lost. By then, and for the rest of the war, U-boats were no longer a serious threat to Allied control of the seas.

The battle had been won by June 1943, many months later than it should have been. On behalf of the War Cabinet, Sinclair congratulated Slessor in August. 'This battle has not paused since the war began', he wrote, 'and your aircrews have flown in all weathers interminable miles over the seas to search out and destroy the enemy, often driving home their attacks with unsurpassed gallantry at low level in the face of heavy opposition.' He went on to emphasize the command's multinational nature: British, Czech and Norwegian squadrons as well as American, Canadian, Australian and New Zealand airmen. It was this bringing together of free peoples, especially those from what he was never ashamed to call 'the Empire', which enthused Slessor at the time and remained for the rest of his life a shining example of what might be.

It is always easier to understand the past than to cope with the present or predict the future, but it does seem – in the light of postwar research, that the battle was 'essentially unwinable' from a German viewpoint. 'Between 1940-45', wrote Geoffrey Till, 'the US alone constructed nearly double the shipping tonnage that the Germans managed to sink. As early as June and July 1943 the Allies found they had a generous surplus of shipping, and as Churchill said later, "All the rest was merely the proper application of overwhelming force."' The air gap had always been the most serious problem, 'and its elimination would have put an end to the wolf-pack attacks with or without Ultra', in the opinion of Marc Milner. 'The failure of the Allies to close the air gap before 1943 remains one of the great unsolved historical problems of the war... For many historians of the Atlantic war the myopia of the airmen who drove the strategic bomber offensive seems incredible.' The 'slavish adherence' (in Buckley's words) of Churchill and the Air Staff 'to the principles of the strategic bombing offensive seemingly blinded them to the harsh realities of the Battle of the Atlantic.'

Slessor's blindness

Eisenhower, Tedder, and their senior colleagues had gone from the Mediterranean Theatre by January 1944 in order to prepare for Operation Overlord, the Allied plan to liberate Occupied Europe. In their place went an American officer, Lieutenant General Ira C. Eaker, as Allied Air Commander-in-Chief, with Slessor as his deputy. 'I was reluctant to leave Coastal Command', he wrote, 'and had been looking forward to taking a hand in Overlord', but he had to go. On January 14th, 'I climbed rather sadly into an old Hudson and took off for Gibraltar and Algiers to start in on a new and very different sort of job. I could at least not complain of lack of variety in my war experience.'

Yet again we see the RAF's random posting policy at work. By January 1944, Slessor had the experience, of men and equipment, to do even better work during the coming critical year. He was replaced by Air Marshal Sir Sholto Douglas, who was brought home from the Mediterranean because he did not fancy the idea of being a mere deputy and to an American at that. Slessor did not then know that he was second choice to Douglas, whose appointment was vetoed by the Americans. They did not relent even when Churchill assured Roosevelt that Douglas was not, as alleged, anti-American. Douglas was therefore given Coastal Command, about which he knew nothing, and like Slessor a year earlier, would spend vital months attempting to master the structure of an enormous new command, and grasping its complicated and often tense relations with British, Canadian and American seamen and airmen. Worse even than that was Douglas's decision to exclude members of his ORS from policy discussions: a foolish decision, given his ignorance of air-sea matters, and one that, as Goulter has said, had 'serious consequence for the early planning of the Overlord operations.'

Just as there can be no doubt that Slessor would have gone on to become a far more effective commander of a bomber group in 1942-3, had he been left at Grantham, so also there can be no doubt that his experience of war at sea in 1943 would have equipped him to give better service at Northwood in 1944-5. Instead – thanks to Douglas's vanity and the willingness of Portal to pander to it – Slessor was told to break into a third unfamiliar field.

Slessor had made a mark in Coastal Command as 'a hard-hitting professional with a clear mind (except when clouded by dogma); above all, he was a leader. He was fortunate in arriving when the command was on the brink of its long-awaited triumph.' Sir Maurice Dean, who knew all the Whitehall Warriors, thought highly of him. 'He was intelligent, experienced, friendly, receptive of ideas, hard working. Coastal Command and the Royal Air Force owe him much.' Yet he failed to understand the significance of the great naval/air victory in which he played a part. This is not surprising, because he had only been involved in the campaign for a few weeks and he remained, throughout his life – as well as his active career – an unflinching bomber champion.

The Atlantic victory, he wrote in May 1943, would mean that 'many of us could be spared to take part in the more direct offensive against objectives on German and Italian soil.' This was indeed 'fairly poor praise'. To tell men who had just achieved a decisive victory that they might now 'be lucky enough to take part in the real work of the war!' confirms Terraine's opinion that Slessor simply did not understand what was at stake in the Atlantic. A thoroughly committed believer in bombing, he was also 'thoroughly imbued with dread of great land battles.' Overlord was a concept he regarded with deep suspicion, whereas he welcomed the growing impact of Harris's offensive even though Bomber Command suffered heavy losses. This, he believed, was 'true air warfare.'

For these reasons, Slessor was blind to the scale of victory that he and his predecessors at Coastal Command had achieved. His 'blinkered view' (in Terraine's words) never broadened. He never grasped the fact that Overlord – not the bomber offensive – was the supreme offensive action of the Western Allies in the war, and it could not have been launched without the Atlantic victory to which Coastal Command made such a vital contribution. Overlord was a campaign lasting 11 months and during that time the Allied forces under Eisenhower totalled nearly five and a half million men, nearly a million vehicles and more than 18 million tons of supplies. 'There can be no conceivable notion', as Terraine wrote, 'of building up and maintaining such a force as this with undefeated U-boats at its back... even so, it did not engage the main body of the enemy' which was engaged by the forces of the Soviet Union. The official naval historian, Captain Stephen Roskill, was more broad-minded than Slessor. The 'prosecution of the entire Allied offensive strategy', he wrote, 'depended on control of sea communications.' Churchill had made the same point, speaking in the House of Commons, in February 1943: 'the defeat of the U-boat and the improvement of the margin of shipbuilding resources are the prelude to all effective aggressive operations.'

Slessor summed up in a very long letter to Trenchard of December 19th 1943 the command's achievements in that year. The U-boat, he told his old master, 'operates not as a true submarine, but as a "submersible": i.e., for his mobility and lethal effect he has to be on the surface, and he uses his submersible quality for evasion. When he is on the surface he is extremely vulnerable, and if the air can find him it stands a very good chance of killing him.' And did so, in 1943, because 'for the first time we have had the tools without which no-one can do the job – especially the very long range Liberators which closed the Atlantic gap.' Coastal Command's success, he emphasized, 'has been due largely to the fact that it is a unified Air Command... We should have been fatally handicapped if the Air had been split up into penny packets under the various naval commands – as it is in the US. In fact, we have been able to handle the U-boat war as an air problem and not as a naval problem.'

'Unlike the navies, British or American,' Slessor continued, 'we do not cover every convoy, only those at risk: they do not understand that a convoy not covered today can easily be covered tomorrow, thus saving time and effort. The aircraft carrier has had an important success since its introduction in June this year as an anti-submarine force – especially the American carriers.' Even so, he thought the carrier 'obsolescent – it is a rather expensive method of getting an aircraft onto the right spot, and where we have the really long range bomber I don't believe any carrier will live long.' Slessor was wrong on this point, both during and after the war, but he knew that Boom thought carriers were useless and that therefore became his opinion.

Writing in the 1950s, Slessor noted that the crews of his old command 'certainly did not get their mead of public recognition at the time; nor have they since', and for this neglect he ventured to criticize Churchill, whose hired writers recorded little about the Atlantic battle in their enormously long memoirs, but Slessor himself – thanks to his blindness – was not entirely guiltless in this connection.

Coastal Command was eclipsed by the glamour and sacrifice of those who served in Fighter and Bomber Commands, so it was not until March 16th 2004, nearly 60 years after the end of the war in Europe, that it received its first national monument, unveiled by the Queen, in Westminster Abbey. A relief carving, depicting an eagle surveying the waves, commemorates in particular the 10,875 men who lost their lives. Some 2,000 aircraft were also lost. By the end of the war, Coastal Command had accounted for 189 U-boats, and another 24 were sunk in joint action with surface vessels. As for the strike squadrons, they destroyed no fewer than 366 vessels in return for suffering the command's heaviest casualties. Following the service, there was a flypast over the Abbey by a Hawker Siddeley Nimrod maritime reconnaissance and anti-submarine aircraft (first flown in 1967), flanked by two Panavia Tornados, a multi-role combat aircraft (1974). The Liberators, Catalinas, Hudsons and the rest had long gone, but veterans in the Abbey welcomed this tribute – though long delayed – from machines far superior in every respect (not least in crew comfort) to anything they even dreamt of during their years of 'Constant Endeavour'.

After the ball was over: in defence of Coastal Command
On October 12th 1946, Slessor wrote to 'My dear PW', Captain D. V. Peyton-Ward, RN (then working at the Air Ministry as an official historian). General Eisenhower had had a long talk on the 11th with Lord Tedder, CAS, about the 'very unsatisfactory relations' between the US Army (and its air forces) and the US Navy, which was 'exceedingly powerful politically', and intending to use that power during the coming session of Congress to prevent American airmen from achieving independence. The admirals and their allies were 'basing themselves on the outworn theory that all operations over the sea or on the sea should be a matter for the navy, completely ignoring the fact that the air is one and that you cannot arbitrarily divide air operations by high water mark.' They were alleging that Coastal Command was a failure during the war, and

therefore the US must not create an equivalent under air control. Some Royal Navy officers were secretly supporting them. Tedder wanted to give Eisenhower 'a really reasoned paper backed up by historical truths of what Coastal Command actually achieved and how the system worked.' Slessor told Tedder that he was sure there was no-one who could do this better than PW, one of the command's best men.

Peyton-Ward offered that 'really reasoned paper' to Tedder, through Slessor, in November 1946. Entitled *The Unified Air Force*, its 'vital principle', Peyton-Ward argued, was the 'flexibility which enables air power to be directed when and where it is most needed', avoiding the 'fatal locking-up of portions of the total on specialized roles.' That flexibility was seen in the successful co-operation between the RAF and the RN during the years 1943-5. The Admiralty had operational control of Coastal Command, delegated to its head, and obtained assistance from Bomber and Fighter Commands by direct negotiation with the Air Ministry. The actual day-to-day operations were handled in the Area Combined Headquarters (ACHQ), where the Admiral and the Air Marshal worked together. The seaman could not himself order air operations, but he did tell the airman what he wanted done.

In March 1947, A. V. Alexander (Minister of Defence) assured Lord Shackleton that 'whatever good work Coastal Command did, the credit was primarily due to Sir Dudley Pound and the other Admirals who fought the Air Ministry and the Air Marshals tooth and nail to get any aircraft at all for Coastal Command.' Slessor responded in a note to Philip Noel-Baker, Secretary of State for Air. He recalled the 'curious alliance' Alexander – then First Lord of the Admiralty – made in the winter of 1940-1 with Lord Beaverbrook and Admiral Sir Roger Keyes to dismember the RAF by handing over Coastal Command to the navy. The upshot was a 'polite fiction about the operational control of Coastal by the Admiralty, which is now decently dead and buried.' As head of Coastal in 1943, Slessor had fought Pound and others over 'a particularly ill-advised attempt on their part to take 190 heavy bombers – with untrained crews and the wrong sort of equipment – away from Bert Harris and give them to me, instead of doing the obvious and sensible thing (which we subsequently did) of getting the Americans to redispose some of their large surplus of properly-trained and equipped anti-submarine aircraft and put them in the vital area of the Atlantic battlefield, the Bay, instead of kicking their heels in the Caribbean and the US Eastern Shore Frontier, where there were virtually no U-boats. On that occasion, I won hands down and the Admirals received a very sharp rocket from Mr Churchill in the U-boat Committee.'

The suggestion that airmen were 'wicked and subversive in not yielding always to each and every demand made upon them by the Admirals really is nonsense', Slessor continued. 'War is a matter of priorities and it is the duty of the Chiefs of Staff to assign resources.'

During the early years of the war, the Naval Staff found it 'extremely difficult to grasp the fact that in war one just cannot afford to concentrate exclusively on one strategic factor until it is insured 100 percent at the expense of every other factor, including our ultimate capacity to win the war by offensive action instead of merely avoiding defeat by blockade.'

Until September 1939, he recalled, we had 'no coherent strategic policy', not even a policy of intervention with the army in support of France. 'As Director of Plans, I was in on every major strategic appreciation from the spring of 1937 till the outbreak of war, and incidentally on the Inskip discussions where Ellington gave away the Fleet Air Arm.' Slessor made three points about the Naval Staff of those days. Firstly, it placed undue reliance on Asdic as the answer to the U-boat. Secondly, 'the almost passionate rejection by the navy's Director of Plans of the idea that the Air could really be a serious menace even to merchant ships, let alone warships.' This was the opinion of Admiral Sir Tom Phillips, who learned better in the last minutes of his life as Japanese torpedo-bombers sank his battleship, the *Prince of Wales* (and the battle cruiser *Repulse*) off the east coast of the Malay Peninsula on December 10th 1941. And thirdly, the emphasis on fleet action: 'which, of course, was as dead as the Dodo and had been since Jutland.'

During 1942, when the Naval Staff at last realized that the U-boat posed a far greater menace than German or Italian surface vessels, essential diversions to Coastal Command delayed the expansion of Bomber Command. 'If the Air Staff had not kept their eye on the ball and resisted the many demands of Ministers, Admirals and Generals to use bombers for any purpose but that for which they were designed, we should never have built up Bomber Command to the strength and efficiency which had such decisive results in the last two years of the war.' By 1943, Slessor concluded, the Allies had in the Atlantic more anti-submarine aircraft than were needed, if they had been in the right places: 'it never occurred to the Naval Staff that the right answer was to do something to redeploy the Allied anti-submarine forces as the strategic situation required – that was left to an Air Marshal to do.' As we shall see below, Slessor devoted many of the best hours of his life, after the war, to rehearsing again and again wartime arguments with the Admiralty. These arguments were a necessary part, he was convinced, of the RAF's defence against current Admiralty claims – which were no less improper than those made in wartime.

In May 1948, he received a friendly letter from Admiral Samuel Morison, USN, who was sending him a signed copy of his book on the Atlantic battle. In return, Slessor sent Morison a copy of his despatch on Coastal Command operations in 1943. 'I am afraid you will find it is somewhat severely critical of the US Navy Department at the time', he wrote. 'I had a great personal respect and some affection for Admiral King, but I do not think he and his staff knew how to fight submarines. I am sure this must be a terrible thing for an RAF officer to say to the Official Historian of the US Navy! But perhaps if you read my draft despatch you will feel that I have some justification for what I say.' On a lighter note, he was able to confirm that he was indeed the son of the Steward of Christ Church whom Morison knew. 'I did not often come to Oxford during the years 1922-5, but used to dine with him in the hall two or three times a year, and always enjoyed drinking champagne out of pewter.'

Slessor wrote a thorough despatch on his year in Coastal Command – 56 closely-printed pages – which was published against Admiralty advice in 1949. 'My Lords Commissioners' objected to the detail, which might be of assistance to an enemy in another war, and to the 'strong criticisms of American ideas and methods... Co-operation with the United States in anti-submarine warfare matters is now particularly close, and My Lords feel that if publicized the criticisms would serve only to harm the cordial relations now existing.' Slessor, quite rightly, wrote 'nonsense' beside this paragraph in his copy of the letter. He reproduced his summary of operations which appeared in the *Coastal Command Review* for 1943 and then turned to 'Some Salient Features of the Operations, and Certain Questions of Policy'. The criticisms he made, temperately, were intended to avoid at least some of the disastrous mistakes which came close to losing the Atlantic battle should there be another war.

CHAPTER 12

RELUCTANT COMMANDERS:
EAKER AND SLESSOR
IN THE MEDITERRANEAN

Bombing Germany and invading France

When writing to Trenchard in December 1943, Slessor already knew that he was to leave Coastal Command for the Mediterranean. He would have preferred to remain at Northwood, once he realized that no place could be found for him to take part in what he really wanted: bombing Germany and preparing for D-Day. 'There has not been a day-raid beyond the range of fighter escort since Schweinfurt [in October]', he reminded Trenchard, when the Americans suffered heavy losses. 'You may have discussed this with Eaker. But my own impression is that he gets a pretty strong lead from Arnold; and the American authorities, themselves inclined to be unduly casualty-conscious, are also particularly susceptible to public and press opinion which, I'm told, was very shocked by the Schweinfurt losses.' But Slessor was convinced that it was vital to knock out the German fighter factories, whatever the cost, and he hoped Trenchard – who was soon to visit Washington – would urge Arnold to do this. Arnold, in fact, needed no urging: he was about to remove Eaker from command of the Eighth Air Force, send him to the Mediterranean, and replace him with Spaatz. A superb long-range fighter – the P-51 Mustang – was then becoming available in ever-increasing numbers and under its protection American bombers gave their whole attention to destroying German air power, as Slessor advocated.

As for the invasion, 'I think it is beyond doubt that if we and the US air force had concentrated our resources on building up the bomber force in the UK (instead of dispersing them on all sorts of things like airborne forces and bombing islands in the Pacific), the war would be over already and we should never have to invade – and it may be that we shan't have to invade – depending on the weather in the next three months... I've always said that when we go into Europe again it will be on a march-table and not an operation order, and I think I may yet turn out to be right.' He turned out to be quite wrong. Meanwhile, he and Eaker found themselves, very reluctantly, leaving England.

The largest single air command in the world

Ira Eaker, formerly head of the Eighth Air Force in England, was sent to the Mediterranean in January 1944 as head of Mediterranean Allied Air Forces (MAAF) with Slessor as his deputy. Eaker thanked Portal for choosing Slessor. 'Nothing could have pleased me more. I also wish to assure you that without question he and I will work together in perfect harmony.' They did so, helped perhaps by the fact that both men were keenly aware that they had been relegated to a secondary theatre, even though they commanded huge numbers of men and aircraft and were responsible for important operations in an enormous area. The days of 'champagne and oysters' gave way to those of 'beer and cheese', as Major-General Kenneth Strong (the departing head of intelligence) rather unkindly put it.

The friendship between Eaker and Slessor outlasted the war. According to James Parton (his aide and biographer), Eaker was 'low-key and unpretentious, speaking in a soft Texas accent, never pompous with rank, and totally without vanity.' He is widely recognized as one of the greatest – and best-liked – American pilots and commanders, and the fact that he chose to keep in touch with Slessor for the rest of their lives supports the high opinion that many contemporaries had of our bomber champion. Slessor greatly admired – and often quoted – Eaker's splendid speech made soon after his arrival in England in February 1942: 'We won't do much talking until we've done more fighting. But this I will say now: after we've gone, we hope you'll be glad we came.'

According to Air Vice-Marshal Stanley Lee, who saw him frequently in 1944-5, Slessor 'was a man who inspired respect and liking from all who served anywhere near him. Unconcernedly sure of himself, and completely without flourish, he had a direct and rational manner that helped greatly with the American officers with whom his own staff was integrated in the Combined Headquarters.'

There is a marvellous map in the British official history showing the enormous extent of MAAF's activities by the middle of 1944. From Algiers in the west to Alexandria in the east, the 12,000 aircraft under the command of Eaker and Slessor were able to reach all the way from eastern France to the western coast of the Black Sea, including most of Germany and southern Poland. Eaker could make the fullest use of the inherent flexibility of air power, concentrating his effort sometimes at short range, sometimes at medium and at other times at long range, always with devastating results.

In 1972, Group Captain Tom Gleave, an official British historian, invited Slessor's comments on a draft of the volume covering Mediterranean events in 1943-4. Gleave and his colleagues, having studied the records, annoyed Slessor – who had not – by praising Tedder: 'I fear I do not share your admiration', a remark confirming the good judgement of those who did not ask Slessor to be an official historian. He would have found it too difficult to separate his personal opinions (not only of Tedder) from either the written record or the oral testimony of others. He then told Gleave that Eaker was keen on strategic bombing, not air support for armies, and 'was bitterly disappointed and hurt at being winkled out of High Wycombe', where he had commanded the Eighth Air Force. Slessor spent much of his time until mid-1944 in Algiers. He was also often in Cairo (where his relations with that great commander, Keith Park, were frosty) until he moved to join Eaker in Caserta Palace, near Naples.

King Charles of Naples began to build that palace in 1738 (revealing, incidentally, the buried city of Pompeii) with the intention of rivalling Versailles. When Eaker set up his headquarters there, 'it impressed his staff as less a rival of Versailles than a parody of the Pentagon Building in Washington', recalled Lieutenant-Colonel James Parton, Eaker's historian. 'Squatting in squalid disorder at the base of the sharp hills separating the Neapolitan Plain from the Volturno Valley, it was an enormous, neo-classic pile of brick and marble laid out in the form of a rectangle... its once exquisite gardens were littered with military camps and motor parks; its once handsome chambers overflowed not only with the harassed headquarters of the Fifteenth Army Group and the Tactical Air Force but also with two centuries' accumulation of fleas and filth. There was no heat, almost no sanitation, and the weak electricity had a habit of fading out altogether at unpredictable moments each evening.' Alexander and Cannon had moved into this 'untidy rabbit warren helter-skelter during the stress of battle', expecting to move on in a couple of weeks. But they remained for six months before pulling out in May, to be replaced by Allied Force Headquarters (AFHQ) from Algiers. An irony lost on Slessor is the fact that Giulio Douhet, the air power theorist whom he so disdained, was born in Caserta.

Slessor soon found that he had acquired massive responsibilities. In addition to his demanding – and sensitive – duties as Eaker's deputy, he was also head of RAF Mediterranean and Middle East. There were subordinate formations in East Africa, Iraq, Persia, the Levant, Aden, and a training group in Palestine. West of about longitude 20 degrees east, Slessor was responsible through Eaker to General Sir Henry Maitland Wilson, Supreme Allied Commander; east of that line, he was responsible to the British Chiefs of Staff through Portal. Although Americans were forbidden by Washington to take any part in Balkan affairs, Eaker 'was allowed, and indeed encouraged, to collaborate in the support of the Yugoslav partisans, and he always went to the very limits of his authority to help us in the Balkans.'

Slessor thrived on responsibility, but he also needed information and support. As early as January 20th he was complaining to Portal: 'I am very much less in the news as to what the Balkan countries are doing than I was back in Coastal Command, where at least I could read *The Times* and the *Daily Telegraph*.' The cause was one which agitated him throughout his time in the Mediterranean: rivalry between AFHQ in Algiers, 'which was started by Americans and has a genuine Allied tradition', as Harold Macmillan (Churchill's Minister Resident in the Mediterranean) observed and Cairo, which is 'somehow connected in their minds with imperialism, Kipling and all that.' Sir Robert Bruce Lockhart (Director of Political Warfare Executive) agreed: Americans regarded Cairo 'as having the atmosphere of George III and 1812', whereas Algiers, in British opinion, was 'a second capital of the Daughters of the Revolution'.

MAAF, wrote Parton, was 'the largest single air command in the world' and, he thought, 'had a decisive influence upon some of the crucial battles in World War II.' There were more Americans (217,000 officers and men) than Britons (104,000), but the RAF operated more than twice as many aircraft (8,850 to 3,750). In the forthcoming Battle for Rome, MAAF produced what Parton claimed to be 'the classic example to date of tactical employment of air power, thereby making a permanent contribution to the basic doctrines of air war.'

MAAF's organization

'It is not altogether easy running a mixed US-British Staff', Slessor confided to his wife Hermione in February 1944, 'but I can say that I like all the Americans in HQ MAAF very much and some of them are extremely able – one in particular, a young second generation Norwegian-American called Norstad, who is the sort of SASO [Senior Air Staff Officer, but actually he was Director of Operations], who is outstandingly efficient and intelligent as well as being extremely nice.' Lauris Norstad, like Slessor, would rise high in his nation's service after the war and the two men would often be in close touch during the years 1950-2. 'In some ways', Slessor continued, 'one is apt to get a little irritated with their apparently amateur methods – I have sometimes to pull myself up and remember that I am in some danger of becoming a pedant as far as staff work is concerned. But the fact remains that whatever their methods, they get the job done and usually done damn well – often rather extravagantly and with a very lavish use of resources, but it is done.'

The guiding principle for MAAF's organization was 'joint operational staffs, but separate administrative staffs'. Hitherto, the policy had been to alternate British and American commanders and staff officers in a vertical organization which merged both operations and administration. The new system proved more efficient and both sides were happier with it. The hub of the headquarters and the only parts which had mixed personnel were the signals, operations, and intelligence sections. These three key sections took orders directly from Eaker and Slessor through their respective chiefs of staff and were the links with the Strategic, Tactical and Coastal Air Forces and MAAF's other operational components.

The administrative organization of MAAF differed sharply from its operational chain of command. 'The hodge-podge was obviously too complex to be readily understood', wrote Parton, 'much less readily re-organized in the heat of a major battle.' So Eaker wisely left it alone for the time being. Slessor reported to Portal on January 20th from Algiers. 'Eaker is up at Caserta with the 15th Army Group, where Wilson is also moving for the Shingle operation.' The services were widely separated for the moment, and Slessor thought it 'quite impossible to exercise effective control over air operations from Algiers – one might just as well do it from London.' AFHQ was to have moved to Caserta, but the soldiers had filled the available accommodation. He ended by assuring Portal that it was 'essential' for him to have John Linnell as his deputy in Caserta, to look after the RAF's interests there.

MAAF Rear, the Plans Section, remained in Algiers, but everyone else found his or her way to 'the pretty little Arab resort of La Marsa, some ten miles outside Tunis on the Mediterranean shore.' La Marsa had originally been only an advanced command post for Tedder and Spaatz, 'who had requisitioned the extraordinary Villa d'Erlanger in the adjacent hamlet of Sidi bou Said after Tunis fell [in May 1943].' Gradually, the command post attracted personnel from Algiers and Constantine (the previous HQ of North-West African Air Forces) until everyone was there except MAAF Rear. 'The result', Parton recalled, 'was a weird patchwork quilt of an establishment with accommodation ranging from the palatial Villa d'Erlanger to squalid hovels and including, among other odds and ends, a former monastery and a former harem.'

In effect, Eaker and Slessor ran a command post, separate from either American or British 'administrative headaches and chores'. They dealt with their 'constant joint operational problems without worrying about any conflict in administrative procedure. The minimum amount of staff overlap between the two nationalities provided the maximum in flexibility of command.' As Parton described it, MAAF was like a motor car with synchromesh transmission: 'either commander could shift from operational to administrative or from joint to separate problems' in a moment and each had a Chief of Staff – Major-General Chauncey for Eaker and Air Marshal Linnell for Slessor – who served as the 'clutch' to ease the change from one task to another.

Oil was provided for the engine by Major (later Lieutenant-Colonel) McCrary, an editor with the New York *Daily Mirror* in civilian life and Eaker's newly-appointed Public Relations Officer. We must 'tell the story of an Air Command that stretches from Dakar to Turkey', he suggested to Eaker on January 25th. 'That story must be told every day. It must compete with the "big show" out of UK if the kids fighting in the air down here are to feel that they are doing an important job in the war.' In working with the RAF, McCrary agreed with Eaker – himself a skilled journalist – that our rule should be 'joint, not mixed'. Slessor also agreed with this principle. Although he found McCrary too American-minded and brash for his taste, he came to realize the value of publicity for the efforts of his multi-national forces in all the capitals of the Allied states.

Slessor wrote to 'My dear Ira' in Caserta from their Rear Headquarters in Algiers on March 8th. It was a typical letter: very long, rambling widely and full of unsolicited advice, but spiced with shrewd observations – especially on matters of organization and office politics. 'I think you would be surprised at how haywire things here are liable to go as far as the air is concerned', he wrote. 'Of course, one must realize that the scope of AFHQ has enlarged enormously since Tedder and Ike's day – then they were only concerned with the battle in North Africa, then Sicily and Italy. Now, in addition to the planning of yet another campaign (Anvil), AFHQ and MAAF are concerned in the whole Mediterranean and all the Balkans as well, and have to do a whole lot of work which was formerly done by HQ Middle East... And, unless you have a really senior representative here who can deal on level terms with Jumbo and Gammell, the navy and Macmillan[12] on the political side, and on service terms with branches like G-2 [intelligence] and G-3 [operations] and Deputy COS (and that's important), you will find MAAF being let in for all sorts of things and committed to policies which are quite unsound from the air point of view.' Slessor insisted, with unnecessary vehemence to a man who was at least as air-minded as himself, that 'anything which may remotely affect air policy must be dealt with by MAAF and not some staff branch in AFHQ... So that, while I shall come up and see you [in Caserta] when I can get away, I have reluctantly come to the conclusion that for the present I should be here [in Algiers] for most of the time. You have a first-class man there in John Linnell of course, which makes it easier for both of us.'

'I hope you will take the first opportunity of having another good blow at Bulgaria', he advised Eaker. 'I believe that with a week of good weather we could put Bulgaria out of the war with the Strategic Air Force. I'm not sure whether you have withdrawn the ban on [bombing] Sofia – if not, I hope you will. There is no reason now why Sofia should not be bombed... And I am very anxious to see that marshalling yard at Bucharest get a good hammering; apart from the practical importance to the oil traffic, it would have a most valuable moral effect in Romania.' No doubt, but Eaker was well aware that Spaatz was most unlikely to approve such a diversion from targets of more immediate concern in Italy or across the Alps.

---

[12] The portly Wilson was known as 'Jumbo'; his Chief of Staff was Lieutenant-General James Gammell; and Churchill's Minister Resident at AFHQ was Mr Harold Macmillan.

Ruminations on Keith Park

One headache Slessor identified was a division of responsibility between AFHQ and all the politicos, diplomats and even generals at Middle East Headquarters in Cairo for action in the Balkans. There was 'a background of tradition' in which Cairo was 'the centre of all military and political activity in the Mediterranean', a tradition which those serving there were determined to keep alive. 'Park, unfortunately, has very little experience of that sort of thing', he told Eaker, 'his strong suit has always been operations.' Slessor was mistaken. He himself had far less experience of Cairo's devious ways than Park, who had actually served there. Also, Park had spent many hours in the company of Tedder and Coningham, men whose own devious ways were a match for those of anyone in Cairo – and Park was bright enough to watch them at it, listen to what they said, and do likewise.

Park and Slessor were in constant and often acrimonious conflict between 1944 and 1946, and Park believed – wrongly – that Slessor engineered what he considered his premature retirement. Slessor thought him 'rather a difficult character – I had many passages of arms with him when later [in 1944] he was under me in the Mediterranean.' Years later, in 1957, he wrote that Park 'was a brilliant commander of fighters; he proved that not only in 11 Group but later in Malta. And I think the major credit for the Battle of Britain should go to him.' Park thought the warmth of this tribute was 'false' and Air Chief Marshal Sir Leslie Hollinghurst, who knew both men well, agreed: it was 'a clear case of a guilty conscience.'

During 1944, Slessor did his best to limit Park's areas of independent action in the Mediterranean. Although admitting that he did not know him well – whereas Portal did – he soon felt it necessary to inform the CAS that Park was incapable of handling the Cairo job, politically unaware, and very stupid. Perhaps Slessor was unwise to meddle in political affairs of which, in fact, he knew little – never having served in the Middle East. Portal, fortunately, was well aware of Slessor's 'tendency to hold dismissive opinions' and not only refused to sack Park but gave him an even more important appointment when opportunity offered. Slessor had a reputation, recalled Group Captain Tom Gleave, for writing adverse reports about practically every officer in the service: 'Keith Park was a first-rate candidate for Jack Slessor's attention. Keith hated bumff. Jack Slessor revelled in it.'

In November 1944, Slessor complained – at great length – to Evill (VCAS) that Park was not capable, in his view, of handling a really big command and strongly objected to any move to appoint Park as his successor. In that same month, Park wrote to Slessor asking that if he had any criticisms to make of his actions, he should direct them to him, and not to other Commanders-in-Chief. This, of course, was a serious charge, but the reality was probably less scandalous than it seems. Slessor had a lifelong urge to advise, instruct, and above all to ruminate at length on paper about matters great and small. While doing so, he would sometimes, perhaps inadvertently, say more than he intended. In this instance, he revealed only too clearly his disdain for Park.

A heated debate followed and Park – who could be as prickly as the next man – refused to destroy the correspondence, despite Slessor's request. Fortunately, a letter from Slessor on December 3rd had 'an unusually conciliatory tone', as he realized that his pen had yet again run away with him and there was a risk of an open breach that might not be resolved as he wished, given Portal's high regard for Park. Years later, Slessor candidly admitted to an official historian, Denis Richards, that there were two occasions in his life when he felt 'scarred'. One was when he objected to the proposal to award a GCB to Park. Portal, usually careful to guard his tongue, responded sharply. 'What are you worried about? Your turn will come.'

Ruminations on Joe Cannon

In a letter to Eaker in early March Slessor allowed himself to propose that Joe Cannon be appointed to command the air side of Anvil, if it were mounted. This was too much for Eaker. He was always prepared to listen to Slessor, but the only opinions that mattered to him were those of Spaatz in London and Arnold in Washington. He put him politely in his place on the 8th. 'In the American Air Force organization, it is not the air force that supports an army in the field, it is an Air Support Command. The latter is given the staff and the communications to accomplish this job. The army opposite number and equivalent is the Army Commander. The Twelfth Air Support Command, therefore, supported the operations in Africa, the landing in Sicily, the landing at Salerno and the landing at Anzio.' These were basic matters which Slessor ought to have grasped before leaping in with an unsolicited suggestion.

Clark and Cannon had assured Eaker that Brigadier-General Gordon P. Saville, as head of that command, was well able to handle Anvil, with Lieutenant-General Alexander M. Patch as Army Commander. Eaker could not degrade Cannon to that position, and Cannon would back Saville as properly as he had backed him elsewhere. 'I believe we are wrong to start out on the assumption that Cannon, as the Twelfth Air Force Commander, will not appreciate the importance of Anvil and will not properly supervise and support the activities of his Air Support Command.' If it should happen that Cannon showed 'any lack of appreciation of his responsibilities', if Anvil were to be mounted, 'you and I sit here to take immediate measures as required.' Eaker agreed that the operation was unlikely to be mounted. 'Practically, there is no prospect for it, bearing in mind the shipping situation, the air force availability, the probable enemy intention and a study of the terrain.' Slessor accepted Eaker's instruction and did not again offer advice on the employment of American officers.

Eaker reported to Arnold on March 21st that Cannon was proving 'an ideal commander' for the Twelfth Air Force. He was respected and trusted both by Alexander and Clark. As for Saville, he too was performing well as Air Support Commander: 'Cannon is highly pleased with his performance and Clark praised him to the skies when I last saw him.' But Eaker regarded the Fifteenth Air Force as 'a pretty disorganized mob.' Until recently, it had been a tactical formation and lacked the formation skills needed to fly deep into Germany, and was unable to bomb accurately when it got there. It needed escort fighters and pathfinder leadership. '[Nathan] Twining [its commander] understands that he has a difficult job on his hands and he has set about it with a will.' Spaatz agreed with Eaker about the Fifteenth's poor performance.

Shifting shingle

Military affairs in the Mediterranean in mid-January were in a state of 'feverish lull'. A combination of bitter weather, difficult terrain, and stern German resistance had brought the ground campaign in Italy to a halt before Cassino, but plans were in train for Operation Shingle, amphibious landings at Anzio (on the Italian west coast, about 40 miles south of Rome) to be launched on January 22nd. Churchill pressed hard for it, overcoming strong American resistance, in a vain bid to demonstrate that British influence over the war's grand strategy was not in decline and that a decisive victory could be achieved in Italy now that a British officer was in supreme command.

The daunting task of moving the Allied air forces from North Africa to Italy was also in train. Eaker and Slessor thus faced a triple task as James Parton has explained: 're-organization of command, completion of the move to Italy and execution of a major military operation which experience at Salerno [in September 1943] had shown would not be easy.' The Americans insisted that the Eighth Air Force in England and the newly-formed Fifteenth Air Force in Italy be yoked under the operational control of a new organization, US Strategic Air Forces in Europe, with its headquarters in England and Spaatz in command. By late in 1943, it was thought that the Combined Bomber Offensive (CBO) from English bases was producing important results and that bases in the Foggia area (near the heel of the Italian boot) would shortly permit 'for the first time a comprehensive program of true strategic bombardment by the heavy bombers in the Mediterranean Theater.' Possible grounds for conflict between Spaatz and Eaker were obvious, but they were old friends and Spaatz readily agreed to communicate with the Fifteenth Air Force only through MAAF and to delegate to Eaker operational control of that air force, except for CBO directives.

In January 1944, it was expected that the heavy bomber bases around Foggia would soon be replaced by bases some 350 miles farther north, in the immense Po valley, anywhere between Milan in the west to Venice in the east. Numerous opportunities would follow for co-ordinated operations with Spaatz's bombers in England against German targets. In fact, on only ten occasions were such operations carried out – all from Foggia – partly because of bad weather, but mostly because of the Allied failure to advance rapidly up the Peninsula. At least 30 joint attacks were cancelled. Consequently, the Fifteenth Air Force was usually employed against targets in Italy.

Slessor had watched the early stages of Shingle from the Advanced Air Headquarters alongside 15 Army Group at Caserta. The army, he thought, was not up to scratch. 'I wish Tedder had stayed as Allied C-in-C', he told Portal on the 27th, 'but I feel confidence in Jumbo [Wilson] and I know Eaker feels the same.' Shingle was not going to be the 'smashing success' it could have been, despite the fact that the Allies had a more complete air superiority over Italy than over Kent. 'The air cannot win a land battle for the army – the army must fight', but Alexander was 'taking counsel of his fears... the old Camberley business – the army busy as usual proving that the war is administratively impossible.' Eaker, he said, fully shared his views – but the American changed his mind, as we shall see shortly. 'The operation, largely owing to Mr Churchill's influence', in the opinion of the British official historian, 'was given quite an extraordinary degree of importance. It was fathered by wishful strategical thinking and was not made the subject of a searching tactical analysis.' Slessor did not probe the matter more deeply in his memoirs.

Next day, the 28th, he added a postscript to his letter on Shingle's failure. 'It really makes one almost despair of our armies', and William J. Donovan (whom he had met in Washington, head of the Office of Strategic Services, and now a Brigadier-General) was 'bitterly disappointed and angry.' Slessor had 'not the slightest doubt that if we had been Germans or Russians', we would probably be in Rome now, 'and the whole right of the enemy line opposite the Fifth Army would have crumpled. As it is, I suppose we shall continue to do next to nothing until the Hun has had time to redeploy and hit us hard.' Thus the instant expert, fresh from contemplating war at sea commented in his usual cavalier fashion on an amphibious operation about which he knew nothing. He admitted that Shingle 'may have been an unsound conception... which had no hope of success once the main Fifth Army attack failed to break through on the Garigliano and Rapido front.'

However, in Slessor's view, no major operation could succeed unless the commander showed 'vigour, audacity and readiness to take chances in exploiting unexpected success.' He had in mind the American General, John P. Lucas, commanding the landing force (designated VI Corps). By midnight on January 22nd, only 22 hours after the first landing craft reached the shore, over 36,000 men, 3,000 vehicles and large amounts of stores had been landed. 'In fact, we know from the enemy's records', wrote Roskill, 'that there was at that moment almost nothing to prevent the landing forces advancing right into Rome.' Whether they could have held on until reinforcements arrived remains a matter much debated.

Slessor offered no criticism of Churchill's part in the 'unsound conception', though the great man himself said later that 'Anzio was my worst moment in the war. I had most to do with it. I didn't want two Suvla Bays in one lifetime.' Parallels with Gallipoli have often been noticed. Michael Howard, for example, wrote that Churchill hoped the appearance of two Allied divisions 'would terrify the enemy, resolve a strategic deadlock and have perhaps decisive consequences for the conduct of the war. As at Suvla Bay, the commander on the spot landed the bulk of his forces without opposition and dug himself in at leisure, while the enemy reacted with lightning speed. As on the Gallipoli peninsula, the Allied forces found themselves hemmed in on a narrow beach-head, every inch of which was under enemy fire.' Although the Allies were not forced to depart, they suffered horrendous casualties: 40,000 dead, wounded or prisoners, and perhaps as many again sick or deserted out of a force of 110,000. Anzio, in fact, leaves as big a blot as Gallipoli on the reputation of a man Slessor regarded as the greatest Englishman who ever lived. 'This whole affair has a strong odour of Gallipoli', remarked Lucas even before it began, 'and apparently the same amateur was still on the coach's bench.'

Samuel Eliot Morison, an official US navy historian, and Major-General Lucian Truscott (a dynamic commander who replaced Lucas) both disparaged the efforts of airmen throughout this operation. According to Morison, 'bombing did no good to the amphibious forces bound for Anzio.' In fact, wrote Slessor, nearly 250 vessels arrived off Anzio undetected and unopposed, thanks to the destruction of an enemy airfield at Perugia in the centre of the peninsula, 120 miles north of Anzio. According to Truscott, 'Air support was – and continued to be – the weak point in all beachhead operations'; airmen were set on fighting their own war, trying in vain to isolate the battlefield by bombing bridges, roads and railways. In fact, wrote Slessor, the air forces 'worked on plans carefully prepared on an inter-Service basis before the landing and afterwards adjusted daily in conference with the responsible army staff. Throughout the Anzio operation there was not a single official complaint about the lack of air support – indeed very much the reverse.' Carlo D'Este, an American historian who has studied this operation in detail, agreed with Slessor. The air support, he wrote, 'was both massive and timely'. Over 12,000 tons of bombs were dropped at a cost of 144 bombers and fighters; the Luftwaffe lost 142 aircraft.

Eaker, backed by Spaatz, wrote to Arnold on March 6th to defend the actions of Alexander and Lieutenant-General Mark W. Clark, Commanding General, US 5th Army. Having seen the ground – which Slessor had not – Eaker thought Lucas would have been destroyed by

German forces driving in from the flanks and cutting him off from his sole supply port if in fact he had pushed inland. Eaker went on to rebuke Arnold. 'I think you know what ardent airmen Tooey [Spaatz] and I are and that we both have the aggressive spirit. When you find the two of us in agreement on this you should be less critical of the ground forces. They were not let down by airmen, and do not say they were. When the navy announces that it cannot unload supplies with a wind of more than force four or with a high tide and rough seas, nobody criticizes the navy. That is an accepted limitation in naval operations. The same is true of the ground forces. When they come to a swollen stream flowing at such a strength that it prevents their laying their pontoon bridges, or when they come to a mined defile, it is well understood that they are halted for the moment. You have not, I am sure, appreciated completely the limitations which the weather has imposed on the air effort here during the last six weeks.'

Slessor would have been less ready to defend Alexander. Years later, in March 1961, he told Field Marshal Sir Claude Auchinleck that 'I became convinced, as a result of serving alongside [Alexander] for a year in Italy, that he is quite the stupidest man who has ever commanded anything more than a Division... he owes his position entirely to Churchill's occasional gross misjudgement of men.' And in October 1962 he wrote to 'My dear Bill' Elliot (whom we shall meet shortly) about Alexander's memoirs. 'The fact is, of course, that Alexander is (a) almost illiterate and (b) the stupidest man I know – nice, but bone stupid and also idle and irresponsible.' Here we have Slessor's considered opinion of a brave soldier with a graceful manner whom Churchill (helped by Brooke) advanced far beyond his ceiling during and after the war. Michael Howard regarded Alexander as 'charming, personally courageous, but ineffectual; like Ian Hamilton at Gallipoli, a gallant gentleman, far out of his depth.' The Italian campaign, over which he presided, was 'an object lesson, even when one has crushing logistical superiority, in the number of things that under indifferent leadership can still go horribly wrong.' As for Major John North, Alexander's ghost writer, he also provoked Slessor: 'not only incompetent but also a loathsome little squirt', who did not check his facts and references. North's mortal sin was that he made no reference in his text either to Eaker or Slessor, and had nothing to say about the part played by Anglo-American air forces in bringing about the victories achieved in the Mediterranean campaigns.

CHAPTER 13

GRINDING TOWARDS VICTORY

Air support for ground forces

Throughout 1944, there was tension between advocates of invading southern France or continuing the Italian campaign, and between those who preferred to back the strategic bombing campaign, rather than focus on direct support for the armies. There was, thought Parton, 'persuasive evidence of the Fifteenth's ability to destroy Ploesti's oil installations.' He also approved 'the evolution of a policy of interdiction of rail lines by the medium and fighter-bombers rather than blunderbuss smashing of rail facilities in marshalling yards.'

The strategic air force, nominally a joint enterprise, was effectively an American formation because the British component – 205 Group – consisted of only four squadrons of night bombers, whereas the Fifteenth contained no fewer than 21 groups of heavies and seven of long-range fighters. To the Fifteenth, therefore, belongs 'the chief credit for the success of the great campaign against oil which began on April 5th. For the elimination of Ploesti, source of 30 percent of the entire Axis oil supply, was the *sine qua non* of the whole counter-oil offensive. The Fifteenth accomplished it with 20 daylight missions (plus four night attacks by 205 Group) which all told constituted the biggest single air battle of the war.' Between April 5th and August 19th, the strategic air force flew more than 5,000 sorties over the continent's third most heavily-defended target and dropped 13,000 tons of bombs. These attacks cost 222 day bombers, 15 RAF night bombers, and 49 fighters.

Slessor thought the 'excellent system evolved by Coningham and Montgomery in the Western Desert' to assist ground forces was improved in Italy. As ever, he could not bring himself to credit Tedder or even mention his name. But the Mediterranean Allied Strategic Air Forces (MASAF: the US 15th Air Force and its tiny RAF partner, the RAF's 205 Group) were commanded not by Eaker but by Spaatz in England. He was reluctant to see heavies employed in support of ground operations in Italy and, as we have seen, many operations against targets across the Alps were planned, though few were actually carried out. The result was that MASAF gave little support to Spaatz and less to Eaker and Slessor than it could have done. They were obliged to accept this handicap to their own plans – a consequence of commanding in what had become a secondary theatre.

As for the use of mediums and fighter-bombers in Italy, there emerged a sharp difference of opinion. Should railway targets (especially marshalling yards with large concentrations of locomotives and rolling stock, also repair shops) be given priority? Or should 'interdiction' be attempted? That is, setting a barrier across the enemy rear, mainly by destroying bridges. Slessor advocated the latter. 'There are now some 17 German divisions in Italy south of Rome', he wrote to Norstad on February 11th, 'I do not believe the army – even with our support – will move them. But I think it more than possible that the Hun, by concentrating all this force so far south, has given us – the air force – an opportunity.'

That opportunity, he continued, was to hammer his lines of communication, already hard pressed, by a 'scientifically planned' attack on the right places. A week later, Eaker approved a new bombing directive. It included attacks by MASAF on northern Italy's big rail centres, attacks on rail links by the Tactical Air Force, and interruption of seaborne traffic by the Coastal Air Force. Both Wilson and Spaatz approved the directive, but in Washington Arnold pressed for a focus on German defensive positions, to blast open a route for the army to advance northwards. As Slessor feared, Arnold's demand did not bring success at Cassino in February or March.

To Slessor's surprise, medium bombers – especially the Martin B-26 Marauders of the 42nd Bombardment Group in Sardinia – proved astonishingly accurate in hitting bridges. So also did the fighter-bombers, attacking at low levels. And yet, as a faithful Trenchardist, he remained convinced that the immediate battlefield was no place for bombers or even fighter-bombers: 'that is the job of the artillery.' Except as a last resort in defence, aircraft could help the army more effectively, he argued, by paralysing the movement of supply lines behind the battlefield. Even heavy bombing could not, by itself, bring about a breakthrough at Cassino. The soldiers needed to be ready, in sufficient strength, to advance as soon as the bombardment ceased, but they were not.

Reflecting later, he confessed that he had been mistaken about the 'enormous importance of the intensive air bombardment of the enemy's rail communications in northern France' before D-Day, June 6th 1944. That was now 'a matter of history'. But he still could not bear to name the chief advocate of that bombardment: the 'Transportation Plan', devised by Tedder and his Chief Scientific Adviser, Solly Zuckerman. Slessor had good reason to resent Tedder on personal grounds – as we shall see – but a bigger man, attempting to write a history of great events, would have acknowledged his exceptional merits both in command of air forces and in support of Eisenhower as Deputy Supreme Allied Commander.

Recognizing the merits of that plan brought Slessor perilously close to agreeing with Zuckerman about the use of Bomber Command. Had he been listened to by Harris, as *The Times* surmised, 'the continuing and wasteful area bombing campaign might have been exchanged for something much more precise and effective in terms of paralysing supplies to the German armies. Zuckerman himself remained convinced to the end that such a re-deployment of air forces to a tactical role would undoubtedly have shortened a war which, in spite of the awesome weight of the strategic air offensive, only ended with the surrender of the enemy on the battlefield.'

Staggering strangle

Then came Operation Strangle in April. Slessor reported on it to Portal at great length on the 16th, a length which he saw no reason to edit when incorporating the report into his memoirs a decade later. No doubt the CAS – or his staff – rescued useful points about the Italian campaign from Slessor's rambling reflections on Great War operations and those proposed for the liberation of Occupied Europe. The most useful point made by Slessor was the fact that German soldiers remained effective despite Allied air superiority. Very bad weather, together with ingenuity and determination were to blame. The Germans built up stocks of fuel, ammunition, food and fodder for their horses by making good use in darkness of numerous small vessels on both coasts – and by living off the country, which they exploited ruthlessly for supplies and labour.

The ability of 'the Hun' to fight effectively despite Allied air power astonished Slessor. 'I cannot conceive that our air superiority in Overlord can be more complete', he told Portal. 'Yet he fights, and fights like hell, not only in defence but in counter-attack. He is undoubtedly the world's finest ground soldier.' Perhaps – though opponents of Japanese and Soviet soldiers might disagree. The lesson that even overwhelming air power can be resisted was soon forgotten, but, as Terraine has said, 'painfully re-taught to the Americans in Vietnam, between 1964-73.'

The German soldier, wrote Slessor, 'lives far harder than we and the Americans do, and gets along with far less. He doesn't worry about ENSA shows or V-cigarettes, coca-cola or chewing-gum, the masses of motor vehicles, or all the luxuries without which it is assumed that the modern British and American soldier cannot wage war.' Whatever truth there was in these assertions, they did not apply to Polish soldiers – or airmen – but Slessor had not been in Italy long enough to take their measure. The main factor in the current stalemate, Slessor emphasized, was that the Allied ground armies were not forcing the Germans to fight constantly, and so use up their precious reserves. He recognized the army's need to rest, refit and train, but argued that quiet periods only made its task harder.

Cassino: abbey and town

The Germans defended the town of Cassino and Monastery Hill overlooking it as a vital part of their Gustav Line, barring Clark's army from advancing on Rome and also preventing relief of the Allied forces at Anzio. 'To attacking troops', wrote the official British historian, 'the ground set vile tactical puzzles one after another.' The ground was 'unspeakably rough and broken with minor ridges, knolls, and hollows jumbled all together. At one point deep clefts might be the obstacle, at another sheer rock faces or steep slabs, or all three might be found in a few acres... This or that knoll or ridge might seem to be promising objectives but would turn out to be commanded from an unlikely direction by another knoll or ridge or by several.' In short, 'The advantages of the ground lay wholly with defending troops.'

The first attempt to break through failed in January. The second attempt was made in mid-February by Lieutenant-General Sir Bernard Freyberg's New Zealand Corps (ordered to take the town) and Major-General Francis Tuker's 4th Indian Division (ordered to take Monastery Hill). Tuker expected the Germans to occupy the famous abbey on top of the hill and requested its destruction. Clark refused because he rightly foresaw that the ruins would offer numerous excellent defensive positions, but Freyberg backed Tuker and Alexander added his support.

The Germans, however, had informed the Vatican that they would not use the abbey – and did not do so until after it was destroyed. 'There is abundant and convincing evidence', recorded the British official historian, 'that the Germans made no military use whatever of the abbey's buildings until after the Allies had wrecked them by bombing.' On the morning of February 15th 135 heavy bombers – B-17 Flying Fortresses – dropped over 300 tons of high explosive and incendiary bombs on the abbey. They were followed a little later by 87 medium bombers – B-25 Mitchells and B-26 Marauders – dropping a further 140 tons. Although this massive raid did not eliminate a single German soldier, it killed or injured at least 300 civilians who had taken refuge in the abbey. The Indians were unable to attack immediately after the bombing ceased, and were repulsed with severe losses when they did. 'After the war the Allies insisted they had irrefutable evidence that the monastery had been part of the German defences and it took until 1969 for the Americans to admit that it had not been.' A British government investigation into the bombing in 1949 – which Slessor presumably knew about – concluded that no such irrefutable evidence existed, but felt unable to release that information to the public for another 30 years.

The air bombardment of Cassino town and abbey were strictly ground force ideas and, as Eaker assured Arnold, MAAF agreed only with 'profound reservations'. Eaker personally pointed out to Freyberg, before his attack on the town, that bomb craters would make it impossible for tanks to operate, but the New Zealand commander asserted – wrongly – that bulldozers would quickly clear a path. The Cassino position was not taken by direct assault, but as a result of outflanking movements, which, as Molony says, were 'made possible not just by dried terrain and increased Allied strength, but chiefly by what has since been accepted as a classic demonstration of the proper employment of air power – Operation Strangle.'

American bombing 'is usually a joy to see', enthused Slessor in a letter to Hermione on February 16th, 'marvellous. You have probably seen in the press that we had to blot out Monte Cassino Abbey, the old Benedictine monastery. Very sad – I believe it was lovely and contained some wonderful old frescoes. But the Hun, of course, was using it as an OP [Observation Post] and machine-gun nest and it had to go – and the US bombers made a superb job of it.' Slessor's 'joy' was not tempered by any critical assessment of what the bombing actually achieved. 'Most of the bombers missed the abbey altogether,' wrote Carlo D'Este, 'and it was only the final bombing runs that did any significant damage. What the bombs failed to accomplish, Allied artillery did, as the ruins were pounded into rubble.' American money helped pay for the re-building of the abbey, but as late as 1991 the monks refused to display signs in English.

When composing his memoirs a decade later, Slessor wisely took a less exuberant line about a shocking miscalculation – political and military – that sullied the reputations of all the commanders concerned. He then described the bombing as 'a tragedy, but an inevitable tragedy.' He claimed that he had 'strongly opposed' it at the time; it is more certain that Eaker did. Like Clark, Eaker doubted whether the Germans were occupying the abbey. 'The evidence that they were not', wrote Slessor in the 1950s, is now so overwhelming as to permit of no further argument', but 'no man among the troops detailed to attack the Cassino position would have believed it for a moment. It was astonishing how that towering hill with the great white building atop dominated the whole scene in that valley of evil memory; and Private Doe from Detroit, Smith from Wigan, Jones from Dunedin or Yusuf Ali from Campbellpore eyed it and felt that behind those windows there must be at least an enemy observer waiting to turn the guns on him personally when the time came to attack.' No doubt; but commanders usually have more compelling reasons for major action than to ease the fancies of their men.

The bombing of the abbey on February 15th, in Molony's words: 'delivered in isolation from the action of the land forces, achieved no military object except a temporary stimulation of the soldiers' morale. The air and artillery bombardment of Cassino town and Monastery Hill on March 15th, amounting to some 2,192 tons of bombs and shells, produced results which were the opposite of those intended. The bombardment turned Cassino town into a chaotic and almost impassable maze of ruins, rubble, and craters. It failed to kill or bury alive the parachute battalion in the town, or even to craze them with fear.'

A study produced by MAAF's Director of Operations and Intelligence concluded that the defenders were not destroyed by the bombing because deep and solid shelters protected them; the army 'was not prepared to attack in sufficient strength immediately after the cessation of bombing'; enemy morale was 'superb' and reinforcements reached them more quickly than the Allies realized; and 'it is now doubted whether this headquarters should have acceded to the army's requests for an attack on such a scale or in the manner in which it was performed.' Portal agreed. These were indeed results bleak enough to give even the most devout bomber champion pause for thought.

Bombing Florence and Rome

Florence was not only world famous for its artistic and architectural treasures, but also an important road and rail centre. As the war drew closer to the great city during 1944 there were fears that the Germans and the Allies might destroy it between them. In February Slessor had set down his thoughts on the issue. 'Florence is one of the shrines of European civilization', he wrote, 'and in my view is of more permanent value to the cause for which we are fighting than a few British or American lives.' Only if bombing were found to be absolutely essential, from a military point of view, would he condone it, but he doubted if this would be the case. 'We must also consider the effect on the reputation of and popular regard for the air forces now and after the war of having been responsible for the destruction or serious damage of Florence.' He did not think 'we should take refuge behind the army in this matter and give in on it under pressure from them. We have always rightly maintained that it was our job to select bombing objectives'. These fine words do not appear to have come back to haunt him after he agreed to the destruction of Monte Cassino. Slessor told Portal on March 1st that Alexander and Eaker were pressing him for permission to bomb marshalling yards only a mile from the Duomo. He proposed to yield to that pressure, so long as 'only the most experienced and accurate bomber squadrons' were employed, and thought it would be 'very bad luck if any of the famous buildings were hit.' The Chiefs of Staff approved, and so did Churchill, next day.

'I had to make a beastly decision this morning', wrote Slessor to his wife on March 2nd: 'to bomb Florence. Unfortunately, there is a damned important marshalling yard there – the Campo di Marte station – and the Hun evidently realizes that we have been holding off it and is deliberately making use of that. The army have been pressing for it for weeks, and the Americans don't attach quite the importance to that sort of thing that we do. I've dug my toes in up to now, and have had one or two strongish arguments with little Eaker about it. But I've had to give in and send him a signal saying I agree to its going ahead. I hope we shall be able to avoid too much damage to the town – the yard is about a mile from the Duomo and it would be very bad luck if any bombs fell anywhere near the really lovely part of the city. But one can never be quite sure. God damn these

Germans! What a foul obscenity they are, leaving their beastly trail of terror and destruction all over the world.'

The bombing achieved little, however, and was not repeated. Then, on June 3rd, Hitler directed that Rome and Florence were to be regarded as 'open cities': all German civil and military headquarters were to move out and demolition of rail and road bridges was forbidden. The Allies were equally anxious to spare Florence, but as in the case of Rome, Alexander declined to issue a declaration to that effect because he knew that Albert Kesselring, the German commander, would contest every yard of ground south of the city and possibly within it whatever Hitler decreed. In the event, there was heavy fighting all around Florence and it did reach into the city. The Germans destroyed five of the six bridges over the Arno and many buildings as they withdrew in early August. Alexander 'is very proud of the fact that so far in this campaign', wrote Macmillan in September, 'he has succeeded in saving Rome, Florence, Pisa, Siena, Assisi, Perugia and Urbino from any except minor damage and that wantonly inflicted by the enemy when retiring.'

Meanwhile, on April 10th, Portal informed the Prime Minister that Britain's Ambassador to the Vatican had reported an air attack on Rome on March 19th which cost about a hundred civilian lives. Slessor, however, had assured Portal that not a single Allied bomber had flown over Rome on that day. If bombs were dropped, the Germans were responsible – but radio monitoring could not confirm this. Slessor supplied a list of attacks that had been carried out on Rome during March. They were all aimed at marshalling yards and very few bombs were known to have fallen outside the areas selected.

Dazzling Diadem

Allied forces surged forwards from Cassino to the sea on the night of May 11th-12th to begin Operation Diadem, the battle for Rome. Strangle and Diadem, in Parton's opinion, 'formed without question the most significant demonstration of tactical air operations in the history of war.' Medium and fighter-bombers gave Field Marshal Kesselring's reserves, moving down from the north, a severe mauling. As Slessor later observed, the Germans were unable to co-ordinate counter-attacks because Allied aircraft – working closely with ground forces – destroyed the enemy's system of control by attacking headquarters, command posts, signals systems, supply dumps, vehicle parks and repair shops. As Molony writes, 'the main feature of air operations was the supremacy of the Allied air forces, a priceless advantage for the Allied armies', and one airmen under the command of Eaker and Slessor did not have to fight for. Although the Luftwaffe in Italy was 'a spent force', airmen suffered heavy casualties from ground fire: 357 aircraft were lost during 25 days between May 12th and June 5th and many others damaged.

Slessor wrote to Trenchard on May 26th about pressure on the air force to knock out guns. 'I think Saville, the US AOC controlling the close support in this battle, is doing very well. He is only putting the absolute minimum of effort onto guns and other battlefield targets, and is keeping his eye on the ball and concentrating on the movement in the back areas, which of course is the answer.' He thought it a conservative estimate to say that well over a thousand vehicles had been destroyed in the past two days. When enemy guns are active in an area which cannot easily be reached by our guns, then fighter-bombers should be used against them. 'But as a rule the fighter-bombers, and in fact all bombers, must be used against communications and supply in the back areas, and that I think is being well done in this battle.'

A few days later, Marshall and Arnold visited Eaker and Slessor in Caserta, and Arnold asked Slessor for his views on what air power had achieved in that battle. By June 1944, Slessor had advanced a long way from the simplicities of pre-war Trenchardism. He began by setting down his musings on what air power had not achieved. 'It cannot by itself defeat a highly organized and disciplined army, even when that army is virtually without air support of its own', he wrote, nor can it 'by itself enforce a withdrawal by drying up the flow of essential supplies', nor can it entirely prevent the movement of strategic reserves to the battlefront... In short, it cannot absolutely isolate the battlefield from enemy supply or reinforcement', nor 'absolutely guarantee the immunity either of our forward formations or back areas, port installations, base depots, airfields, convoys at sea, etc, against the occasional air attack or reconnaissance.'

On the other hand, Slessor continued, air power had made it impossible 'for the most highly organized and disciplined army to offer prolonged resistance to a determined offensive on the ground – even in a country almost ideally suited for defence; it can turn an orderly retreat into a rout; and virtually eliminate an entire army as an effective fighting force.' The Allies had so dominated the air that ground forces were able to move troops and supplies freely in daylight or darkness. Not only were enemy forces unable to move with equal freedom, they were denied accurate and detailed information about Allied dispositions and could not prevent Allied aircraft from observing and reporting their own. Slessor ended with his usual plug for Trenchard. He had said that 'all land battles are confusion and muddle, and the job of the air is to accentuate that confusion and muddle in the enemy's army to a point where it gets beyond the capacity of anyone to control. This is exactly what the air did to the German army in Italy in the critical last days of May and first days of June.' And yet the confused and muddled Germans somehow managed to fight on for another eleven months.

Rome fell into Clark's eager hands on June 4th without hard fighting because the Germans simply withdrew to yet another defensive line north of the city. Its capture justified the code-name Diadem, in Molony's words, 'although every workaday soldier, airman, and sailor had earned this royal badge of distinction and honour, it is unlikely that any one of them felt that "a broad white fillet set with pearls" encircled his old tin hat.' Diadem cost the Allied forces more than 40,000 casualties, the Germans over 50,000, and another year of hard fighting lay ahead. Even so, it was a victory. The week of June 4th-10th 1944 marked 'the beginning of the end' for Hitler: Rome fell on the 4th, the liberation of Normandy began on the 6th; and on the 10th the Soviet Union launched an attack on Finland that would end in Berlin. The bravery and determination of numerous soldiers in Italy from many lands has never been questioned, but the 'masterly dispositions' of their field commanders 'would have remained on paper, an interesting matter for readers of military history to discuss' – in the words of Molony's British official history – 'if the Mediterranean Allied Air Forces had not first defeated the German Air Force in the Mediterranean Theatre and driven it from the Italian sky.'

Anger over Anvil

Slessor, backed by Eaker, strongly opposed Operation Anvil, the Allied landings on the coast of southern France. No operation anywhere from start to finish of Anglo-American efforts in the Second World War generated more animosity than Anvil; in part because the military arguments for and against seemed finely balanced, but mostly because the decision to proceed made it painfully clear to the British that the Americans were now able and willing to do as they pleased. The operation had at first been intended to begin at the same time as Overlord, but shortage of shipping ruled out simultaneous landings. Without the great ports of Marseille and Toulon, however, Eisenhower's armies could not be adequately supplied. Anvil proved to be anything but the 'bleak and sterile... tomfoolery' Churchill had confidently predicted, and by the end of October the southern French ports were handling nearly 40 percent of all American supplies reaching Europe, and transporting them along a rail network deliberately left intact by Tedder.

The Allied threat to the Mediterranean coast had been obvious for months, but the hard-pressed Germans were obliged to withdraw forces northward to meet an even greater crisis pending there, and they were very weak at sea and in the air. Even so, ten divisions lay south of the Loire and seven of these guarded the coast. They had the use of well-sited batteries at all the obvious landing points and plenty of guns, both heavy and light, and there was no chance of achieving tactical surprise because the Allied build-up in Corsica was regularly monitored by German reconnaissance aircraft.

The British Chiefs of Staff preferred to keep up the pressure in northern Italy and the Balkans, but the American Chiefs backed an operation that would greatly assist Eisenhower's advance towards Germany after the Normandy breakout. Slessor, however, pressed hard to 'establish a base somewhere like Udine [in north-eastern Italy, close to the border with Slovenia, then part of Yugoslavia]; thence we should either strike east in the direction of Zagreb, to turn the right of the enemy's northern line of defence into the Balkans – the River Save line – or break into southern Austria in the area Villach-Klagenfurt. But what I really hankered after was to see Anglo-American forces on the Danube before the war came to an end.'

Even a decade later, when he had had time to consider the supply problems faced by the Allies in north-west Europe – quite apart from Roosevelt's need to focus attention on that campaign and avoid entanglements farther east – Slessor still thought his proposal the right thing to do. 'I was always a confirmed Balkanite', he told Eisenhower as early as January 1949, 'because I felt in my bones that it would be a bad thing on a long term view if the war ended without an Anglo-American force on the Danube. Whether in the long run, as it has turned out, that would have made any difference, I don't know.' Slessor meant in thwarting Soviet postwar aggression. No-one can know, of course, but the supply problems would certainly have been even greater than those he overlooked in north-west Europe in 1944.

The British, wrote Brigadier Molony, 'were accustomed to make war on a shoe-string, and therefore to strategic improvisation, following where fortune led... The Americans, on the other hand, confident in their almost unlimited resources, believed in marching to their strategic goal by a series of predetermined, ponderous, and inexorable steps. Their strategic goal in the European theatre was to reach the heart of Germany in the shortest possible time in overwhelming strength.' By 1944, as the balance of power within the western alliance shifted, the Americans 'felt that they had graduated as masters in the art of war, and had every reason to follow their own way, subject only to the duty of showing themselves to be, in their own way, true and faithful allies.'

Roosevelt, up for re-election in November, was under constant pressure from the Pacific lobby, led by the formidable Admiral King, and well aware that many Americans believed diversions farther east suited only British imperial interests. 'This damned business of Anvil will continue to hang over our heads for a while', Slessor had told Eaker in March, 'but I'm prepared to bet any odds against it coming off.' Another bet he would have lost. Nevertheless, he regarded himself as an Allied commander, obedient to the policies of the Combined Chiefs of Staff, even when they conflicted with his own opinions or those of the head of his own service.

General Wilson was reluctant to take the same view, as Slessor had informed Portal on March 20th. Wilson, he wrote, was 'a very loyal and perhaps rather conventional soldier and, I think, tends still to regard himself a bit too much as a British General who should do what the CIGS wants [General Sir Alan Brooke], instead of as an Allied C-in-C who should do what he believes right in the light of approved COS policy. But he is constantly telling me that Brooke is all against Anvil and wants him to kill it.' Wilson, thought Slessor, was out of his depth: 'He appears to have been unable quickly to think out the purpose of operations in Italy or the method of conducting them.'

Slessor was off to Cairo next day, to discuss the Balkan situation, Aegean operations, co-ordination of transport priorities, Liberator training and other matters. 'I do wish we could get AFHQ up to Caserta', he complained – not for the first time – to the CAS, 'it is a frightful handicap having it stuck back here [in Algiers]. It is regrettable but nevertheless a fact that if there is not someone really senior here on the air side, the air force simply gets quietly relegated to the background – not by Wilson or deliberately by Gammell, but by the US army staff system on which this extraordinary HQ is worked.'

Anvil was postponed in April, but revived by the Americans in June, after the fall of Rome, and timed to begin on August 15th. The arguments for and against went on and on – at a level above Slessor's – and were prolonged by Churchill's passionate refusal to recognize the strength of the American case, but he was eventually obliged to accept that British strategic opinions only mattered if they agreed with American opinions. Worse still, for an alleged Francophile, he ignored the fact that the French had raised half a million troops in North Africa and refused to take part in any venture not on their own soil. He did, however, achieve the petty victory of having it re-named Dragoon – allegedly for security reasons, but actually because he had been 'dragooned' into reluctant agreement. Under Saville, the Twelfth Tactical Air Command was ready to go by D-Day, with more than 2,000 aircraft from 14 airfields in 'primitive, malarial Corsica'; some 300 ships lay in the western bays of that island. Anvil/Dragoon was assisted by a re-born French air force, 'one of the brightest accomplishments of Allied teamwork in the Mediterranean', Parton thought. It was a minor part, carried out with Anglo-American ground support in British or American aircraft, but promised well for the postwar revival of France. Overall, thanks to hard-won experience at Sicily, Salerno and Anzio, and allowing for German weakness in that area, the assault was admirably planned and executed. The subsequent pursuit, however, cost inexperienced French and American soldiers dearly, as skilled and fierce Germans lived to fight on too many other days – in southern France as everywhere else, to the exasperated admiration of Slessor and other commanders.

Saville's move to Corsica meant that the Desert Air Force alone would be responsible for air operations in support of the 5th and 8th Armies in Italy, but Slessor managed to strengthen that air force by transferring units from Coastal Air Force and from the eastern Mediterranean; also by holding on to fighter pilots due for relief. In the end, 30 squadrons, all British, were left to support the Italian campaign, while no fewer than 64 were assigned to Anvil/Dragoon.

CHAPTER 14

TROUBLES COME IN THREES: YUGOSLAVIA, POLAND, GREECE

Backing the partisans

Yugoslavia was a very important part of Hitler's empire. From there, the main German routes to Greece and Bulgaria and hence to the eastern and northern shores of the Aegean could be controlled. From the Dalmatian coast much of Allied traffic along the opposite Italian coast could at least be challenged. Yugoslavia's rail and river communications were a vital link in the transport of oil from Romania and other raw materials from the eastern Balkans. Her first resistance movement had been organized by General Draza Mihailovic, backed by the exiled royalist government in Cairo and supported by both London and Washington. Known as Cetniks, they were mostly Orthodox Serbians, strongly nationalist, fervently anti-communist.

Another movement, known as the partisans and composed largely of Catholic Croats, was led by Josip Broz, a communist later known as Tito. There were Fascist Croats – the Ustasas – led by Ante Pavelic, who were brutal even by German standards, and there were also many Muslims, who rarely fitted easily into any faction. They all opposed each other bitterly, and the Cetniks at times collaborated with the German and Italian rulers of Yugoslavia. After long cogitation, London decided to back Tito.

In May 1943, the first British mission under Captain William Deakin was dropped in by air to join his headquarters, followed in September by Brigadier Fitzroy Maclean, MP, representing Churchill, and Tito set up a provisional government in November. There were no language difficulties. Maclean quickly learned that Tito spoke fluent German and Russian, 'and was also very ready to help me out in my first attempts at Serbo-Croat. After a couple of rounds of plum brandy we were deep in conversation.' One reason for British interest in Yugoslavia was a 'T.E. Lawrence complex – the idea that Britain could control the manner and timing of each country's liberation, as she had done with the Arabs after the First World War.' Maclean freely admitted his fascination with Lawrence – blowing up trains and bridges, living rough with guerillas –

and was enthralled by his words: 'We had won a province when we had taught the civilians in it to die for our ideal of freedom. The presence or absence of the enemy was a secondary matter.' In fact the partisans proved to be 'a hundred times more formidable than Feisal and his Hashemites' and Tito became a greater guerilla leader than Lawrence, for he successfully defied both Berlin and Moscow and got most of what he wanted out of London and Washington.

Eaker and Slessor strongly supported 'Special Duties' operations intended to supply 'knives, guns and explosives to the Balkan patriots.' 'Wild Bill' Donovan (head of OSS) backed them, pressing for aircraft to be assigned permanently to this work. Slessor had already told Donovan that they were badly needed because 'he was convinced that the only way to divert forces from the coming invasion of Europe was to "raise Hell in the Balkans."' Some heavy bombers were based at Blida, near Algiers, and gave valuable help to Tito's forces, though Eaker, Slessor and Donovan always felt much more could have been done if authorities in Washington and Whitehall had looked more kindly upon 'unconventional' methods of war-making. In fact, for all his apparent friendliness towards Slessor, Donovan was an 'Irish-American anti-colonialist', determined to set up a large intelligence-gathering mission in both Yugoslavia and Greece. He was, moreover, opposed to the Communist Partisans and backed their royalist opponents. Fortunately, Roosevelt and Marshall resisted Donovan and the anti-Tito State Department.

Although Slessor got on well with Eaker and Donovan, he soon became aware of US resistance to seeing their men drawn into the Balkans. Lincoln McVeagh, Ambassador to the Yugoslav and Greek governments-in-exile, told President Roosevelt in February 1944 that British policy, in his opinion, was 'directed primarily at the preservation of the Empire connections and the sea route to India... It is very far from a policy aimed at the reconstruction of the occupied countries as free and independent states.' Adding to friction on those grounds was American fear of being drawn into postwar support for Britain's interest in the eastern Mediterranean against growing Soviet influence there. The War Department even opposed direct US involvement in relief schemes as the first stage of what was likely to become an endless involvement – restoring war damage, keeping the peace, and working closely with the British. Given such strong American suspicions of British motives, Slessor soon found that fighting the Germans was the easy part of his new job.

He reported to Portal on April 16th 1944 that Tito was firmly in the saddle and Britain should not back King Peter II as a counter to Soviet influence. Slessor hoped to see an Allied force on the Danube at the end of the war, exerting strong influence throughout the Balkans. He wrote again to Portal on the 28th to say that the Allies were in danger of becoming 'helpless spectators', despite their air power. As Field Marshal Jan Christian Smuts had recently remarked, 'although we have a huge army on hand we can only employ a fraction of it because of our lack of shipping.' Slessor thought we should use 'all the irregular troops we could lay our hands on and re-organize some regular troops on Commando lines, put in paratroops in small parties all over the Balkans to fight with the partisans, lay on a lot of small landings to seize islands, destroy small enemy garrisons all over the place, and meanwhile give Tito all he could use in the shape of weapons and transport.' Portal, himself a confirmed 'Balkanite', agreed. But the Italian campaign made slower progress than expected, and the need to prepare for Operation Anvil/Dragoon drew away valuable resources.

Slessor wrote again to Portal on April 28th about the need for more and better organized operations in the Balkans. 'Given the shortage of shipping, they must be mainly air operations.' Eaker was supportive, 'though he regards the Balkans as my province and is precluded by US policy from taking any very active part, other than allowing US aircraft to continue helping in supplying Tito.' Slessor had in mind a specific air force for the Balkans, but needed Portal's strong backing because 'the first reaction' of soldiers here, 'when a requirement for a new command crops up, is to look around for some general and a corps HQ that happens to be out of a job... the predominant partner in any project must be a man in a khaki coat.' Slessor had in mind Elliot. 'I can't think of anyone who would fill the bill half as well.' He got his way, with reluctant agreement from Admiral Andrew Cunningham – whose objections, in Wilson's view, amounted to 'deliberate and tendentious obstruction' – in early June.

The Germans made a determined attack on Tito's headquarters at Drvar (a remote mountain village on the Unac river, near the northern end of the Dinaric Alps) on May 25th. It nearly succeeded, but he escaped and was flown to Bari (on the east coast of Italy's heel) in a Soviet DC-3 Dakota, together with some staff officers and members of the Soviet Mission. Heavy air attacks inflicted a severe defeat on the Germans during the next few days.

Slessor met Tito in Bari in June and was greatly impressed: 'much more than a guerilla leader – an outstanding personality and potentially a statesman of no mean order... a Yugoslav patriot first and a Communist second.' He told Slessor that he needed air superiority if he was to wage a successful campaign, plus weapons and ammunition, and a reliable means of evacuating his wounded because the partisans lacked doctors, nurses and medical stores; the Germans killed any wounded they caught and the desperate efforts to protect their wounded gravely reduced the partisans' fighting strength. Several airstrips needed to be roughed out in mountainous country and most flights – both in and out – would have to be made under the cover of darkness. Slessor was able to tell Tito in June that the Chiefs of Staff had approved the creation of a 'Trans-Adriatic

Command at Bari under a Senior Air Force Officer'. Fortunately, someone came up with 'Balkan Air Force' as a rather more memorable name.

The Balkan Air Force

The partisans had already received significant help from the Desert Air Force, now based in Italy, and 242 Group of the Coastal Air Force, with its headquarters in Taranto, on the west coast of Italy's heel. There were also the so-called 'forces' of the Special Operations Executive (SOE), and an organization known as Force 133, directed from Cairo. Clearly, there was a need for creating a single commander to bring all these units together. This demanding – but exciting – job went to one of the RAF's greatest officers, William Elliot. Among the highlights of his exceptional career (thus far) were service as a combat pilot in both Palestine and south Russia, a rare double; a year as a recruiting officer with W. E. Johns, the immortal creator of Biggles; four years as Assistant Secretary (Air) to the Committee of Imperial Defence and to the War Cabinet; head of Night Operations at Fighter Command headquarters; and Director of Plans in the Air Ministry. Had his health been good enough, he would probably have succeeded Slessor as CAS in 1953, but he suffered a heart attack in that year and retired in 1954.

Elliot was to be responsible for 'ensuring the co-ordination both of the planning and of the conduct of combined amphibious operations and raids by Allied air, sea and land forces on the islands and eastern shores of the Adriatic and Ionian Seas.' He was to contain and destroy enemy forces in the Balkans and Greece; and to open a channel of large-scale supply to 'Marshal' Tito, giving 'the greatest measure of support' to his Yugoslav National Army of Liberation (YNAL). Elliot was given an inter-service secretariat and set up a combined operations room, intelligence and communications centre for himself and representatives of the Flag Officer Taranto, the Commander Land Forces Adriatic, Brigadier Maclean and Special Operations agents. He was also given British and American political advisers.

In other words, he was handed a hot potato that might easily turn into a can of worms. As it happened, the BAF became an excellent example of inter-service co-operation, thanks to Elliot's wisdom and skill. All his decisions were backed wholeheartedly by Slessor. The BAF had its headquarters in Bari and eventually operated 24 squadrons of at least eight nationalities. 'At last we had a tidy and workable organization', wrote Slessor, 'to tie up all these loose ends in the Balkans and give the necessary guidance and impetus to operations in that important area.' Owen Reed, of Britain's Secret Intelligence Service, provided essential information to help guide Allied bombers to their targets throughout this period.

An operation splendidly codenamed Ratweek began on September 1st.

Proposed by Maclean, it was timed to coincide with the German withdrawal. The BAF and the US Fifteenth Air Force would help the partisans to move on from simply harassing Germans to seeking a decisive victory over them. Ratweek provoked a counter-attack and under its cover the Germans made frantic attempts to repair damaged rail links, 'but they reckoned without the Balkan Air Force. Every time that we received reports of a breakdown gang at work,' exulted Maclean, 'we signalled its location to Bari, and within a few hours our fighters were on to it. Each evening towards sunset would come the cry of "Avioni!" and, looking up, we would see the familiar shapes of two or three Junkers 52 transport planes winging their way ponderously northwards... The evacuation of Greece and Macedonia had already begun and these, no doubt, were senior staff officers and others who preferred not to attempt the journey by train and were getting out by air while the going was good. Here was a loophole which needed blocking up. A signal to Bill Elliot, giving the time and approximate route of these flights, did the trick. Somewhere or other our fighters must have swooped down on them for after that we did not see them again.'

Bulgaria joined the Allies, now that Soviet forces were arriving in that region, and a German retreat from everywhere in the Balkans and the Greek islands began. By the end of the year, this 'thoroughly cosmopolitan force' included two partisan squadrons – one equipped with Spitfires, the other with Hurricanes – proudly displaying 'the partisan red star in place of our red ball in the middle of the roundel.' Two Soviet squadrons, one of Dakotas and one of Yak fighters, also arrived and reluctantly accepted Elliot's operational control. There were Italian, Greek, South African and Polish squadrons (as well as British) and Dakotas of the USAAF helped, 'though they could not be officially included in BAF since Washington wished to have no overt responsibility for operations in the Balkans.' Elliot's most exasperating problem, with which Slessor could do no more than sympathise, was to discover what was happening 'in the field' because guerillas cannot risk sticking to regular plans or use radios freely, and must usually operate under cover of darkness and be prepared to scatter at a moment's notice. The BAF's most valuable work was evacuating wounded, saving partisans the difficulty of carrying their wounded with them and thereby enabling them to move quickly. During four months, June to September, the BAF evacuated over 10,000 men and women – figures which indicate the scale and intensity of the fighting.

Slessor assumed that the British would remain in the Middle East after the war and transform the BAF into an international force – including Turkey – to face the growing danger of Soviet aggression. He had hopes of forging with Tito 'a bridge of common interest', despite his Communist background. On September 17th, he suggested to Portal that as soon as Germany was defeated, Britain should give Yugoslavia aircraft and equipment, assign officers and men to work with the partisans, and arrange for them to receive further training in the Middle East and in Britain. 'The partisans', he wrote, 'had always been suspicious of naval or army intervention', but were 'very forthcoming' with airmen: 'soldiers in khaki are – in traditional memory – people who occupy other people's countries and as such are liable to be suspect. Airmen in blue somehow seem to fall into a different category; perhaps because their airfields are usually in relatively remote places, and they are not so much in evidence in large centres of population.'

Belgrade was liberated in October 1944 and Slessor later attended a celebration there. 'Tito was in great form, resplendent in a lovely new uniform, a very different person from the hunted guerrilla leader in rough serge and heavy boots that I had first met in Bari the previous June.' The capture of Belgrade ended the guerilla phase of the Balkan war and the Germans were in full retreat. 'In the space of two or three months', Maclean recalled, 'the war, from being a guerilla war, a war of movement, had become a war of position, a type of war which was completely new to the partisans. Politically, too, the capture of Belgrade marked the beginning of an entirely new phase. The days were past when partisan statesmen and administrators needed to creep through the enemy lines at night to transact their affairs. Tito and the members of his National Council were now safely installed in the capital', and had come to stay.

Slessor backed a plan outlined by Air Commodore Leonard Pankhurst to build an East Mediterranean Air Force, combining the air forces of Greece, Yugoslavia and Turkey with the BAF. This force, they hoped, might be strong enough to deter Soviet aggression. Romania and Bulgaria would be welcome to join, but Slessor was rightly aware that both states were likely to be controlled by the Soviet Union after Germany's defeat. He flew to London at the end of September, where Portal and Sir Orme Sargent of the Foreign Office expressed approval of the plan.

Back in Italy by October 25th, Slessor reported to Portal. 'We must face the fact that the offensive in Italy has, figuratively and literally, bogged down... In the Po valley, we are battering our heads against a co-ordinated and strongly-defended front. On the other side of the Adriatic, the enemy is in an already disorganized retreat which we have a chance of turning into a catastrophe. In the bag between the Russians and Bulgarians on the east, the British in Greece on the south, and the Adriatic on the west, are some 300,000 enemy troops of whose escape routes northwards the best are already cut. The only forces who can in time pull tight the string of the bag in the north and in conjunction with the winter, when it comes, destroy the enemy forces in the Balkans are the Russians, the partisans and the air force.'

The Russians intended to turn north, in Slessor's opinion, to capture Budapest, and he thought the partisans – helped by Elliot's air force – must act. Otherwise, 'Kesselring will have those additional forces to help him hold the south-east approaches to Austria, which will make it much easier for the enemy to withdraw divisions from the south-east to the defence of Germany proper. To that extent, immediate action on an adequate scale in the Balkans is of direct importance to the main offensive on the western front.' Slessor ended by warning Portal that Wilson and Alexander would resist a Balkan campaign because their eyes were firmly fixed on Italy.

'Early this week', wrote Slessor to Portal on November 9th, 'Alexander produced a plan for future strategy this winter which I think was about the silliest I have yet seen. Briefly, he proposed after the capture of Bologna to split his forces neatly in half and put half each side of the Adriatic, thus making quite sure that he would have insufficient strength for a decisive offensive on either side. His plan also showed a grand disregard for such minor details as the fact that the available Yugoslav ports and communications would not sustain the forces he proposed to put in there. One of his main preoccupations seems to be to get control of operations in Yugoslavia, which I am equally determined he should not have as long as I can prevent it. I have no regard for his strategy of power or command.' For the present, Slessor concluded, 'we are going ahead opening up Zara, Split and Sibenik and doing the necessary reconnaissance; going into the problem of opening up an all-weather airfield at Zara; getting as many supplies into the partisans as possible; and seeing what can be done to put in artillery and armour.'

Slessor wrote again to Portal on December 9th about Yugoslavia. 'Subasic and Velebit came through here [Caserta] yesterday on their way back to London. The latter is a personal friend of mine. He is quite unlike the average partisan officer, being a well-educated, highly intelligent and cultured person... a chap to whom one can talk quite freely as to another Englishman, and I believe he has a big future in Yugoslavia after the war.' Slessor had told him that Tito's long absence in Moscow had harmed relations with the western Allies; 'we were all dismayed at Tito's apparent suspicion of us because we had no designs whatever on Yugoslavia after the war.' Velebit shared Slessor's concern about the 'ill-mannered stupidity' of some partisans and Slessor urged Portal to spare him some time in London.

In December, Slessor went to Cairo, where Anthony Eden (Foreign Secretary) told him about a proposal agreed with Stalin to share influence in Yugoslavia after the war on a 50-50 basis. Although annoyed that Sargent had not passed his own proposal to Eden, Slessor suggested that the Soviet Union be invited to organize, equip and train the postwar Yugoslav army, while Britain did the same for the air force and the navy. Eden agreed and thought work should begin even before Hitler's overthrow. But nothing was done. The Americans were reluctant to supply aircraft and the Soviet Union was not interested in sharing power. Seven years later, in 1951 – when Tito had broken with Stalin – Slessor, then

CAS, was able to give him some Mosquitos. 'And today [about 1955] we see in one of the subordinate commands of SHAPE [Supreme Headquarters, Allied Powers in Europe] a military organization under American direction in south-east Europe, which (though it does not include Yugoslavia) has at least something in common with what was in 1944 a somewhat premature conception.'

During the early months of 1945, Slessor was deeply worried about the prospect of conflict between the Allies and the partisans over control of Venezia Giulia, a territory at the head of the Adriatic, north of Venice, including Trieste (formerly the principal port of the Austro-Hungarian Empire) and the great 'pear drop' of the Istrian Peninsula, which had been acquired by Italy in 1919. Allied forces expected to drive out the Germans and set up an 'Allied Military Government' (AMG), pending a peace settlement, but it gradually became clear to them that Tito intended to make the whole territory part of his new Yugoslavia. It was vital to avoid an outbreak of fighting, especially now that civil war had broken out in Greece (as we shall see shortly) and Slessor found himself in a tense situation involving British, American, Yugoslav and Italian interests – with Stalin brooding in the background. Slessor had returned to England on the eve of this first clash of what became 'the Cold War', born in Warsaw during August and September 1944. New Zealand troops, partisans and Italians were all in Trieste by early May and Churchill signalled President Truman on the 12th to say that an 'Iron Curtain' had been drawn across eastern Europe. But a month later, on June 9th, an agreement was signed in Belgrade and the partisans withdrew from Trieste. A treaty signed in Paris in 1947 created 'The Free Territory of Trieste', but this failed and eventually the area was partitioned with the port remaining in Italian hands.

Meanwhile, in August 1946, Slessor was invited to comment on Wilson's official despatch on the Yugoslav campaign. He found it hard to say anything, 'other than that I should have regarded it as a moderate effort for a first-term student at the Staff College.' He agreed with Elliot 'that it is a scrappy, disjointed and pedestrian series of notes.' As for the suggestion that airmen should comment only on air operations, Slessor rejected it. Wilson was a Supreme Allied Commander, not an army commander appointed by the War Office. 'We have just as much right to comment on the strategic and political issues as the War Office has; in fact, for the period after the formation of the Balkan Air Force more right, because Air Vice-Marshal Elliot was definitely SACMED's representative in the Balkan countries on strategic and political issues.'

The Battle for Warsaw[13]

As one of Britain's pre-war planners, Slessor felt 'a sense of obligation' to Poland, as well he might, for Britain gave a guarantee of independence to her 'First Ally' that proved to be the deadest of dead letters as soon as the Germans invaded in September 1939. Later, he saw at first hand how brave and skilful many Polish airmen and soldiers were. He also knew, though he could not say so in his memoirs, what an essential help Polish mathematicians had been, on the eve of war, in revealing Germany's Ultra secrets to the French and British. Although Stalin had joined Hitler in the conquest of Poland, 'I was still guileless enough to believe' in the middle of 1944, three years after Hitler turned on Stalin, 'that the single-minded concern of our Russian allies, like our own, was the defeat of the Germans, to which the efforts of the Polish underground resistance groups could make a valuable contribution.'

Allied armies were on the move during July 1944 towards Germany from west and east. Most leaders of the Polish Home Army (AK, Armia Krajowa) agreed that Warsaw was too large to seize without sacrificing countless Polish lives and that it would be best to wait until the Germans were compelled by the growing danger to their homeland to abandon the city – and then attack their rearguards. A sensible if unheroic strategy, given that the AK had very few weapons, little ammunition, and the Germans had plenty of everything and would crush a rising with the utmost ferocity. Unless the Red Army came promptly to the rescue, thousands of Poles would be slaughtered. But some AK leaders, aware that the Soviets had Polish collaborators in tow who were eager to set up a Communist government, argued that Poland must free herself from cruel German rulers if she were to have any chance of escaping rule by equally cruel Soviet rulers. As Andrzej Sitkowski (who fought in the AK) later wrote: 'this was the same Red Army that in collusion with Germany had invaded Poland in 1939. The Soviets had also executed thousands of Polish officers in Katyn [near Smolensk] in 1940.' Doing nothing 'would have meant handing the capital over to the Soviets and their puppets.'

At 5 pm on August 1st General Tadeusz Bor-Komorowski, head of the AK, ordered a rising against the Germans in Warsaw. A week earlier, the Soviet Foreign Office had declared that the Red Army's sole purpose was 'to help the Polish people to re-establish an independent, strong, and democratic state', and on July 29th Radio Moscow urged the citizens of Warsaw to join the battle. 'From that point', John Connelly wrote, 'everything went wrong that could go wrong.' Fewer than 30,000

---

[13] Norman Davies writes 'the Underground fighters who launched "the Warsaw Rising" did not themselves use the term. For reasons connected with developments on the Eastern Front, they called it "the Battle for Warsaw". It was only after the city had been destroyed, and especially after the war, that "the Warsaw Rising" or "Uprising" came to be widely used, but by different people for different purposes.'

Top left: Jack Slessor aged three months, in September 1897, with his mother Adelaide. *(Slessor family)*

Top right: Jack (centre) with his father Major Arthur Slessor and his brother Rodney, on their return to England in 1903. Rodney died in April 1945, aged forty-six. *(Slessor family)*

Bottom: At the Dragoon School in Oxford, circa 1910. *(Slessor family)*

Top left: The formroom block at Haileybury School as Jack would have known it. The inscription over the archway reads *ostium mihi apertum est magnum* (a great opportunity is open to me). *(Imogen Thomas)*

Top right: Jack as a Haileybury schoolboy in 1912 *(Slessor family)*

Bottom: Promotional photograph of a Haileybury dormitory in Slessor's day. *(Slessor family)*

Top: Slessor liked to doodle, even in his First World War logbook, though few of his efforts survive. Apart from airmen and aircraft, he evidently took a keen interest in ladies' footwear. *(RAF Museum, Hendon)*

Bottom: More examples of Slessor's artwork. The right-hand page includes his doggerel, 'Push off when the Hun is in sight'. *(RAF Museum, Hendon)*

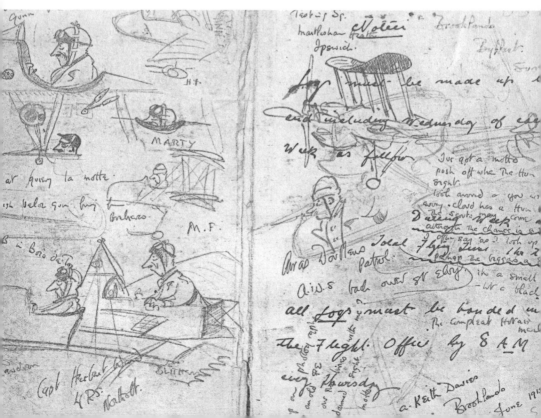

Top left: Lieutenant Slessor on leave in London during the summer of 1916, recovering from his adventures in Darfur (south-west of Khartoum) for which he would be awarded the MC.
(Slessor family)

Top right: Joachim Breithaupt commanded Zeppelin L.15, one of five which raided London on October 13th 1915. Slessor made what he later called 'a very amateur and wholly ineffectual' effort to attack L.15.
(Kenneth Poolman)

Bottom right: Self-portrait. The caption reads 'This officer has a regrettable preference for being improperly dressed. JCS, France, 1917.' *(Slessor family)*

"This Officer has a regrettable preference for being improperly dressed. JCS France 1917"

Court Leys,
Toot Baldon,
Oxford.

Top left: The three flight commanders of 5 Squadron at Acq, near Arras, on the First Army front in 1917. Slessor (centre) with Captain Smart on his right and Captain Illingworth on his left. (*Slessor,* Central Blue)

Top right: Thanksgiving service at Haileybury on Armistice Day, November 11th, 1918. (*Imogen Thomas*)

Bottom left: In April 1921 Slessor was sent to Parachinar on the North-West Frontier. As well as sketching soldiers and attempting to draw a camel, he enjoyed polo three times a week, tennis, fishing, shooting and cricket. (*Slessor family*)

Top left: With his son John at Farnborough, 1926. *(Slessor family)*

Top right: An action shot of Slessor taking part in the Staff College hunter trials in 1934. *(Slessor family)*

Middle: The Slessors' damaged bungalow in Quetta after the earthquake in May 1935. *(Slessor family)*

Bottom right: Waziristan (now north-east Pakistan) in December 1936. Slessor is on the far right. *(Slessor, Central Blue)*

Top left: Slessor upon being appointed Air ADC to the King in March 1939. *(Slessor family)*

Top right: As head of 5 Group, Bomber Command, in May 1941. This portrait, by Cuthbert Orde, has for years been a treasured possession of the head of the Air Historical Branch, Ministry of Defence. *(Slessor family)*

Bottom: The Hawker Henley, first flown in 1937. A sturdy single-engined two-seater, it was able to carry a useful bomb load far and fast, but only 200 were built and all were used merely as target tugs. *(J. Goulding and P. Moyes)*

Slessor upon being appointed head of Coastal Command, February 1943. *(Slessor family)*

Top: 5 Group was equipped with the Handley Page Hampden, a weapon of little value, used as a night bomber.
(J. Goulding and P. Moyes)

Middle: A Consolidated Liberator B-24. This plane made an essential contribution to Allied victory in the Battle of the Atlantic by sinking, damaging or frightening more U-boats than any other aircraft.
(RAF Coastal Command Year Book)

Bottom: With Captain D. V. Peyton-Ward, RN, the Admiralty's representative at Coastal Command Headquarters in 1943.
(Illustrated *magazine*)

Top: A Group Commanders' conference at Coastal Command Headquarters, Northwood, near Watford, in 1943. Slessor is in the centre. (*Slessor*, Central Blue)

Bottom: Slessor greeted by Tedder in January 1944 on arriving in Tunis to take up his new job as Deputy Commander of Mediterranean Allied Air Forces (MAAF). *(Owen A. Phillipps)*

Top: The end of Slessor's operational career. He left Marchionese, near Naples, on March 15th 1945 in his 'civilianized' B-25 Mitchell bomber. Slessor's PA, Lady Hermione Ranfurly (right) waves a temporary farewell. *(Owen A. Phillipps)*

Middle right: Lieutenant-General Ira C. Eaker, USAAF, was appointed head of MAAF in January 1944 with Slessor as his deputy. *(Slessor, Central Blue)*

Left: King George VI visiting Slessor, Commandant of the Imperial Defence College in London, in June 1948. *(Brig. T. I. G. Gray)*

Top: A magnificent seven of Old Haileyburians in 1948 at Old Sarum, Wiltshire. Left to right: Air Marshals Sir Brian Baker, Sir Arthur Sanders, Prime Minister Clement Attlee, AVM Geoffrey Pidcock, Slessor, Group Captain Harry Day, AM Sir William Dickson. *(Imogen Thomas)*

Bottom left: The portrait (which Slessor disliked) by A. R. Thomson, which hangs in the dining room at Haileybury. *(Haileybury School)*

Bottom right: Off duty with his dog Maxi at Strand on the Green, circa 1950. *(Slessor family)*

left: Shortly before taking over as CAS, 1950.
(Slessor family)

right: At Heathrow airport with Lady Slessor,
his way to meet General Eisenhower, 1951.
(Slessor family)

Bottom: Arriving at Westminster Abbey,
accompanied by Lady Slessor, for the Battle of
Britain memorial service in 1952. *(Slessor family)*

Top left: Slessor with an Australian friend in Brisbane, 1959. *(Slessor family)*

Top right: Three Blackburn Buccaneer low-level strike bombers. This aircraft proved so successful in Fleet Air Arm service from 1962 that by 1969 the RAF was obliged to accept it. (RAF Coastal Command Year Book)

Bottom: Slessor, far right, with Her Majesty the Queen, Prince Philip, and Slessor's son John far left, RAF Scampton, June 10th, 1963. *(Slessor family)*

Top: At Rimpton with his dog Sophie, circa 1975. Like most airman of his vintage, he preferred his RFC tie to all others.*(Slessor family)*

Bottom: The Avro Vulcan, pick of Britain's V-bomber force, capable of dropping nuclear weapons on Soviet targets, but here carrying a Blue Steel air-to-surface missile. (RAF Year Book, 1978)

Yousuf Karsh became one of the world's most famous photographers during and after the Second World War. A meticulous man, he caught Slessor looking his best, as CAS in 1950. (*Slessor*, Central Blue)

of the available 40,000 soldiers responded. 'They occupied several districts of the city, but failed to secure major strategic objectives, such as bridges and ammunition supplies. In less than a week, the AK had yielded the offensive, and began sacrificing block after city block in heavy fighting.'

By mid-September, Soviet forces were watching the fighting from positions across the broad, shallow and fordable Vistula river running through Warsaw. They did nothing to help the rising and Stalin even refused landing rights to British and American aircraft that were attempting to bring in weapons, ammunition, medical supplies and food. What was left of the AK surrendered on October 2nd. Along with the city's surviving civilians, they were taken to internment camps, and from there to slave labour in Germany. Most surviving buildings were then systematically dynamited, leaving Warsaw 'the most extensively demolished urban area in Europe.'

However, three points may be made in Stalin's defence that Slessor might have considered in his memoirs. Firstly, the Soviet offensive was halted not only at the Vistula but along a front stretching for hundreds of miles: a pause to re-equip and bring up reinforcements after such a long, rapid and costly advance was essential. Secondly, the Germans were still formidable enemies, and during the seven weeks after August 1st inflicted over 160,000 casualties on the Red Army: the impression – common in the west – that the army was enjoying a holiday during these weeks is entirely mistaken. And thirdly, it was in Stalin's interest to press on into Germany as quickly as possible. He had good reason to fear that the Germans would allow American and British forces easy victories in the west, perhaps even make a separate peace with Hitler, and so cheat the Soviet Union of the rewards of victory. 'He correctly believed', wrote Marshall Brement (an American diplomat and historian) 'that his postwar political position and the security of the Soviet Union would depend to a great extent on where the Red Army was physically located when hostilities ended.'

The months of August and September, Slessor recalled, were the worst of his career, despite the utmost gallantry shown by his airmen – Polish, British, South African – and by the Poles in Warsaw. They were fighting against 'the blackest-hearted, coldest-blooded treachery on the part of the Russians', and he hoped there might be 'some very special hell reserved for the brutes in the Kremlin who betrayed Bor's army, and led to the fruitless sacrifice of some 200 airmen of 205 Group and 334 Wing.' Although Slessor had good grounds for anger, the fact remains that Soviet prestige in 1944 was very great. Ruling circles in Britain and the United States were eager to back 'Uncle Joe' whatever he did (or did not do) because the final overthrow of Hitler's armies, weakened as they were, would take much longer and be much bloodier without the fanatical aggression of Stalin's hordes. Also, as Churchill and especially Roosevelt agreed, Poland lay within his 'sphere of influence' and her people, for all their bravery, had a long record as ill-disciplined nuisances (from the prejudiced viewpoint of their neighbours). But Stalin's refusal either to help Warsaw himself or co-operate with the Anglo-American air forces marked a turning-point. Here is where the Cold War began, as more and more members of those ruling circles were reluctantly brought to admit that 'Uncle Joe' was as vile a monster as Hitler.

In memoriam

During 1947, Slessor persuaded the Air Ministry to recognize the Polish Air Force Association and in December he was invited to be its patron. The association's members served Britain gallantly and skilfully on the ground as well as in the air in every European theatre from start to finish of the Second World War. They were men who were wise enough, or lucky enough, to avoid returning to a Poland now under the heel of another foreign tyrant. During Battle of Britain Week each September, Slessor would appeal for donations, however small, to be made to the association on behalf of 'the dauntless Polish airmen who, when their own country had been overrun, found their way out by devious means to carry on the fight at our side.'

Privately he thought the British government should have given more generous help, but he knew that was not going to happen. 'It is terribly difficult for many of these Poles to carry on – women as well as men, exiled from their native land and in many cases separated from their families.' By 1954, there were seven branches of the association in Britain, helping those in need. 'Many who apply to the association for aid', reported *The Times*, depend on National Assistance Board grants as their only income; most are the widows and elderly parents of killed airmen. In the past year, 157 applications for help reached the association from Poland. Requests for food, medicine, and clothing were most frequent, and 89 parcels of an average value of just over £4 were sent out in response. Officials in London state that these parcels reach without interference the families to whom they are addressed.'

The last of Slessor's many letters to *The Times* was about the Poles. On September 18th 1976, he wrote, 'a memorial is to be unveiled in London to some 14,000 Polish officers killed or missing in Russia during the Second World War, including over 4,000 butchered in cold blood at Katyn. Eight nations are to be represented, including the United States, France and Germany', but he had been told that a Foreign Office spokesman alleged that 'the responsibility for the Katyn murders is a controversial one, and the British government [of James Callaghan, a Socialist] cannot involve itself by formal representation at the unveiling ceremony. 'For gross bad manners and craven ingratitude', raged Slessor, 'this is surely unbeatable. It is, alas, only one more example of the sort of thing that makes it difficult nowadays to be proud of being British.' This,

his last letter, shows Slessor at his splendid best – as indeed did his conduct throughout the Warsaw Rising and his postwar efforts (unsupported by any government, Conservative as well as Socialist), to help the survivors of that terrible time. On May 1st 2004, when Poland became a member of the European Union, President Alexander Kwasniewski said: 'At last the Second World War is over.' Millions of Poles shed tears of joy that day, joined in spirit – one likes to think – by their good friend, Jack Slessor.

A sea change

However, back in 1944, Slessor was not blind to the failings of the Poles in London and Warsaw: 'tactless and stupid' as they sometimes were, or infuriating in their refusal to face up to military realities. He understood their refusal to talk to Russians (who murdered or deported many resisters prior to August 1st), but they also failed to discuss their plans with the British or Americans. Bor-Komorowski made four demands for 'indispensable' air support. These 'demands', Slessor argued, should have been made in time for the Polish general to be told that it was quite impossible to meet any of them, and his plans must therefore be changed.

Firstly, Bor-Komorowski wanted air raids on certain Warsaw suburbs, and also on Cracow and Lodz. Easily done by the Red Air Force; impossible for Allied bombers operating out of England or Italy, even with Soviet co-operation, which had been rarely, grudgingly and often ineptly provided for any military task during the past three years of 'alliance'. Secondly, he wanted Polish fighter squadrons to land in the Warsaw area and fight from there. A fantastic notion, for they could not have been kept supplied with fuel, ammunition or necessary servicing. Bor-Komorowski's third demand, for the Polish Parachute Brigade to be sent from England to Warsaw, was equally unrealistic. The transporting aircraft could not be escorted throughout such a long journey (out and home) and very few would have survived German flak or fighters. Bor's fourth demand, for air supply, 'was the only one that had a chance of being met,' wrote Slessor, but it was difficult and dangerous. The dropping-zones lay 7-900 miles from Allied bases in Italy – a very long way over rugged country, much of it still held by a well-armed enemy, with no help from ground radio stations and no weather information.

On the other hand, western air power was a crucial element in planning risings anywhere in occupied Europe. By mid-1944, all resisters knew that the Allies were able to supply them from the air, bomb airfields, disrupt troop concentrations and send in paratroopers. If, as was generally agreed, resisters must help Allied armies, the Allies must help resisters. Both sides paid special attention to capital cities. As Davies says, the Germans hung on to 'symbols of their all-conquering supremacy'; resisters wanted their capitals 'to emphasize the restoration of national independence.' Both Rome and Paris were liberated from within as Allied armies approached and the Germans fled. Why should that not happen in Warsaw?

Portal was reluctant to help: 'Our supreme task in the air was to sustain the battle which was being waged by Bomber Command, and which might prove decisive if we did not allow ourselves to be drawn away by less essential calls on our resources.' Despite pressure from Churchill, Eden and Lord Selborne (the Minister responsible for Special Operations Executive: SOE), just over 150 tons of supplies were dropped on Poland during the critical middle months of 1944. According to Harrison, 'Over 3,400 tons of supplies were dropped on Yugoslavia during the same period. The tonnage dropped to Poland was barely sufficient for a limited programme of sabotage, never mind an uprising.' In fact, SOE unwisely encouraged the Poles – both those in Warsaw and those in London – to expect more help than there was any prospect of them getting: 'neither SOE's Polish Section nor the VI Bureau (Polish GHQ) had it in them to tell the home army that, owing to the impossibility of providing adequate air support, their plans were plain rubbish.'

Slessor was advised by the Chiefs of Staff on August 3rd that a rising had begun in Warsaw, and that he should help if he could. Next day, he reported to Portal – with General Wilson's agreement – that 'air supply to Warsaw was not a practical proposition, even if the weather was favourable; the aircraft would have to fly part of the way out and back in daylight and, with the moon at the full, would be bound to suffer some loss en route; to drop supplies accurately from a low altitude over a city which was bound to contain AA and machine-gun defences would mean that only a few would get through, and much of the drop would fall into the wrong hand.' He pointed out that this project was the equivalent of the Russians attempting from bases in Poland to support a resistance group in Florence and urged Portal to make it clear to the Russians that they were far better placed to help the resisters. Nevertheless, he did send out 13 Handley Page Halifax four-engined bombers that night, to various points between Cracow and Warsaw, and five failed to return.

Although Slessor understood that political necessity must sometimes outweigh military practicality, he was convinced that the Russians would soon come to the rescue of the Poles. The Chiefs of Staff agreed and the British Mission in Moscow was told to discuss the rising, and how best to assist it, with the Soviet General Staff. Meanwhile, Polish pressure – from London and Warsaw – for immediate action became intense. The Polish Section of SOE even ordered Squadron Leader Waclaw Król of 1586 Flight to lead his men to Warsaw, but Slessor prevented him from doing so. The London Poles protested vehemently, Portal urged Slessor to give way – and he did so, reluctantly. Seven Halifaxes flew to Warsaw, some of their cargo reached the right hands, and all seven aircraft returned safely. This success proved to be, in the long run, a misfortune because it raised hopes that were bound to be dashed. Churchill was then in Italy and Slessor told him that if the Russians would not supply Warsaw the only sensible alternative was for the US Eighth Air Force to do it from England, and then fly on to land at bases in the Soviet Union.

Between August 12th-17th, 17 out of 91 aircraft sent from Italy to Warsaw failed to return. Another three, hit by flak, crashed on landing; many of the rest suffered damage and injuries to crew members; and most of the supplies carried at such cost did not reach the men, women and children resisting ever more desperately in the city. Slessor told Churchill on the 17th that they were beyond help, unless supplies could be sent from England or the Red Army chose to rescue them. The London Poles refused to see reason, however, and demanded the transfer of crews from 300 (Polish) Squadron in Bomber Command to Italy. Harris protested against what he – and Slessor – regarded as 'a useless political gesture'. But Sinclair and Portal pressed Slessor to permit flights with volunteer crews. More losses were suffered and few supplies got through. All told, in operations on 22 nights, 31 heavies were lost out of 181 despatched. There was even an equally useless military gesture to send out Short Stirlings, which were significantly inferior to the barely-adequate Halifaxes.

Flight Lieutenant Ryszard Chmiel left a vivid account of a gallant effort in near-impossible conditions on the night of August 20th-21st. 'We had been ordered to carry out the sortie regardless of weather conditions', he wrote. 'So, though the Met forecast was exceptionally despondent, we took off. It's funny how only the gloomy predictions come true: sure enough, right from the Yugoslav coast fog stretched from the ground to 6,000 feet above. Fog was hardly the word for it – water vapour or steam would be more appropriate. We had no navigational aid from the ground; I tried map reading at first but even rivers were so obscured that we finally flew on solely with star fixes.' In addition to these hazards, there were night fighters to look out for, intense ground fire, numerous searchlights to avoid, and the need to drop their containers from no higher than one hundred feet when at last they found Warsaw. 'We got through all the usual flak on the way home and landed safely at base. The other Halifaxes – five of them – that had taken off with us never returned. The Home Army people signalled that a supply was received on Krasinski Square on August 20th at the time we noted in our log book. So we knew that at least our flight had not been in vain.'

According to Norman Davies, this was 'one of the great unsung sagas of the Second World War.' In courage and skill, it ranks with the RAF's 'finest hours' elsewhere and yet it was on a very small scale, compared with the enormous number of American and British bombers sent out from England to Germany day after day, night after night. Was it not possible to send Slessor more bombers? Would he have accepted the Warsaw Airlift as a legitimate reason for diverting bombers from the assault on German targets? More could certainly have been done in the time available, though it would still not have been enough, given Soviet refusal to help, if

Churchill and Roosevelt had jointly insisted on relief being given top priority. Whether they should have done so are questions of strategy, politics and morality that Slessor did not explore in his memoirs.

The British Ambassador in Moscow, Sir Archibald Clark Kerr, reported to London on September 11th that the Soviet Union was now prepared to co-operate with its western allies in organizing aid to Warsaw. In daylight on the 15th, the US Eighth Air Force sent off 108 B-17s from England, but all were recalled because of very bad weather. During the night of the 17th-18th, 107 B-17s tried again. They dropped nearly 1,300 containers before flying on some 600 miles to Poltava, in the Ukraine. About 80 percent of these containers fell into German hands. No repeat operation was permitted and Roosevelt did not insist.

As early as August 15th, Slessor suspected that the Soviet failure to help the Poles was deliberate. He sent a long signal to Clark Kerr on the 18th, giving details of his efforts and asking him to press the Russians to help. On the 22nd, Vyacheslav Molotov (Foreign Minister) informed the Ambassador that the Soviet government objected to British or American aircraft landing in territory 'liberated' by the Red Army after dropping supplies over Warsaw. This meant, Slessor recalled, not only that American flights to Poltava were barred, but that British aircraft, even when damaged and with wounded men on board, had to face the long grind back through the enemy defences to their bases in Italy.

Molotov informed the Ambassador in November that the Soviet High Command had not been consulted before the rising, and would have advised against it: 'because by the time the Red Army reached Warsaw it was too tired to take the place by storm.' Slessor, by then, was convinced that 'the Kremlin never intended the rising to succeed.' Even if the Soviet ground forces were exhausted, Stalin could still have ordered his air force to drop supplies to the Poles and attack German targets outside the city; he could certainly have allowed American and British bombers use of airfields in 'liberated' territory.

Although the Anglo-American alliance with the Soviet Union held, there was what Gerhard Weinberg called 'a sea change at the top in both countries... There was nothing they could do in an area far from their military power and a few miles from the Red Army, but having themselves sent aid to the Soviet Union and to Marshal Tito's partisans, they remembered Stalin's attitude toward an independent Poland. And so did the people of Poland.'

Greece: liberation and civil war

In Greece, as in Yugoslavia, two rival resistance groups fought against the Germans – and against each other. The largest was devoutly Communist: EAM (its political arm), ELAS (its military arm) led by General Stephanos Saraphis. British leaders at first backed EAM/ELAS for the same reason that they supported Tito (he killed Germans), but Greek resisters produced no individual with Tito's authority – or with a Fitzroy Maclean to sell him to Churchill – and they gradually became convinced that Greek Communists were devoted Moscow lackeys, poised to seize power in Athens as soon as the Germans departed. 'There seems to be no limit to the baseness and treachery of ELAS', wrote Churchill to Eden as early as February 6th 1944, 'and we ought not to touch them with a bargepole.' The other resistance group – smaller and weaker – was no less devoutly Nationalist: EDES, led by General Napoleon Zervas. Although EDES was much more to Churchill's taste, he assured Eden in December 1944 that: 'We can easily at any time, when we are victors, compel obedience from the Right Wing by threatening to withdraw our forces.' But because EAM/ELAS was so strong, and eagerly killed Germans (as well as fellow-Greeks), the British Chiefs of Staff were readier than Churchill or the Foreign Office to avoid a break with the Communists. It would be a tragedy for Greece that no leader of Tito's stature in military and political affairs arose to harness opposition to the German occupiers and at least aim at national unity before and after they were driven out.

Churchill had presided over a meeting in Naples in August, attended by General Wilson, Admiral John Cunningham and Slessor, where it was agreed to form a force under Lieutenant-General Ronald Scobie to go into Greece with the support of the Balkan Air Force and the navy as soon as the Germans began to withdraw. This was Operation Manna. His main task was officially 'relief and rehabilitation', but he was also to help set up a civilian government, pursue the retreating Germans and – not least – prevent a Russian advance into Greece. As Baerentzen and Close state, 'Indeed, a British "interest" in the eastern Mediterranean including Greece was a policy of such venerable age – antedating by far the creation of the Greek state in the 1830s – that British politicians, diplomats, and soldiers often took it for granted.'

At another meeting in September the Greeks agreed that both movements would come under Scobie's orders. The plan included dropping a parachute brigade on airfields in the Athens area. Slessor objected. 'We were going into an Allied country', he said, 'to harass the retreating enemy and to help the Greeks to organize the relief and reconstruction of their country, which had suffered so sorely under the German heel.' He thought it 'slightly bizarre' to make such a fuss 'in an area that we had no intention of entering until the Germans had left it.' Slessor did not know – few people did – that when Churchill went to Moscow in October, he gave Stalin a paper with percentages of influence – British, Soviet – suggested for all Balkan countries. Stalin was to have Bulgaria, Romania, and half of Yugoslavia; Churchill to have Greece and control of the eastern Mediterranean. 'Stalin gave this paper a great blue tick. With that tick, EAM/ELAS went into the dustbin of history.' Consequently, for political reasons, Churchill ruled that the Allied return to Greece 'should be rather a showy affair.'

Greece was clear of Germans by early November, but heavy fighting had already begun and degenerated into civil war on December 4th, provoked – the British believed – by the Communists, who were now well supplied with arms and ammunition, thoughtfully left for them by the retreating Germans. Scobie, who, as Richard Clogg has it, 'lacked political imagination or recent combat experience', gravely under-estimated the danger and, like Churchill, thought a 'volley from British troops' would serve to restore order. Britons and Greeks were soon engaged in fierce street fighting and Churchill told Scobie – in a telegram leaked to the American press – that he must treat Athens as a conquered city. The Americans in Greece, already sharply opposed to British policy, now showed themselves to be ostentatiously neutral; the Soviets likewise stood aloof from this vicious conflict, unique in the Second World War, between erstwhile allies.

Alexander replaced Scobie with Major-General John Hawkesworth, who had recent Italian experience, and a brigade of 4 Indian Division was flown in from southern Italy to support him. As was often the way in the British army, Scobie was not fired, but stayed to remain responsible for the general direction of policy. The brigade was obliged to travel in the Liberator and Wellington bombers of 205 Group, thanks to the RAF's lack of a transport fleet – an aspect of air power insufficiently valued by Slessor and his colleagues in their pre-war planning. Slessor had supposed that airmen could do little to help soldiers in street fighting. 'I turned out to be quite wrong', he admitted: 'the Spitfires with their 20-mm cannon proved invaluable in close support of the troops... Moreover, most unexpectedly, the Beaufighter, of all things, proved a most accurate and effective street-fighting weapon.' Its crews became so adept they could be briefed to attack a particular house by giving them its street number. At Scobie's request, Slessor brought in 39 Squadron (Beaufighters armed with 60 pound high-explosive rockets) to hit the Averof prison, where ELAS had seized a British garrison and 700 rebels being held there. 'A rocket Beau blew a hole in the side of the ·prison through which a coach and four could have driven, and the men of 2 Parachute Brigade, who were concealed in the villas opposite, were across the boulevard and into the prison before the surviving defenders knew what had happened to them.'

On December 7th, however, Portal signalled Slessor from London to tell him that that day's *Evening Standard* claimed that a large group of guerillas west of Moulki were marching on Athens when Spitfires, patrolling at tree-top height, dispersed them by firing over their heads. Portal realized that the aircraft were operating under Scobie's orders, but he wondered if such restrictions merely encouraged ELAS rebels. 'I imagine also that half-hearted action by any of the armed forces cannot fail to cause doubt about our determination to see this business through.' Portal instructed Slessor to put these points privately to the Supreme Commander. He did so, but by this time his relations with Alexander were worse than ever.

Slessor had written to Portal on December 3rd about Alexander's proposed re-organization of the command. 'I can only think that Alexander cannot have very much idea of what goes on anywhere in or from the Mediterranean theatre other than within a few miles of the front line in Italy.' Worse still, he fails to realize that 'he is not a British General responsible to the War Office, but an international inter-service commander responsible to the Chiefs of Staff.' He knows nothing about the Balkan campaign and his intermittent interference merely adds to the problems we are facing there. He will have to learn that 'when one reaches the level of Supreme Command one cannot behave like a bull in a china shop – least of all an Irish bull in an Anglo-American china shop.'

On December 9th Churchill asked Portal to explain what Slessor meant by saying his communications with Air Commodore Geoffrey Tuttle (in charge of air operations) and Scobie 'are not of the best, which is understandable in the circumstances.' Not for the first time, Portal found himself admitting to Churchill that Slessor's messages were too long and contained 'certain irrelevancies', but as for communications, 'with the limited staff and W/T facilities which were included in the expedition, and with local commanders as busy as they must be with their daily work, Slessor does not receive from Greece the constant and detailed reports which one might expect from a well-established theatre of operations.'

'This damned Greek business is like a lead weight in one's heart', Slessor wrote to Hermione on December 19th. 'I hate every moment of it', but we could not let ELAS take over. 'Geoff Tuttle is doing very well', he thought, but 'I'm not very happy about Anglo-American relations. I'm afraid our temperamental cousins are going though one of their "lows", but I don't take things too tragically.'

Although Churchill was known to be obsessed with Greek affairs, he nevertheless astonished most of his advisers when he decided to attend to them in person. He arrived in Naples with Eden on Christmas morning and was met by Slessor and John Cunningham. He then flew on to Athens. 'Not even Churchill's great prestige could effect a deal, but he was now aware of the pressing need to establish a regency and, on his return to London, pressured King George into appointing Archbishop Damaskinos as regent.' The Prime Minister, George Papandreou, who had accompanied Scobie to Greece in October, was replaced by a general. 'The insurgency was essentially suppressed by military means, in which British control of the air was vital.' The liberation of Greece from Axis occupation, concluded Richard Clogg, 'proved to be the prelude to a bitterly-fought civil war (1946-9) which was to set back the process of postwar reconstruction for a further five years.'

Slessor visited Athens several times in January 1945 to consider the revival of a Greek air force. Although his American colleagues in the Mediterranean kept their deep reservations about British policies in

Greece (also in Italy and Yugoslavia) to themselves, Edward Stettinius – newly-appointed Secretary of State – announced publicly that it was US policy to encourage all liberated peoples to 'develop their own form of government without interference from outside.' As Slessor noted, Stettinius seemed unaware – in those days – that the Communists were determined to impose their own rule, if they could, and kill those who objected. According to Admiral William D. Leahy (formerly US Ambassador to Vichy France and one of Roosevelt's closest advisers), the civil war began as a result of 'active and aggressive action' by the British.

Some Britons, added Slessor, were equally foolish in failing to see in ELAS 'a gang of the most bloodthirsty cut-throats that ever existed.' 'I think we must remember', he wrote to Sir Edward Grigg (Minister of State in the Middle East) in March 1945 'that even the most pro-British American has been brought up against a vivid background of sturdy settlers being driven by Imperialist oppression to take up arms to defend their freedom against the redcoats. The British, when outside the British Isles, are always in the wrong. What happened in Greece in 1944 was just the British up to their old games again, just like North America in 1776, and the ELAS cut throat at Kiffisia [suburb of Athens] was just the same sort of chap as the rugged colonial of Bunkers Hill.'

These rather light-hearted, though perceptive, remarks contrast sharply with the very real concern Slessor had expressed to Portal some three months earlier in two letters, of December 12th and 15th 1944. In the first he said 'the days when HMG could send a cruiser to Constantinople or wherever it might be, without by your leave to anyone, are dead whether we like it or not. The US (and incidentally the Dominions) are entitled to insist on that.' In his better moments, Churchill knew this as well as Slessor, but he was most reluctant to admit it. The Greek affair was not merely a military shambles, it caused severe and long-lasting harm to relations between Whitehall and Washington. Slessor, observing it at close range, had both the knowledge and the intelligence to compose a devastating analysis, but his memoirs appeared long before he had the time to reflect calmly and deeply on any of the great events of his lifetime.

The second letter was provoked by Churchill's insistence on appointing Alexander to succeed Wilson as Supreme Allied Commander in the Mediterranean. He did this against the wishes of senior officers in all three services, British and American, who knew Alexander for an idle lightweight of undoubted charm and little intelligence. The Americans already suspected that Alexander received instructions direct from Churchill, behind their backs, and if this were confirmed, 'there will be hell to pay, and this system of command will break down, to the permanent prejudice of Anglo-American relations.' Portal agreed, and with his fellow-Chiefs continued the arduous task of limiting the circulation of the ailing, frustrated Prime Minister's worst blusters and keeping his favourite general on a tight rein.

Slessor's part in the liberation of Greece and defeat of Communists there was recognised in August 1946 when he fronted up at the Greek Embassy in London to be awarded the Grand Cross of the Order of the Phoenix by the King of the Hellenes. After the war, Slessor's wife took a particular interest in Greece, as he did in Poland. 'The RAF does not forget its friends', Hermione wrote in July 1951. 'Unfortunately we cannot help everyone who has helped us. So we have thought it best to adopt this one village,' Aidhonokhori, near the airfield at Yanina in Epirus. 'These Greek frontier villages have had an appalling time since 1940. Aidhonokhori is typical. Four times it has been sacked, its homes burnt and its villagers murdered by the invader and by the Communist enemy.' She appealed to all readers of *The Times* to send her parcels of food and clothing or money to buy essentials. In November, that newspaper was able to tell readers that a grand total of £3,750 had already been raised, together with about 350 cases of clothing, shoes and household goods.

Meanwhile, Slessor left his last operational command in March 1945. Harold Macmillan called on his successor, Guy Garrod, on the 29th. 'He was friendly and pleasant; but he is not quite the character that Jack was.' During his time in the Mediterranean, Slessor attended numerous meetings with Macmillan, who said of him as early as March 1944 that he was 'concise, firm, hitting every nail on the head – the most impressive of the lot.' In May, when he thought Alexander was missing his chances, he did not fail to say so publicly. In short, concluded Macmillan in January 1945, Slessor 'is a very clever and co-operative man.'

In November 1946 Slessor was invited to comment on Wilson's official account of the Greek campaign. 'I really do hope and trust', he began, 'that in the interests both of historical accuracy and of Field Marshal Wilson's reputation, the War Office will not publish this so-called despatch.' Slessor had made it perfectly clear to Churchill, he said, that he had no transport aircraft to permit an airborne descent upon the Athens area as part of his 'showy affair'. Eaker 'was under orders from his Chiefs of Staff not to engage American forces in the Greek affair at all – indeed that was the policy of the Combined COS at the time – it was to be a purely British affair; except, of course, that the Americans were to cash in and get the credit by organizing relief. Mr Churchill then decided that he would make a personal appeal to the President to allow US transport aircraft to take the British airborne brigade in and I spent the afternoon in his bedroom at the Villa Reale with him while he composed a despatch to the President telling him of the object of the exercise and asking him for the use of the American aircraft. This request was granted by the President personally, and the reason why that is so important is that it disposes of any suggestion (and the Americans made many of them when we got into trouble in December) that this was a purely British venture which did not have sanction from American authority.'

CHAPTER 15

SLESSOR'S NEXT APPOINTMENT

Air Member for Personnel?

On May 25th 1944, Air Chief Marshal Sir Wilfrid Freeman (now Chief Executive at the Ministry of Aircraft Production) wrote to Portal about the front runners for an Air Member for Personnel (AMP) to replace Sir Bertine Sutton. It had always been an important Air Ministry position and would become more so, as an end to the war began to look likely. AMP would have to arrange for the systematic release of thousands of officers and men, while at the same time trying to retain key personnel for demanding postwar tasks. Freeman thought Slessor 'as good as Tedder in almost every respect. I am inclined to think he would be much better as a future CAS than as an AMP. He has the advantage that he can be spared almost at once. He is a snob... He is rather inclined to be intolerant of people who are not quite as quick on the uptake as himself. To a certain extent, therefore, he is an intellectual snob. He is inclined to make mistakes now and again and disinclined to admit them even when they are obvious to himself. His wife is dangerously indiscreet, although I am quite sure she would never hear operational matters discussed in her presence; it would not be the same thing where personalities were concerned.'

Overall, Freeman thought Slessor 'the only possible choice for CAS', after Portal, 'and in this respect would be far better than Tedder.' Portal evidently welcomed his former right-hand man's opinions about personalities near the top of the RAF, though he made his own decisions. In this case, Freeman's bizarre suggestion that Slessor could step into Tedder's shoes as Deputy Supreme Commander within a few days of the launching of the greatest combined operation in history indicated how far Freeman had drifted away from reality. Slessor's next appointment would be as AMP – but Portal made it very clear to Churchill (and then to Attlee) that Tedder should be the next CAS.

Portal had been on the receiving end of many very long messages from Slessor and was acutely aware of his massive self-confidence. 'Slessor, as you know can teach everyone else their job very easily and well,' he wrote to Sinclair in June. Keith Park, then commanding in Cairo, had quarrelled bitterly with Slessor during 1944 and would have agreed with Portal. As early as June 29th, Portal had told Eaker that Slessor might soon be brought back to England, but Slessor did not learn that he was to go until November – and that his replacement would be Park. Slessor's response was only too typical. 'I am not awfully happy about him in this job', he informed Portal. 'Have you considered Norman Bottomley as an alternative?' He admitted that Park 'has come on a lot since early this year, but he's a bit slow on the uptake and had very little experience of strategic planning, which is a rather important part of the job here.' Portal's response – silence – was equally typical.

As it happened, Sinclair was reluctant to appoint Slessor as AMP. 'I fully share your high opinion of Slessor's dynamic qualities', he told Portal on September 2nd, 'but all qualities have their defects and I think that his would be serious in such a post as that of AMP. His imagination, his wealth of ideas, his forcefulness in argument and his clarity of expression on paper will all be invaluable in the high councils of imperial strategy after the war and in command or in high staff appointments during it. The new AMP ought to remain in his job for two or three years, and I cannot help thinking that it would be a pity to lock Slessor up in that office at this critical period.' But Churchill insisted that Slessor remain where he was until March 1945.

Air Commander, South-East Asia?

Sir Trafford Leigh-Mallory, en route to Kandy in Ceylon (now Sri Lanka) as Allied Air Commander, South-East Asia Command, had just been killed in November 1944 in a flying accident, and Slessor immediately offered to replace him. He was only just finding his feet in a massive command, and yet he was already happy to depart for yet another job about which he would know nothing on arrival. Portal, however, chose Park to succeed Leigh-Mallory because, as he told Sinclair, 'Park probably has the better operational sense, just as Slessor has the better political and strategical sense', and the war against Japan was then expected to last until some time in 1946, offering ample scope for Park's particular strength. 'Park will give three-quarters of his time to the air force and one-quarter to the higher strategy, politics, etc., with which Mountbatten [Supreme Allied Commander, South-East Asia] is primarily concerned. Slessor on the other hand will probably give two-thirds of his time to matters of higher command and strategy, and one-third to the RAF. Park is the more inspiring leader and will probably get more out of his subordinate commanders than Slessor, simply because he will see more of them and know more about what they are doing. Slessor on the other hand will probably get on better with the Americans, the Government of India and with Mountbatten (unless they hold different views on strategy, in which case we can look out for trouble).'

Slessor was deeply miffed both at being overlooked himself and at the further elevation of an officer whom he regarded with contempt and expressed his surprise in another long letter to Portal in December. However, he was nothing if not magnanimous: 'no doubt you have weighed up all the pros and cons of that.' Such was Slessor's high regard for his own opinions that he would have been even more surprised if Portal had objected to being thus patronized.

Slessor then moaned to Freeman about Park's appointment. 'I agree with all you wrote about Park', replied that sour creature: 'there is no doubt that he is loyal and hardworking, but he is stupid.' This from one excellent deskman to another, men for whom bureaucratic skills were indeed the highest form of intelligence; men who would not have known where to begin if given the responsibility for commanding fighters either in the Battle of Britain, Egypt, Malta or anywhere else. Freeman went on: 'You will see that you and I are at one on this question of senior appointment and generally speaking Boom [Trenchard] agrees with us.' Trenchard, of course, was long retired and undeniably 'stupid', as his strident advocacy of 'strategic' bombing in 1939-40 sadly demonstrates, confirmed by his bizarre memorandum to the British Chiefs of Staff in May 1941 about German morale. In any case, serving officers had no business consulting him about appointments even if he had not been ignorant of modern air power, men and materials.

Oxford professor?

Slessor sent Portal yet another very long letter, this time hand-written about his personal affairs, on September 12th 1944. It was a time when Portal was over his ears with worries about the faltering progress of Operation Overlord. Slessor had persuaded himself that he was in the running for a Chair in Military History at Oxford University after the war. 'It has for some years been my secret and cherished ambition', he confessed to Portal, despite the fact that he had never even attended a university, let alone obtained a degree. 'I have no [service] ambitions', he went on, 'and, if I had my way, would clear out as soon as the war is over', but it would be 'false modesty' were he to pretend that he would not also be in the running for senior positions in the postwar RAF.

At Oxford, however, Slessor believed that 'no don is ever unduly burdened by his professional duties', and there would be many servicemen undergraduates whom he could get thinking on the right lines about air power. He would also be able to assist in the compilation of official histories and writing for the newspapers. Slessor did not get a Chair, nor any other academic position, nor did he take part in the writing of official histories, but in September 1944 fancies that were equally absurd filled his mind. 'I believe there is nothing against a professor being a Member of Parliament', he told Portal, 'and I have before now considered standing for Parliament if I could find anyone mug enough to get me a nice safe seat.' For all his air power enthusiasm, Slessor was in other respects very much a man of the Victorian Age when, at times, comfortable offices could be 'found' in Church, State or Oxbridge for suitable gentlemen with useful family connections.

He hated bothering Portal personally at this busy time, 'but I think possibly this matter has some importance to the RAF. I have asked Boom's advice, but shall abide by your decision.' The matter was urgent – at least in Slessor's mind – because he had his eye on a nice house in Iffley which was to come up for sale in October. If Portal thought Slessor should stay on, would he consider seeking the appointment himself? Or commending Edgar Ludlow-Hewitt? Portal's reply, if any, has not survived. The letter is most revealing about Slessor's flaky grip on reality outside service circles. Apparently he believed that 'selective and controlled nepotism', which got him into the RAF, would now waft him into Oxford and even the House of Commons. This is a man, remember, who thought many other senior officers – in all three services – were stupid.

Air Member for Personnel

Portal had decided by December 1944 that Slessor should put Oxford and/or Westminster behind him and return yet again to the Air Ministry, this time as Air Member for Personnel. But Churchill, who disliked the RAF's enthusiasm for shuffling its senior officers from one position to another at short intervals, wanted written reasons before he would agree to Slessor's departure from MAAF. Having consulted Portal, Sinclair did as the Prime Minister asked on December 17th. 'A strong, fresh and imaginative officer is now required' as AMP, wrote Sinclair. 'The demobilization period will be difficult and perhaps stormy. Our plans for educational and vocational training, for release, and for cutting down the wartime RAF will test the capabilities of the ablest officer we can find in the always exacting post of AMP.' Above all, he concluded, 'a major share of the task of building up the new peacetime air force on sound lines will fall to him.' Churchill was unconvinced and so Slessor remained in Italy for another three months.

As AMP from April 1945 until September 1947, Slessor would spend more than two exhausting years managing an efficient system of release and at the same time trying to retain enough experienced officers and men to permit the RAF to meet its world-wide obligations. He was rewarded on New Year's Day, 1946, with promotion to the rank of Air Chief Marshal (full General). These obligations remained ill defined in the uncertain postwar years, as did the terms of service for regulars and short-term conscripts. Slessor well remembered the chaos following the Armistice in November 1918. Matters were handled much more skilfully and sensibly after the Second World War ended. He paid tribute to Ernest Bevin (Minister of Labour) and to Air Vice-Marshal John Cordingley (Director-General of Manning): he 'held my hand in Kingsway, and I'm sure prevented me from doing too many silly things as AMP.' The 'Demobforms' were a great success, setting out situations in simple, accurate language, although 'Misunderstandings were bound to arise', Slessor recalled, 'too often thanks to the chicken-witted muck-rakers of some sections of the popular press.'

These 'misunderstandings' were rife in India and South-East Asia, as Park informed Slessor in October 1945. Slessor drew his attention to a statement in the House of Commons by John Strachey (Under-Secretary of State for Air). An immense transport task faced the RAF during the next nine months, said Strachey, when over one million service personnel had to be moved – most of them brought home, but many sent out to replace them. A larger proportion of airmen than of other servicemen must therefore be retained to do this, which was not a task for recruits. Park told Slessor later that month that he had addressed large gatherings of airmen in Bangkok, Saigon, Hong Kong, Kunming, Calcutta and Madras and found general acceptance of Strachey's statement. The fact remained, however, that when airmen were released, they were likely to find army and navy men in the civilian jobs they had hoped to get. Park thought the government should guarantee jobs to airmen on late release, or permit them to stay on in the service until work was available. He also recommended that the tour of duty overseas be reduced to three years and told airmen at several mass meetings that the Air Ministry had agreed to accept his recommendation. Slessor thought he had gone too far. There was no prospect, he told Park on November 20th, of the tour being reduced to three years in the near future and he denied that he had ever mentioned such a reduction. Park retorted that Slessor had in fact agreed on August 2nd and that it should become effective on April 1st 1946. Park was right, Slessor wrong.

During January 1946, there was serious unrest at several stations in India and Singapore, which kept Park busy though privately he was not too distressed: 'Better than 1919 by 90 percent', he wrote in the margin of one letter. On February 7th he received an unusually encouraging signal from Slessor who was sure, he said, that the situations were being well handled by all concerned. Park had Slessor's fullest confidence and would not be receiving orders because he was best placed to know what to say and do. Slessor would offer advice, send information, and try to keep the press in order. These exchanges brought the two men closer together than they had ever been and they would remain on good terms after Park was required to leave the RAF in September. At first, Park blamed Slessor for what he considered his premature retirement, but Tedder (now CAS) made it clear that the decision was his.

By December 1946, demobilization was largely completed. Over 4,250,000 men had been released since VJ-Day and of the 750,000 who remained in uniform, many were on regular engagements. As for the related problem of building a postwar air force, Slessor was unable to get from the Treasury authority 'even for an interim establishment, on which to give permanent commissions or long-term engagements.' He was therefore restricted to 'the very obsolete prewar' figures. Another depressing duty was the need to retire many good officers, made worse by the fact that he was unable to ensure that their pensions kept pace with an ever-rising cost of living. However, one moment of unalloyed pleasure came his way in October 1945 when he was able to present wings to his own son, John, at Cranwell's first passing-out parade since the war. Young John – not known as Jack – made his career in the RAF and retired in January 1978 as a Group Captain.

Among those officers leaving the service while still full of life was the famous head of Bomber Command, Sir Arthur Harris. Slessor wrote to Sinclair and Portal on May 17th 1945 about the prospect of finding a colonial governorship for him. Meanwhile, he should be sent on leave and relieved of his command as soon as possible. He is not well, and 'his staff are finding things very difficult, as he feels his job is done and finds it hard to take an active interest or give the necessary decisions now that the spur of active operations is no longer present.' He had said he would not accept another RAF job, but he needed something for he only turned 53 that year. Slessor suggested sending him and his wife to southern Africa for three months. 'I would suggest telling him frankly that this is designed to give him a rest in his own part of the world and that we should not expect him to do much in the way of work, while we looked for something permanent. Perhaps Bermuda? I believe he would do it all right', Slessor went on, 'though I admit he would probably be a great nuisance to the Colonial Office.'

Nothing came of that suggestion, and a month later – on June 20th – Slessor wrote again to Portal, this time about the possibility of appointing Harris as Inspector General of the RAF. He would not take it on, said Slessor, and if he did, 'would do more harm than good. He is an entirely selfish man and is gravely lacking in balance and judgement.' This is a severe dismissal of a man whom Slessor recommended as Governor of Bermuda! 'I don't think he is capable of curbing his tongue', he continued, 'or suppressing his own individuality in the interests of the service as a whole... Anyway, he is a sick man and has never been any good at going round units.' Nevertheless, concluded Slessor, 'We must do everything possible to get him some suitable job after retirement – though his own violent and intolerant personality is the worst impediment.'

Freeman wrote to Portal on August 1st 1945. Portal had shown him this letter from Slessor, which was 'a nasty shock and the shock doesn't get less. It's almost unthinkable that a man holding that position should have written in that sense. Supposing his name is proposed and the Secretary of State asks his views – then in my view AS [Archibald Sinclair] would be right to object and say why he does so. He, JS [Jack Slessor] has done himself sufficient harm by having that Ranfurly woman in his office and now comes this. There is a great deal in Tedder's contention that JS is still very unstable.' Hermione Ranfurly had been Jumbo Wilson's Private Secretary. She later acted as Slessor's Personal Assistant in Algiers, Caserta and London, becoming a particular friend. Self-confident, assertive and (like Tedder's second wife) far from deferential towards Freeman, she naturally incurred the same hearty dislike.

As soon as the war ended, the army head, Alan Brooke, resumed his agitation for aircraft to meet what he called the army's 'domestic needs': in particular, communications, reconnaissance and casualty evacuation. 'If we give way at all', wrote Slessor to Portal on November 1st 1945, 'we should draw an absolutely firm line under the light unarmed single-engined aircraft. Once we go beyond that we open the floodgates and there will be no stopping it.' But army and navy pressure gradually proved irresistible. In May 1954, at the request of his successor, Dickson, he expressed his views on helicopter policy. The army should have them, but let us not 'go mad about helicopters and rush to extremes just because the Americans (who are notoriously extravagant and very rich) are doing so. But if the General Staff can make a case (as I think they can) that helicopters are essential to enable the modern British army to fight the sort of wars it may have to fight in our day, and the Chiefs of Staff agree – then they should be provided.' But they must remain part of the RAF: 'a lorry can belong to any service because it does its work on the ground where we all live. An aeroplane exists to do its work in the air; it must be controlled operationally by the Air Force Commander' and a helicopter 'is an aeroplane.' A decade later, in August 1964, Slessor had his say about 'the present craze for helicopters.' They obviously had many uses, but would be useless in wartime even if the Allies had air superiority because they are such easy meat for ground gunners. They were, moreover, increasingly acquired by the other services and thereby offended the Trenchardist principle that only airmen should operate aircraft.

Throughout his time as AMP, Slessor spoke frequently at Air Council meetings about intractable problems which filled his working day: recruiting, training, paying, accommodating and retaining skilled officers and men, serving on the ground as well as in the air. There were times when the recruitment situation was 'well nigh desperate', but he also thought the RAF was 'extremely wasteful of manpower' and could use what it had far more efficiently. Although he often got Council support, what really mattered was Treasury support, and that was very hard to obtain in cash-strapped Britain after a colossally expensive war.

Tedder's unofficial adviser
However demanding his work as AMP was, Slessor always found time to keep an eye on all other branches of the RAF and especially on any aggressive move, as he saw it, from either the Admiralty or the War

Office. In March 1946, for instance, he wrote to Tedder (and others) about an Admiralty plan to control all air forces allocated to operations over the sea. But control of the Atlantic, argued Slessor, 'depends primarily today on our ability to occupy and hold Iceland, the Azores, Gibraltar and West Africa and to deny the French and Spanish ports to an enemy. The control of the Mediterranean depends entirely on our ability to control the North African coast and to maintain air superiority against air forces based on the European lands to the north. The control of the Red Sea depends on our ability to deny Egypt, the Sudan, Somaliland and Arabia to a potential enemy. And so on. So let us forget this phrase "control of sea communications" in this connection. Actually, the control of sea communications is the heart and core of all British imperial strategy and as such the authority responsible to HM Government is the Chiefs of Staff.' Clearly, Slessor did not foresee any diminution of Britain's role as a first-class imperial power, even at the end of a war that left her heavily in debt to the United States and facing massive tasks at home, to remove bomb damage, build houses and factories, educate children, prepare ex-servicemen and women for peacetime employment, modernize obsolete industries and earn money from overseas trade.

A few weeks later, in May, he wrote to Tedder again – the usual long, rambling, thoughtful, but unsolicited note – to counter Admiralty criticism of the RAF's conduct in the war at sea. His note traced 'a long wrangle' beginning in 1937 when the government separated the Fleet Air Arm from the RAF leading to a current request that all 'maritime' squadrons be placed under the operational control of the local naval commander. In Slessor's view, such a request threatened that integrity of air power 'on which this nation today and tomorrow doth chiefly depend for its continued existence.' The Air Staff must therefore take up this challenge 'and contest it with all the vigour at their disposal.' As Slessor argued, 'Where is the great potential enemy battle fleet against which we must train a large, highly-specialized FAA, versed in all the tactics and techniques of the type of naval battle which has not taken place since Jutland and which I firmly believe will never take place again?'

No sensible airman, he insisted, would be found to decry 'the magnificent services' of the Royal Navy during the recent war, but 'it would be fatal to drift back into the atmosphere of inter-service strife which, in the thirties, did so much to poison inter-service relations and, incidentally, contributed materially to the disasters of the early war years.' But appeasement, he continued, was no more effective in inter-service than in international relations. And when it was suggested that control of sea communications was the 'exclusive responsibility' of the Admiralty, or that air operations against enemy naval units or merchant shipping could only be conducted by men trained from youth in the navy, 'then that is flying in the face of all modern experience.'

According to Slessor, more than 80 percent of the enemy surface vessels over 400 tons sunk or damaged in Home Waters should be credited to airmen, including 50 of the German heavy ships. In the Mediterranean, over 700 enemy vessels were destroyed – not by specialized squadrons alone but more by, for instance, rocket Hurricanes that yesterday were attacking German land forces in Yugoslavia or Wellingtons that tomorrow would be attacking Rommel's communications in the desert. Virtually all the offensive mining which took such a terrible toll of German shipping, 'and which called for a degree of precise navigation at sea that in 1937 would have been claimed by the Admiralty as the exclusive property of the professional sailor, was done by Bomber Command.'

As for the U-boat, 'greatest of all dangers to our sea communications', the RAF sunk half of those claimed by British forces. In 1943, Slessor told Tedder, 'Coastal Command sank 83, more than the surface ships of the British and American navies put together; and we have it on Doenitz's own authority that but for the Bomber Offensive, the Mark XXI U-boat (which might have reversed the decision of 1943) would have been at sea by the autumn of 1944 – a fact which Doenitz claimed might be said to have won the war for the Allies.' Slessor thought these facts enough to prove that young RAF airmen, 'who had never been in anything more nautical than a Channel steamer', were just as capable of operating over the sea as their sea-faring brothers. 'Finally they prove, what the Air Staff have consistently claimed and what the army fully accepted, that air operations are a matter for airmen, wherever they are conducted.'

Can it really be maintained, he asked in conclusion, 'that there is any justification whatever for the continued separation of the FAA from the RAF? This is not a matter between the RAF and the navy alone. It is a matter in which the army is vitally concerned', because these were days of extreme financial stringency. 'We cannot afford the men or money for these expensive luxuries, large overheads, reduplicated establishments and preparations for a type of war that can never recur... The Germans lost the war at sea largely because they did not concentrate on essentials, as Doenitz himself has told us. In particular, it is vital that we should never again find ourselves faced with the shortage of destroyers and escort vessels that was so nearly fatal at one stage of the late war.'

Slessor thanked Spaatz in May 1946 for sending him a copy of an excellent paper on strategic air power. 'I wish to God more people realized the truth of what you say. It is terrifying to me – the extent to which in one short year my country and yours have thrown away [sic] their one great war-winning weapon.' There was a report in the day's press about a loan to Britain by the US. 'Financially, I don't know how important that is', he admitted; 'politically, it seems to me profoundly important. The one hope for the future of the world today seems to me to be Anglo-US solidarity.'

In June Slessor sent Tedder (and others) a copy of his reaction to

Montgomery's paper on 'The Army Aspect of the Future Development of Combined Army/Air Force Action'. It was obviously written with the last 12 months of the European war in mind, when there was plenty of everything needed to overthrow the Third Reich. But 'we have got to face up to present-day realities and the impression grows as one reads through the paper that in the cold light of 1946 the Field Marshal is asking for the moon.'

Slessor was anxious to re-affirm the principle – already engraven on Tedder's soul – that it was the army commander's duty to state what he wanted done, in what order of priority, and the air commander's duty to get it done. 'I think this is really a question of intelligence and the proper integration of the air and army intelligence staffs', Slessor argued. He thought Tedder would agree that when there were differences of opinion between the soldier and the airman, it usually boiled down to questions of fact. 'An example which comes to my mind, which I think you will remember, was the argument about the bombing of the marshalling yards at Florence.'

Among other criticisms of Montgomery's paper, Slessor emphasized the army's resonsibility for constructing airfields. In the Mediterranean, as Tedder knew very well, 'if it had not been for the American army engineers, we should have been quite incapable of constructing the airfields that were essential in the back areas away from the Tactical Air Force zone.' Another point on which he and Tedder were in complete agreement was over Montgomery's demand for a specialized ground attack aircraft. 'If ever a policy was justified,' wrote Slessor, 'it was the policy which the Air Staff fought so doggedly in the teeth of War Office opposition, that the dual-purpose fighter-bomber was the answer to close support, and not the specialized dive-bomber.' And finally the two men were at one regarding Allied aircraft production policy. By agreement with the Americans, Britain 'did not produce transport aircraft, but concentrated on combat types; and though the Americans were very generous up to a point, they did not meet their undertakings to provide us with transport aircraft in sufficient quantities.'

Slessor thanked Tedder on June 3rd for letting him see a Joint Technical Warfare Committee report. He noticed that guided weapons were believed likely to render obsolete the strategic bomber travelling at nearly supersonic speeds in the stratosphere, but – according to Admiralty experts – the same weapons would not sink an aircraft carrier travelling at a mere 40-50 knots on the surface of the sea. He also thought it 'the very greatest mistake to have reduced our deception organization in the way we have; we were first-class experts at it in the war... I have always thought that deception should be maintained as a very special concern, under the same umbrella with SIS and SOE (in fact, I produced a paper to this effect in 1944 that I think you will find in your archives).' But if deception were to be revived, Slessor hoped that Brigadier Dudley Clarke would be put in charge.

On January 13th 1947, Slessor replied to Tedder, who had asked for his comments on a paper submitted to him. Firstly, it under-estimated the importance of strategic air power in the Mediterranean. Secondly, the Dominions must shoulder more responsibility for defence in peacetime. And thirdly, more work was needed on acquiring accurate intelligence. He was pleased with a paper composed in the Imperial Defence College, but dismayed at the suggestion that disarmament would be mutually beneficial. In his opinion, it would suit only the Soviet Union, with its vast reserves of expendable manpower, and thereby hand them the initiative.

Tedder had been invited to deliver four lectures in the prestigious Lees-Knowles series in February and March 1947 at Cambridge University. They were published as an Air Ministry pamphlet for service use in September and commercially in 1948 as a small book entitled *Air Power in War*, reprinted by the Greenwood Press, New York, in 1975. Tedder asked Slessor to read them before publication and offer comments. They were 'quite first class', replied Slessor on March 28th. 'I think it is extremely important that they should have a wide circulation to the service as soon as possible.'

At some later date he claimed in a marginal note that they were actually written by Bill Elliot (ACAS (Policy)) and his staff. Elliot, an outstanding officer and close to Tedder in these years, may well have been consulted about them, but they reflect Tedder's long-standing and often-expressed opinions – and do so in Tedder's distinctive voice. Slessor's comments added little of substance to an analysis with which he was in wholehearted agreement. It cannot often have happened (one hopes) that two fine senior officers with so much in common became so irretrievably estranged. Tedder made four points in particular. Firstly, that Britain and the US must not draw conclusions about military operations from a time of plenty in 1944-5 against an enemy already severely weakened by massive campaigns on the eastern front. Secondly, air power would be a 'dominant factor' in future wars, great or small. Thirdly, sea power would be vital as long as Britain remained an island. And fourthly, that an attempt at merely passive defence would be slow suicide.

Slessor sent Tedder a 'strictly private and secret' handwritten letter (eight pages) on April 6th 1947 about the government's decision to reduce the term of National Service from 18 to 12 months.[14] In his opinion, the decision was made for purely political reasons and seemed to him 'more than lamentable – I think it is very sinister.' It had 'seriously shaken' his belief that officers should implement government policy – even that of a

---

[14] The National Service Bill set service at 18 months. This was reduced to 12, following Labour Party pressure, but raised again to 18 months before the Bill came into force on January 1st 1949; after war broke out in Korea in June 1950 it was raised to two years.

Labour government – without question. Although Montgomery, head of the army, had agreed to the cut, Tedder had not, 'but what hope had you when the professional head of the army, who had previously made all the running for the 18 month term, lets you down as he did?' Montgomery had an 'olympian ignorance' of the essential details of the manpower problem and did not grasp the implications of his actions. The decision would cost the RAF about 25,000 men in any single year after 1949 – and, of course, the army many more.

It is difficult to know whether this or any other Slessor letter galvanised Tedder into action which he would not otherwise have taken. Given Tedder's concern for Britain's security and offensive capacity – not less than Slessor's – and the quality of his advisers, it seems unlikely. He agreed with almost everything Slessor wrote, although the sheer length and frequency of his messages must have made his heart sink, especially on a busy day. However, in this instance, Tedder wrote bluntly – and with typical brevity – to A.V. Alexander on April 11th. Press accounts of the discussion and decisions taken about the reduced National Service period were, he wrote, 'remarkable for their similarity and for their inaccuracy.' Alexander's claims that the Chiefs of Staff were given time to consider the proposal and that they agreed to it was 'of course, quite incorrect.' But it went through, for the time being.

Slessor had the great pleasure on June 27th 1947 of speaking at Haileybury, his old school. It was the first Speech Day, he said, 'since an event which will affect all your lives in the near future – I mean the decision of His Majesty's Government to introduce permanent compulsory National Service in peacetime.' This was nothing new, Slessor continued, for the Public School boy. 'For 12 out of the last 33 years, boys have had to accustom themselves to the idea of military service on leaving – in ten of those years it was for an indefinite period and with the virtual certainty that they would actually have to fight and maybe give their lives for their country.' But he was certain that that possibility 'has never deterred any man from this school. On the contrary, the fact that we were at war provided the great incentive; the cause for which no-one worth considering has ever hesitated to make any sacrifice; as so tragically many old boys of this school have proved. Today that great incentive is missing. But in my opinion a greater incentive and a no less noble cause will be yours – the prevention of war.' Slessor became a Life Governor and Member of the Council of his old school. He was President of the Old Haileyburian Society in 1954 and returned to Haileybury on several occasions to make much the same speech.

CHAPTER 16

THE SUCCESSION

Commandant, Imperial Defence College

On practically every issue that came before Tedder as CAS, he and Slessor were agreed. When Tedder chose to retire – he had not been appointed for a fixed term – it was supposed, not least by Slessor, that Slessor, who was seven years younger, would succeed him. His qualities, good and bad, had long been recognized. He had opinions on every aspect of past history, current problems, and future strategy in all three services, but he was incapable either of waiting to be asked for those opinions – or of brevity, when asked. He was usually friendly and helpful, especially to men with whom he had served or to junior officers in general, but he dismissed too many senior officers with a contempt that seems undeserved. Also, he rarely resisted the temptation to instruct senior as well as junior officers, and always at inordinate length. But he was a man of exceptional energy and ability with important contacts across the Atlantic. The differences between Tedder and Slessor were of style and manner, rarely of substance.

On June 13th 1947, Tedder sent a handwritten note to 'My dear Jack', inviting him to accept nomination as Commandant of the Imperial Defence College (IDC) in London. The invitation was obviously important and Tedder had no good reason for not discussing it in person with a man whom he regularly met, face to face, on other important matters. Outstandng medium-rank officers in all three services, British and Commonwealth, were there introduced to those inter-service and national issues that would concern them if they achieved high rank. No-one, Tedder assured Slessor, in any of the services could fill the post better. On the back of his copy of this letter, however, Tedder noted what he really thought of him: 'fluent, verbose, favourites, erratic, ambitious, personal publicity, political, clubs, conventional, snob, refusal to accept appointments.'

Even so, the offer was a good one. Since its foundation in 1927, there had been eight Commandants, only two of them airmen – Sir Robert Brooke-Popham (1931-2) and Sir Arthur Longmore (1937-8). It was high time for another airman and the position was, moreover, the closest in the

RAF to master of an Oxbridge college and thus entirely suitable for a 'fluent, verbose' man who had expressed a fancy for an academic career while the war was still to be won. 'There is no-one in any of the services who can fill the post with the same standing and authority as you can,' wrote Tedder, 'and I know your appointment would command universal approbation with the General Public as well as throughout the services.'

But Slessor only turned 50 in June 1947 and was unwilling to accept any position, however agreeable, that might weaken his prospects of succeeding Tedder. Although well aware that the office was not in the holder's gift – CAS proposed, Prime Minister disposed – he thought of the IDC job as a last resting-place before retirement. He was mistaken. The current Commandant – Sir William Slim, a far more distinguished officer than Slessor – would succeed Montgomery as head of the army from 1948-52 and then served as Governor-General of Australia from 1953-60.

Slessor complained to Trenchard, Portal and Freeman, angling with their support for a promise – if not a guarantee – that if he accepted Tedder's offer he might later return to the Air Ministry as CAS. At Slessor's request, Freeman asked Tedder on June 13th what he had against him. His answers, reported Freeman to Portal, were unconvincing: 'he is influenced solely by a dislike for Jack, a strong wish to remain on, and by his wife.' Freeman passed on these opinions to Slessor, who wrote to Portal for advice on the 17th. He did not fancy the IDC job; he was tempted to retire at the end of the year; and he had no idea why Tedder disliked him. Portal then invited Tedder (though not in writing) to promise Slessor (though not in so many words) that he might become CAS when he, Tedder, retired.

Angered by all this nudging and winking, Tedder tried to pin Slessor down on June 19th. 'I am more sorry than I can say that he [Portal] should have given you such advice... To make any appointment – however senior – subject to an undertaking or promise as to subsequent appointments would, in my view, be to go against one of the fundamentals of our service code... As Trenchard put it when we were discussing things last night, "no-one can say who will go where two years ahead." To put the matter in its simplest terms – I believe it to be your duty to the RAF and to our national security to take charge of the IDC.'

These words shook Slessor, who protested that he had never sought a guarantee of the succession. After further correspondence, now involving Noel-Baker and Prime Minister Attlee, the words 'should not be passed over' were selected to apply to his prospects. He informed Noel-Baker and Tedder on July 10th that he had decided not to retire, and would accept the IDC appointment. 'I cannot pretend to enjoy the prospect of serving on in the circumstances as they are', he complained, but manfully did so – for another 29 months (until December 31st 1949) when Tedder at last retired. Hugh Saunders took over as AMP on October 1st 1947 and

Slessor succeeded Slim on January 1st 1948. The pill was more than sweetened in the glorious month of June when the King had lunch at the college with Slessor; he was made a Knight Grand Cross of the Order of the Bath (GCB); and he learned that he was to be the King's Principal Air Aide-de-Camp with effect from July 1st.

Sir Basil Liddell Hart, the military historian, wrote to Slessor in May 1965 to tell him that he had heard recently from Sir James Barnes, formerly Permanent Under-Secretary of State for Air, whom Slessor had recruited for his succession campaign. Liddell Hart sent Slessor a copy of his reply to Barnes. 'It may interest you to know that in 1948-9 I went on a round of visits to stay with the AOCs-in-C and found that they were inclined to argue against the appointment of Jack – so Tedder had evidently been active in swaying opinion. Their preference was for Ralph Cochrane. One of the reasons they gave against Jack's appointment was that he would be too inclined to defer to the other services, and not uphold the interests of the RAF strongly enough!' Liddell Hart may be mistaken in supposing that the AOCs-in-C needed 'swaying' by Tedder, when they were quite capable of making up their own minds. He is certainly mistaken in supposing that Slessor would 'defer' either to the Admiralty or to the War Office: 'oppose', root and branch, is a word far closer to his natural instincts.

A year later, in 1966, Slessor set down what he then remembered – less what he had forgotten – about these agitating events. 'I admit I should have been happier if anyone other than Tedder had taken over from Portal as CAS. I had known him for many years[15] and am afraid I had never liked him. I had never been at ease with his extraordinary manner – a sort of compound of nonchalant detachment, mischievous impishness and roguish humour which baffled and irritated me.'

Setting aside Tedder's 'extraordinary manner', the issue which most grated with Slessor concerned the Malcolm Clubs. Founded by Tedder and his second wife, Toppy, in Algiers in July 1943, to offer airmen a higher standard of comfort, food and drink than the basic NAAFI, fare that most generals and some air marshals thought sufficient for 'the men', there were ultimately over a hundred clubs, formed into a self-financing charity. One is surprised that Slessor – wise and humane as he often showed himself – did not wholeheartedly approve of the Tedders' splendid achievement, but it is a sad fact that many senior officers (especially Whitehall Warriors, ancient or modern) waged a long campaign to close them down. Nevertheless, they outlived both Tedder and Slessor, who bitterly recalled the 'tiresome trouble' he had 'about those damned Malcolm Clubs', which became 'a perfect nuisance to me.'

---

[15] This is not so. They met, briefly, for the first time in Singapore in February 1937; again briefly in Tunis in January 1944; and only began to serve together in January 1946, while Slessor was AMP and when Tedder became CAS.

Slessor came to believe that only his friendship with one Lancie Royle, Chairman of NAAFI, prevented 'a real row between the NAAFI, the army and the RAF over these clubs.' In precisely what particulars they offended him and others, he was unable to say.

Slessor regarded Tedder as 'an under-bred bounder', an amusing insult when set down in 1966, though perhaps a fitting one from a man of Victorian tastes who was a life-long advocate of 'judicious and controlled nepotism.' Although Tedder's father ended his life as a Knight of the Realm and a Companion of the Order of the Bath, he achieved both distinctions by mere effort and his father was undeniably a grocer, so Slessor's verdict may have some merit. Three years later, in 1969, Slessor had persuaded himself that his move to the IDC was fortunate. 'I still believe it to be an ideal prelude to becoming one of the Chiefs of Staff', he wrote, 'and think it a pity that Slim and I are the only two who have enjoyed that advantage.' Tedder's 'mischievous impishness and roguish humour' would have relished these words – it may be that even Trenchard, Portal, Freeman, Noel-Baker, Barnes and Attlee would have raised a wry smile.

Calm before storm

Slessor wrote to Tedder on October 26th 1948 about command in the Atlantic, one of his favourite hobby horses. He believed that the North Atlantic must be treated as a single battlefield – not a divided one, as in 1943. There should be a Supreme Commander, North Atlantic; he must be an American sailor with an RAF deputy, and his headquarters must be in Britain. In a covering letter, he commended Tedder's memorandum on the subject: 'admirable – it exactly reflects the feeling which has steadily grown upon us during a series of exercises [at the IDC] this year.'

In November 1948, Slessor delivered a lecture at Camberley on 'The Development of Air Power: A Lecture Mainly Designed for Army Officers.' During the Battle of the Atlantic, he began, Coastal Command played a vital part in defeating the U-boat. Without that victory in 1943, Operation Overlord could not have been launched. 'There you have air power, working away unseen, hundreds and hundreds of miles away out there in the North Atlantic, unheard of, unknown to all but a very few soldiers – yet exerting an influence on their destiny and on their capacity to fight, just as surely and vitally as the Spitfires and rocket Typhoons that were a daily commonplace in their lives when action was joined.'

The 'primary agent' of air power, said Slessor, is the bomber: but 'our actual practical experience of air power is infinitesimal compared to our knowledge and experience of sea or land warfare. After all, we have been fighting at sea and on land for thousands of years; we have a vast literature on the subject; and certain principles have emerged from the experiences of hundreds of great sea and land commanders of all nationalities.' The air situation was different. 'I'm not a very old man [he was then 51], but the first aeroplane made its first flight when I was a small boy, and it isn't 40 years yet since the first man flew the English Channel and we, to our great misfortune, ceased to be an island.'

'Although we are still learning about air power, we can safely say that the methods and weapons used in the last war, which ended only a little over three years ago, are already obsolete: because of the atomic bomb, the jet-propelled aircraft, and the guided missile. The heavy bomber will one day be as obsolete as the battleship: I expect to see one mounted on concrete at Cranwell, as HMS *Victory* is at Portsmouth.' Yet air power had grown at a phenomenal rate. 'In 1918, 150 miles was a good range. In 1945, the American B-29s in the Pacific were bombing at ten times that range... I am still serving, but as a young officer I flew a 50 hp Blériot monoplane with a top speed of about 55 mph', whereas today's standard fighter can reach 600 mph and 'I expect to live to see fighters operating at well beyond the sonic barrier – I suggest that in another 20 years' time 1,000 mph will be quite a commonplace for a fighter.' Slessor thought the manned bomber already obsolete, 'except perhaps as a marker for the unmanned bomber', which, he thought, would soon be in service.

He then turned to the bomber offensive in the late war, which was 'primarily responsible for the almost amazing degree of air superiority that we enjoyed in the last two and a half years of war', although he admitted that it did not become a war-winning factor until 1944. He also admitted that the Air Staff 'over-estimated the effect of bombing on morale, and we under-estimated the recovery factor. I still think these two factors were among the greatest miracles of history. I would never have believed that the morale of a people would stand up to what the Germans endured. Would we have stood it, I wonder?... Again, who, having seen Germany after VE-Day, would have believed that, as one example only, late in 1944 the German aircraft industry under the supreme direction of that genius Albert Speer was producing over 2,000 fighters a month?'

Slessor urged his audience to read Lord Tedder's four lectures on 'Air Power in War', Sir Norman Bottomley's lecture in the *RUSI Journal* and the report on Exercise Thunderbolt, a detailed study carried out over four days in August 1947 at the School of Air Support, Old Sarum, Wiltshire, of strategic bombing issues between January 1943 and the end of the European war. 'I do not under-rate the importance of the tactical air forces', Slessor insisted, 'but I am speaking to an audience of soldiers, and any soldier who does not know that no army can fight without the close co-operation of a good tactical air force had better go back to school.' Montgomery often said 'you must win the air battle before you embark on the land or sea battle.' Slessor disagreed. You must begin the air battle first, but he thought it would be dangerous for the army to think it could not fight without air superiority. The Germans did, 'and did damned well in defence', but they could not win without it. As for the future, he concluded, 'It may be that the destructive capacity of the atom bomb has been somewhat exaggerated', nor did he think germ warfare a practical proposition. However, 'unless we command the air over these islands we are sunk – even more certainly than we should have been last time', and unless 'we can protect our convoys from air attack we shall starve.'

On January 14th 1949, Tedder forwarded to 'My dear Jack' some 'bumph' about command organization for the Atlantic. 'I feel that one of the troubles is that none of the chaps who have been considering all this', wrote Tedder in a covering letter, 'have any practical knowledge of the subject. So I am most grateful to you for your offer to give me the benefit of your experience.' Slessor replied next day. 'If they had set themselves out to produce a scheme which entirely ignores the essential lessons of the Battle of the Atlantic, they could not possibly have done better... I never thought I should live to see the day when the Air Staff submitted to the CAS a paper recommending that Coastal Command "should be placed under the operational control of C-in-C North Atlantic."' Yet in October 1948 he had advocated an American sailor as 'Supreme Commander, North Atlantic', who would presumably have Coastal Command under his 'operational control'.

Slessor found time at the end of March 1949 to offer Tedder his thoughts on seeking better pay for servicemen. Britain, he said, spent over two thousand million pounds on drink, cigarettes and betting, so the economy would not crash if 40 million pounds were added to the defence budget. Tedder did not reply. Years of experience at the top table, seasoned by his own commonsense, had taught him that – rightly or wrongly – Treasury officials and government ministers alike would regard such a simple assertion with, at best, amused contempt. A few days later, on April 1st, Slessor wrote to Hugh Saunders (his successor as AMP) about his dislike of a 'Report of a Working Party on the Attitude of Serving Airmen'. He criticized its membership: three scientists, a trade union official, and two young officers. 'What the RAF really needs', he told Saunders, 'is leadership, better pay and conditions, more and better food, and no more working parties.' True enough, perhaps, but Saunders and Tedder were on the field of play – and not, like Slessor, on the sidelines – and could rarely afford themselves the satisfaction of 'sounding off'.

During his time at IDC, Slessor kept many irons in the fire, among them a permanent concern for the pay and living conditions of both officers and men. In February 1949 he wrote to Arthur Henderson about a case brought to his attention by the wife of Nigel Maynard (formerly his PA in the Mediterranean). A young married Flying Officer on Maynard's station was living in squalor: 'if the RAF is to live in slum conditions it will soon be manned only by slum types.' He and his wife – and scores like them – were worse off than farm labourers. Accommodation was the greatest problem. The army and navy, being so much longer-established in or near towns used to providing temporary homes, were better able to cope than the RAF, which had many stations far from reasonable prospects of affordable rooms. Slessor sent a copy of that letter to Sir Edward Bridges at the Treasury, telling him: 'I have a son-in-law, a son and a nephew in the RAF and I know what I am talking about, and I assure you that this is a vividly true account of the sort of conditions of life for the younger married officers in the RAF today.' In May he wrote again to Bridges, following a week-long tour of South Wales, when he visited 12 factories and collieries, to collect information about how civilians lived and worked. He told Bridges, not for the first time, that the disparity between service and civilian conditions was far too great. Bridges replied, as Slessor expected, with smooth words, but only 18 months later – to his surprise – the pay of servicemen was actually increased and steps were undertaken to improve living conditions.

Cochrane or Slessor?

Until May 1949, it seemed that Tedder accepted the overwhelming weight of influential – though retired – air force opinion in favour of Slessor as his successor. They had exchanged letters throughout 1948 and Tedder sometimes asked 'My dear Jack' for his advice on matters great and small. On April 6th, for example, Tedder's immediate response to a Slessor letter showed that they were completely at one over a vital issue. 'Have people completely forgotten, or have they ever learned,' asked Tedder, 'some of the elementary lessons of the last war?' A rhetorical question, of course, but one to which both men gave identical answers. 'Have they forgotten', Tedder continued, preaching to the converted, 'that it was Bomber Command and the Eighth Air Force that really won the battle for air superiority over Europe? Have they forgotten that it was Bomber Command that in 1944 strangled German communications and utterly disorganized their whole land operations?' Moving on to current worries, Tedder wondered if it was wise – or even safe – to rely on the Americans (who were concentrating on the technique of atom-bombing vital targets at long range) to intervene in operations in Germany or other areas calculated to help the land campaign or to defend Britain. He recalled how reluctant they had been to divert their heavy bombers to assist Overlord.

Tedder also wondered how effective the new American aircraft would prove to be in practice. In order to fend off agitation by the US navy for carrier-borne atomic bombers, the USAF was developing the enormous Convair B-36, named Peacemaker, which was intended to reach Soviet targets from North American bases. But they were too heavy for British airfields, and Tedder doubted whether they had the speed or agility to penetrate Soviet defences. He rejected the suggestion that Britain leave strategic bombing to the Americans. 'If we deprive ourselves of our air striking force', Tedder argued, 'I think we are not merely, as some people say, relegating ourselves to being a second-class power, but writing ourselves off completely as a power. As you quite rightly quote Winston's remark: "Air mastery is today the supreme expression of military power", and the punch that gives mastery is the bomber.'

Naturally, Slessor responded at once to a letter giving him every reason to suppose their differences of 1947 were far behind them. 'I don't think there is much chance of my forgetting the supreme importance of the bomber', he assured the CAS. Nevertheless, the only current British bomber – the Avro Lincoln – was an 'unenterprising' design (in the opinion of later aviation experts) with an 'unremarkable' performance (by the standards required in and after 1949). It was utterly incapable of successful raids on Soviet targets from British bases. Had war returned to Europe in these years, the Lincoln would have proven as useless as the Whitleys over Germany a decade earlier. Some American-operated Boeing B-29 Superfortresses were based in eastern England, and others were bought by the RAF (re-named Washingtons), but they too were inadequate war machines by 1949 and would have been destroyed just as easily by Soviet ground and air defences, if war had broken out. In other words, Tedder and Slessor were not only in agreement, they were whistling in the dark to keep up their faith in Bomber Command's prospective punch.

Slessor therefore agreed with his master that leaving long-range bombing to the Americans was 'dangerous bunkum', and was 'very attracted' to Tedder's idea of strengthening the bomber force at the expense of Transport Command after 1952. 'It would be sad to have no Transport Force', wrote Slessor in what seems a magnificent understatement even for so ardent a bomber champion, 'but obviously if by that means we could have a really worthwhile Bomber Force we should not hesitate.' Despite the RAF's many embarrassments during and after the war – not least during the still-current Berlin Airlift – in scraping together enough transport aircraft for essential tasks, neither Tedder nor Slessor ever accepted, in their Trenchardist souls, that such types were an integral part of a properly-balanced air force. During the 1950s, fortunately, the RAF's first fleet of adequate British-built transport aircraft gradually emerged.

Why did Tedder and Slessor refer to 1952? They did so because by then the superb English Electric Canberra (a twin-engined jet-bomber) would be in squadron service, but it was a medium-range tactical bomber, incapable of carrying either heavy conventional bombs or an atomic bomb. It was one of the few British aircraft taken into US service, as the Martin B-57. Genuine strategic bombers – the Vickers Valiant, the Avro Vulcan and the Handley Page Victor – flew in 1951-2, but only became operational between 1955-8, long after both Tedder and Slessor were sidelined. Meanwhile, continuing his reply to Tedder in April 1949,

Slessor hoped the Americans would soon settle their 'futile inter-service squabbles' and plan an effective response to any prospective Soviet invasion of western Europe. It must be launched from British bases. 'At present, I am afraid they are thinking far too much in terms of stunt flights from American soil.'

Such exchanges – cordial, thoughtful, and extending over many months – persuaded Slessor that Tedder now agreed with their mentors about the succession. Instead, in a letter to Arthur Henderson (Secretary of State for Air) on May 23rd, Tedder recommended that Ralph Cochrane succeed him from January 1st 1950. 'Since the war', he wrote, 'his outstanding achievement has been the organization and training of Transport Command to the pitch of efficiency and morale which made possible the Berlin Airlift.' As head of 5 Group from February 1943, Cochrane had made it Bomber Command's sharpest weapon during the last two years of the war. 'But for the luck of the draw', wrote Harris after Cochrane's death, 'he would have made an outstanding Chief of the Air Staff and, in my opinion, an incomparable Chief of the Defence Staff.' That may be so, but Tedder failed to provide him with Air Council experience and – unlike Slessor – he had little inter-service experience, and none at all with Americans. His dour personality would surely have dismayed them. All his life he had a lean and hungry look, a face not made for easy laughter, and a manner that was at best distant. On the other hand, intelligent men of every class and rank who valued efficiency and hard work as highly as Cochrane did never looked to him in vain for wholehearted support.

By late July, however, Prime Minister Clement Attlee had rejected that recommendation and selected Slessor. As he recalled, 20 years later, 'I was lucky enough (and this sort of thing always involves a large element of luck) to be selected' by Attlee. 'Probably few people realize how very much the appointment of Chiefs of Staff depend on the decision of the Prime Minister; and I am sure Attlee's decision was in no way influenced by the fact that he too was a devoted Old Haileyburian!' Devoted is the word: at the height of the Korean War Attlee found time to exult with Slessor over the first XV's successful rugby season and Denis Healey (Secretary of Defence, 1964-70, who knew Attlee well) wrote that his 'only interests outside politics were cricket and his public school, Haileybury. He favoured anyone who came from Haileybury', so Slessor may again have reaped the benefit of a good background. No mention, even in 1969, of the part played by Freeman, Portal and Trenchard (among others) – or the opposition offered by Tedder. Slessor was appointed for only a two-year term, later extended by one year.

Tedder did not accept his rebuff gracefully. On September 1st, he chose to break into Slessor's holiday at Auchnacraig, Isle of Mull, south-west Scotland, by sending him a list of proposed senior postings. Slessor wasted at least a day – as Tedder had maliciously intended – in offering detailed comments, not one of which resulted in a change. 'I had imagined', Slessor concluded, 'that Pirie would stay put [as Air Member for Supply and Organization, AMSO] for another couple of years [he did not], that Holly [Hollinghurst] was definite for Washington [he was not], I'd hoped that Ding [Saunders] might do another year [as AMP; he did not] and thought John Baker a good bet as AMP [he was not]. And I hoped it would not be necessary to relieve Dickie [Dickson, as AMSO] for some time to come [it was].' Slessor, however, would have the last laugh. During December, he invited Cochrane – whom he regarded as 'the best group commander that Bomber Command ever had' – to accept appointment as his Vice-CAS; he did accept and remained in that high office until he retired at the end of October 1952. According to Group Captain Sir Leonard Cheshire, VC, one of Bomber Command's most famous pilots, the European war might well have ended sooner if Cochrane had replaced Harris in late 1944 because he would have co-operated more eagerly and intelligently in implementing Tedder's transportation plan. Meanwhile, with Tedder's blessing, Slessor enjoyed a tour lasting two months, in October and November, of all overseas bases: this to prepare himself for command after his time at the IDC.

In November 1956, Air Vice-Marshal Edgar Kingston-McCloughry wrote to Air Chief Marshal Sir Leslie Hollinghurst (who had retired as AMP in October 1952) to express – at length – his dislike of Slessor's life-long preference for anyone who had been at Haileybury; his part in 'hustling' Kingston-McCloughry out of the service; his resentment of Tedder's choice of Hollinghurst as AMP ('the only man strong enough to put a break on him'); and his 'most disappointing' memoirs, *The Central Blue*. He knew about Tedder's efforts to have Cochrane succeed him as CAS and also that Slessor, 'with his burning ambition' had pulled every string he could find to get to the top.

Ambition is not, of course, a sin and neither Portal nor Tedder – to name no other top men – were any less determined than Slessor to climb as high up the greasy pole as they could. He might well have made a name as an operational commander in either Bomber or Coastal Command, had he been allowed to serve there longer. Whatever reservations one may have about him as a bomber champion, strategist or author, his demanding service in Whitehall, Washington and Italy were an excellent preparation for three more years in the corridors of power, occupying the plushest office open to a British airman.

CHAPTER 17

CHIEF OF THE AIR STAFF

A hard year

Let us hope that Jack Slessor enjoyed a deep sense of satisfaction on New Year's Day 1950 when, at long last, he occupied the seat once warmed by his heroes Trenchard, Newall and Portal; a satisfaction enhanced by the knowledge that – also at long last – Tedder was out. Fortunately, he did not then know that Prime Minister Attlee (and he an Old Haileyburian) would shortly bring the 'under-bred bounder' back in. On March 14th, Tedder was appointed head of a joint-services mission in Washington and Britain's first representative on the 'Standing Group', a newly-formed executive committee of the North Atlantic Treaty (NATO). NATO had been created in 1949 as a means of deterring aggression by committing the US to nuclear retaliation against the Soviet Union if western Europe were attacked. The Soviet Union had detonated its first atom bomb a few weeks after the treaty was signed, but it then had no means of landing a bomb on an American target; the US had no means of landing one on a Soviet target without bases in western Europe. Britain's willingness to provide such bases was a major fact in persuading the US to join several states in NATO.

Slessor would have no choice but to work closely with Tedder in precisely those areas of his new office where he most wished to make his own mark as a global strategist. 'I had to see something of him in Washington', recorded Slessor in 1966, 'when I was CAS and he was our representative on the Standing Group – an appointment which I found difficult to stomach and only agreed to because, as ex-deputy to Ike (who by then had become President) and as a MRAF and ex-CAS [as well as being a noble lord, with many close contacts in the American military establishment], I thought he would carry the desirable amount of weight on behalf of the British Chiefs of Staff on the Standing Group. Actually, he did not cut much ice as it turned out and was nothing like the success that Bill Elliot was when he succeeded him. The fact is he is a flat-catcher [another long-forgotten Victorian insult, akin to 'under-bred bounder'] and though he has caught a good many flats in his day, "You can't fool all the people all the time", etc.'

Here we see Slessor at his worst: quite unable to separate his personal detestation from an objective assessment, even years later, of an outstanding Allied officer. Slessor was also mistaken in his facts. He was not consulted about Tedder's appointment; Eisenhower was not elected President until November 1952, long after Tedder had left Washington; and when the appointment was announced General Omar N. Bradley (head of the US army and Chairman of the Joint Chiefs of Staff) greeted it warmly: 'I consider Marshal Tedder one of the United Kingdom's most outstanding men. I am glad to have him with us.' When Tedder left Washington in April 1951, at his own insistence, General Walter Bedell Smith (formerly Eisenhower's Chief of Staff, currently head of the Central Intelligence Agency) wrote equally warmly to Portal: 'I saw Arthur Tedder off last week with great regret. The old ties are very strong and, in addition, it was a great comfort to have him close at hand', during the gravest days of the Korean War.

It is unlikely, however, that untroubled satisfaction long outlasted New Year's Day, 1950, once the new CAS began to receive and open the files. Neither the RAF's equipment (ground as well as air) nor its manpower (especially in the crucial areas of experienced middle-rank officers and senior non-commissioned officers) were adequate for the Cold War and imperial challenges of 1950. As he told Basil Embry (head of Fighter Command) on January 9th: 'One must remember that we are at the moment operating under financial riding orders (which only this morning were repeated in no uncertain terms), which accept the situation that we are in no sense prepared for war and won't be for a long time to come.' Worse still, in cash-strapped Britain there was unlikely to be serious money made available to help remedy the situation. His own elevation to the rank of Marshal of the Royal Air Force (Field Marshal) did not come through, with the appropriate pay rise, until June 1950.

Slessor's first concern was with 'the size and shape' of the armed forces during the next three years, to March 31st 1953. 'I should make it clear', he told Francis Fogarty (head of the Far East Air Force in Singapore) on January 20th, 'that the forces proposed are not those which are considered necessary for a major war against Russia, and the Chiefs of Staff made it clear to the Defence Committee that a period of warning, amounting to 18 months at least, would be necessary to enable us to bring the services up to an adequate state of preparedness for war.' Much anxious discussion followed on how best to spread too few aircraft – many of them obsolescent – over too many commitments, world wide.

On March 1st, he raised with Ralph Cochrane several matters of deep concern throughout their time at the head of the RAF. Above all, was development of a British atomic bomb and a new long-range aircraft to deliver it, at need. Scarcely less important were the development of a guided air-to-air missile, a fighter to carry it, a ground-to-air missile and an effective control and reporting radar system. 'But I was relieved to find the other day', he told Cochrane, 'that you agreed with me that while "the basic weapon of the air force is the bomber, and the basic strategy of air power must be offensive", the realities of our time and geographical position demand that our first duty as the Air Staff is to put HMG in a position to stand firm in the face of an ultimatum backed by an atomic threat – possibly earlier than 1957.' At a practical level, he accepted that Bomber Command was under-equipped, under-manned, and would remain so despite the arrival of American B-29 bombers. The Lincoln was inadequate and the Canberra as yet untried. All other commands – Fighter, Coastal and Transport – were in an even more parlous state.

The other two Chiefs of Staff were General Sir William (later Field Marshal the Viscount) Slim and Admiral Lord Fraser of North Cape. Slessor added value to the team in that they were commanders first and foremost, whereas he had made his name mainly as a master of staff work. 'His great strength', wrote two distinguished soldiers and Whitehall Warriors, 'lay in his ability to argue a case – and herein lay the rub. He was a devotee of the Trenchard theory that the RAF could fight wars more effectively and cheaply than the older services, and of the doctrine of centralization of air power, which led him to clash with Fraser over carriers and naval aviation.' Now began the carrier battle that raged in Whitehall throughout the 1950s and 1960s. Attlee had won a General Election in February 1950 and replaced A. V. Alexander as Minister of Defence with the more alert Emmanuel Shinwell, who shared the Prime Minister's opinion that naval demands were unrealistic. 'Slessor stepped in with a radical proposal for merging his former Coastal Command with naval aviation to form a joint Maritime Air Force', but Fraser could not accept that. An enquiry followed, but while it was deliberating, the Korean War broke out, 'the Fleet was able to display the versatility of its larger existing carriers', and suddenly – as is usually the case in wartime – there was enough money to keep all three Chiefs moderately happy.

On February 3rd Slessor had written a difficult letter to General Hoyt Vandenberg (head of the USAF). He was obliged to admit that he could not afford the cost of preparing four bases in Britain for the new, heavier generation of American bombers. The cost, £7 million, must come from the RAF's budget, and he was committed to giving military assistance to other NATO countries. 'Between you and me, we in the RAF (and in fact all three services) are being squeezed like lemons for money and there is jolly little juice left... I'm pretty nearly at my wits' end to know how we are going to do our stuff with the money we have got.'

Slessor re-organized the Air Staff with effect from March 1st into two main groups: one under the Vice-CAS (Cochrane), the other under a new Deputy Chief (Sir Arthur Sanders, with whom he had flown in 5 Squadron in 1917) and made both directly responsible to himself. Under Tedder, the Deputy Chief had reported to the Vice-CAS. Cochrane would be concerned with questions affecting strength and efficiency; Sanders would be concerned with inter-service policy and planning, and with work involving co-operation with Commonwealth and Allied air forces. Slessor had three reasons for his re-organization. Firstly, the growing pressure of work arising from international commitments, such as Western Union and the North Atlantic and Brussels treaties. Secondly, he was anxious to reduce the number of men and women serving in the Air Ministry. And thirdly, he needed to consider training problems created by the planned introduction of new aircraft types.

Slessor was invited to reply to the toast of 'The Armed Forces of the Crown' at the first postwar Royal Academy dinner held at Burlington House on April 27th 1950. It was a great occasion: Prime Minister Attlee, Mr Churchill, the Speaker of the House of Commons, the Headmaster of Eton and the President of the Royal Academy headed a glittering assembly. In 1944-5, said Slessor, three revolutionary developments transformed the face of war: 'the atomic weapon, the rocket missile and the jet-propelled aircraft.' There was no 'short cut to security' via the bomb alone. Western nations must build up their conventional defences, but we would be in trouble if every nation tried to create its own balanced forces. Only by accepting 'the principle of integration', with each nation making the contribution to which it was best suited would the West get a truly balanced force, backed by aircraft capable of carrying atomic weapons, and thereby deter aggressors.

Shortage of money for modern equipment and skilled personnel would be a major theme of Slessor's official life in 1950 and, indeed, throughout his term as CAS. For example, on May 8th he asked his old Balkan Air Force friend Bill Elliot (then back in Whitehall as Chief Staff Officer to the Minister of Defence and Deputy Secretary (Military) to the Cabinet) to tell those who mattered that the services could not fight a cold war and prepare for a hot one on just £780 million a year. 'If the real crisis comes in the next few years, we shall be defeated unless we spend more money and devote more manpower to defence.' He did not think war 'immediately imminent or inevitable', but the government's belief that a crisis was unlikely before 1957 was 'entirely meaningless – a most dangerous alibi for inaction.'

Another major theme of Slessor's official life was the ever-sensitive business of keeping allies sweet. He wrote to Sir George Pirie – head of the RAF Delegation in Washington – on June 19th 1950 to advise him that at a meeting next day with the Western Union Chiefs of Staff he would tell the Dutch to scale down the size of their proposed navy, which he was certain they could not afford. French plans, he thought, were 'even more fantastic.' The British Admiralty had led both nations astray: 'they all pipe each other aboard and have a marvellous time without any relation whatever to the real needs of balanced defence in Western Europe.'

Of greater importance, however, was the difficulty of 'selling' British opinions across the Atlantic. Slessor had become acutely aware of a potentially dangerous rift between Britons and Americans when he served under Eaker in the Mediterranean and for the rest of his life he would do his best to reduce that rift. Although he had many good friends in Washington, it was often uphill work, especially before the outbreak of war in Korea. For example, in August 1951 he wrote to Bill Elliot in Washington: 'I am amazed to see in my *Times* that the Congress are now busying themselves with a resolution to unify Ireland… Well, well!' He wrote again to Elliot in October about American pressure to introduce eight American instructors – all of Colonel rank – at the Turkish Air Staff College in place of the three RAF officers currently employed there.

Korea

In June 1950, to everyone's surprise in Whitehall and Washington, came an outbreak of war: not in central Europe or the Middle East, as many pundits half-expected, but in Korea. Since August 1945, the 38th Parallel of Latitude had separated the interests of the Soviet Union and the United States in that country. By June 1950, a communist state existed in the north and an officially democratic republic in the south. When North Korean forces invaded South Korea on the 25th, it was widely supposed to be a Kremlin-inspired attempt to draw Anglo-American forces to the Far East while the Soviet Union 'destabilized' the politically-shaky states of western Europe (notably France, Italy and Greece) where there were large, well-disciplined communist parties.

Although President Truman and his advisers recognized this danger, they believed they must act in support of South Korea. Britain was anxious to help, despite her heavy commitments in Europe, the Middle East, Malaya and Hong Kong as well as her interest in balancing trade prospects with the new People's Republic of China and diplomatic links with the Nationalist regime in Taiwan. Prime Minister Attlee at once sent Britain's Far East fleet to join US warships in operations off Korean coasts, where they were joined by several Commonwealth warships. The Americans wanted a British presence on the ground and in the air as well as at sea, and Attlee agreed. Slessor (and Tedder, then representing the British Chiefs of Staff in Washington) shared Vandenberg's fear that nuclear weapons might be used. 'Every day that passes', wrote General Curtis LeMay to Vandenberg on June 30th, 'makes more possible the total destruction of Washington by several atomic bombs or a single hydrogen bomb, leaving our nation temporarily without top-level direction.' Vandenberg approved his request to respond promptly, but privately shared British suspicion that 'old ironpants' was itching to get his retaliation in first. In late November, when United Nations forces under the command of General Douglas MacArthur were in retreat, LeMay calmly supposed that nuclear weapons would be used to prevent their defeat.

Slessor summoned all his senior officers and station commanders to a meeting on September 11th to tell them that the term of National Service had been increased to two years, that all regulars would be retained 'for a period beyond the due date of termination of their engagements', and everyone's pay had been increased. He was anxious that the reasons for these changes be carefully explained to all ranks. If we can get through the present dangers in Korea, he said, a third world war is less likely. But we must be on guard – and from now on will have more and better equipment and accommodation. We must all not only work harder but also train more reservists, in all trades, against the day when they may be needed full-time. We cannot afford headlines in the popular press about 'Skilled tradesmen peeling potatoes' or 'National Servicemen with nothing do but mow the Officers' Mess lawns.' We are short of men (and women) and must use everyone we have efficiently – and we must keep postings to a minimum.

Finally, he made a point of great importance to him personally and one which he wanted all his senior officers to have in mind when encouraging recruiting. 'None of us joined the RAF to make money – or anyway we were clean out of luck if we did. What always attracted the right sort of chap to the service was love of flying, an interesting job, the spirit of adventure, a cheerful existence among congenial companions – plus a rate of pay which, while never equal to the higher rewards of civil life, was enough to enable one to lead a reasonably decent and carefree existence, provided one wasn't extravagant.' That led him to reflect on marriage. It was the married NCO and junior officer who worried him most. 'No less than 79.5 percent of the officers in the RAF today are married. That is far too many – and incidentally a far higher proportion than it was 20 years ago. I'm all for a chap being married when he is the right age, but the right age is not when he is barely out of a recruit centre or a young officer in a squadron.' In Slessor's opinion, 25 – the age at which one qualified for a marriage allowance – was too young. 'I know that unfortunately you cannot forbid an officer or airman to get married, or make him send in his papers if he did, as was the custom in the old days', but he urged his senior officers to do all they could to dissuade their junior officers and men from taking this step until they were close to 30. Married life greatly harmed off-duty life, which should be a major and enjoyable part of everyone's career in the services. He himself married when a few days short of his 26th birthday.

US and British Chiefs of Staff had met in Washington during October and by November 6th Slessor and the other British Chiefs were desperate to know from General Omar Bradley (head of the US army) if MacArthur realized that Chinese forces were now helping their North Korean comrades, and if he had been authorized to cross the Yalu river into Manchuria. 'We look like being in for a prolonged containment at best', they told Tedder, 'and war with China at worst.' Tedder replied on the 8th that he had spoken with Bradley, who assured him that the US wished to avoid war with China, but South Korea had to be made safe from another invasion, and that MacArthur did not regard Chinese assistance for the north as serious.

MacArthur was mistaken. On November 24th, in response to his advance into North Korea, massive Chinese forces poured across the Yalu and drove the Allies back in disorder. The British Chiefs signalled 'a catalogue of anxiety' to Tedder on the 28th, of which the main item was a fear that MacArthur was eager to escalate the conflict into all-out war with China and even with the Soviet Union. Tedder showed most of this signal to Bradley – wisely deleting a few of the more 'unhelpful', if not hysterical, sentences – and was told, yet again, that Truman opposed escalation. Military opinion remained more steadfast in Washington than in Whitehall, but at a press conference on November 30th the President said: 'We will take whatever steps are necessary' to win this war. When asked if that included the use of atomic bombs, he replied: 'That includes every weapon we have.'

Attlee flew to Washington on December 3rd, taking his Chiefs with him. Five formal meetings of the principal American and British leaders, civilian and military, were held during the next few days, in addition to many private talks. MacArthur's conduct and capacity, Chinese and Soviet intentions, the scale of British and Commonwealth support in Korea, and the fragility of western Europe (both economically and militarily) under Soviet pressure were anxiously discussed. On the 7th Truman promised Attlee – but only verbally – that he would never authorize the use of nuclear weapons without informing him first.

On January 5th 1951 the British Chiefs again pressed Tedder for information about MacArthur's intentions. The effect of being 'kicked out of Korea would be calamitous', they alleged. They saw no military reason why the UN forces should be beaten, unless the morale and determination of certain American units faltered. Tedder discussed this message (suitably sanitized) with Bradley and then assured Slessor and his colleagues that there were over 450,000 Chinese troops in Korea – far more than the British realized – and that they were supported by Russian-built MiG-15 jet fighters. The Chiefs thereupon decided to send Slessor back to Washington to consider this 'very grave situation.' In fact, however, the tide of battle was already turning in UN favour under the command of General Matthew B. Ridgway and to the relief of Slessor and most of his colleagues, British or American, Truman sacked MacArthur on April 11th. A Chinese attack began on the 22nd, but it failed; the Kremlin backed off; the conflict did not spiral out of control; and an armistice was eventually agreed in July 1953.

Slessor had written to his friend George Fielding Eliot in New York in October 1951 to tell him that 'the thing which above all shook our faith in American leadership was the Korea débâcle of last winter... It is the brutal fact that your own leaders were panic-stricken, when MacArthur took his knock on the Yalu. We had advised against pressing on north. You had ignored our advice – or rather the Pentagon had completely failed to exercise any sort of control over MacArthur and had allowed him to do so. And you were being pushed into the sea by the Chinese – in spite of your overwhelming air and sea power – because the American army would not fight.' Fortunately, Ridgway came along 'and did to your Eighth Army what Monty did to our Eighth Army before Alamein.' Even so, 'we are in the atomic front line and you are still the hell of a long way from it, and the experience of the Korean panic last winter does make us wonder a bit what you are likely to do in another really critical situation.'

A decade later, in March 1960, Slessor returned to these themes in a letter to Barton Leach, of Harvard Law School. Both the US Navy and Air Force were 'extremely efficient' in Korea, he thought, but the army was a problem: a low standard of discipline, a narrow gap between officers and men (so that orders were regarded merely as a basis for discussion), too high a standard of living: 'too much central heating, Coca Cola and doughnuts, too high pay and a general tendency to be soft.' All of which reinforced his doubts about American leadership of the free world in the event of a major war.

These were easy jibes, like those he so often made about soldiers during the Italian campaign in 1944-5. By 1960, however, Slessor had the leisure, energy and top-brass contacts in all three services on both sides of the Atlantic (as well as his personal involvement) to have made a serious study of the use of air power and the quality of inter-service co-operation in Korea. Instead, it was left to Richard Hallion to observe, years later, that strategic bombing of enemy bases in Manchuria was impossible for political reasons. 'Accordingly, air power simply could not function in the same way as it had in World War II.' But by 1960 Slessor had become fixated by the bomb.

Meanwhile, back in the Korean War, three squadrons of Sunderland flying-boats, already based in the Far East, were hard worked in co-operation with UN naval forces to patrol and blockade the sea approaches to North Korea. The only other RAF contribution was in fighter pilots, many of whom flew with American F-86 Sabre wings. These were bitter pills for the proud, patriotic Slessor to swallow. Not only did the RAF lack a strategic bomber force, if war should break out in Europe, but it also lacked fighters that could usefully support American Sabres against Russian-built MiGs.

Strengthening NATO, reviving Eisenhower

At Farnborough on July 7th 1950 the RAF gave its first 'full-scale demonstration' since the last of the Hendon pageants in 1937. It was a memorable occasion: over 400 aircraft, almost a thousand aircrew and a total of 5,400 airmen and airwomen took part. The outbreak of war in Korea added zest to the occasion, although no-one then knew how small a part would be played by the RAF – or how close the world would come to a nuclear catastrophe. At least 80,000 spectators attended, among them the King and the Queen, and they enjoyed a massive flypast of 225 aircraft. Six Commonwealth countries, the US, France, Belgium and the Netherlands took part. Among the events was, as *The Times* reported, 'a most realistic portrayal of the role of fighter-bombers in support of ground troops... This was the first public demonstration of a rocket attack by jet fighter-bombers, and awe-inspiring it was.' As well as the sight of jets hurtling about, there was also 'some graceful formation flying' by Harvards of the Central Flying School. In three flypasts they formed 'RAF', 'GRVI' and the Prince of Wales's Feathers.

Continuing tension in Europe and the Middle East, together with outright war in Korea, encouraged Attlee's government to strengthen Britain's armed forces. Although National Service – increased to two years after the outbreak of war in Korea – was now a normal part of a young man's life, the RAF remained underpowered until September 1950, when a new pay and trade structure was introduced which greatly improved regular recruitment. New squadrons were formed for service in Germany, equipped with de Havilland Vampires, and new types of fighters were ordered in October and November – the Supermarine Swift and Hawker Hunter. To fill the gap before they came into service, 430 Canadian-built Sabres were ordered. This decision was much criticized, but Slessor and his colleagues were seen to have acted wisely to remedy Fighter Command's 'outrageous obsolescence', especially when the Swift failed to match expectations.

Slessor flew to Ottawa on October 8th and then on to Washington for talks about how best to defend the West. The military committee of NATO met on the 24th under General Bradley for the last time before the chairmanship passed to Belgium. Slim and Admiral Fraser were present, as were Slessor and Tedder. The question of integrated armed forces was to be discussed again. 'The most controversial problem – that of German re-armament – will not even be considered until the Defence Ministers meet', reported *The Times*. 'The French members of the Standing Group are not even allowed to discuss it, and it does not appear on the military committee's agenda.' Eisenhower was thought likely to be appointed Supreme Allied Commander in Europe (SACEUR) – for the second time in his career.

The military committee of NATO met in London on December 12th. Defence Ministers had considered a 'German contribution to European defence and the command structure' in October in Washington and now it was agreed to recommend full German participation, as Dr Adenauer (head of the new West German state) insisted. Members of the 12 delegations then met in Brussels on the 16th to take part in meetings of the Defence Committee (Defence Ministers) and the Atlantic Council (Foreign Ministers). As *The Times* reported, 'much emphasis is laid by officials here on the fact that the discussion of the integrated force is really the main task, since the question of the German contribution to it is only one aspect of the whole problem.' The names of the Supreme Commander (Eisenhower) and his Chief of Staff (Lieutenant-General Alfred M. Gruenther) would be officially revealed. Integration should include fitting the Western Union military organization into the organization of the Supreme Headquarters of the Atlantic Powers in Europe (SHAPE).

An easier year

Slessor wrote to Arthur Henderson, Secretary of State for Air, on January 31st 1951. The Canadians, he said, had become very NATO-minded and therefore wanted any military aid from them to go through NATO and not through the RAF. He feared a bureaucratic logjam, but Tedder – still representing British interests in Washington – was aware of the danger. Slessor wrote to Tedder on the same day about the RAF's need to set up three training schools in Canada. 'I know you are keenly aware of the danger of the Standing Group machinery becoming an instrument of delay,' he said, and asked him to do his best to get permission for these schools to begin work soon. As was often the case, Tedder and Slessor were in complete agreement over particular issues, though colder than ever personally, and – with one pulling and the other pushing – the schools were opened. No doubt good working relations were helped by having the whole width of the Atlantic between them. One ludicrous problem faced by Slessor (and Tedder before him) was that the Canadians preferred to be based on the continent, rather than in England. Partly because they 'didn't like our rations – wanted cereals for breakfast and whatnot.'

A week later, on February 5th, Slessor wrote again to Tedder, this time about the organization in Paris of SHAPE. He asked Tedder to urge Eisenhower, the Supreme Commander, to have 'a really senior RAF officer on his HQ level who can act for him with his authority'; otherwise, 'the air will tend to get shouldered out at every turn.' Tedder agreed entirely that Hugh Saunders, Air C-in-C Western Europe – and for years a close friend – was just the man to be Air Deputy under Eisenhower. Slessor then wrote to Gruenther, Eisenhower's Chief of Staff, on the 7th about his fear that air interests were under-represented at SHAPE, and on the 26th he told Montgomery, Deputy Supreme Commander, that he had had four hours with Eisenhower recently. His ideas were moving in the right direction, but he relied too much on carrier-borne aircraft to challenge Soviet power from north and south. His Overlord experience, when the U-boats had been beaten and he enjoyed air superiority, weighed too much with him. The 'row in the Commons on Thursday' served to show that Britain was unwilling to accept Norstad as Eisenhower's Air Deputy. The post should go to Saunders. Eisenhower,

Gruenther, Slessor and others met on March 1st and agreed to appoint
Saunders – a satisfactory result for both Slessor and Tedder.

   Unlike Tedder, however, Slessor felt it necessary on March 12th to
offer advice to Saunders without being asked for it. 'Ike, in a typically
American way, is against any clear-cut directive on the division of
responsibilities between you and Larry [Norstad]', he wrote, but Saunders
should stand firm on two points. Firstly, as the senior airman in SHAPE,
he was entitled to a wide area of personal authority in relation to all air
forces, including the USAF, and must not allow himself to be regarded as
a mere adviser. Eisenhower and Gruenther must not deal directly with
Norstad in matters that were properly Saunders' concern. Secondly,
Eisenhower preferred to see an organization 'evolve', but Slessor urged
Saunders to get his job description set down on paper. 'Ike is liable to get
a little impatient with outside advice', but Slessor was determined to offer
it, because the RAF had committed a third of its strength to the integrated
force. Did Saunders need such elementary instruction? Nothing in this
letter could have been news to him, but he knew Slessor of old as a man
of immense enthusiasm who always wanted to help, even at the risk of
interfering. Saunders had reached the rank of Air Chief Marshal, thanks
to a record of service in combat, command and management roles that
was longer, more varied and more distinguished than Slessor's. He did not
need to have his hand held. In any case, nothing said or done by a British
officer (or politician) changed American minds, once they were made up.
Such had been the case since at least 1944, as Slessor well knew – when
he stopped to think about it.

More tactical than strategic

Slessor was usually at his best – thoughtful, well-informed – when
considering officers for promotion, or a new appointment, or a decoration.
He was particularly good at writing – often in his own hand – a friendly,
informal word of thanks from on high to long-serving officers on the eve
of a retirement that was not always welcome. For example, he wrote to
Lieutenant-General Sir Robert Mansergh (Commander of British Forces
in Hong Kong) on January 30th 1951 about Air Commodore David
Bonham-Carter, the new AOC Hong Kong. 'You may on first sight think
he is rather a funny old thing, with his hearing-aid – he is very deaf. I
would like to assure you that he is a really first-class chap. I've known
him for the best part of 25 years, ever since he was a young officer out of
Cranwell. He is chock full of guts and will make a first-rate fighting
commander, if it comes to trouble.' He commanded a station in Bomber
Command and although he was well into his forties (born in February
1901) often flew on operations, especially with crews whom he thought
needed a bit of bucking up – and was awarded a well-earned DFC. He
intended to fly a de Havilland Vampire jet fighter out to Hong Kong,
'which is typical of him. You can rest assured that in old Bonham you

have a really indomitable Air Force Commander.' Slessor was also realistic and occasionally came up with a vivid image. 'We just cannot afford to find diamonds for every hole in the watch', he said when answering objections in February 1951 to the appointment of Air Vice-Marshal Sir Alexander Davidson (recently retired) as Commandant of the Royal Observer Corps.

He wrote to 'My dear Larry', Lieutenant-General Lauris Norstad, head of Allied Air Forces in Europe at Fontainebleau in April 1951, commending Tom Pike for appointment as his Senior Staff Officer. 'Tom is one of our very best young Air Vice-Marshals – a chap who is generally regarded in the RAF as bound to go to the top of the tree. He is now commanding 11 Fighter Group and was one of our best-known fighter pilots in the Battle of Britain. So he has excellent air defence experience as well as Tactical Air Force experience. He was a student under me at the IDC in '49 and was one of the star turns of his year... He is a teetotaler and a non-smoker and to my mind it is a measure of his character that he is none the worse for that!' Norstad accepted Slessor's recommendation and Pike was appointed Deputy Chief of Staff (Operations) at Fontainebleau. He did indeed climb to the top of the tree, as CAS (1960-3) and then as Deputy SACEUR until 1967.

In April it was announced that the American, British, Canadian and French air chiefs were shortly to meet in Washington 'to discuss matters of mutual interest'; they would be accompanied by their supply advisers. Britain had asked the US to provide about 400 Sabres to increase Fighter Command's strength until new British types could be produced. A major question was whether such a large number could be supplied at a time when the USAF was expanding its own fighter strength. The Sabre was already being built in Canada, under licence, for the RCAF. Before leaving for Washington, Slessor wrote to Saunders in Paris on April 21st, inviting him to raise certain important matters with Eisenhower. The expansion of the RAF, he said, depends *entirely* [his emphasis] on our obtaining an appropriate share of the raw materials and machine-tools available to the North Atlantic coalition', but these were not being supplied, thanks to American stockpiling and its own expansion. 'So you should be under no delusions about the fact that unless we do get our proper share of these things, this RAF expansion programme is not worth the paper it is written on. We have got (or are building) the factories; we have got the skills; we can – though with difficulty – find the labour; we can find most of the material. But unless we can secure the vital machine-tools and the necessary quote of essential scarce raw materials – particularly things like sulphur, molybdenum and tungsten – then all the rest will be of no avail... On every ground', he concluded, 'miltary, political, psychological, it would be fatal to find America armed to the teeth, including the defences of the continental US, and backed with great stockpiles of strategic raw materials, while her Allies in the front line are still comparatively defenceless.'

The meetings began at the Pentagon on April 30th and five weeks later, on June 7th, they all met again in Paris. Three subjects were discussed in Paris: an increase in aircraft production in NATO countries; accelerated training of pilots and technicians in the US and Canada; and the building of more and better air bases. They would also consider whether it might one day be possible to standardize aircraft manufacture on both sides of the Atlantic. Some NATO countries were producing aircraft and equipment in numbers too small to be useful and obsolescent anyway. They should be encouraged to divert to 'other fields of war production.' The question of 'air preparedness' particularly concerned France, as *The Times* reported, because 'her strategic position makes her a natural advance base for the air forces of the western allies.'

Slessor had spoken at the Mansion House, London, to members of the Air League of the British Empire on April 20th 1951. He admitted that Bomber Command was at present 'and for some years to come would be primarily a tactical bomber force, this limited role had been forced upon us by circumstances and did not represent a permanent policy.' Although only the USAF had, 'for the present, the ability to strike back at an aggressor with the bomber', the first order for Britain's four-engined long-range jet bombers had been placed, 'and in due course' they would replace the Lincolns and Washingtons. 'We should never have very many of them in peacetime – nothing like the great bomber fleets we knew in 1945' because they were so expensive, but they would be able to carry the atomic bomb.

Meanwhile, Slessor continued, the RAF had a very heavy commitment to Eisenhower's integrated air force defending western Europe. 'People were far too prone to think and speak of European defence in terms of divisions. There must be divisions, but the outstanding lesson of the last war campaigns – a lesson reinforced by events in Korea – was that a campaign on land was a two-fisted affair, one fist being on the ground and the other in the air.' The RAF was greatly expanding its tactical air force in Germany and Slessor foresaw 'difficulties in many directions – machine-tools, raw materials, works services for airfields, and radar stations' – but he believed they would be overcome. Since the introduction of new pay rates, he concluded, 'recruiting was going well, though he could wish to see more men entering on long-service engagements.' His main concern was in the air, not on the ground: 'we were not getting enough young men of the right quality coming forward as aircrew.'

Dangerous times

President Truman recommended to Congress on April 30th 1951 a massive increase in spending on defence. Quoted in *The Times*, he said that if the Soviet Union chose to 'unleash a general war, the free world must be in a position to stop the attack and strike back decisively and at once at the seats of Soviet power.' In Britain, on May Day, the House of Commons debated an Opposition motion expressing anxiety that 'the re-armament programme which it approved in February was based on estimates of defence production which were not accepted by the ministers principally concerned.'

In May Slessor firmly rejected a request by Sir Oliver Harvey, Britain's Ambassador in France, that a very popular Air Attaché, Air Vice-Marshal Sir Robert George, remain in office. Slessor told the Secretary of State for Air that George had spent nearly seven years in Paris and must now go – which he did. Slessor liked him very well and quite understood that the Ambassador felt the same way. The French air force had been riven by 'intrigues, personal jealousies, moves and counter-moves on political and senior air force levels about which George, owing to his many contacts, has been able to keep us well informed. We also owe to him our knowledge about the lack of security in the French Air Ministry.' But Slessor thought the RAF now needed a man in Paris who was better informed about technical and operational matters.

He wrote to 'My dear Dick', Air Vice-Marshal Richard Atcherley, on May 21st to calm his fears about complaints that he had upset influential persons while head of the Pakistan air force during the past two years. 'Don't you worry', said Slessor, 'I know what difficulties you had to contend with and how well you did it. The trouble is, of course, that practically no-one of the old Indian army – except a few like Slim and Auchinleck – learnt anything in the war about the basic principles of land/air warfare and army/air co-operation.' General Sir Douglas Gracey, head of the Pakistan army from 1947, 'certainly did not.' A legend in his lifetime, 'Batchy' was one of a kind, on the ground and in the air; inspiring and entertaining many, infuriating a few, throughout his brilliant career. It is greatly to Slessor's credit that he backed this maverick in Pakistan and then made him head of 12 Group, Fighter Command, where he was an outstanding success.

Slessor spoke at a dinner arranged by Hawker Siddeley on May 31st 1951 to celebrate the tenth anniversary of the first flight of the first British jet aircraft with the original Whittle engine, aptly named Pioneer. As in May 1941, he said, the RAF was in the middle of a great expansion – and the times, in some ways, were more dangerous now than then. Fortunately, Britain no longer stood alone: 'today we are a member of a great Atlantic coalition which includes the United States.' Slessor believed that Anglo-American air power could ensure world peace for another century, as British sea power did for a century after Waterloo.

During August, a long-pending crisis with Persia (later Iran) over production and control of the oil industry came closer to a head. Dr Mossadeq, the Prime Minister, had nationalized all foreign oil assets on May 2nd. Churchill (then Leader of the Opposition in the British Parliament) wrote to President Truman on June 29th in support of Prime

Minister Attlee. 'Short of an invasion of Western Europe', he wrote, 'I cannot think of any Soviet aggression more dangerous to our common cause than for the region between the Caspian Sea and the Persian Gulf to fall under Russian-stimulated Tudeh Communist control... Limitless supplies of oil would remove the greatest deterrent upon a major Russian aggression.' A 'special meeting' in Downing Street took place on the evening of August 20th to discuss the situation. Attlee presided and Slessor was present as well as ministers and the chairman of the Anglo-Iranian Oil Company. Nothing was done, to Slessor's fury – which was not eased two years later when it suited the Americans to act as Britain so often had in the good old days and toppled Mossadeq.

Only rarely did Slessor find time even to contemplate the pleasures he enjoyed so much between the wars: hunting, shooting, fishing, sailing – and relishing an unspoiled countryside. He wrote to his old Mediterranean boss, Ira Eaker, on August 31st to say that he had no chance of joining him and Carl Spaatz in October for a few days' fishing on the Rogue river. He confessed that he could not even get away from Whitehall to attend the wedding of his son John in Southern Rhodesia (later Zimbabwe) and so Hermione would be going alone.[16] He felt obliged to attend major exercises, and then to take part in an important Atlantic Council meeting in Rome to discuss German re-armament, Middle East Command, and the possible admission of Turkey to NATO.

Slessor wrote to Sir Keith Park, his old sparring partner – now living in Auckland, New Zealand – on October 11th. 'I should be grateful', he wrote, 'if you could let me know whether you think there is any ill feeling anywhere in the RNZAF about having an RAF officer there. As you will by now have seen, Donald Hardman has been appointed CAS Australia. I am sure you will agree that he is a first-class man for the job. But I think that this is a direction in which you may be able, if necessary, to help out the relations between the RAF and the RAAF. As you know, there is a rather unfortunate background to all this (Ellington's visit and the subsequent appointment of Charles Burnett [1940-2], which caused a good deal of disgruntlement in the RAAF).' Slessor had talked to Prime Minister Menzies and Tommy White (Minister for Air), who both pressed for an RAF officer. 'The direction in which I think your influence may be useful is in removing any impression that this appointment was in any way at the insistence of the RAF.' Air Marshal Sir Donald Hardman succeeded an Australian, George Jones, in January 1952. During the next two years, he sought to strengthen British influence over the RAAF, encouraging it to see itself as an adjunct to the RAF.

Not all Slessor's letters were friendly or sympathetic. He was, after all, a seasoned Whitehall Warrior and well able to fight for his corner. In October he wrote to Lieutenant-General Sir Kenneth McLean at the

---

[16] Flight Lieutenant Slessor married Ann Gibson in Bulawayo, Southern Rhodesia, on October 6th.

Cabinet Offices. 'I have had dealings in the past with [Sir Robert] Knox, who is Secretary of the Honours Committee, but habitually regards himself as final arbiter in matters of awards.' Slessor was not prepared to accept that a CMG [Companion of St Michael and St George] for Air Vice-Marshal Cecil Bouchier was not on simply because Knox refused to recommend it. 'It is all nonsense to talk about these "strict rules"', he told McLean, 'rules are made for man and not the other way round'; an exception could be made if the services and the Foreign Office agreed. Incidentally, he added, Bouchier's reports [from Japan] were used just as much by the Foreign Office and other ministries as by the Chiefs of Staff.

'Boy' Bouchier, an old friend of Park's, had made a fine reputation in Fighter Command. In 1944, however, Slessor had refused Park's request that Bouchier be appointed to command Aden, but was obliged to give way. Then, in 1945, when Park recommended Bouchier as British Senior Officer in Japan, Slessor again objected, and was again obliged to back down. Bouchier's record – in England and in the Far East – suggests that Park's judgement of his merits was superior to Slessor's. By 1951, however, Slessor had changed his mind about Bouchier and pressed for him to be knighted in recognition of his services in Japan.

Bouchier was awarded a CB, but not the CMG. Slessor, however, returned to the charge in August 1952. He wrote to 'My dear Bill', Field Marshal Sir William Slim, at the War Office, making a stout defence of Bouchier's postwar service in Japan and especially as the personal representative of the British Chiefs of Staff to the Supreme Commander of the United Nations forces in Korea, General Douglas MacArthur. 'I know he is sometimes apt to be tactless and get people's backs up. But I have been a bit unhappy for some time about the way he has been treated, and your Military Attaché in Tokyo has been working against him.' Bouchier had served us well and it was he who was 'largely responsible for putting right the grossly wasteful way in which the US air force was being employed.' We must not allow him to come home under a cloud. The Foreign Office refused a CMG for him, but Slessor proposed a KBE [Knight Commander of the Order of the British Empire: less distinguished than the KCB, but far more so than a mere CMG] in the New Year's Honours List, which was awarded. He sent a friendly letter to 'My dear Boy' next day, August 13th.

At a General Election on October 25th 1951 the Conservatives gained a narrow victory and Churchill (who would be 77 in November) replaced Attlee as Prime Minister. 'Thank God', wrote Field Marshal Montgomery. 'At last we have you back again and in charge of the ship. May you stay there for five years and more.' It was not an opinion Slessor shared even though he was a staunch Conservative. He would describe Churchill, in his usual extravagant language when discussing the great and the good, as 'by a long chalk the greatest Englishman that ever lived', but working within his unpredictable range was a different matter.

A successful year

Although Slessor's main concerns remained the Cold War, the Middle East and Korea, the RAF was constantly engaged in operations against Communists in Malaya. The Far East Air Force provided reconnaissance, communications, casualty evacuation, air support and supply for ground forces – all difficult enough, but made far more dangerous when operating over mountains or jungle in turbulent, unpredictable weather. From the airfield at Tengah in Singapore, bombing and strafing sorties were carried out by Lincoln and later by Canberra bombers, also by Vampires and Venoms (an improved version of the Vampire), armed with rockets. They were supported by Australian and New Zealand squadrons and played a vital part in a long – and successful – campaign to stabilize the Malay Peninsula.

On January 23rd, Slessor outlined for Lord De L'Isle and Dudley (Secretary of State) his thoughts on bombers and fighters. 'There is no school of thought in the RAF that wishes to plunge heavily on the largest class of bomber', he told him. 'We are making no effort to produce a modern heavy bomber like the American B-36 or B-52. We know we cannot afford it. The Valiant is not a heavy bomber. It is only a modern medium bomber to replace the old Lincolns which did us so well in the late war, but are now seven years out of date.' He was well aware that bombers were costly, but they must be modern types: 'otherwise we may as well have none at all.' As for fighters, he continued, 'there is no more dangerous fallacy than the belief that fighters alone can protect us from destruction. We must have the essential minimum – and that is a very large figure, nearly one thousand for the defence of UK alone. But the counter-offensive is an absolutely indispensable element in air defence and without it no number of fighters can save us in the long run.' It would be fatal, he believed, 'to surrender our bomber arm to the Americans or any other ally. There is of course also the point that we are committed to our NATO partners to produce a bomber force for the defence of Europe – and hence of ourselves.'

Slessor privately regarded the noble lord as 'that little fool', totally under Churchill's thumb, and was therefore provoked into setting out for him the facts of life – as Slessor understood them – with unusual brevity. On March 1st, for instance, he outlined 'British Bomber Policy.' The RAF, he wrote, 'can certainly not afford to build up a great strategic bomber force on the lines of Bomber Command in 1945 and the Air Staff have no thought that it should do so. The strategic air offensive against Russia must always be primarily a responsibility of the United States.' He went on to explain, in simple terms, his deepest beliefs. 'In the defence of these islands, it has always been a cardinal point in British air policy that the counter-offensive is an indispensable element in air defence. The amazing degree of air mastery enjoyed on all battlefronts, and the virtual immunity of the United Kingdom from air attack after the spring of 1941, was due in the main to the fact that the enemy's air resources were increasingly, and in the end entirely, thrown back on the close defence of the Reich by the Allied bomber offensive.' The RAF, he repeated, must have a V-bomber force, capable of carrying an atomic bomb, as well as defensive fighters, and we must not rely on the US to protect us.

At the end of March Slessor held his annual conference with Commanders-in-Chief – a practice begun by Tedder in 1946 – at the School of Land-Air Warfare, Old Sarum, near Salisbury in Wiltshire. The conference in 1952, entitled *Unicorn*, was to discuss how best to build up RAF strength to meet new commitments, actual and potential, and lasted for five days. In addition to Cs-in-C, senior officers from SHAPE, Commonwealth air forces and the USAF attended, together with Royal Navy and army officers and civilians from various ministries.

'The RAF', reported *The Times*, 'is actively engaged in Malaya and Korea, and because of the disturbances in Egypt its strength in the Suez Canal zone was recently increased. During the past 18 months the size of the RAF Second Tactical Air Force stationed in Germany has been steadily built up', and Anthony Eden (Foreign Secretary) had said that – subject to the requirements of the SACEUR – British forces on the continent would operate as closely as possible with European defence forces in matters of training, administration and supplies. By the end of 1952, there would be 4,000 Allied aircraft in western Europe, one-third of them RAF. All fighter squadrons were now equipped with jet aircraft, 'though they compare unfavourably with the American Sabre and the Russian MiG-15', while radar-equipped all-weather and night fighters were 'coming into use'. Prime Minister Churchill had recently announced that 'super-priority' was being given to new types: the Hawker Hunter and the Supermarine Swift, 'swept-wing fighters of high performance which will replace the existing Meteor and Vampire day fighters. Bomber Command was being greatly strengthened by the arrival of twin-jet Canberras, to be followed – one day – by larger and more powerful V-bombers.'

Coastal Command was also being strengthened, partly by the introduction of four-engined Avro Shackletons (a useful development of the elderly Lancaster) to support the even more elderly Short Sunderland flying-boats, but mostly by the acquisition – from the US Military Defence Aid Program – of the excellent Lockheed P2V Neptune. Few aircraft, in the opinion of Mick Ensor, a veteran of the wartime Coastal Command, have been better loved and few have lasted longer in front-line service. 'More than a thousand of these superb machines would be built by Lockheed between 1946 and 1962, with a further 82 built by Kawasaki Industries for the Japanese Self-Defense Force between 1966 and 1979. Some were employed on intelligence-gathering missions around the periphery of the Soviet Union; some flew patrols over the South China Sea during the Vietnam War; and some were used as late as 1982 by the

Argentine navy to stalk the British fleet during the Falklands War.' Of particular interest to Slessor – both during his term as CAS and afterwards – was the fact that the Neptune was capable of taking off from an aircraft carrier loaded with an atomic bomb.

In early April 1952, Slessor attended a 'tactical exercise without troops' in Paris for senior officers in all three services under Eisenhower's command and NATO representatives. 'The greatest discretion is being observed about it', reported *The Times*, 'and all that can officially be said of its object is that it is "to study staff procedures and resolve certain problems that might be encountered in the defence of western Europe."' Later in April, Slessor issued a memorandum on ground defence to all Cs-in-C at home and overseas. 'Both officers and airmen are now getting a sound basic training in ground combat when they first enter the service', he wrote. 'If they are kept up to the mark thereafter, and their capabilities are further developed by the interest and direction of their superiors, as well as by adequate unit and station exercises, we shall soon create a body of men to whom the essentials of station defence are part of the normal scheme of things.'

Slessor addressed the General Assembly of the Church of Scotland in Edinburgh on May 22nd. It was not true, he said, that the National Service recruit wasted his time. Young men were returned to civilian life as good citizens with useful skills. He regretted the passing of the compulsory church parade 'as a central feature of the pleasant community life of the service as they knew it of old', but perhaps the 'padre's hour' offered 'even better opportunities to the young minister.'

The Global Strategy Paper

An eminent British historian, Sir Michael Howard, thought Slessor as CAS established 'a doctrine of nuclear deterrence that was to provide a basis for all our strategic thinking until the end of the Cold War.' An impressive tribute from an outstanding scholar, who believed that Slessor's many writings, speeches, radio broadcasts and letters to *The Times* had a significant impact on both British and American thought. He was influenced by Dean Acheson, President Truman's Secretary of State from 1949 to 1953, who both 'censured and served' the next four presidents. For him, as for Slessor, NATO was the shield and the Soviet Union the enemy; he was also a good hater and neither man was distressed at news of the death in 1959 of John Foster Dulles, Eisenhower's Secretary of State, whom they regarded as Ike's evil genius. Like Slessor, Acheson rejected any suggestion that negotiations with the Soviet Union would lessen Cold War tensions: only power, and a readiness to use that power, got through to the Kremlin's rulers.

Shortly after the election of October 1951, the new Churchill government decided that Britain's defence policy must be revised. This was partly because Britain could not afford the ambitious re-armament programme begun under Attlee in 1949, nor the increase in armed forces agreed by NATO in Lisbon in February 1952 – which Slessor dismissed as 'an economic impossibility, a logistical nightmare, and a strategic nonsense' – and partly because Churchill thought more account should be taken of nuclear weapons. The Chiefs of Staff were therefore instructed to review British strategy.

On Slessor's suggestion, they agreed to escape from their offices for five days (April 28th to May 2nd) and Admiral Sir Rhoderick McGrigor – who had succeeded Fraser as First Sea Lord – offered the magnificent Royal Naval College, Greenwich, as an ideal place to reflect calmly – they hoped – away from the hassles of daily routine. Ian Jacob, Chief Staff Officer to the Minister of Defence, attended in order to give the Chiefs the benefit of his wartime experience in drafting papers for Cabinet perusal. One is surprised to learn, given Slessor's reputation as a 'paper man', that Jacob's skills were found necessary, but the Chiefs' own draft – which must have been largely Slessor's work – was 'a patchwork of uneasy compromises between the three services' views, and lacked coherence.' May and June were spent refining it, with Jacob's help, and that of Sir Frederick Brundrett (Chief Scientific Officer) and Sir Pierson Dickson (Foreign Office).

More than 40 years later, in 1993, their report – the 1952 Global Strategy Paper – remains, in the words of Bayliss and MacMillan, 'perhaps the best-known, the most often discussed, and also the most highly regarded defence document of the post-war period.' Ronald Lewin regarded it as 'the most important strategic review since 1945 and set the tone of British defence doctrine (if not entirely of practice) during the next decade.' Its basic theme was the need for increased effort to win the Cold War; success could be achieved by deterrence; Britain should complement the US's nuclear strength; and unnecessary commitments should be cut, in Europe and the Middle East. According to some commentators, it made Britain 'the first nation to base its national security planning almost entirely upon a declaratory policy of nuclear deterrence.' It has also been credited with influencing the Eisenhower administration's 'New Look' at defence policy in 1953.

The paper was similar to earlier ones concocted in May 1947 and June 1950 in that all three emphasised Britain's recognition of her dependence on allies – especially the US – for security. But the Chiefs of Staff now argued that NATO planners had not taken sufficient account of nuclear weapons. After visiting the US with Churchill, the Chiefs became aware of the size of the nuclear arsenal there and the ability of the Strategic Air Command to wipe out many vital centres in the event of Soviet aggression. This fact alone required a re-think about overall strategy.

Also, Britain, the Commonwealth and western Europe were facing economic crisis in early 1952. It seemed so severe that the Chiefs feared a 'bloodless victory' for the Soviet Union. Yet in February 1952, NATO had agreed in Lisbon to build up a force of 96 divisions and 9,000 aircraft by 1954 to counter a perceived Soviet superiority in conventional forces. Even with American aid, which the Chiefs did not believe would be forthcoming on a sufficient scale, neither Britain nor the states of western Europe could finance anything like such forces. Moreover, a central argument of the paper was that the West should prepare to meet a long cold war, rather than an immediate hot one. Defence spending must therefore be kept at a level which could be sustained for years.

Slessor and his colleagues were convinced of 'the implacable and unlimited aims' of the Soviet Union. As for China, they believed in 1950 that her xenophobia would make relations with the Soviets awkward and that she should not be driven into their embrace, but her intervention in Korea had changed that opinion by 1952. China, they thought, was 'a potentially great military power'. Even so, the Chiefs opposed using the bomb against the Chinese, partly because they had so few, but mostly because its use in China would alienate most Asians. There could be no question of using the bomb in minor wars. These must be won by conventional forces. The West's Cold War policy required the backing of 'the great deterrent': this stress on deterrence is a prime feature of the paper, and one evident in British thinking ever since 1945 because Britain was so vulnerable to nuclear attack. Possession of the bomb was now intended to give British negotiators arguments to use against American pressure for greater contribution to conventional defence, as agreed in Lisbon.

The Chiefs were sure that in the event of war, Britain would be 'the first and principal target of the Russian atomic attack', and she must therefore have her own weapons ready to deal with the bases of enemy long-range bombers and submarines. Although the support of the US would be essential in the long run, only a nuclear-armed Britain could hope to exercise any influence over US actions – and receive atomic bombs from the US. As well as nuclear weapons, the Chiefs were prepared to use chemical or biological weapons, in retaliation, if this were to Britain's advantage. They differed over the likely course of events after bombs were dropped. Slessor did not think there would be much military activity, but McGrigor thought both sides would fight on with any surviving forces. This 'broken-backed' warfare, as they called it, would be waged more at sea than elsewhere. The navy would thus have a role to play, a consideration which helped McGrigor support the rest of the paper. That notion would disappear in November 1952, when the Americans detonated a hydrogen bomb – many times more destructive than the atom bombs the Chiefs had in mind.

Conventional forces must be kept at a high state of readiness in western Europe, to convince the Soviet Union that a non-nuclear attack would make slow progress at a high cost. But could adequate forces be afforded? Should not Germany now be involved in the defence of the

West? And re-united? What risk was there of her joining – or being joined to – the Soviet Union? The Chiefs thought the Soviet Union would shrink from direct confrontation in Europe and exploit the West's weakness elsewhere. They also thought the US was too narrowly focussed on NATO and needed to pay more attention to the Middle and Far East – and to France: because despite her 'weakness and inefficiency', she had important possessions in Africa and the Far East.

The Global Strategy Paper was inspired by economic pressure and the Chiefs believed their recommendations would save money, but within six months the government undertook another review in a vain attempt, for a crumbling empire, to cut defence spending and match 'commitments to capabilities.' The paper was the basis of a British move to change western military policy, beginning in mid-1952 when Slessor went to Washington in an attempt to gain American backing for British plans. He failed, though the paper found favour with the US air force. Later that year, the Eisenhower administration, facing similar economic pressure to the British, adopted its 'New Look' defence policy which, like the British paper, emphasised nuclear weapons.

That paper had been coolly received both by Truman and Eisenhower. The US was rapidly acquiring massive power which Britain could not hope to match, and American decisions about how and where best to use that power were only marginally influenced by British wishes, whatever soft words were used in Whitehall or Washington. Slessor believed the paper influenced the 'New Look', but only British commentators agree. In his *Strategy for the West* (1954), he is not specific about a connection between the two, but in 1962, in *What Price Co-Existence?* he claimed that the 'New Look' originated in Whitehall.

When or where should the bomb be used?

Slessor wrote in March 1952 that General Eisenhower (expected to be the Republican candidate in that year's presidential election) had 'established this extraordinary position as a sort of military demi-god' and would probably be unable to control the right-wing of his party, where there was talk of 'liberating' eastern Europe. Slessor (among others) was anxious to prevent John Foster Dulles – generally supposed to be an enthusiast for action – from becoming Secretary of State, if Eisenhower won in November. He therefore hoped that Thomas Dewey, Governor of New York, would run and win. Hoyt Vandenberg (head of the USAF) suspected that the British were trying to back out of commitments to allow the US free use of air bases in Britain. There was increasing tension between American 'freedom of action' on the one hand and Britain's 'extreme vulnerability' on the other. This tension divided the two nations over nuclear strategy throughout Eisenhower's administration.

The British Chiefs argued that the Allies must not retreat from Communist aggression in Indochina, but doubted if the Chinese could be deterred even with atomic weapons, for they were used to 'cataclysmic disasters'. General Omar Bradley, who had evidently observed film of nuclear tests more closely than Slessor and his colleagues, and read the resulting reports more carefully, disagreed. Nothing in any nation's most 'cataclysmic' past even began to compare with the bomb's impact. The Americans, he told Slessor at their meeting in Washington July 29th-30th 1952, believed the bomb would be effective against any state. A prohibition on its use in Asia would encourage aggression and force the West into 'a series of Koreas'. In Whitehall, however, there was more fear of new MacArthurs than fear of new Koreas: that is, fear of American readiness to use the bomb in areas of marginal concern to Britain. The debate was not over whether the bomb dominated western strategy, but over who controlled it and where it would be used. On this key point the Americans and British were, and remained, far apart.

Clean sweep of old gang

As early as May 1952, when he still had more than half a year to serve, Slessor felt it necessary to write to Lord De L'Isle and Dudley (Secretary of State for Air) about the 'speculation and gossip going on in the service and places like the RAF Club' about his successor. 'Press correspondents like Dundas of the *Express*, who are always out for sensation and trouble-making, know that I am due to go at the end of this year and that Saunders, Lloyd, Hollinghurst and Cochrane are approaching their retiring age.' Slessor feared such headlines in the 'stunt press' as 'Clean Sweep of Old Gang' – which, of course, is what even the non-stunting broadsheets would report, though under more respectful headlines. *The Times* announced, as soberly as anyone could wish, on June 9th that Sir William Dickson was to take over from Slessor on January 1st 1953.

Meanwhile, Slessor took the trouble to write to Hollinghurst in July about three junior officers, all pilots, who had failed promotion exams in Germany. He had met and liked them, they all had good records, and he wondered if the RAF was not being too strict. 'Promotion exams should be a sieve to stop the wooden-head getting promoted and let through the ordinary chap even if he is not a potential star at the Staff College.' He had been told by Norstad that the USAF had a system whereby an officer's CO was able to award a certain number of marks, based on personal knowledge, which were included in the result. Slessor, always an advocate of 'selective and controlled nepotism', thought we should look into this. Four year later, he again made the point that 'the first requirement of an RAF officer is not the ability to do sums or answer questions glibly, but "fire in the belly", the quality of leadership and the invincible morale that through the years characterised the men who fought from what I shall always think of as Sutton's Farm, Hornchurch, in Essex.'

'The supreme deterrent to active aggression', wrote Slessor in the July issue of *Les Ailes*, 'and the instrument under whose cover we are building up our strength and holding the line in the Cold War is atomic air power.' He admitted that the RAF could never equal the USAF, 'but the medium force of Bomber Command is even now playing its small part and will do so to an increasing extent as the new four-engined jet bombers – the best in the world – come into the line.' He had not, of course, made a systematic comparison of these unproven bombers with those actually serving in the American or Russian air forces. They were British built and therefore, in his opinion, the world's best.

The RAF had three tasks, he continued. One was to contribute to NATO's integrated air forces; a second was to protect sea lanes of communication; and the third was to defend the United Kingdom, 'a vitally important allied base in war.' Should there be another world war, the modern submarine would pose an even greater threat than Hitler's U-boats. 'Coastal Command is far smaller today than it was in the crucial year 1943, but it is expanding steadily and re-equipping with the Shackleton, which is proving itself [he claimed] a first-class anti-submarine aircraft.' As for Fighter Command, it had undergone a great expansion during the past 18 months and its new swept-wing fighters, are 'of incomparable performance', he thought, even though they were not yet in service. Overall, he concluded, with our NATO partners 'we should again prove invincible and irresistible if the disaster of a third world war came upon us, but our first job was to make sure that it did not.' A few days later, on July 13th, he attended the first 'air demonstration' organized by NATO at Brussels airport. About 1,500 airmen from all NATO countries took part in a display, 'which was a demonstration of the need for vigilance and the fact that the organization of security cannot be confined to one country.' Swift and Hunter fighters showed their paces, as did Canberras and Vampires.

Throughout his time as CAS Slessor was irritated by 'this absurd business whereby no-one but US officers are supposed to know anything about the A-bomb.' He talked it over with Hugh Saunders (at SHAPE) in August. Several US airmen were trying to reduce the restrictions, but 'the word "MacMahon" is written on their hearts and they are terrified of giving anything away officially – even though all we need know has already appeared in papers like the *Saturday Evening Post* and in unclassified US documents like their Civil Defense Manual.' He wondered whether it would therefore help if, when Saunders ended his tour of duty, he was replaced by an American, Norstad.

In September 1952 Slessor exploded with rage at American objections to British sales of aircraft to states in the Middle East. Since the war, he said, the US had 'taken advantage of our difficulties – which are largely due to the extent to which we have beggared ourselves in two world wars in lives and treasure – to extend their influence (and hence their trade, sales of aircraft etc.) all over the world.' He thought Britain's withdrawal from Palestine was largely forced by Americans; they played a part in getting the British out of India; 'having refused to back us in Greece in the troubles of 1944-5 they have since moved in and taken over the influence which we used to exert'; they had made Turkey 'virtually an American satellite', and in short, wrote Slessor, 'American imperialism has become far more intolerant and selfish than British imperialism at its ripest.'

As he drew near to the end of his days in office, in October, Slessor summarized his thoughts on command and organization in NATO for Ridgway, the Supreme Commander. In the event of war, air power would be vital and should be controlled from SHAPE – by an airman, who was Ridgway's deputy. Slessor would prefer a Briton, but had no rooted objection to an American. The aim should be that achieved by Montgomery and Coningham in the desert, and again in France and Germany, and the way Bradley and Vandenberg co-operated. 'We know it works', he assured Ridgway. What he strongly objected to was a French general in a senior position.

On November 12th, Slessor spoke at a lunch organized by the Institute of Transport in London about the need to 'transform our present balance of payments position, but also enormously reduce our mortally dangerous dependence on the sea transport of imports in war – namely, a revolutionary increase in the home production of food.' Also, a 'merchant air fleet' must be built up with more modern machines to replace the improvised aircraft that have been used for too long. On the military front, said Slessor, 'two long-range four-engined jet transports, with two more in operating reserve, at a reasonable rate of use, would lift in a year between the United Kingdom, the Middle East and the Far East more troops more cheaply than two of the latest troop ships.' Never before had he spoken out so boldly in favour of cargo and personnel carriers, but it would be years before such aircraft appeared.

Slessor had his last conference with his Commanders-in-Chief on November 17th in the Air Council Room, Whitehall Gardens. He told them that the main assumptions of the Chiefs of Staff's current strategy were that war was less likely than it had previously been thought; that we should pin our faith on the strategic deterrent, with the V-bomber as its instrument; and that we should plan for a short intensive war with one month's reserves at maximum rates. Money was tight, aircraft numbers dangerously reduced, and the RAF was seriously short of skilled manpower: too many postings, poorer working conditions than in civil employment and lower pay were the causes. Many junior officers lacked initiative and personal authority, in Basil Embry's view, and had a 'factory whistle' attitude – too ready to stop work. Hugh Lloyd then expressed everyone's regret that Slessor was leaving and 'wished him happy landings for the future.' On that more cheerful note, our bomber champion ended his Whitehall career. Always 'a rapid and voluble speaker, full of ideas, he tended to monopolise meetings; indeed some felt he upset the balance of the Chiefs of Staff by his domineering manner.' But Lord Cherwell (Churchill's scientific advisor and a man slow to praise others) regarded him as 'undoubtedly one of the ablest men I ever met in the air force', adding words that Slessor would have valued: he had 'sympathy with the problems and needs of the other services.'

Slessor took his last parade as CAS a month later, on December 17th 1952, at Cranwell's graduation ceremony. 'Untimely hard weather – at times the wind reached 65 knots – drove the parade into the comparative peace and shelter of a hangar.' In his address to more than 300 future officers, he said that today the 'Pax Atlantica' rested as firmly on Anglo-American air power as the 'Pax Britannica' rested on the British fleet for a hundred years up to 1914.

Ira Eaker had received a cheerful note from him in September announcing his forthcoming liberation: he would be 'a free man' next New Year's Day. 'I can't tell you how much I look forward to that. We have bought a lovely old 15th century manor house in Dorset – 120 miles from London.[17] I am going to write a book or two, and sundry articles for the papers about air power. I hope to be able to help old Boom Trenchard in keeping air power in the public eye.'

He had, he said, been asked to go to SHAPE as the top airman, but used his lameness as an excuse for declining. If so, it was a decision he would soon regret, for he was at the height of his powers and his enthusiasm for advocating and managing air power was undiminished. He used the same excuse – perhaps with more reason – for refusing a governorship in one of the British Dominions – he did not say which one. 'They have tried to get me to go on the Coal Board – but what the hell do I know about coal!' To which one might reply that he knew nothing about war at sea before he went to Coastal Command and yet he made a success of it and, moreover, enjoyed himself more than in any other appointment, including that of CAS. It seems there was also a suggestion that he become Commissioner of the Metropolitan Police. However, he had not turned down 'one or two directorships, which will help out with the pennies.'

Slessor was not awarded a peerage, even by the Tories, but he must soon have regretted not taking on another full-time job. On January 1st 1953, when he became unemployed, he was only half-way through his 55th year. Apart from his life-long lameness, he enjoyed excellent health and would live for another 26 years. He was far from idle during those years: he wrote numerous articles collected into several books; lectured on both sides of the Atlantic as well as in Australia; spoke regularly on radio; and fired off many letters to the Editor of *The Times*. These were not of petty interest: that newspaper then had 'an importance in British

---

[17] Rimpton Manor, near Yeovil, which is actually just across the border, in Somerset.

public life which is difficult in these days [2005] to appreciate', wrote A. N. Wilson. 'It was the in-house journal of the Establishment, a term first used in 1923.'

Slessor was a director of the Blackburn aircraft company, a consultant with General Dynamics, an active member of several committees (especially those concerned with former servicemen) and he attended countless lunches, dinners, garden parties, funerals and memorial services. In November 1955 he was delighted to learn that he had been awarded the C. P. Robertson Memorial Trophy for his work in 'interpreting the RAF to the public' since his retirement. But for a man of his temperament and energy, it may not have been enough. He was, in short, a spectator – calling out loudly and often from a privileged seat in the grandstand about a game he knew well. Those on the field of play heard his voice, but they made their own decisions.

Looking back in 1969, Slessor said he was happy to retire at the end of 1952. Churchill, who had returned to power in October 1951, 'was not the easiest of men to work under and he did not particularly care for me.' Slessor later claimed that he was asked to stay on for a fourth year, but declined. 'I had done a year under the Conservative Government and had found serving under Churchill so difficult that I was reluctant to do another year of it.' Churchill had always been very difficult to work with. He became more so in the 1950s as his mental and physical powers weakened, and he was compelled to recognize Britain's declining status as a world power. We know that Slessor and Tedder had more in common than either man cared to admit, and here we see another point in common: both were happier to recognize Churchill's greatness from a distance, when they were no longer obliged to see him regularly and put up with his unpredictable moods and methods of business that suited no-one but himself. Churchill's doctor, Lord Moran, observed that he was slow to recognize the merits of anyone who was not congenial to him. 'Efficiency in itself did not appear to influence his likes or dislikes.'

Slessor wrote a careful, heart-felt letter to Churchill on December 30th. 'Tomorrow I am leaving the employed list of the RAF after near 38 years in the air service and shall have no more share in the responsibility for shaping our military programmes. While it is clear from our Global Strategy paper that the Chiefs of Staff themselves fully understand the importance of the bomber in British policy, I have sometimes felt that it is not universally recognized as the vital thing it is. May I express the hope that you will, perhaps during your voyage to New York, find time to read the attached note, which summarizes a conviction based on many years of experience and study of air power.'

The note began by quoting Churchill's speech in Boston in 1949 when he said: 'For good or ill, air mastery is today the supreme expression of military power and fleets and armies, however necessary, must accept a subordinate rank.' Slessor then quoted Churchill's words in 1940: 'The navy can lose us the war, but only the air force can win it. Therefore our supreme effort must be to gain overwhelming mastery in the air. The fighters are our salvation, but the bombers alone provide the means of victory.' Slessor then told the Prime Minister that today 'it is the bomber which holds out to us the greatest, perhaps the only, hope of achieving our hearts' desire – the prevention of war. It is the great deterrent.' We must not leave it to the Americans. 'If we did that, we should sink to the level of a third-class power. We cannot live on our historical tradition or on the credit of our past achievements. In war, we should have little or no influence on the direction of Allied strategy or on the determination of terms of peace. In peace, we should lose what influence we have – and it is still important – upon American policy and strategic planning.' But these heartfelt words fell on stony ground. As Slessor later noted, his last message to Churchill was not even acknowledged.

CHAPTER 18

SAGE OF YEOVIL, 1953-1956

NATO and Everest

On January 6th 1953, during his first week 'as one very new to the unemployed list', Slessor wrote to *The Times* to comment on a letter from the Chairman of the Navy League. Everyone owes a debt to that league 'for its assiduous vigilance in keeping before the public eye the importance of sea power to the Commonwealth and Empire', but Slessor hoped to see an end of ill-informed criticism by sailors of airmen. It was simply not true, he wrote, that 'the only possible counter' to the threat by shore-based aircraft to British sea communications lay in carrier-borne fighters and anti-submarine bombers. 'But actually the one thing, more than any combination of other causes, that led to the extraordinary degree of air supremacy over our sea communications – as over this island and the theatres of land warfare – was the bomber offensive. It could not have been achieved earlier by any other means, certainly not by carrier-borne fighters, nor could it be in any future war.' Slessor ended by asking naval champions to make the case for their service without denigrating air champions. 'We had too much of that in the old days. Not only was it very bad for inter-service relationships, but it resulted in a great deal of nonsense being written which darkened counsel and, in retrospect, must be a matter of some embarrassment to its authors.'

Stalin's death in March 1953 offered a chance of thaw in the Cold War, but Dulles and the American military worried over the growing size of the Soviet nuclear arsenal during the rest of that year and throughout 1954. The problem they faced was not, as Slessor believed, trying to convince the Soviets that the West could hurt them, but trying to avoid a Soviet strike from the blue that might negate America's most-loved military asset. The Americans were determined to strike swiftly, at need, and feared that their allies might prevent action or the use of their bases. Vandenberg had thought this last a motive behind the 1952 paper.

A 'British Atlantic Committee' was set up in May 1953 with Sir David Kelly as President and Slessor as Vice-President. Its purpose was 'to promote in the United Kingdom the fullest possible knowledge and understanding' of NATO and was equivalent to similar committees created in Norway, Denmark and the Netherlands. It was backed by the 'British Society for International Understanding'. A conference was shortly to be held in Paris, to discuss 'NATO and the Re-Armament of the West', at which Slessor would lead the British delegation.

It was learned in July 1953 that a Frenchman, Marshal Alphonse Juin, was to become 'the most important field commander in the west', exercising greater power – according to a leader writer in *The Times* – than either Bradley or Montgomery did during the Second World War. At present, Juin was in command only of ground forces and 'the true seat of war, should it come' was at the headquarters of an American general, Matthew Ridgway, in Paris. In August, however, control would shift to Juin's headquarters in Fontainebleau. He would take charge of the Second and Fourth Allied Tactical Air Forces, under Air Chief Marshal Sir Basil Embry, who was to succeed Lauris Norstad. The British Army of the Rhine had for some time been under the central ground command in Europe, but the Second ATAF had not. This important departure from precedent merited careful scrutiny, thought *The Times*. Only a few days previously, Slessor had reiterated in *International Affairs* his strongly-held view that no-one understands air power 'who has not had to wield it.' Juin had not.

The strategic air forces would remain in other hands, and General Ridgway had stressed that the new Air Deputy at SHAPE was to be Norstad, an outstanding airman. 'But control of the tactical air forces is to be severed from the rest and the 14 governments of NATO have turned their backs on the principle which Lord Tedder took special care to stress in his Cambridge lectures in 1947. Air warfare cannot be separated into little packets. It knows no boundaries on land or sea other than those imposed by the radius of action of the aircraft; it is a unity, and demands unity of command. Now things have changed, apparently; General Ridgway is to split his – still inadequate – air power into two packets in his vital zone.'

Slessor addressed a European Youth Conference at Middleton Camp, near Edinburgh, on August 25th 1953. More than 200 young men and women, representing nearly every country west of the Iron Curtain attended. It was, he thought, 'ludicrous to imagine that Russian divisions could roll across Europe to the Channel as if they were on a field day – even against inferior opposition – if an atomic deluge was descending upon Russian cities and communications behind their forces.' He also thought many generals ignored or underrated the influence of 'the terrible power of the atom-bomber force of the United States and Britain.' We must be on guard for many years to come. The object of NATO was not like Mount Everest where, having reached the summit, one could plant a few flags and come back down again: one must stay at the top.

Ira Eaker, fishing friend, aviation colleague

By July 1953, the Slessors were living at Rimpton Manor in Yeovil, Somerset, about 120 miles west of the capital. From October 1953 onwards, 'Jack' wrote many letters to 'Ira' Eaker. They had become good friends after the war, visiting each other's homes and sharing a keen interest in fishing, as well as similar views on strategic bombing and the need to be able to respond promptly and effectively to Soviet aggression. There was much talk about him joining Ira and Tooey Spaatz on the Rogue river. He would at last be able to accept a standing invitation, because he had been invited to lecture at several colleges in the US and Canada.

In a letter of November 7th 1953 he raised a delicate subject regarding his visit to the US. 'One trouble which I'm sure you'll understand is that we can't get dollars except just to meet day-to-day routine expenses. So we are dependent for our passage to California and back either on the USAF or your company.' A month later, on December 9th, as befits one unable to pay his way, Slessor gushingly thanked 'My dear old Ira' and 'dear Ruth for the marvellous time you gave us.' He went on to say how much he wished Ike (now President) 'had a bit more comprehension of the complete revolution in human affairs that has been brought about by air power.' In July 1955, Slessor told Eaker he was to undertake a lecture tour of the US for four weeks in February/March 1956. 'We shall never get to first base with these Kremlin chaps', he added, 'as long as we persist in imagining that they are people with whom we can negotiate normal civilized agreements.'

Slessor had been appointed a director of Blackburn and General Aircraft in June 1954. 'He is so well known in aviation circles throughout the world', said Mr Robert Blackburn, chairman, at the company's annual general meeting in August, 'that it seems almost unnecessary for me to say how greatly our deliberations will be assisted by the breadth of his knowledge, experience, and vision.' A year later, on June 1st, Slessor wrote to Eaker to commend the technical director of Blackburn, Mr N. E. Rowe, a good friend. He was going to the US and would have with him the chief designer, Barry Laight, 'who is also an excellent chap and is responsible for the design of a new maritime strike aircraft for which we have just had a development order in the face of competition from four or five of the bigger aircraft firms like the Hawker Siddeley Group. Do get in touch with Rowe when he is in Los Angeles – you'll like him and I know he would like to have a talk with you about the weapons system which we are building into this new aircraft.' This was the Buccaneer, one of Britain's greatest aviation achievements.

No doubt Slessor came to appreciate the irony of his association with the Buccaneer, the finest aircraft used by both the FAA and the RAF. The Royal Navy had invested in very expensive carriers after 1945 and needed aircraft of first-class quality for them. A specification was issued for a two-seat tactical strike bomber capable of operating at very low levels. The Blackburn B.103, designed by Laight, was chosen during May 1955. In October 1959 it was ordered for the Fleet Air Arm as the Buccaneer S. Mark I and the first production model flew in January 1962; an improved Mark II entered FAA service in June 1964. It proved so successful that by 1969 the Air Staff had been obliged to use it in the RAF: reluctantly, because the animosities in which Slessor himself played so active a part were still alive. It could have been in service years earlier – saving all the money wasted on the TSR.2, as we shall see below – had it not been for the traditional 'internecine warfare' between the RAF and the Royal Navy.

As early as January 1958 Slessor had written to Geoffrey Tuttle (Deputy CAS) in the Air Ministry to commend the Buccaneer. 'I hope there is no conscious or subconscious prejudice in the Air Staff against taking an originally naval design. That surely would be very silly. If the aeroplane is a good one for the job, surely that should be the only criterion – especially if, as I believe, the practical arguments in favour of a virtually identical aeroplane for the two services doing the same job are as strong as they are.' In October 1958 he wrote to George Brown, a senior Labour politician (then in opposition), about the Air Staff's antagonism to the Buccaneer. The delay in deciding whether or not to go ahead (and in what numbers) was, of course, harmful to Blackburn, but was also costing Britain millions in American and possibly German sales. Slessor wanted Brown to press Sandys in the House of Commons on these points.

There was much talk of supplying the Buccaneer to the German navy in 1959, but Blackburn's hopes were dashed in part by German insistence that only a reconnaissance capability was required (which was nonsense, in Slessor's opinion) and in part by US pressure to buy Lockheed's F-104 Starfighter (which could not operate successfully in the Baltic either to attack shipping or lay mines). A year later, in June 1960, Slessor wrote sadly to John Orme (in the Cabinet Office) about Air Staff opposition to the Buccaneer and the lack of government backing in selling it to the Germans.

British Egypt?

The Sage of Yeovil had his say in September 1953 regarding the Suez Canal and Britain's military base in Egypt. 'However childishly unreasonable it may appear to us', he wrote, 'that the Egyptians should consider it inconsonant with their dignity as a foreign state to allow allied bases on their soil, when we see nothing undignified in having allied troops quartered in England, we must face the realities of the times we live in.' Britain no longer had the strength to defend either Egypt or the canal and the fact that Turkey was now a NATO ally changed the strategic situation. 'I would be the last to advocate any policy of scuttle', Slessor added, because stability in the Middle East was important to NATO and the British Commonwealth. There may be criticisms of Churchill's policies, but 'the surrender of a vital British interest to bluff or violence by Egypt or anyone else seems to me exceedingly unlikely to be one of them.'

Lieutenant-General W. G. Lindsell questioned Slessor's opinion that Turkey's entry into NATO reduced the need for a main base in Egypt. 'Just as we now require, and are building, an advanced base in the Antwerp area to maintain our forces in Europe, whose main base is in the United Kingdom, so forces operating in defence of Turkey or the Persian Gulf area would require a main base in Egypt with perhaps smaller advanced bases nearer the forces deployed in action with the enemy.' Only at Suez, Port Said, Alexandria and the canal itself were there facilities to supply armed forces on a grand scale.

Strategy for the West

Slessor's *Strategy for the West*, published in June 1954, was based on lectures given in Britain and the US during 1953 and reflected his time at the Imperial Defence College and as CAS. It is a work by a passionate Cold Warrior, putting the case for unrelenting opposition to the Soviet Union in blunt language. Sir Michael Howard regarded it as 'a seminal work. In it he laid out a strategy for the conduct of the Cold War that was to be followed, and followed successfully, for the next 35 years.' Howard, writing in 1998, found it 'immensely refreshing' to read it again and be reminded of the author's 'sterling common sense, which was as evident in his political judgements as in his military.' The West's task, argued Slessor, was to drive Communism back behind its current frontiers and keep it there. He had no patience with the crusading ardour of many Americans, who believed they had a God-given mission to destroy it, whatever the cost. Given time, and a readiness to spend heavily on armaments, the West would show the Kremlin – and those it ruled – that overt aggression would prove too costly, also that the western way of life, with all its faults, was superior. 'Few policies', concluded Howard, 'either political or military, have ever been so triumphantly vindicated.' He found it hard to think of any other retired senior officer in any service who made so substantial a contribution to the strategic thinking of his time.

But what if nuclear war did break out? Here Slessor was less than convincing. He admitted that defence of the British Isles was impossible and citizens must grin and bear it, taking 'what comes to them, knowing that thereby they are playing as essential a part in the country's defences as the pilot in the fighter and the man behind the gun.' This was nonsense, in Howard's opinion: Slessor had 'lost touch with reality. There could be no comparison between the aftermath of a nuclear, let alone a thermonuclear, strike and the German blitz of 1940.' Nuclear weapons, however, were preventing major war and therefore, as Slessor wrote, 'the greatest disservice that anyone could possibly do to the cause of peace would be to abolish nuclear armaments on either side.' There was in effect a balance of terror: an uneasy truce, but the best solution available.

The book was the subject of a long, thoughtful, critical, but generally approving editorial in *The Times*. General Gruenther (the American head of SHAPE) had recently stated that he expected atomic weapons to be used if war broke out in Europe; so too had his British deputy, Field Marshal Montgomery; and now Slessor 'states categorically in his new book *Strategy for the West* that there is no chance whatever of another great war being waged without recourse to the nuclear weapon. All three are telling the plain truth as they see it, and echoing the strategic doctrines of their governments – doctrines which Sir John Slessor, perhaps more than any other single man, has helped to shape.' In the opinion of that newspaper – regarded in those days as a reliable guide to government thinking – Slessor's book was 'the most authoritative exposition yet to hand on what is loosely called the "new look" strategy. He believes passionately in the capacity of the Strategic Air Command and Britain's own Bomber Command to deter aggression. He believes that this country does not need to maintain the whole of the regular army on first-line scales of equipment; that it is "only realistic" to recognize that three-quarters of the Territorial Army ought really to be training for Civil Defence; that the make and shape of the navy are not right for modern war. He will not tolerate any suggestion that the Atlantic alliance should delegate responsibility for strategic bombing to the United States: "the RAF without Bomber Command would be like Nelson's fleet without its Line of Battle... We should sooner than later sink to the level of a fourth-rate Power."'

Two points troubled the leader writer. One was the assumption that while the RAF awaited its V-bombers and the Americans built more and better aircraft and atomic weapons, the Soviet Union would not overtake the West's lead. It may not use its power 'with western perfection', but it is always dangerous to underrate that state. Slessor thought it would be 'hopeless' for the Russians to try and destroy the US by air attack and their own cities were vulnerable. 'But the danger will grow, until a great war would be "almost" as suicidal for the United States as for Russia.' The second point was this: 'Is it not possible that, as the deterrent effect of atomic stockpiles dwindles, air forces armed at great cost with atomic bombers may find themselves virtually excluded even from Korea-type local wars, until they are relegated one day to the role of Household troops? Very soon almost every kind of aircraft will be potentially the carrier of a mass destruction weapon capable of converting a local war into a global conflict.' Liddell Hart had suggested that any air force action risked being mistaken for an atomic attack. 'It has been clear for some time that atomic bombers, in the process of deterring global aggression, are likely to increase the frequency of local wars. Is it impossible that in the process they may end by sounding the knell of air attack altogether, even of the tactical kind?' Slessor would 'certainly dismiss any such suggestion with contempt. He expounds with perfect clarity the orthodox doctrines of 1952 and 1953. But what of 1956?'

Strategy, Slessor thought, was 'the management of the political, military, economic and industrial resources of the Western coalition in such a way as to achieve the objects of the Free World.' To do this, the 'Free World' must base its strategy on 'spiritual values'. Slessor did not define these slogans – 'Free World' or 'spiritual values' – he merely regarded them as if they were immutable given assets, like aircraft or tanks. We may dislike and despise, he wrote, 'the crazy philosophy of dialectical materialism', but we cannot force our values on the Soviet Union or Communist China. Their choice is 'no business of ours', unless they tried to impose it on others and we must resist, 'by every effective means, military or political.' But they already had imposed their 'choice' in many places – and what military means would be 'effective' in obliging them to withdraw?

Unless 'the West takes leave of its senses', Slessor believed there would be no third world war because the Communists were totally foiled by atomic strategy. Their devious campaign was to stir up 'peace activists' in the West who would accuse everyone else of being warmongers. Sadly, this campaign worked only too well with the 'muddled vanity of ecclesiastical and scientific exhibitionists' and the feeble minds of others. To give up nuclear weapons would be to ruin the prospects of long-term peace. We were, in fact, engaged now in a third world war and had been for years.

What did it mean to 'negotiate' with Russians? It cannot involve such concepts as honour, compromise, sacrifice. Their words meant only what they said they meant. They were not reasonable men. Nevertheless, we should still meet them, but with no expectations of a satisfactory outcome, and we should avoid making useless treaties. Diplomacy needed the backing of force and NATO hitherto had been unrealistic. The Soviet Union, as always, pursued world domination. Although it was very strong, in Slessor's opinion, it was vulnerable: certainly to aerial attack and the satellites were likely to prove a source of weakness in a crisis.

On our side of the fence, Slessor wrote, we must avoid lapsing into 'the infantile intolerance of McCarthyism', and the US should be more cautious about condemning Britain's colonial rule because premature independence would open the door for Communists. He did not consider whether Britain could afford colonial rule indefinitely or whether colonies might not reject Communism as firmly as an ever-growing number of their people seemed to be prepared to reject British rule. One way to reduce the size of the British army, the Sage of Yeovil seriously suggested, would be to train up 'locals in the various areas to fight for us, as has been done for years.' For good or ill, as Slessor seemed unable to realize, those days were long gone. Although air power kept the Cold War cold, the main burden fell on the armies – and we needed compulsory military service for our young men.

The primary weapon of the free world

The Allies needed enough force both to prevent war or to fight it, if need be, but not so much as to sap their economies. 'To arm ourselves into bankruptcy would be to accept self-imposed defeat.' We were, Slessor thought, at a 'strategic crossroads', where we could build a force to equal the Red Army and bankrupt ourselves, or maintain atomic air power with an army of sufficient size to deter but not to bring economic ruin – and so we should not hesitate to trade with Communist states.' These resounding assertions of the obvious were nowhere backed by the figures or numbers that alone could make them mean something to senior members of governments.

The West might see more limited wars – like Korea – and should not shrink from them. Air power was not decisive there, because it was a limited war and 'air power is an unlimited weapon.' Its 'strategic function' in small wars was to keep them small: 'to hold the ring and prevent them spreading.' How easy Slessor made it sound! But what if a small war lasted for years, at an ever-growing cost in men and materials, undermining the resolve of a nation's citizens to continue – or encouraging that nation to enlarge the war or even to use the bomb?

Although he claimed an 'affectionate regard' for the Royal Navy, the aircraft carrier did not, in his opinion, justify the expense involved. But did it not provide precisely that flexibility in the use of air power which he so often preached elsewhere? He harped on about 'the most deadly enemy of the U-boat was the radar-fitted shore-based aircraft of Coastal Command', and though that might well have been true up to 1945, was it still true a decade later? The days of the aircraft carrier, he asserted, 'are no doubt numbered.' As was so often the case, Slessor's forecast proved mistaken. For the rest of his life, the carrier remained a vital part of sea power and still is.

Lord Granville, President of the Navy League, was among the many who disagreed with Slessor. 'Unquestionably, in coastal or narrow waters', he wrote in November 1954, 'land-based aircraft have their important part to play in defence of our shipping, but there is not in sight at present any substitute for carrier-based aircraft for providing air cover for convoys in the wide oceans.' This he claimed, was in fact the opinion of Slessor (among others) 'who have stated that the navy must have its own carrier-borne aircraft. It may well be, in the future, that these aircraft, like the fighter and bombing forces, will be largely replaced by guided missiles, but these too will need floating bases with the convoys.' Trenchard, concluded Granville, had 'strong views as to the cost and great vulnerability of aircraft carriers, but it is perhaps significant that in the last war no British carrier was sunk by land-based aircraft and only one by naval aircraft.'

World War III

Slessor lectured at the Royal United Services Institute on 'Air Power and the Future of War' in 1954. If air power was used wisely, he said, total war had no future. The lecture is yet another regurgitation of old – not necessarily bad – ideas, but he had said it all so often before. This ardent bomber champion repeated his conviction – one much disputed by historians – that 'if we had been able to concentrate a rather higher proportion of the national resources of Britain and America on the bomber offensive against the heart of Germany', the Allies would have won the war sooner.

Slessor gave the Pollak Memorial Lecture at Harvard in the same year on 'A British View of the World Strategic Situation Today'. The Communists used what he called 'the tactics of the termite'. They constantly advocated atomic disarmament in a 'natural and transparently obvious gambit', aimed at putting 'the Free World at a fatal military disadvantage.' We were fighting World War III now, and had been for years, but he was willing to bet that there would be no Anglo-American forces on continental soil in 20 years – that is, in 1974. He would have lost the bet, and knew it, long before he died in 1979. He was right, however, about China not remaining a satellite or a permanent ally of the Soviet Union and becoming a world power.

He greatly relished a rare opportunity to lecture at Oxford in 1955 on 'A Policy of Deterrence'. He was totally obsessed with what was (and still is) a major issue, but he was now long out of office, a self-appointed expert, the Sage of Yeovil, merely repeating himself to whoever on either side of the Atlantic would offer him a platform. His analysis is simple and shallow, as if the world were divided into two armed camps. He shows little awareness of changes since 1945. In fact, except for his fixation on air power – and in particular the bomber – he remains what he literally just was, a Victorian Englishman, of good Home Counties family and breeding, a family with several members who had served the state in or out of uniform. He disagreed with those who wanted to 'ban the bomb' because he was certain it kept the peace. A study of history should convince those 'kindly Christian people' that they were wrong. Britain must keep her own bomber force and nuclear weapons, although we remained part of an alliance and could not take on the role of arbitrator between the US and the Soviet Union. 'If we want to remain a Great Power, we must face up to the cost.'

But that is what many Britons in 1955, who were not wealthy retired officers living in comfort, did not want. This was the year when wartime austerity at last began to fade away, and they wanted a greater share in those comforts that men and women of Slessor's class had so long enjoyed, together with the goodies now appearing: cars, televisions, kitchenware and foreign holidays. 'Great Power' status did not enthuse them, and except for a vocal minority, they did not dwell on the prospect of instant incineration any more than they did on death and taxes.

Slessor wrote an article for the *New York Reporter* in 1955 on 'Disarmament and Security after Geneva'. German reunification and Soviet withdrawal from East Germany and eastern Europe should be prior conditions to any disarmament decisions, reinforced with regular inspection. Despite the risk, he advocated withdrawing British and American forces from the continent, except from West Berlin, because air power would remain a sufficient deterrent to the Soviet Union. For the first time he proposed that nuclear weapons might be eliminated from world armouries, but 'smaller tactical atomic weapons' must be retained. If there was disarmament, and the Soviet Union broke the agreement, these and bigger weapons could quickly be built. Really? Quicker than the Soviets could, and quickly enough? Air Power would remain 'the supreme expression' of military power. We must seek disarmament, he wrote. The West spent heavily on defence, and 'no-one in his sane senses does not long to see a reduction in the present gross misapplication of wealth to armaments.' An admirable sentiment, but meaningless – as anyone in the West's massive defence industry or in its very large armed forces, could have told him.

An international system of defence
In November 1955, Slessor had contributed to a discussion on the hydrogen bomb, a weapon even more terrible, if ever used, than the atomic bombs produced and tested during the past 11 years. The idea that 'the object in war is the destruction of the enemy's armed forces was finally disposed of with the advent of the atomic and the hydrogen bombs.' Today, he argued, 'perhaps unfortunately', victory could be achieved simply by massive destruction. What was the 'great deterrent' designed to deter? The prevention of a potential aggressor from undertaking total war as an instrument of policy, as Hitler did in 1939. It would not prevent 'minor aggression, such as the North Koreans walking across the 38th Parallel in 1950.' Bertrand Russell, for whom Slessor expressed 'a great admiration and respect', had written that the world's rulers only valued the bomb because it prevented war, but there was a much cheaper way of preventing war, and that was mutual admission that war could no longer further the interests of either party. That would not be the case if nuclear weapons did not exist. The West could not declare that any Soviet potential target be regarded as immune from attack, as Admiral Sir Anthony Buzzard suggested. 'Destruction would be confined to NATO soil', if the Admiral had his way, 'particularly to Germany, and possibly also to satellites like Poland and Czechoslovakia.' Slessor maintained that that would seem 'a good bargain' from a Russian viewpoint, for they would much prefer 'to capture places like Paris and the Channel ports intact than as masses of radio-active rubble.'

Clement Attlee had rightly said in June 1954 that when national existence was at stake, 'any weapon will be used as a last resort.' Slessor argued that 'no-one suggests that we should immediately drop a hydrogen bomb on Moscow the moment there is a frontier incident', but there must be conventional forces based in Germany – and there must also be a West German army. 'We cannot afford to wake up one fine morning to find that some peace-loving democrats have liberated Hamburg, with the help of the peace-loving East German army.' The last resort was reached, said Slessor, when it became 'absolutely clear' that the Kremlin had decided on the gamble of total war.

As he so often did, Slessor advocated the 'air control' procedure practised by the RAF between the wars to deal with the Soviet threat. The first step would be to give ample warning before bombs were dropped on urban areas to enable non-combatants to flee. The second step was to designate 'prohibited areas' and notify these to the enemy before any action took place. Finally came the third step of bombing these places without further warning. It was a procedure that worked against a people without ground or air defences, but one which would undoubtedly have made it easier for the Soviet Union to focus its defences on 'prohibitive areas' – including the routes to and from them. As Sir Michael Howard observed, air control proved to be 'a pretty disastrous policy when the United States adopted it in Vietnam with their "free-fire zones"'. Slessor was quite right, however, to warn that modern western armies were top-heavy and used to living comfortably. He pined for an army more akin 'to that of the old Punjab frontier force', which 'went cheerfully to war on foot with a rifle, a couple of bandoliers, a bag of raisins and a chupatti or two, and a water bottle.' The Americans did not go to war in Vietnam like that, but their adversaries did.

In January 1955, General Gruenther – then SACEUR – had announced that Soviet armies could still march through western Europe to the Channel. If they did so, NATO had in the B-47 Stratojet a weapon for which the Russians had as yet no equivalent, but he was greatly concerned about the West's incomplete early warning system. It had already cost serious money and would cost much more. So too would the acquisition and construction of airfields. When Gruenther arrived in Paris with Eisenhower in January 1951 there had been only 15 airfields in the whole of western Europe. Now there were 125 and that figure would soon rise to 175. In the event of war, Soviet forces would seek to destroy these and so Gruenther was encouraging the building of aircraft carriers: 'we should welcome all the platforms afloat and ashore we could be given. They would all be needed and the side which survived the first phase of an atomic attack with the most airfields – afloat or ashore – in an operational condition, would clearly hold the advantage for further phases of the war.'

That early warning system was completed and by 1961 NATO maintained an air alert over Europe with fully-armed fighters poised, night and day, to scramble and challenge Soviet intruders. This international system of defence had been painstakingly created during the 1950s and was backed by, in Ian Forrest's words, 'a hefty punch in the form of a nuclear air strike force which is contributed to by its 15 nation membership, and extends across free Europe from Norway to Turkey.' The entire network was under the overall direction in 1961 of Lauris Norstad, now SACEUR at SHAPE, near Paris. He had at his disposal over 6,000 aircraft 'and since 1954 all operational plans have hinged on the use of tactical nuclear weapons for both air and ground forces.' At first, most of the aircraft were American, 'but the current policy is to encourage indigenous industries within the NATO countries to build themselves up by the construction of selected designs under licence.'

Norway and Denmark formed NATO's Northern Command, guarding against Soviet threats from the Baltic or Arctic waters into the North Sea. Allied Forces Central Europe, with a headquarters at Fontainebleau, was a fully-integrated command drawn from the air forces of seven states, including West Germany, as well as Canada and the United States. Allied Air Forces Southern Europe had a headquarters in Naples and included air units from Italy, Greece and Turkey. There was also the US Sixth Fleet, on permanent cruise in the Mediterranean, with three large aircraft carriers among its 50 vessels. These NATO forces offered a formidable deterrent, by no means only in nuclear weapons, to any aggressive spirits in the Kremlin, who reasonably preferred other methods of spreading Communist influence. Nevertheless, all this carefully-deployed hardware ought to have calmed the apprehensions of any bomber champion: it was just what Slessor devoted the best years of his life to asking for.

The first six weeks

Slessor attacked a declaration by nine eminent British scientists in July 1955 as 'a curious mixture of realism and – well, the reverse, to put it mildly.' They thought an atomic war might well put an end to the human race and no agreement to ban hydrogen bombs would stand in time of war. 'So far so good', he commented, 'and it is to be hoped that this part of the declaration will receive as much publicity in Communist countries as it has here.' Unfortunately, the scientists went on to ask for the renunciation of thermo-nuclear weapons by the world's governments. 'I should have thought that all historical experience goes to prove that this sort of pledge to renounce war as an instrument of policy is never worth the paper it is written on.' It was widely agreed – nowadays – that war could not be made to pay, but that was only because of the existence of the terrible weapons which these scientists wish to renounce. Nuclear disarmament may one day become possible, but only when conventional armaments have been drastically reduced and that day was a long way off.

As late as 1956 Britain had no hard information about the targetting plans of even those American bombers based in Britain. By the end of 1953, Slessor had hoped that Bomber Command would have its first V-bombers in service. Only then, he came to realize, would there be any prospect of soft words about co-operation being translated into hard commitments. Meanwhile, as S. J. Ball explains, Fighter Command would remain a vital component in the defence of Britain and other NATO countries; and Transport Command would be enlarged (not before time) 'to give the army strategic and tactical mobility in Cold War operations and to enable overseas garrisons to be reduced, once emergency air reinforcements and routine air trooping proved practicable.' But in considering Cold War problems, 'both the Chiefs and the Foreign Office misjudged the threat. They expected Chinese Communist subversion to create increasing instability in the Far East, and to prevent the reduction of force levels east of Suez, whereas a successful outcome of the current re-negotiations of the Anglo-Egyptian Treaty was confidently expected to lead to a substantial saving of troops in the Middle East.' As it happened, King Farouk of Egypt was expelled a few weeks later and Gamal Abdul Nasser, destined to cause Slessor much heartache, would shortly emerge as one of the great villains of the age, in the opinion of many Britons.

Churchill's son-in-law, Duncan Sandys (Minister of Supply) demanded that the conclusions of the Global Strategy Paper be more 'starkly defined: only forces that contributed to Britain's position as a world power in the Cold War and were relevant to the first six weeks of a hot war should be maintained.' Much to Slessor's exasperation, Harold Alexander (Churchill's favourite wartime general and now, to the astonishment of everyone who knew him, Minister of Defence) backed Sandys. Churchill suffered a stroke in June 1953 and in his absence Sandys attacked the navy's cruiser and carrier programme. This was much more to Slessor's liking. However, it was now learned that the Soviet Union was building powerful cruisers capable of disrupting Britain's sea links, and that Soviet air defences were more likely than ever to pick off strategic bombers. As Jackson and Bramall explain, 'Carrier-borne low-level strike aircraft, armed with atomic weapons, would be a sensible precautionary supplement to the British deterrent. And to cap the navy's good fortune, the NATO force planners required three carrier groups in the north-east Atlantic, which could only be provided by the Royal Navy in the initial phases of a war at sea because the American carriers could not arrive until about D+15 (i.e. 15 days after war had been declared).'

'If the air force would cease its attacks on the navy's new Carrier Strike Force concept', declared Rhoderick McGrigor (First Sea Lord), 'the navy would not re-open its offensive for the transfer of Coastal Command to Admiralty control.' The assumptions of the Global Strategy Paper regarding both the Middle and Far East were seen to be mistaken by 1954 and McGrigor's forecast, 'The Navy of the Future', proved to be more useful: 'the introduction of strategic ballistic missiles, carrying nuclear warheads; atomic-powered submarines and surface ships; the replacement of gun-armed battleships and cruisers with missile-equipped destroyers and frigates; and the design of smaller carriers with vertical take-off strike aircraft and air defence missiles.' Slessor's thinking and writing failed to take in any of these changes.

The V-bombers

In Slessor's opinion, as we have seen, the bomber was the primary weapon of the Free World, but the British must not leave it to the USAF. We British, he thought, were very good at 'this bomber trade; the RAF would be nothing without it.' Even for so devout a bomber champion, this is a narrow view. Quite apart from the vital contributions made independently of Bomber Command by all other commands during and after the war (including the wonderful Berlin Airlift), Slessor ignored the fact that postwar bombers were even more vulnerable to ground fire than they had been up to 1945, and required either fighter escort or the absence of enemy fighters if they were to cause anything like the damage their champions hoped from them. Nor did he have any comment to make about the economic and military folly – for a nation as impoverished and short of skilled labour as Britain – of producing three different types of immensely complex and expensive long-range strategic bombers to do the same job.

The Vickers-Armstrong Valiant (intended as a 'stop gap', pending the appearance of the more sophisticated Hawker Siddeley Vulcan and the Handley Page Victor) came into service in January 1955. During the next decade it did well in several roles, but would not have survived exposure to Soviet defences. Vulcans and Victors were appearing in small numbers by 1958 and a V-force was steadily built up as the main prop of British defence policy. Crews – both air and ground – were carefully trained and kept at a high state of readiness, ready to take off at the first radar warning of Soviet attack. All three were excellent flying machines, but would have been easy meat for Soviet fighters or missiles. American bombers – the B-47 Stratojet and the B-52 Stratofortress – would also have suffered, but they were larger, faster, far more numerous, equipped with more electronic devices, and most of them would be operating from less vulnerable bases.

Without a bomber force, argued Slessor, we would lose not only influence, but also – he asserted – moral backbone. 'This thing is so much a matter of life and death to us all that no British family of the requisite quality should rest content until they have at least one son serving his country in the air.' Thus did he set down two beliefs of equal force that lay at the very core of his being. On the one hand, he was absolutely convinced, as a devout bomber champion should be, that it was a matchless weapon. On the other hand, he was no less certain, given his own family's long and honourable record of service to the Crown, that there were indeed families of the 'requisite quality' whose sons should be entrusted with that weapon. Air power, he insisted yet again, was not inhumane. It had worked well in Iraq before the Second World War in reducing casualties on both sides. Although there was some truth in that then, it is difficult to see how his argument could be applied to the entirely different world of the 1950s. As it happened, the V-bombers and a variety of ballistic missiles (American and British) were Britain's nuclear deterrent force from 1958 to 1969. Much to Slessor's chagrin, the task was then handed over to the Royal Navy's nuclear-powered submarines, armed with Polaris missiles.

The bomb as peacemaker

In May 1949, long before he became CAS, Slessor had expressed to Lord Pakenham (Minister of Civil Aviation) a major theme not only of his term of office but of the rest of his active life. He agreed with Pakenham that the Rhine was an excellent line of defence against the danger of Soviet invasion, but he preferred a line further east, 'to rid civilized Europe of this filthy fungus. And it is perfectly obvious that to have any hope of doing that we must re-arm Germany.' To defend only the Rhine would be to abandon Germany – which could then turn towards the Soviet Union, forging an unbeatable combination. But the French would not, at this time, agree to German re-armament. 'It's a damned dilemma. But I'm sure we've got to face it.'

Efforts must be made to reduce the Soviet Union's hold on the states of eastern Europe in the hope of making them 'benevolently neutral'. In the Middle East, oil sources and bomber bases were vital, but Britain could not afford to maintain its current level of forces there. As for Asia, Chinese expansion must be resisted: 'the road to Paris', declared the Chiefs in a phrase almost certainly fashioned by Slessor, 'might well be via Peking and Delhi.' The fate of Indo-China (Vietnam) was crucial. The French would have to be offered assistance, if Communism were not to triumph there. Slessor does not explain what was 'crucial' to western security – let alone survival – in that corner of the world. Although the French received 'assistance', they were driven out of Indo-China, and replaced by Americans who soon found themselves in an apparently limitless bog.

Slessor contributed to a series of radio broadcasts in February 1954 on 'The Revolution in Strategy'. He thought there was 'not the smallest chance' of agreement with Communists 'by the normal methods of international negotiation.' Fortunately, no-one would force a major war if he knew that to do so would 'bring down the annihilating force of atomic air power on his head. I believe that that knowledge is a predominating factor in Soviet policy.' The Brussels Treaty, he proposed, should be amended to include 'a solemn undertaking that in the event of aggression the aggressor will be subjected to the full weight of Anglo-American air power, using the atom and in due course the hydrogen bomb.' The Soviet

Union and her satellites should be invited to adhere to the new treaty. 'If they refused, as they inevitably would in the first instance, we should say: "Then you remain subject to its sanctions, but you do not get the advantage of its safeguards."' West Germany should be re-armed and, when she is strong enough, British, American and French forces should be withdrawn from Germany. 'We should demand that the Russians should withdraw the Red Army into Russia at the same time; but should make it clear that we propose to withdraw whether the Russians do or not – except from Berlin, where we shall stay as long as they do – leaving the protection of Germany to the German forces.'

To forestall one criticism, Slessor said he did not anticipate bomber fleets 'taking off at the drop of a hat to slaughter millions of defenceless civilians by atom bombing their cities.' What he had in mind – as he advocated time and time again – was the method by which the RAF exercised control 'humanely and effectively' in Iraq and the North-West Frontier of India between the wars. 'In no circumstances', he asserted for the umpteenth time, 'did we bomb without ample warning notice to the tribes to get their non-combatants away in safety.' Surely this is a false parallel? A few dozen or even hundreds might flee a village or a small town, but millions could not be evacuated from a great city. In any case, the 'safety' Slessor spoke of was relative and temporary. What would even a small number of persons do for food, shelter and clothing away from their homes? Had he already forgotten the refugees he had seen in many parts of Europe in 1945 and 1946?

The creation of a hydrogen bomb, Slessor told a radio audience in January 1955, 'carries for us a message, not of despair but of hope.' No-one could win a nuclear war, but what about the rise of another mad dictator? Hitler, he admitted, would have used it, but 'I do not believe the Kremlin would run the risk... chess is the Russian national game, not poker.' He did not delude himself into believing the Soviet Union would flinch from any course, 'however murderous, by ethical considerations or any feelings of humanity. Their wearisomely consistent advocacy of atomic disarmament is merely a natural and transparently obvious gambit, to put the free world at a fatal military disadvantage. But they know as well as anyone that they cannot conceivably derive any advantage from hydrogen warfare.'

Nuclear strategy, argued Slessor in a lecture at London University in January 1956, 'meant a change in the function of armies and tactical air forces. Their role in Europe was not to fight a modernized edition of the last war, but to act as a tripwire to ensure that the enemy could not gain his ends by military force without provoking total war. We had to have something between the hydrogen bomb and the frontier policeman.'

How special is the relationship?

Both the US and Britain were anxious 'to remain on Europe's periphery', despite their commitment to NATO – the former confident in its own strength, the latter, still ruled by men who could remember when Britain had that strength, believing it had a special relationship with the US that outweighed any links with the states of continental Europe. The British Chiefs were eager to restore the Combined Chiefs of Staff, formed with the Americans during the war, and perhaps enlarged to include a Frenchman. Their purpose, as Washington understood it, was to get the US to help Britain cling on to her global interests in the face of inadequate resources.

Slessor feared the Americans would be tempted to a showdown with the Soviet Union, rather than endure a long Cold War grind. He had expressed this fear to Sir Roger Makins, British Ambassador in Washington, as early as May 1951. 'The American people are impulsive and a people of extremes and, though they are fundamentally peace-loving, let's face it, they are capable through ignorance and prejudice of forcing their government to precipitate a war. Isolationism and anti-British sentiment and the "hell, let's get this thing over" feeling thrives on ignorance, and the ignorance of the British point of view throughout America is appalling.' Thus Slessor, the broad sweeper, though not so wide of the mark. His knowledge of the US was confined to official circles in Washington and New York; his knowledge of Britain to official circles in London. Nevertheless, it was in those circles that most key decisions were made.

CHAPTER 19

DISASTER AT SUEZ

Allies at odds

Gamal Abdul Nasser – Prime Minister, President, Dictator – of Egypt and leader of Arab nationalism, nationalized the Suez Canal on July 26th 1956. This was one of the most influential actions of the second half of the 20th century. Among the consequences were two confirmations: of Britain and France as middleweight powers, the United States and the Soviet Union as the only heavyweights. Until then, as Jackson and Bramall explain, 'efforts had been directed towards converting Empire into Commonwealth at a responsible pace'; thereafter came a 'precipitate shedding of colonial responsibilities.' As the crisis developed, the British Chiefs of Staff became baffled by 'the confused political and foreign policy aims against which the military operations had to be planned, mounted and conducted. They became unhappier still when secret Franco-Israeli collusion was thrust upon them to provide an internationally-implausible *casus belli*.'

Despite the best efforts of governing circles in Britain, France, the United States and Israel to conceal their conduct, including the activities of their secret services, the actual course of events is now well known and only Slessor's thoughts and actions have a place here. He sent to *The Times* on June 14th 1964 a letter published on the 16th, provoked by reading Herman Finer's book, *Dulles over Suez* in which he wrote of President Eisenhower's 'terrible anger' with Britain and other 'lesser nations' for flouting his will at the time of the crisis. Finer exaggerated, thought Slessor. 'I was the first (and I believe for some weeks the only) Englishman to see the President after Eden's ultimatum on October 30th 1956, having been summoned to the White House at 2.30 pm on the 31st.' Eisenhower was not angry, in Slessor's opinion, rather he was amazed at Britain's rash unilateral use of force, especially just before a presidential election. There was 'an atmosphere of mystified ignorance in Washington about what was actually going on in the Middle East that day.' Eisenhower showed him a tape: 'British aircraft are now bombing Cairo'. All Slessor could say was that he felt sure it could only be airfields. Eisenhower then asked him what he thought of the attack. Slessor expressed concern about the impact on Anglo-American relations and on the Commonwealth, but the President assured him that the alliance would survive – an opinion confirmed by Emmet Hughes in *The Ordeal of Power*.

Air Marshal Sir Anthony Selway (head of the RAF Mission in Washington at the time of Suez) wrote to Slessor on June 16th 1964. Slessor had dined in Washington on October 30th 1956 with the Selways, Nathan Twining, head of the USAF, James Douglas, Under-Secretary for Air (plus their wives) and Frank Nash. Eisenhower was re-elected on November 7th, the day after the cease-fire at Suez. Selwyn Lloyd (Foreign Secretary) went to Washington in mid-November, but no-one would see him and John Foster Dulles (Secretary of State) was in hospital. Selway was writing now, some eight years later, to remind Slessor that they had agreed to do their utmost to preserve friendly relations with the Americans. 'All through the crisis period I sent personally to [General] Tommy White [Chief of Staff, USAF] our accurate top secret operational summaries, as I felt it was important that somebody in the Pentagon should have the true facts. I never received any acknowledgement of these messages and in fact had no contact with four-star level for many weeks afterwards, but when it was over our relations were even more cordial than before and those with Tommy White especially so.'

On January 12th 1957, Slessor set down privately – not for publication – his thoughts on Suez. He was 'bitterly critical' of Eden's Middle Eastern policy. Throughout his CAS years, the Middle East had been 'a constant source of concern to us. We had the Tripartite Declaration of May 25th 1950, with which I was in full agreement, believing (mistakenly) that thereby the US were committing themselves to positive action which held out some hope of ultimately solving the Arab-Israeli impasse.' Then came the military coup in Cairo in July 1952 and General Mohamed Neguib's assumption of power, followed by endless talks about the Suez Canal base, though the agreement to leave the canal zone was reached only in October 1954, when Slessor had been out of office for nearly two years.

He had been constantly irritated, though 'there can be few British officers who know and like America better than I', by the 'unhelpful and sometimes almost openly inimical attitude of the State Department and their usually very amateur "diplomats" in the Middle East – in Turkey and Egypt particularly.' It was based on their sentimental, outdated, and hypocritical obsession with the alleged evils of British colonialism. Dulles could be so foolish. For example, he presented Neguib with a silver-plated pistol the day after describing the British as 'the enemy'. As Lord Chandos said, Dulles thus conveyed 'a doubtless unintended message' to Neguib. As early as 1948, Slessor had been corresponding 'more in sorrow than in anger' with George Fielding Elliot about the way Americans were embarrassing Britain in Palestine. Slessor agreed with

Chandos that during the critical years in Egypt, American influence –
directed from the embassy in Cairo – was anti-British and influenced in
part by American oil interests.

Time to go?

'If it was militarily acceptable in October 1954 to agree to evacuate the
canal zone', thought Slessor, it was equally so four years earlier; another
example of our common fault of hanging on in the face of the inevitable
and losing all the kudos in the process.' The Chiefs of Staff were pressed
by Ernest Bevin (Foreign Secretary) to make concessions, but the British
hung on too long. By late 1952, Slessor was arguing – with the support of
John Harding (head of the British army) – 'that this huge base in a
politically-hostile country was neither essential nor really practicable in a
nuclear age.'

During 1955, it seemed obvious to Slessor that the agreement of
October 1954 was not improving relations with Egypt. Nasser deposed
Neguib within three weeks of its signing and made himself dictator. He
wished to create an 'Arab' (that is, Egyptian) empire from the Atlantic
coast to the Persian Gulf. He was anti-British; he openly threatened to
destroy Israel by refusing to allow that state use of the canal, by
concentrating troops in Sinai, building up supply dumps close to the
Israeli frontiers and by organizing a tripartite command – Egypt, Syria,
Saudi Arabia – under an Egyptian general, with the declared intention of
attacking Israel; and he looked for support to the Soviet Union. The US
and Britain nevertheless offered this tyrant a huge sum to build a massive
dam on the Nile river at Aswan, near the Sudan border. This would be the
largest civil engineering project in the world. When completed, the dam
– with a huge lake reservoir – would regulate the river's flow, 'on whose
caprices Egypt had always depended for her very existence, and provide
as well a major generator of electricity and a source of irrigation.'

Eden visited Washington in January 1956 to discuss the Middle East
with Eisenhower, but got nowhere. Slessor was then in the US, making
speeches in which he urged the Americans to help re-create stability there,
now that British influence had declined. He urged them to recognize the
danger of growing Soviet influence and the threat to Israel's existence, but
Eisenhower's government was not prepared to act, and therefore must
bear 'a heavy responsibility' for what followed.

In February 1956, there were still powerful British forces in the canal
zone. If Eden really took such a serious view of Egyptian aggression (as
he would claim in October), why did he not cancel the evacuation of the
zone, with or without American agreement? He could have made it clear
to Nasser and to Israel that whatever the US and France did, Britain meant
to stand by the Tripartite Declaration of 1950. Britain would remain in the
zone until the UN provided a force to settle the Arab-Israeli conflict and
would, meanwhile, escort Israeli ships through the canal – implementing

a UN resolution already five years old. Such action, Slessor realized, would have cost Britain dearly and exposed her to terrorist action. 'Mr Dulles would no doubt have preached us Sermons, and a lot of Americans, whose fathers hijacked the Panama Canal only about 50 years ago, would have called us Colonial Imperialists, but that would not have mattered.'

The Americans put a resolution to the Security Council in April 1956, urging the Arabs and Israelis to stop raiding each other, which the unfortunate [General Tommy] Burns [head of the UN Emergency Force] and his observers in white jeeps had been failing to do for years. On May 9th, [Dag] Hammerskjold [UN Secretary-General] reported that both sides had agreed to a cease-fire. The Americans 'were provided with a nice alibi to get on with their election campaign and talk about Eisenhower's genius as a peacemaker.' But on July 12th Dulles told the Egyptians that the US would not finance the Aswan dam project – and gave the news to London only one hour before giving it to Cairo. Slessor agreed with the American and British governments that it was right to cancel the project, given the fortune Nasser was spending on Soviet arms. Two weeks later, on the 26th, Nasser nationalized the canal and declared that he would use the income to build the dam.

Asiatic Hitler or Moslem Mussolini?
Slessor regarded this as an act of infamous bad faith, despite some admitted provocation. He lost his temper, uttered angry words, drafted yet another letter to *The Times*, cooled down, tore it up and sent another, published on August 1st. He described himself as 'an obscure retired officer living in Somerset' – which is by no means how he really regarded himself – who could afford to lose his temper, but the Prime Minister could not. 'What lethal rubbish it is', he wrote, 'this idea that we cannot afford to be strong! Shall we never learn anything from history? Can our people never be made to understand that what we really cannot afford is to be weak and yet continue to enjoy a standard of living astronomically high compared to that of most of the world's population? We are faced today with a challenge in the Middle East potentially no less mortal than that in the Europe of 1938 – though far more easily countered if only we have the courage. We shall never have another last chance as we did in 1939-40. Unless we and our American allies now act together in defence of interests which in the long run are vital to us both, and not only retain military strength but use it if necessary, then indeed for us both the bell will toll.'

During the following days, Slessor became convinced that Eden had taken leave of his senses and was determined to join with the French to invade Egypt. Slessor wrote to Dickson on August 4th advising him that if he had to use force, use enough promptly, and suggesting that the only reasons for invading should be to secure the uninterrupted flow of shipping and protect British lives. A week later, on August 11th, Slessor had another letter published in *The Times*. Britain must ensure that no single state or combination of states cuts sea and air communications or stops the oil flow upon which depend the economy and the military capacity of NATO. If that were to happen, we should resort to force. 'Nothing but good can come of making it quite clear in advance that in the last resort we shall not shrink from using force for that purpose.' During the next three months came the 'woolly moralistic platitudes which were to characterize what passed for US policy', but Slessor remained convinced that Eden intended to destroy Nasser whatever the Americans or anyone else thought. On August 1st, Eisenhower – 'the obedient loud-speaker of Dulles on foreign affairs' – had declared that the canal was vital to the US economy and its future welfare. In Slessor's opinion, it was no such thing.

Eden made an ill-judged broadcast on August 8th, alleging that the issues were a 'matter of life and death to us all' and that Nasser could not be left in 'unfettered' control of the canal. On the 11th, Slessor's letter of the 9th to *The Times* was published: 'to re-occupy Egypt to ensure against any temporary interference with the communications and the flow of oil... would defeat its own object as well as incurring all sorts of other disadvantages which must be obvious.'

Slessor spoke to Sir Robert Menzies, Prime Minister of Australia, on August 15th. He had attended all the Cabinet meetings on Suez. Slessor thought him, as usual, 'pragmatic and sensible'. Nasser must not be allowed to do as he liked, but what could be done to stop him? International control of the canal? Refusal to pay transit dues? Readiness to use force to get ships through the canal? On August 23rd it was agreed to send a group under Menzies to commend the international control plan to Nasser, but Eisenhower and Dulles were weak and seemed to have no idea how to deal with a man whom Slessor regarded as 'an Asiatic Hitler'. Apart from the puzzling location of this minor dictator, one flinches at the comparison with Hitler. Whatever crimes Nasser committed, only Stalin in recent centuries deserves to be linked to that universal tyrant. Eden, more accurate than Slessor, referred to Nasser as a 'Moslem Mussolini.' Menzies began talks with Nasser in Cairo on September 3rd.

Meanwhile, French troops moved to Cyprus, which Slessor thought 'unnecessary and unwise'. He thought the Foreign Secretary Selwyn Lloyd's remarks about 'the pattern of events in the thirties' at Northolt on September 5th were unhelpful, and also the comments of the Trades Union Council, which opposed force except with UN consent. 'I wished, for the umpteenth time, that these damned Trade Unionists would mind their own business, get on with their own important job, and not always go babbling about matters on which they have neither the experience nor the information to form a judgement.' Despite Slessor's exasperated disdain, many citizens of 'the better sort' (in his reckoning) agreed with the 'damned Trade Unionists' on this issue. As Jackson and Bramall wrote 'the high-handedness of the Anglo-French international "police action" smacked too much of 19th century gunboat diplomacy, and it united most of the world and half of Britain against Eden and his closest colleagues.'

The Menzies talks broke down on September 10th. Next day, the British and French governments announced their determination to resist arbitrary interference with their rights, although they would do their best to avoid fighting. Dulles favoured talk rather than action at one of his 'interminable press conferences', where he made an 'infantile statement' and used words which were 'idiotic even for him'. He was, in Slessor's opinion, guilty of 'crass, sanctimonious, muddle-headed ineptitude' throughout his time as Secretary of State. Slessor was not alone in his exasperation with Dulles, a learned international lawyer, but also a sombre lay preacher much given to endless sermons called press conferences. 'He doesn't stumble into booby traps', wrote James Reston in the *New York Times*, 'he digs them to size, studies them carefully, and then jumps.' Churchill detested him: he was, he said, 'clever enough to be stupid on a rather large scale.' And yet Dulles asked Selwyn Lloyd on November 18th: 'Why did you stop? Why didn't you go through with it and get Nasser down?' On his death bed three years later he reckoned he had been wrong about Suez.

Parliament met in special session on September 12th and a week later a meeting of the Canal Users' Association expressed determination to keep it open, but Eisenhower and Dulles – their minds on the election and deeply suspicious of 'colonial' actions – made it clear that they would not back a forceful solution. The British and French governments referred the matter to the Security Council on September 23rd. On October 13th, Britain and France got 9 out of 11 votes in the Council – plus a Soviet veto. Their resolution sought free and open transit through the canal; respect for Egyptian sovereignty; canal operations to be insulated from the politics of any state; tolls and charges to be fixed between Egypt and the canal users; a fair proportion to go towards canal development; and any dispute to be settled by arbitration. Slessor was happy with all these points and had yet another letter published on the 15th: 'Suez should surely teach us that we cannot possibly go it alone.' He flew to Philadelphia on October 25th, supposing the crisis to be over.

The President blows off steam

Meanwhile, tension was mounting between Israel and her neighbours. Eisenhower warned David Ben-Gurion, Prime Minister of Israel, against aggression. Slessor was in a New York office on the afternoon of October 29th when news came that Israel had invaded Sinai. He flew to Washington next evening and was met at the airport by Selway with news of the Anglo-French ultimatum, 'which at first I found impossible to believe.' At the Selways' dinner party, Nathan Twining asked Slessor:

'What else could you have done?' But he was still in a daze and could think of no sensible answer. No-one then realized the ultimatum had been sent without informing Eisenhower. Slessor was mistaken. 'Despite Eisenhower's later public declaration', wrote Thorpe, 'with one eye firmly on the impending presidential election, that the United States had not been informed in advance, he had in fact heard unofficially on October 24th that Britain would shortly be attacking Egypt... He had also received regular updates through the official channels from Eden.'

Next morning, October 31st, in Selway's office, Slessor got some information about the progress of operations in Sinai from Salmon (the Israeli attaché), rang Bill Jackson, special assistant for foreign affairs, at the White House and was summoned to meet the President at 2.30 pm. 'One of the most staggering things about this whole story is the way in which all our senior representatives abroad were kept in the dark. Bob Dickson – our Ambassador at the UN – heard of our ultimatum through his Soviet opposite number.'

Jackson met Slessor at the rear of the White House. In Eisenhower's study, Bob Montgomery was fixing up a nationwide broadcast for that evening and Jackson told Slessor later that it was supposed Dulles would write the text. As they waited to meet the President, there came a report of a British air raid on Cairo. Although Slessor hoped it meant only airfields, it was 'an evil moment' for him. He met the President alone. For some 15 minutes Eisenhower 'blew off steam'. The previous day, he said, had been the worst of his life. He had taken his political future in his hands by condemning Israel as an aggressor. He was not playing politics and did not want another four years in this 'God-damned job'.

Slessor found it hard to believe that Eden gave the President no warning, though accepted his word that this was so. Eisenhower had approved the six principles and thought Britain should have accepted them at once. He thought King Saud of Saudi Arabia was a man to back. Slessor agreed that his father had been a great man, but thought little of this son. He did not warn Eisenhower that, in his opinion, 'Saud would double cross him as soon as look at him. Why a US President should think it a good thing to back a lecherous, treacherous, slave-dealing oriental tyrant like Saud rather than – say – King Feisal [of Iraq] and Nuri-es-Said [his Prime Minister], I could not understand.' Perhaps Slessor got his answer, some two years later, when Feisal, Nuri-es-Said – a born intriguer – and many others were killed in Baghdad. The meeting with Eisenhower lasted about 40 minutes. Not a lot was said and Eisenhower later told Bill Elliot that 'Jack sat there with his head in his hands.'

Slessor returned to New York on November 1st and flew home next evening. He let the Chiefs of Staff, through Dickson, know only of Eisenhower's intention to keep the alliance alive. Slessor's 'first dazed impression in Washington as to the ineptitude and imbecility of our actions were fully justified.' Then came news of the cease fire. 'I am now sure that we could do nothing else, but at the time one's reaction was that we had committed the folly of intervention and now were not going to do the only thing that could possibly excuse it, namely, make a job of it.'

He was asked to protest publicly, but Dickson urged him not to – and he agreed, reluctantly, on January 11th 1957 (the day on which he set down these thoughts). 'Always hypersensitive to criticism – a defect most crippling in a leader', wrote John Grigg, Eden 'was provoked into ill-considered, and eventually crazy, acts by the dread of being thought less masterful than Churchill.' His health gave way, he fled to Jamaica on November 23rd for three weeks and in his absence R. A. Butler (Leader of the House of Commons), Harold Macmillan (Chancellor of the Exchequer) and Lord Salisbury (Lord President of the Council) 'worked as a triumvirate in disloyal collusion, not to say conspiracy, with the Americans.' Eden could not recover either health or authority and resigned on January 9th 1957, whereupon Macmillan 'evolved' as his successor, easily defeating Butler, who had been widely regarded as next in line. 'Macmillan's emergence as the victor was amazingly reminiscent of Churchill's in 1940', wrote Keith Kyle, 'with triumph rapidly crowning failure.' Macmillan had been more hotly opposed to Nasser even than Eden and Macmillan was responsible for Britain's most serious misjudgement – of Eisenhower's likely reaction to the Anglo-French ultimatum.

As a devout Tory, it hurt Slessor to believe that Tory ministers could behave so badly and he feared a long spell of Socialist rule after the next election. If Nasser were to be attacked at all, it should have been early in the year and certainly no later than July 26th. But no force was poised to do this and when action was decided upon it was poorly carried out – so poorly that Slessor doubted if there really had been collusion with the French and Israelis. In fact, there had been: at Sèvres, in Paris, where senior members of French, Israeli and British governments met secretly on October 21st and 22nd. They agreed to strike at Egypt, taking advantage of Soviet distraction in Poland and Hungary and US focus on the forthcoming presidential election. Lies were then told to the British public about why their armed forces went into combat and many years passed before the truth dribbled out.

Israeli forces invaded Egypt on October 29th to destroy, they said, guerilla bases. The British and French governments immediately announced that freedom of movement for shipping through the canal was in danger and called for a cease-fire. When Nasser refused, they launched an air attack, followed by a sea-borne invasion. The Americans, fearing Soviet intervention, used financial pressure to force a cease-fire and a humiliating withdrawal. The British suffered most, thought John Roberts: Suez 'cost them much goodwill, particularly within the Commonwealth, and squandered confidence in the sincerity of their retreat from empire. It confirmed the Arabs' hatred of Israel; the suspicion that she was indissolubly linked to the West made them yet more receptive to Soviet blandishment.' As for Nasser, he enjoyed a brief glory, but he had many enemies, limited ability and suffered a shattering defeat at Israeli hands in 1967. He had been in poor health for years and was only 52 when he died in 1970.

It was obvious that the canal would be blocked and oil pipelines cut. Slessor was surprised that a massacre of British and French citizens in Egypt did not follow. Soviet influence in the Middle East, already growing, was made easier. 'The real fact – let me repeat – is that on July 26th Eden lost his temper and was absolutely determined to go in and depose Nasser and impose a solution to the canal problem favourable to us.' Slessor thought the world 'a happier place' when Britain was able to behave as she had in 1882, but it was 'sheer unadulterated imbecility' in 1956, in the face of African and Asian nationalism, America's rise to global power and Britain's relative decline. Eden was always more concerned with 'speeches than principles'; he was a sick, weak man, 'a tragic failure and a disaster to his country.' If Slessor and Tedder had been speaking to each other, they would have agreed entirely about Suez. Tedder had his say in the House of Lords on December 12th 1956. The ultimatum to Nasser was 'a tragic mistake' that split the nation and 'how in the name of heaven did our political intelligence come to be so utterly out of touch with feeling in this country and throughout the world?'

Aftermath

Slessor dined with Menzies in Sydney in January 1959 and learned that he had had a private talk with Nasser on August 30th or 31st 1956. Menzies told Nasser that Britain wanted a peaceful settlement, but would fight to resist total Egyptian control of the canal. He thought he had impressed Nasser, but then came news of Eisenhower's weak words at a press conference on the 31st, which restored Nasser's determination to yield nothing. On his way home to Australia, Menzies visited Eisenhower and was, he told Slessor, 'brutally frank' with him. He found the President 'weak and dithering' and reminded him that his job was to lead. Slessor unwisely took Menzies, a flexible politician, at face value; following most British politicians and military men, Menzies under-rated Eisenhower as: 'a mover and shaker behind the scenes, who took the big decisions and stuck by them, yet was mistakenly underestimated as a mere golfing bumbler by unenlightened outsiders.'

'What the Suez crisis did expose', reflected a leading article in *The Times* on December 11th 1956, 'was the hollowness of some of the claims put forward for the British share of the allied nuclear deterrent. This 'contribution, by admitting Britain to the select nuclear club and giving Britain the prestige of a great power, was supposed to make us masters of our fate. It has not done so, and could not, because Britain is not economically independent. The British nuclear deterrent was amply justified militarily, but it is going far beyond military need in some of its forms. The problem now is to decide how little we need to spend on it to deter global war.'

Slessor had recently claimed that the cost of the V-bomber force over the coming years, including its nuclear weapons, amounted to a mere ten percent of Britain's total defence expenditure. 'But this figure cannot include the cost of developing and producing the hydrogen bomb. It does not include the cost of developing new methods of delivery such as the ballistic missile, on which, according to the last Statement on Defence, increasing emphasis is being placed. And what about the preparations judged necessary for defending the deterrent force: the air defence of the United Kingdom, for instance, which includes expensive guided missile systems? Or civil defence? Or those naval preparations that appear to presuppose global war, such as the minesweeper programme and the construction of nuclear-powered submarines?'

Reflecting on his 1957 notes, Slessor was surprised that the Conservatives had not in fact suffered electoral defeat following Suez. He had not feared outright war with the Soviet Union, as did both Eden and Macmillan, who grossly over-rated British power and influence. By 1962, Slessor believed that Suez had been more ineptly managed even than he supposed at the time. 'It was terribly unfortunate that the chairman of the Chiefs of Staff should have been a weak little man, hopelessly inadequate for the job.' Such was Slessor's bitter assessment of Sir William Dickson, his successor as CAS, from January 1st 1953 to December 31st 1955. Yet Dickson must have given satisfaction in some quarters because next day he was appointed chairman of the COS Committee and then Chief of the Defence Staff on January 1st 1959, a position he held for six months.

Dickson had enjoyed high office under both Tedder and Slessor. His appointment as CAS was 'good news', wrote the historians of the Chiefs. 'Although he was no less devoted to his own service, he was not so wedded to the "RAF über alles" syndrome of many of his predecessors.' He was 'a seasoned and up-to-date Whitehall Warrior', according to an official RAF historian, when he took over from Slessor. He was also 'a great believer in joint-service co-operation; there could have been no better choice for the first Chief of the Defence Staff.' Slessor would certainly have been consulted during 1952 when Dickson's initial elevation was under consideration. At that time – one presumes – the future Sage of Yeovil had not dismissed Dickson in such contemptuous terms. But one cannot be certain: we already knew that he had a very rough edge to his tongue. On the other hand, Dickson's health had declined alarmingly in 1956 and he proved to be something of a liability during the crisis.

The lesson Slessor drew from his reflections was that the appointment of a Chief of Defence was not only unnecessary but a menace. He had said this – and much more – in a long discussion with Walter Monckton

(Minister of Defence) in June 1956. 'I can't help thinking that, under the old system, at least one of the Chiefs of Staff would have resigned before the end of October and brought the thing to a head – I like to believe that I certainly would have.' Easily said, from the comfort of retirement. One must realize, however, as Slessor certainly should have done, that the Chiefs were faced with 'one of the classic dilemmas of democratic government', as Jackson and Bramall put it. 'Refusal by officials, for that is what the Chiefs are, to implement the policy of elected leaders would be both unconstitutional and an abuse of power. For the country's military leaders to do so when war was imminent, or had actually begun, would have amounted to dereliction of duty.'

British and American historians have often noted that the Americans moved smartly in 1953 to set up Shah Reza Pahlavi in Iran and topple Prime Minister Mohammed Mossadeq when he threatened to invite Soviet aid. Their reward was a 40 percent stake in the country's oil production. The difference in 1956 was that Eden did not move smartly to topple Nasser and thereby gave many Americans and Britons a golden opportunity to moralise about Third World self-determination and mouth banalities about universal brotherhood. Also, as Andrew Roberts observed, 'without secret diplomacy and alliances, let alone plans of attack, this country would not have won the Napoleonic wars ... Without collusion the Israelis would not have destroyed one third of the Soviet-built Egyptian air force, which would otherwise have been directed against our servicemen.' Suez, concluded Thorpe, 'was a sudden bright meteor that soon burned itself out; more symbolic than seminal, more an effect than a cause of national decline; it had few consequences, good or bad.'

CHAPTER 20

CASSANDRA OF YEOVIL, 1956-1968[18]

The real World War III

Slessor visited 'the Convair people' in San Diego, California, in early
1956 and wrote to Nigel Birch, Secretary of State for Air, in February.
'All that I have seen and heard here [in Los Angeles, where he was staying
with Eaker, head of the Aircraft Division of the Howard Hughes
Corporation] and in San Diego confirms me in my conviction that we
should and could go for a policy of building US military aircraft under
licence. Indeed, I am now sure that we are much further behind the US
than I privately thought – I would say something like five years.' He
returned to England in April and wrote to Frank Pace, of General
Dynamics in New York (by whom Slessor was employed as a consultant).
Birch, he said, shared Slessor's concern about British fighter development
and was interested in a Canadian project – the Canadair CF 105 Arrow,
later cancelled – 'largely I think because the parent firm and a good deal
of the senior design staff being British he thought it might be easier than
going for an American type.' Slessor pointed out that the CF 105 was
years away from service, whereas excellent American fighters were
already available. But do we need any fighters, 'when we know damn
well that no amount of the best fighters could ensure the necessary 99
percent kill-rate against the hydrogen bomber? There are even some who
are now questioning whether we should not drop Fighter Command
altogether, concentrating on the guided missile and the strategic bomber
for the deterrent.'

Slessor, however, thought there was still a place for the defensive
fighter, but would it have the latest radar and weapons systems? Only with
American co-operation. As a result of 'brooding in the bathroom', Slessor
wondered if that might best be obtained by the purchase of American
fighters or by the Americans buying British Blackburn Beverley
transports or Vickers Viscount airliners? If Pace agreed, would he look
into this? For the first time since VE-Day, he ended, 'I am really worried
about the world situation. We have scotched one sort of World War III in

---

[18] Cassandra: A Trojan prophetess fated to prophesy truly and be disbelieved.

which I never really believed – the shooting war', but 'we seem to run a very fair chance of losing the real World War III – the political and economic war in which we are now engaged.'

Slessor reflected on the need to amend Britain's defence policy in October 1956. The Ministry of Supply should be abolished, and research, development and production should return to the service ministries. As for weapons, Britain should retain her share of the nuclear deterrent, but leave the ballistic rocket to the US, which can afford the high costs. 'The really cardinal decision to be made is this: Are we to prepare for another prolonged global war – a modernized version of 1939-45? Or are we to face what I believe to be the certainty that another great war would inevitably involve the use of the hydrogen weapon, and so could not possibly last for any length of time? At present we are having the worst of both worlds: we are not getting the savings we could get if we faced the short war policy; and we are not fitting ourselves to fight another long, global war.' Slessor made four points in conclusion. One, that Britain must maintain a nuclear bomber force, absolutely battle-ready, like the US Strategic Air Command. Two, she must continue to bear her share of the cost of a tripwire force in Europe, ready to resist an initial invasion by Soviet forces. Three, she must also create a strategic reserve of land and air forces 'including, in these days when our fixed bases are being reduced, carrier-borne air.' And four, Transport Command must be greatly enlarged in order to transport very quickly all or part of this reserve to wherever it was needed.

Hatchet man

Harold Macmillan succeeded Eden as Prime Minister in January 1957. Improving standards of living demanded swingeing cuts in defence spending to release skilled manpower into the economy; closer collaboration with the United States could reduce weapon development costs; and an imaginative defence policy, which was perceived as providing adequate security at much lower cost, could help his [Conservative] Party's electoral image. Macmillan had a sure grasp of global strategy, an acute awareness of Britain's declining power, and ensured that the new Minister of Defence was given the power to overrule the special pleadings of the Admiralty, War Office and Air Ministry.

Duncan Sandys – able, abrasive, energetic and technically literate – was his 'hatchet man'. He submitted to Parliament in April 1957 a White Paper setting out a five-year programme of reforms. National Service was to be abolished, nuclear weapons and missile systems developed. As Jackson and Bramall say, the Chiefs argued for quick-reaction forces, 'equipped with the necessary transport aircraft, helicopters and amphibious shipping so that trouble could be quickly snuffed out by centrally-held reserves, thus reducing the need for large overseas garrisons and enabling National Service to be phased out with less risk to national interests.'

Slessor commented in April on this White Paper which had created 'some uncertainty and despondency' in all three services. The days of the RAF were by no means numbered, he thought, and it would be more than a few years before manned aircraft were replaced by push-button missiles. 'The time, no doubt, will come when the defence of our deterrent bases in this country will be taken over by an effective ground-to-air missile in Fighter Command. But let us wait until there is at least a prospect of such a missile being in service within the reasonably foreseeable future before we start talking about the manned fighter being obsolete.' A smaller RAF, made up entirely of regular officers and men, will be more highly-trained and efficient. 'What more worthwhile career can there be than service in a force that makes such a vital contribution to peace?'

He also wrote privately to Sandys on April 24th. He had little criticism to make of his White Paper as far as the RAF or the navy were concerned, but was worried about the army: 160,000 men (including a minimum of 30,000 recruits, trainees and instructors) was too few. 'Anyway, I beg of you to put an end as quickly as possible to the doubt and uncertainty that must be rampant in the army even more than in the RAF – though God knows it is bad enough there.' As for the cost, he recalled that before September 1939 we were told there was little money to spend on defence, but plenty was found after that day: 'it is not really true that we cannot afford it. The truth is we will not afford it – we prefer the 40 hour week and lots of drink and smoke, television sets and football pools.' Sandys replied civilly but formally, on May 15th.

On that day, Slessor wrote to Frank Pace, of General Dynamics, in New York. He had been asked for a critique of the White Paper by Hamilton Fish Armstrong for the July issue of *Foreign Affairs* and decided to send Pace a copy of that article, together with copies of the White Paper itself and an Air Ministry memorandum on the costing of it. He was more worried by the White Paper than he let on in his critique because it was not, in his view, based on an honest appreciation of the military situation but solely by financial and electoral considerations. He thought the decision to abolish National Service 'entirely unjustified' and made without regard for British commitments in NATO and its impact on the weaker allies. 'I think the trouble largely is that we have a very ambitious and opinionated young man (in spite of his admitted good qualities) as Defence Minister and a cipher as Foreign Secretary. I cannot see Sir Edward Grey 40 years ago or Ernest Bevin ten years ago allowing foreign policy to be ignored to the extent that Selwyn Lloyd has allowed it in recent months.'

He repeated to Pace his great concern for the British army and its need to be able to fight limited wars in the future – without nuclear weapons. 'That means plenty of conventional weapons, stockpiles of supplies and (not least) ample air transport.' He invited Pace to let him have information about the real status and progress of missile development in the US, 'for me to use confidentially to impress upon people that matter that the missile is not yet in shape to replace the manned bomber or fighter (as opposed to supplementing them).'

Sandys provoked furious arguments in Whitehall until after the election of October 1959, when Macmillan was returned to power with a massive majority. He accepted that the hatchet had been swung too vigorously (as well as inaccurately) and gave Sandys a new ministry (Aviation). Slessor had agreed with him that Britain needed neither aircraft carriers nor naval aircraft, that 'the RAF can do it all and it is their job', but he also agreed with the Chiefs that while nuclear deterrence 'was the right policy for preventing a Third World War breaking out in Europe, it had little relevance elsewhere. Wars would still be fought outside Europe with conventional weapons, unless a nuclear power's vital interests were threatened.' The three service ministries preserved their independent powers and the Royal Navy would not merely survive, but grow stronger.

Integration?

In March 1957, Dickson invited Slessor's opinion on a possible integration of the Royal Navy and the RAF. 'I am sure integration must come', he replied, but by evolution rather than administrative action. 'You may remember that when I tried to take the first steps in this direction with Bruce Fraser [First Sea Lord] seven years ago, the principle I suggested was a merging in those areas where we already overlap – i.e., the shore establishments of the Fleet Air Arm and Coastal Command. I now think that under the pressure of events and financial stringency we must and can go faster and farther than I proposed in 1950.'

He advised Dickson to merge the two services, 'not take chunks of one and "hand it over" to the other.' A major war could not last more than two or three months and that means that the safe and timely arrival of convoys becomes irrelevant: 'and that means that Coastal Command becomes redundant. I naturally hate the idea; but the RAF will take that', when they see that the other convoy protection forces – naval escorts – also become redundant. 'I also agree that (however much old Boom would have deplored it) modern politico-strategic conditions, uncertainty about and actual loss of bases, etc., means that the carrier task forces must take over many of the responsibilities that used to be exercised by the overseas commands of the RAF.' Personnel in the two services should be interchangeable: 'the young chap taking up service aviation as a career accepts from the beginning as a matter of course that he is liable to serve in any sort of air unit, regardless of the colour of his coat. The boy from Dartmouth should know that he may become a captain of a V-bomber, and the boy from Cranwell that he may serve at sea in a carrier... We must not be narrow "one-service-minded", but equally we must be frightfully careful not to wreck what has been built up by blood, sweat, toil and tears.'

Dermot Boyle (CAS) also invited Slessor's views and he replied on May 9th 1957. Both major British political parties favoured the idea of integrating the services, in the hope of saving money. 'But, if you will forgive my saying so, we shall not avert that by saying that all who fly must be in the RAF and that we never ought to have "permitted the sailors to dabble in the air business." The brutal fact – whether we like it or not – is that the sailors are in the air business, and to a very important extent.' The fundamental point, in Slessor's thinking, was what sort of war should we be preparing for if the deterrent fails? The White Paper does not ask this question and the Chiefs of Staff are not agreed on the answer: 'in particular because the blue-water-control-of-sea-communications, safe-and-timely-arrival-of-convoys school of thought still holds the reins on the Board of Admiralty.' That used to be the navy's main purpose, and still would be – if a future war were non-nuclear and long; not if it is short and nuclear.

'The basic yardstick', Slessor went on, 'should be that of function. The function of the RAF, and of the new navy arising from the White Paper, is primarily the application of air power (in manned or missile form) direct against the enemy and in support of land forces.' As for the army, he thought they should concentrate on being good conventional soldiers: able to seize and hold ground in Europe or elsewhere. 'If they have any sense, they will leave the missile and nuclear support to the air forces, shore-based and sea-borne, and stick to their honourable and indispensable last.' Let us, he urged, merge where we already overlap. A joint Flying Training Command should follow and a common Technical Training Command: 'the navy after all has a longer experience and tradition of engineering training than we have... in time we might even come to a common Staff College.' Then would follow joint research and development: 'particularly perhaps in the missile field – after all, a missile is a missile whether it is fired from a floating or a fixed base.'

The great deterrent

By 1957, the debate between separate service strategies and a national joint strategy was still going on. In naval eyes, the value of strategic bombing had been accepted and inter-service conflict focussed on whether aircraft should be carrier-borne or shore-based. As for the army, it too accepted strategic bombing and now wished to have its own transport aircraft and helicopters. Air force strategy was concerned more than ever with strategic bombing, the new missiles available, and their control.

In September 1957, Slessor had another book published, entitled *The Great Deterrent*. It had a foreword written by Al Gruenther. In Slessor's opinion, he and Walter Bedell Smith (Eisenhower's right-hand man) were 'two of the finest staff officers I have ever known.' He certainly knew the former – though not at close range – but never served with the latter. This book, like the others, is a collection of lectures rambling round familiar themes as wordily as ever. His avowed aim was to show how strategic thinking had evolved over the past 20 years and his main conclusion – hardly remarkable – was his belief that the Soviet Union would not provoke a total, atomic war because it would not benefit even from victory. The book was briefly noticed in *The Times* by the usual anonymous reviewer who observed that it 'carries the argument no farther than it has already been taken in public controversy.'

Slessor included a lecture given at the US Air War College in 1948 on 'The Chances of War'. We must not panic, he said, over the Soviet Union: strong forces in Germany would deter her, though 'Russians are not governed by reason.' The key factor was a powerful air striking force, but he rejected the idea of a pre-emptive strike, before the Soviet Union had its own atomic bombs. Another lecture, delivered to Allied General Officers of the Western Union on 'Air Power in War' in 1950, argued that Allied air power must work closely with ground forces to resist a Red Army advance, in the event of war, even though its major targets would be far from the battle front. Here, as elsewhere, he wrote as though there were no Soviet aircraft or ground defences – and assumed that the British bomber of 1950 was an effective weapon. It is difficult to know which to admire more, his diligence or his vanity in re-cycling so many ancient pieces. 'The terrible potential power of the long-range atomic bomber' was not – he asserted – generally understood. The bomber had replaced the navy as the keeper of international peace, it was the great deterrent.

In July 1957, Slessor reviewed a book by Henry Kissinger, a Harvard academic who became President Nixon's Adviser on National Security Affairs a decade later, in 1968. He praised Kissinger's criticism of 'a doctrine which left no room for intermediate positions between total peace and total war.' He also agreed that 'a new war will inevitably start with a surprise attack on the US.' The Americans, thought Slessor, had the idea that 'any war can only be all-out, leading to unconditional surrender.' Over Korea, for example, 'it was not the possibility of a Soviet onslaught on Europe that led to the hesitations of America's allies (as Dr Kissinger suggests)', but their fear that 'to spread the war into China – with or without the atom bomb' would have unpredictable 'political repercussions, especially in Asia.'

Even so, Slessor believed that 'the Free World' was indebted to Americans for their 'brave and generous assumption of leadership, both in the military sphere and on the no less vital economic battlefields.' But he disagreed with Kissinger over the doctrine of 'graduated deterrence'. It was possible, thought Slessor, to limit – if not avoid – nuclear war, partly because both sides would want this, but mostly because sufficient retaliatory ground forces would deter the Soviet Union. Graduated deterrence, however, was unrealistic. Once shooting started, the consequences were unpredictable. Slessor had often advocated, in an attempt to reduce the horrors of war for non-combatants, 'some adaptation of the RAF methods of air control in tribal warfare.' Prior warning could be given and 'proscribed areas' set aside.

Kissinger had suggested that if the Red Army attacked in Europe to disarm West Germany and offered immunity from bombing to Britain and the US, the offer should be accepted. Slessor derided this suggestion. 'I do not for a moment believe that a war involving a major Soviet attack on western Europe could conceivably be kept limited for any length of time. It would be a matter of life and death.' NATO forces in Europe were there 'not to fight another great war, but to prevent it.' They were a fire brigade, required to smother a local outbreak before it became a massive conflagration. Slessor did not share Kissinger's anxiety to see all the allies of the US equipped with nuclear weaons: their money would be better spent on conventional forces, and Britain – though a major nuclear power – should also maintain strong conventional forces.

A French bomb
The Soviet Union launched an artificial moon, a man-made satellite named Sputnik-1, in October 1957. It seemed that it would not be long, as Michael Carver wrote, 'before it could deliver megaton weapons onto the cities of the United States' and European members of NATO realized they could no longer make only token contributions to their own defence. A few months later, Charles de Gaulle returned to power in France, 'with all his antipathy to Anglo-Saxon hegemony and his ambitions to restore France's self-confidence after the humiliations of Indo-China and Algeria.'

Britain would retain her own nuclear weapons because, so Slessor claimed in September 1959, she had more experience of bomber operations than anyone else. France therefore ought not to put herself to the enormous expense of building her own strategic nuclear striking force, but rely on her British and American partners in NATO to defend her, if the need arose. Whatever grasp he had of air power issues, his understanding of French opinions about 'perfidious Albion' was sadly deficient. However, he went on to reflect that 'History sometimes repeats itself' and recalled that in the spring of 1939 he was the British air representative at Anglo-French staff talks. 'After a heated discussion on the role of Bomber Command in the opening stages of a war in Europe, I handed to our French colleagues a written assurance' that the British 'would regard collaboration with the French army and air force in the land battle as the primary commitment of the British Bomber Command during any critical phase of the invasion.' Eleven years later, as CAS, he repeated that assurance to a conference of General Officers of Western Union and now, in his complacent, anglocentric way, he was at a loss to understand why the French were not content.

Basil Collier, a fine air power historian, thought Slessor's invocation of history would make 'odd reading', even to those who agreed that NATO should be the West's main defence: several states, firmly bound together, should impress the Kremlin more vividly than any one of them, seeking to follow an independent line in military strength or political influence. 'The assurance conveyed by Sir John Slessor at the Anglo-French talks in 1939 was misleading, not because it lacked good faith (it did not) but because it was coloured by the Air Staff's woefully mistaken estimate of Bomber Command's ability to contribute effectively to the defence of western Europe at that time.' It would be a pity, concluded Collier, if the French 'were left with the impression that we are incapable of understanding the lessons of history and of learning from our mistakes.'

Slessor replied as best he could. 'I have always been frank to admit that, lacking as we did any practical experience of real air warfare before 1939, we did over-estimate the potential value of air bombardment with the primitive equipment of that time.' That being the case, it was unwise of him (and unnecessary) to link his case for France remaining under an Anglo-American nuclear shield with an unqualified disaster in 1939-40. He claimed that he had 'constantly, and sometimes heatedly' warned the French against 'setting too much store by what Bomber Command could actually do to help stem an invasion.' In fact, though, Slessor and his colleagues were still confident of Bomber Command's capacity to wreck Germany's war economy – which he believed was stretched to the limit – even with the bombers then available.

That confidence, whatever reservations Slessor expressed at the eleventh hour, was well known to the French. Bomber Command achieved so little in the years 1939-41 even to damage Germany's war economy, let alone wreck it, that the French could be forgiven in 1959 for looking askance at any British assurance, however sincerely meant. Setting aside the red herring of who believed what in 1939, Slessor and Collier were agreed about 1959: 'Bomber Command would be used to help France – next time, as a partner in NATO.' But the French, Slessor seemed surprised to discover, were a people as proud and independent-minded as the British, and preferred to put themselves to the immense expense of building their own nuclear weapons. They exploded their first nuclear bomb in the Sahara in February 1960.

A new decade for defence

By 1960, an Atomic Energy Defence Agreement, signed by the US and Britain in July 1958, was permitting 'the unprecedented exchange of a wide range of vital nuclear secrets and established a framework for an Anglo-American nuclear partnership that remained in force throughout the Cold War and continues in the late 1990s.' It marked the culmination of strenuous efforts, especially on the British side, and is widely regarded as 'one of the most remarkable agreements ever reached between two sovereign states.' Until his retirement in December 1952, Slessor had a part to play in those efforts, but thereafter – despite undiminished energy and contacts in Whitehall and Washington – he was 'out of the loop': privy to some high-level general discussion in ante-rooms certainly, but excluded from the highest-level decision-making that takes place behind closed doors.

For example, he gave a radio talk on January 31st 1960 entitled 'A New Decade for Defence' in which he argued that the service chiefs should be allowed a greater say in formulating defence policy. Their standing had 'undoubtedly diminished' since the introduction of an independent chairman in 1955. 'By far their most important job', he said, 'still is, or should be, to tender collective advice to the Minister of Defence and the Cabinet. He had a point, but there was nothing he could do if or when this or any other point was ignored. For good or ill, the day of the 'three wise men' had gone: a fourth man as chairman had arrived, and soon (April 1964) there would be a United Ministry of Defence. Taken together, these amounted to fundamental changes in the Whitehall world which had once been Slessor's real home.

In May 1960, Slessor had his say in the uproar following the shooting down of an American Lockheed U-2B reconnaissance aircraft over Sverdlovsk in the Ukraine. The Soviet Union had detonated its first hydrogen bomb in August 1953; in May 1954 appeared the Myasishchev Mya-4 (Bison), a large jet bomber capable of carrying such a weapon; the U-2 first flew in August 1955 and began to photograph military installations in the Soviet Union from July 1956. Washington's handling of the incident may have been unwise, Slessor thought, but to suggest as Philip Noel-Baker – once a Secretary of State for Air – did, 'that "spy-flights" were the real cause of the Paris fiasco is the sort of gross over-simplification that plays straight into the hands of those in Moscow who are striving to divide America from her allies.' The Russian leader, Khrushchev, had known about the flights for years and simply used the fact that one had at last been shot down to wreck the summit conference 'with a show of righteous moral indignation that is nauseating', when one recalls that his own vile regime spies relentlessly on its own people as well as on those in all western states. Slessor suggested that we 'confront the Kremlin with a practical, down-to-earth scheme for an area of mutual control, inspection, and limitation of forces in Europe, making the fullest possible use of United Nations' agency.' We must also preserve 'a strong working consensus in NATO', and member states must stand solidly together.

Slessor had another book published in 1962, entitled *What Price Co-Existence? A Policy for the Western Alliance*. Most of it was written in January and February 1961, with some additions in mid-June of that year, but it broke no new ground. His theme was that 'when we sit down to negotiate with the men of Moscow, we do so from strength, as long as we understand clearly that they will stab us in the back without the slightest compunction if we allow them to imagine they can do so with impunity.' In the opinion of one reviewer, his touch – when dealing with concepts outside the immediate sphere of tactics and strategy – was 'less than sure'. His views on unilateralists, nuclear disarmers, striking trade unionists and immigrants were commonplace and reveal 'the limitations of military analysis' as a solution for contemporary problems. Although he opposed the idea of turning NATO into a fourth nuclear power, 'he insists upon the need for a British contribution to the strategic deterrent and brushes aside the suggestion that his arguments might apply equally to other nations in search of a national nuclear striking force.'

This insistence naturally attracted criticism. 'What really bedevills the issue', wrote J. H. Barnett, 'is our pretence to be a nuclear power in the military sense, and thinking of our contribution to general western defence in nuclear rather than conventional terms.' If only Britain's 'grandiose pretensions' were abandoned and its nuclear weapons were offered to other NATO powers, France – deeply suspicious of the Anglo-Americans – would welcome the initiative and the West would be stronger.

The coming of Polaris

'I believe our defence and foreign policy has never been in such a shocking mess as it is at present', wrote Slessor in February 1963. Our male Cassandra had evidently forgotten the 'shocking mess' of the late 1930s, when he was actually on the field of play, not – as now – shouting from the sidelines. Even so, this letter is the most passionate of all those he sent to *The Times* in the last 20-odd years of his life. The reason was simple. For years past, 'foreign policy has been following one line and defence policy a line leading in an almost diametrically opposite direction.'

Britain had allowed the army and the RAF under SHAPE to decline to an utterly inadequate level, he believed, both in strength and equipment. We had abolished conscription and yet clung to our status as a first-class power with world-wide responsibilities. We also clung 'to the myth of an independent British Nuclear Deterrent' and talked loosely about reducing still further the armed forces based in Germany. We cancelled 'an excellent tactical weapon (Blue Water) on the score of expense, and now propose to spend vast sums on a few Polaris submarines – single purpose weapons of which the Americans already have plenty to deal with Russia and which are useless for our treaty obligations or other potential commitments outside Europe.' We have waited until de Gaulle (the French President) rejected our bid to join the Common Market before assigning Bomber Command to NATO, 'a course I have been advocating for several years', but with no apparent idea of what its strategic role in the alliance would be. As a life-long Conservative it angered Slessor that the fault lay entirely with a Conservative government. It failed to make proper use of the Chiefs of Staff in formulating strategic policy and until it did nothing would save us 'from getting into an even worse bog than we are in at the moment, if that is possible.'

That diatribe, like his others, provoked no response in Whitehall. Although keenly aware that he was very much 'yesterday's man' (if not the day before) with no specific influence, he felt obliged to have his say in any forum open to him. In June 1963, his essay, 'After Nassau: "Folly" of a small Polaris Submarine Force', took up a whole page – with photographs – of *The Times Supplement on British Aviation*. President Kennedy and Prime Minister Macmillan had met at Nassau in the Bahamas in December 1962 and there agreed that Britain would be allowed to buy Polaris missiles in return for agreeing to assign those missiles, their V-bombers and tactical nuclear weapons to SACEUR. 'Thus it came about', wrote the historians of the British Chiefs of Staff, 'that the RAF lost primacy in British Defence priorities that it had enjoyed in varying forms since Hitler came to power in the early 1930s.' The Polaris deal, as Denis Healey observed but Slessor did not, made it certain that President de Gaulle would veto Britain's entry into the European Common Market.

'To those of us whose memories go back to the 1920s', Slessor wrote, 'much of the contemporary comment on the future of the RAF has a familiar ring. Few of us would have believed, in the light of history of the past 30 years, that we should again hear it suggested that the RAF should be abolished as an autonomous service and split up between the army and navy, yet even this has not been lacking.' There was, in fact, no such move in contemplation and such extravagant language did not make it easier for Slessor to sway opinion in the corridors of power. Never before, he believed, had Britain's defence policy been so bedevilled by 'muddled thinking'. The main problem, as he saw it, was the government's insistence on an independent nuclear deterrent. 'To most people that is what Bomber Command is – or was. But since the potential aggressor we have to deter is Russia, and since in the foreseeable future the V-bombers may be unable to penetrate Russian defences without Skybolt – and Skybolt is no more – therefore Bomber Command has no future, and thus the future of the RAF is at stake.' Skybolt was an American air-to-surface missile, costly and plagued with technical problems which was kept alive longer than it should have been because of British interest.

Slessor thought it wrong to build up a small force of very costly Polaris-armed submarines when the US already had over 40 of them. The expense would mean that Britain could no longer pull her weight elsewhere. Bomber Command would suffer and yet it was, in Slessor's opinion, 'a superlatively efficient striking force with equipment second to none in the world, capable of finding and hitting accurately with nuclear or conventional weapons, and without prohibitive loss, whatever targets it may be called upon to attack.' These were large claims to make, and may have been accurate, but Slessor had no first-hand means of assessing them or of comparing them with the striking forces of the US or the Soviet Union; as with his claims for the prewar bomber force, they were assertions.

In September 1963 he again condemned the Polaris submarine programme as 'a fantastic waste of resources' and went on to speak of Britain's 'enormous stake in Australasia and Malaysia.' He could not believe that a British government would leave them to the protection of the US and their own resources. Britain, he was convinced, remained 'whether we like it or not... a World Power and member of a world-wide alliance'; the great material advantages of that status could only be secured by paying an adequate premium in the form of defence expenditure.

That conviction inspired yet another letter to *The Times* in May 1964. 'To allow ourselves to be hustled out of our few remaining overseas bases', Slessor declared, 'by the psychological warfare of Khrushchev and his friends in the United Nations, backed by the aggressive hostility of people like Nasser and Soekarno [ruler of Indonesia], could only result in "throwing our friends to the wolves" and giving a green light to the overweening ambitions of these African and Asiatic dictators – to say nothing of the potentially more formidable threat from Communist China.'

The going of TSR.2

Soon after Slessor's retirement at the end of 1952, the search was on for a Canberra replacement. Serious thought began in 1956 and a combined team from English Electric and Vickers-Armstrong (later to be amalgamated into the British Aircraft Corporation) started work in January 1959 on an aircraft capable of all-weather operations at very high speed at high or low levels in the 'Tactical Strike and Reconnaissance' role. The result, with the uninspiring name of TSR.2 (implying that the Canberra had been TSR.1) first flew in September 1964. But it was cancelled only seven months later, in April 1965. It is widely regarded as the greatest aircraft the RAF never got. It would also have been by far the most expensive. It 'shares with the Anglo-French Concorde a nerve-wracking and politically-dominated gestation', wrote Bill Gunston, 'plus development costs that make a king's ransom pale into insignificance.' The original estimate of its cost in 1960 was £250 million; by 1964 that had climbed to £750 million; and it would not reach squadron service until at least 1967, so Healey killed it. 'The real tragedy', he wrote, 'is that the TSR.2 should ever have been begun; it would have been possible to develop the naval Buccaneer strike aircraft to meet the RAF's needs much faster and at far less cost.'

As a director of the company making the Buccaneer, Slessor presumably had some knowledge of its capabilities and yet he chose to regard the cancellation of a rival (and far more costly) project as 'a major disaster for the British aircraft industry'. However, he hoped for 'a really drastic rationalization of British aviation as a whole – government direction, design, production and use, both military and civil – which is long overdue.' Britain needed a strong strike and reconnaissance force, with a nuclear as well as conventional capability. 'We have seen how our Communist co-existers make a habit of supplying arms to anyone like Nasser or Soekarno – on whom they can rely to use them irresponsibly – not only sophisticated radars and anti-aircraft weapons, but aircraft of high performance and range, such as the MiG-21 and the Badger bomber. We must be able to compete at least on equal terms.'

But modern weapons were fearfully expensive, he went on to argue. Must Britain therefore rely on the US, which could afford them? Not if we looked to Europe: a point which had extra force as it became clear that the government's choice of a replacement for the TSR.2 was an American aircraft that also took an age to produce at enormous cost: the General Dynamics F-111 – and Healey was obliged to cancel it too. It was in Europe, Slessor thought, that the fate of Britain's aircraft industry would be decided. This was not the place to regret the shortcomings of politicians when dealing with European states since 1945, culminating in the folly of the Nassau Conference and Britain's exclusion from the Common Market. Nor was it any use complaining about high-pressure American salesmen: that was their job, to sell.

The lesson of TSR.2, in Cassandra Slessor's view, was 'the need to break through our traditional British attitude of complacent self-sufficiency into the sphere of collaboration and integration with the very efficient aircraft industries of Europe': as, for example, in the development by Britain and France of a supersonic airliner, the Concorde. Not, as it happened, a good example. Work on that project began in February 1965, it first flew in March 1969, but did not enter enter service until January 1976. A marvellous achievement, technically and aesthetically, but it cost a fortune to produce, carried very few passengers, and never made its sole users – Britain and France – any money. It was 'a good example', in Healey's opinion, 'of how a government can find itself supporting a glamorous scientific breakthrough which does not make commercial sense.'

Slessor broke into television in September 1965, taking part in a discussion on Granada ITV about the 'relative and changing importance of each service', and the equipment it should have. 'I've no doubt the V-bombers could demolish some Russian cities', he said, 'at a high cost in casualties. But that sort of thing today has become the role of the long-range missile – Minuteman, Polaris, and so on.' Bomber Command's task, Slessor believed, 'would be to destroy targets east of the Iron Curtain allotted to it by the NATO Supreme Commander in accordance with his plan for the defence of free Europe against Soviet invasion.' He then attacked Polaris again: the navy was 'let in by Macmillan – for purely political reasons, not military at all – for the Polaris submarine programme in the Nassau agreement, which I regard as a bit of political folly on the part of the late government second only to Suez.' The navy should be spending its money on the things it really needed: hunter-killer submarines, anti-aircraft ships, missile ships, commando carriers and not on the 'useless' Polaris submarines. They were useless because they will never be fired in anger and are too few to be a credible deterrent. Service Chiefs, he concluded, 'were more often in conflict with the Treasury than each other, and the late government was far too ready to say, in effect, I'm not going to give you the tools you say you need, but you must still do the job without them.'

Whatever mistakes had been made in Washington, wrote Slessor in November 1965, the fact remained that the US had stood between Britain and disaster on several occasions during the past twenty years, and so Britain must continue to pull her weight east of Suez. That meant maintaining adequate reserves of land forces at home and abroad, properly equipped and trained, capable of being moved swiftly in response to crises – unencumbered, 'how one wishes', by the present enormous tail of dependents. Sadly, like so much else that Slessor held dear, the days when servicemen accepted long-term separation from their families were almost done. 'If ever the day comes', he ended, 'when there are no bases that we can use east of Suez, then we shall no longer be able to play any military part outside Europe. That would be a poor outlook for our Commonwealth partners and allies in the Far East and... for our economic and commercial interests.'

That 'poor outlook' had many bright intervals during the rest of Slessor's life – and many more since his death, greatly helped by the collapse of the 'evil empire in the east', which he would so much have enjoyed. But the fact remains that the 1960s confirmed what seems to be a permanent change for Britain in world affairs, from a player with (at least) major aspirations to one acutely aware of its lost prestige and medium rank. His beloved service suffered grievous changes that hurt him deeply. Charles (always known as Sam) Elworthy was CAS and then Chief of the Defence Staff, from September 1963 to April 1971. Together with Denis Healey, Secretary of State for Defence in the government of Harold Wilson, he presided over 'one of the most fundamental re-orientations of British defence policy since World War II': TSR.2 was cancelled, so too was its replacement, the F-111; the Valiant disappeared; cadet entry to Cranwell ended; and Polaris submarines took over the deterrent role. By the time Elworthy departed, concluded Henry Probert, 'the main withdrawal from the Far East was virtually complete, and United Kingdom defence policy was firmly set towards concentration on the support of NATO in Europe and the north Atlantic.' For good or ill, the RAF and the other services would operate in an environment quite unlike that which Slessor had grown up with and tried so hard to preserve. Like Slessor, Elworthy was an unheeded Cassandra who repeatedly warned against what seemed to both men dangerously rapid changes. Many officers and men would leave the service disappointed and disillusioned.

Sandys had certainly deprived the RAF of supersonic successors to the best-selling Vampires, Meteors, Canberras and Hunters for a whole generation. But: 'Guilt did not wholly lie with the politicians', as Healey pointed out. 'The RAF continually changed its operational requirements, and the aircraft firms often submitted quite unrealistic estimates of the cost and delivery time for a new aircraft, so as to get the contract to produce it.' Slessor had nothing to say about the financial consequences of these changes and never opposed the fixation with shifting 'General Duties' officers rapidly from post to post. 'A man who had been commanding a fighter squadron in Cyprus', recalled Healey, 'would be made responsible in the Ministry for controlling the expenditure of millions of pounds, knowing that he would move on after three years to do intelligence work in Singapore; it would be a miracle if he had the ability or incentive to establish effective control over the full-time experts at the British Aircraft Corporation or Marconi.'

The end of the aircraft carrier?
In February 1966, Slessor commented on 'the wholly erroneous idea now current that the demise of aircraft carriers would mean the eclipse of the Royal Navy and the end of British sea power.' Carriers, he wrote (not for the first time) had always been 'a very uneconomical form of force... the modern embodiment of the old capital ship complex, which cost us so dear in 1939-45 because the Admiralty had insisted on building battleships at the expense of the vitally essential submarine escorts.' Here he quoted (again not for the first time) his own figures for RAF achievements in the war at sea, achievements which outmatched those of the navy. In its 'proper role', he allowed that the navy remained important: 'the protection of shipping and naval support of operations on and over land.' Instead of squandering resources on 'status symbols' such as Polaris submarines and strike carriers, we had devoted them to the really essential requirements – submarine hunter-killers, fast surface hunting craft and escorts, to more assault ships and commando carriers, missile ships and modern light inshore craft', the navy would be in far better shape.

For once, this diatribe attracted several rebuttals – all polite, all devastating. Admiral Sir Peter Gretton, one of the heroes of the Atlantic battle and a recent Admiralty Board member responsible for naval aviation, hit Slessor with a brief salvo. He invited him to explain how assault ships and commando carriers would be defended against aerial attack. 'Surely', argued Gretton, 'carrier-based aircraft, on the spot, are the only solution.' Admiral Sir Caspar John chimed in next day, aiming heavier blows. He had ended his career as First Sea Lord (1960-3) with an 'honest but unsuccessful' attempt to get the navy and the RAF 'to see eye-to-eye on the matter of the deployment of the nation's tactical air power.' He tried again in 1965, as a member of a Chiefs of Staff committee. Admiral John had never regarded aircraft carriers as 'more than an important alternative means of operating aircraft – i.e., as mobile floating air bases complementary to and not in competition with static bases ashore.' They were not 'naval gimmicks', but vital components of a defence system. Then came the Admiral's exasperated plea, echoing cries reverberating round Whitehall for many years – before, during, and after Slessor's career ended. Surely, in an unpredictable future it would be wise for the champions of air power to recognize that there is more than one way of deploying it, and that there are great advantages to be had from mobile take-off and landing points.' Sadly, 'my friend' Slessor felt it necessary to dismiss the carrier and refer, yet again, to the Battle of the Atlantic. 'I do not know of anyone in charge of the navy's affairs in recent years', John ended, 'who bases any part of the case for the aircraft carrier on a need to be prepared to fight that kind of battle again.'

Finally the naval historian Stephen Roskill had his say. Slessor's letter, he wrote, 'contains too many over-simplifications and questionable statements to allow it to pass unchallenged. Even accepting as correct (which I do not) his figures for the relative effectiveness of carrier-borne and shore-based aircraft in the Atlantic battle, he totally ignores the fact that the war against Japan supports entirely the opposite conclusion to that which he draws. It was the Japanese aircraft carriers which smashed British and American sea power in December 1941, and it was the American carriers which reversed that result at Coral Sea, Midway, Leyte Gulf, etc., in 1942-4.' It was carriers which proved their worth, from the Solomons to Okinawa, 'by supplying constant local air superiority; and that could not have been done by shore-based aircraft operating from distant bases.' Roskill then turned to today's world. Britain was still concerned with the defence of shipping and support of military operations 'in the vast ocean spaces east of Suez', so the lessons of the war against Japan are more useful than those of the Atlantic battle, in which shore-based aircraft enjoyed the use of relatively numerous and closely-spaced bases', in Britain, Iceland, North America, Gibraltar, West Africa and the Azores.

Nevertheless, Healey cancelled the new carrier desired by the navy. It would be most useful, he agreed, east of Suez, but given the need for regular re-fits, a three-carrier force would have provided only one carrier permanently in service at horrendous cost. 'I asked the navy to invent a plausible scenario in which the carrier would be essential. The only one they could conceive was a prolonged naval battle in the Straits of Sumatra in which the enemy had Russian MiGs on the adjoining coast, but we had given up our bases in the area; this seemed too unlikely to be worth preparing against.' These comments would have gratified Slessor and so too would Healey's conclusion. 'The navy argued its case for the carrier badly; I had to keep sending its papers back to be made more persuasive. The air force, on the other hand, was represented by two able lawyers – Sam Elworthy himself, the Chief of the Air Staff, and Peter Fletcher, the Air Marshal concerned with policy. They made rings round the navy, carrying the army and the Chief of Defence Staff, Dick Hull, with them.'

Even so, Slessor's belief in the death of aircraft carriers was much exaggerated. More than 26 years after his death, as *The Times* reported, the Royal Navy was hoping to acquire two new carriers, 'capable of switching roles, from launching large-scale air assaults on land targets to carrying special forces and attack helicopters', as well as missile-armed submarines. Although carriers are astoundingly expensive to build and operate, 'both the Americans and the British recognize that they will remain essential in providing mobile bases for the aircraft to support future land operations'; they also 'substitute for costly and politically controversial bases overseas.'

EPILOGUE

These remain

Four of the most important volumes published on the Second World War in the air appeared in October 1961. They were written by Sir Charles Webster and Noble Frankland, entitled *The Strategic Air Offensive against Germany, 1939-1945*. It was an immense undertaking and the result is now regarded as a masterpiece of scholarship, but during the 1950s – as it became known what Webster and Frankland were about – determined attempts were made by Air Marshals and civil servants to suppress or at least bowdlerize it. Portal (coldly) and Harris (hotly) opposed publication, backed by various Whitehall Warriors on the familiar ground that citizens should not know what really goes on in wartime (or peacetime, for that matter). It gives one great pleasure to record that both Tedder and Slessor – so estranged, yet so often thinking alike – were entirely supportive of this great work. Both men were closely involved in aspects of that offensive and therefore well aware that careful scrutiny of their words and deeds might not always show them in a shining light. As it happened, Tedder was highly praised for his achievements in 1944 and Slessor's pre-war efforts were treated with respect.

Slessor's comments on the draft were calm and collected. He was surprised at Frankland's 'insistence on the pre-eminence of contemporary documentation over the recollections of the principal characters.' He had himself followed too often the easy path of memory in his own writings, rather than struggling through thickets of documents, but he frankly admitted that memories could be 'damned unreliable'. As for Tedder, he praised the draft as 'masterly and courageous', adding that he never thought 'anything so near the truth would ever be likely to go on the record.' Its three main conclusions – with which Tedder and Slessor agreed – were firstly that the Anglo-American strategic air offensive made a vital contribution to Germany's defeat; secondly that that contribution depended upon air superiority; and thirdly that aerial bombing took far longer to become effective than anyone had anticipated in 1939.

Very few Air Marshals have been invited to write for *Punch*, a great British institution (now, alas, defunct), but Slessor was. He contributed an introduction to an issue celebrating the 50th anniversary of the RAF's foundation, April 1st 1918. 'It was a rather typically British affair', he thought, 'stemming as it did mainly from some inadequate and ill-judged causes', but if it had not happened then 'it is at least a fair bet that the Royal Flying Corps in the years between the wars would have suffered the fate of the Tank Corps; and then, I wonder, what would have happened to Britain in 1940?' There were a few riotous guest-nights early in that April, but by then there was not much glamour left in the war, 'though we of the new RAF, in our relatively comfortable billets or in Nissen huts on some rather soggy cow-pasture behind the balloon line, knew full well that our discomforts were small beer compared to what the poor devils in the trenches and battery positions had to put up with.'

On a lighter note, suitable for a humour magazine, he recalled the horrors of the RAF's first uniform: 'a dreadful pale blue confection embellished with gold', which nobody would buy and so it soon gave way 'to the more sober slate-blue known all over the world today'. He ended with words which had come to mean so much to him since 1945. 'It is surely permissable to hope that nuclear air power means the end of World War as we old boys have known it twice in our generation.'

Last book

Slessor's last book, *These Remain: A Personal Anthology: Memories of Flying, Fighting and Field Sports*, appeared in 1969 and is perhaps his best; certainly his most readable. 'He reveals himself', wrote a reviewer in *Flight International*, 'as a man with views firmly based on his service, empire, and "huntin'-and-shootin'" experiences; life has consisted of the things he likes doing, either professionally or for recreation.' It is another bunch of essays collected this time to celebrate the 50th anniversary of the creation of the RAF on April 1st 1918. Unusually for anything written by Slessor, one could wish it longer. He had in mind recovering some 'nostalgic memories' for other ex-Haileyburians and attempting to convince the younger generation 'that a career in the RAF has still much to be said for it.' Sadly, the service had changed a great deal since the inter-war years, 'and will change still more if or when the unhappy day comes when we shall have pulled out our garrisons from east of Suez.'

He struck a more cheerful and delightfully evocative note in 1965, when invited to contribute a foreword to a short history of the Royal Flying Corps. 'Aviation today', he wrote, 'is as different from 50 years ago as a tank is from an Egyptian war-chariot.' Nevertheless, like so many of his contemporaries, he was proud to be among 'the old gentlemen' entitled to wear 'the rather gaudy tie of the Royal Flying Corps' and was always 'filled with rather uneasy admiration of the men who fly these great modern jets in weather in which – as the old saying had it – even the gulls are walking.' Modern pilots had to be more serious than Slessor and his early flying friends: 'you'd have to be pretty irresponsible to take the same liberties with a V-bomber that we used to take with our old Henri Farmans, Camels and DH4s, each of which cost a good deal less than one leg of the undercarriage of a Vulcan II.'

Slessor was sure that modern pilots enjoyed flying, 'but I wonder if they get the same thrill out of it as we did? Not the same sort of thrill, I suspect... I am sure my son [John], commanding a V-bomber squadron, gets no more kick out of slipping across to Canada for a couple of days than I did from my first cross-country in an old 50 Blériot from Gosport to Farnborough, when I recall having some doubts about my ability to climb over the Hog's Back. The modern pilot has to be more serious than his father was in the maternity jacket and puttees of the RFC. He has to be, and is, a superbly-trained, highly-disciplined professional.' At this point, Slessor does not miss the opportunity for yet another swipe at the Royal Navy of long ago. Its officers, he admitted, were 'more professional' than RFC officers, 'but they, too, neglected some vitally important aspects of their profession; if they had thought more about what we should now call "operational requirements", Beatty would have been less surprised than he was by our battle-cruisers blowing up at Jutland.'

By the late 1960s, although only just over 70, Slessor felt 'too old and out of touch with current affairs' – in which he too often harked back to old quarrels or situations now irretrievably changed – to go on airing his opinions. Moreover, 'increasing lameness makes it difficult for me to lead as active a life as I used to.' He had been lame since childhood and perhaps his most admirable quality was the fact that he so rarely referred to the pain his legs gave him, or used his handicap as an excuse to evade even the dullest chores. On the contrary, for most years after his 'retirement' he was positively hyperactive in attending committees, lunches, dinners and funerals. 'There can never have been an air force officer less technically-minded', than himself, he confessed: which helps to explain his armchair theorizing, lacking an under-pinning of what men and weapons could actually do. For example, he never once discussed with his son John what he, as commander of a V-bomber squadron, actually did on training or operational flights; and what he and his crews really thought – privately – of their chances of successfully carrying out an attack on a target in the Soviet Union.

The Empire he grew up in had gone by 1967, 'and today Britain ranks in the second category of power and influence... I used to hope that the free multi-racial Commonwealth that followed Empire would be able to exert an influence even stronger, because more broadly based and more generally acceptable; but I am afraid it is only realistic to admit that in the sphere of international politics it has ceased to mean much – and in the strategic field means even less.'

As for southern Africa, he castigated 'the cardboard Canutes of the Rhodesian Front', but deeply regretted the estrangement of Rhodesians and South Africans: 'the soldiers who fought with us at Delville Wood and in the desert, the aircrews who served under me in Italy and shared with their British and Polish comrades the glory of that desperate forlorn hope over Warsaw.' He could not see into the future, except to be certain 'no-one will be the better off, least of all perhaps the White Rhodesians.' As Cassandra, that accurate prophecy was certainly ignored.

As for Europe, the prospect of nuclear war had declined, but the Berlin Wall remained, and 'the hopeful trend towards Europeanism and the Atlantic ideal has been brutally halted – one must hope only temporarily – by the paranoiac chauvinism of an aged Frenchman [Charles de Gaulle] and the lack of guts in most French politicians.' In January 1962, Slessor was one of a hundred representatives of Allied Powers nominated by their governments who produced a 'Declaration of Paris', which included a unanimous recommendation in favour of developing NATO and OECD (Organization for Economic Co-operation and Development) into an Atlantic Community, with its own institutions, consultative assembly, high court, etc. It came to nothing, but it remained 'an article of faith' with Slessor that 'the future for Britain lies in playing a leading part in this Atlantic community.'

Last days

Slessor's wife, Hermione, had died on September 14th 1970, peacefully, after a long illness. The funeral was private and he asked that he be spared letters. A memorial service was held in the RAF's particular church, St Clement Danes in the Strand, on October 13th. There was a huge attendance of family, friends and colleagues in and out of the services. A year later, in October 1971, it was announced that a marriage would shortly take place, privately, between Slessor and Marcella Priest, widow of Brigadier R. T. Priest, late of the Royal Artillery. They were married at Rimpton Manor on November 27th. That marriage, sadly, did not prosper and ended with a judicial separation in 1978. Jack Slessor's last years were thus blighted and he died on July 12th 1979 at the age of 82 in Princess Alexandra Hospital, Wroughton, near Swindon in Wiltshire.

A long obituary did not appear in *The Times* until November (thanks to a protracted strike, which would have confirmed Slessor's opinion that Britain was in serious decline). It described him as one of Trenchard's outstanding disciples and outlined his career. 'Slessor did not come out of the last war as one of the great popular figures', wrote the anonymous obituarist. 'He was not a commander whose attributes caught the attention of the man in the street, or the wartime serviceman for that matter. He created an impression of brusqueness in those who did not know him, although to those who did he was an affable and most sociable man.' Slessor's son John wrote to Eaker on August 6th. 'Poor father, he had an unhappy last few months, I'm afraid, and we console ourselves with the thought that he would never have wanted to linger on when life no longer held any meaning for him.' There was to be a memorial service in London on September 25th. Eaker attended, as a member of the USAF delegation.

It was, he recalled, a 'nostalgic ceremony for a close collaborator and a valued friend from the Second World War.'

Sir Michael Howard remembered Jack Slessor warmly nearly 20 years after his death. Howard was one of those who founded the International Institute for Strategic Studies in London and Slessor became one of the earliest members of its council. 'He was a regular attender at our seminars, discussions and conferences, and never for a moment tried to pull rank. He always expressed himself with force and precision, but listened courteously to dissenting views, made thoughtful interventions in discussions and, without ever abandoning his principles, allowed himself to be moved along by the arguments. He never made you feel a fool, but if you disagreed with him it was wise first to think through exactly what you were going to say. His was always the voice of experience, realism and sanity, and kept us all on track. Although he himself would have denied it, he was indeed a truly great man. His contribution to the winning of the war had been outstanding. No less was his contribution to the subsequent keeping of the peace.'

High praise indeed from a most distinguished historian, but perhaps Jack Slessor – who always had plenty to say for himself – deserves the last word. 'It is customary in democratic countries', he wrote, 'to deplore expenditure on armaments as conflicting with the requirements of the social services. There is a tendency to forget that the most important social service that a government can do for its people is to keep them alive and free.'

ACKNOWLEDGEMENTS

I am most grateful to all members of the Slessor family, who have entertained me (in every sense of that word) on several occasions, allowing me unrestricted access to their papers, photographs and memories and graciously understanding why it took me so long to complete this task. Without their help, and that of Tim Cooper and Errol Martyn (to whom it is warmly dedicated) there would be no book. I am also grateful to the History Department and the University of Canterbury who, in the days when I taught there, granted me leave and money for research. My former student and colleague, Andrew Conway, was helpful in the early stages. The Air Marshals who talked to me about Park, Coningham, Cross and Tedder have now passed away, but they all had memories or opinions of Jack Slessor; so too had Denis Richards and John Terraine. Other friends overseas are still with us and have given essential help: Sebastian Cox and Sebastian Ritchie (of the Air Historical Branch, Ministry of Defence) and their ever-welcoming colleagues at Great Scotland Yard and now at Bentley Priory. It has been a great pleasure to work in the public Record Office at Kew (now renamed British National Archives) where friendly help is always on tap even though the systems are truly idiot-proof. In Washington DC, I have spent many a happy hour with Jo Kincaid, his wife Yvonne, and her inspiring colleagues at Bolling AFB; National Archives and the Library of Congress are also great places to work. Those Americans, plus Phillip Meilinger, Tami Davis Biddle and James Corum keep the 'special relationship' very much alive for me. I thank Henry and Audrey Probert, Humphrey Wynn, Owen Phillipps and the late George Westlake for their friendship as well as their information. John Davies and Lizzie Platt (of Grub Street) know how much I owe them. Andrew Hambling and Victoria Sheppard (of Haileybury School) gave me a memorable day. Not least, I wish to thank all those wonderful students I had the privilege of teaching in Christchurch. Between them, they provided the inspiration to keep me going in times good and bad. Finally, in the place of most honour, is my dear wife Sandra. She makes it easy for me to potter away hour after hour and pacifies the computer when it gets uppity.

SOURCES

Books and Journals

Air Ministry Air Publication 3368, *The Origins and Development of Operational Research in the Royal Air Force* (London: HMSO, 1963)

Andrew, Christopher, *Secret Service; The Making of the British Intelligence Community* (London: Guild Publishing, 1985)

Ball, S.J., 'Military Nuclear Relations between the United States and Great Britain under the terms of the McMahon Act, 1946-1958', in *Historical Journal*, vol. 38, no. 2 (1995)

Barker, Ralph, *The Royal Air Force, 1918-1968: Part II – Into the Nuclear Age* (London: RAF Association, 1968)

Barnett, Correlli, *The Lost Victories: British Dreams, British Realities, 1945-1950* (London: Macmillan, 1995)

Baylis, John, and Alan MacMillan, 'The British Global Strategy Paper of 1952', in *Journal of Strategic Studies*, vol. 16, no. 2 (June 1993)

Beaumont, Roger A., 'A New Lease on Empire: Air Policing, 1919-1939', in *Aerospace Historian*, vol. 26, no. 2 (Summer/June 1979)

Beevor, Anthony, *Berlin: The Downfall, 1945* (London: Penguin Viking, 2002)

Biddle, Tami Davis, *Rhetoric and Reality in Air Warfare: The Evolution of British and American Ideas about Strategic Bombing, 1914-1945* (Princeton University Press, 2002)

Bond, Brian, & Ian Roy (eds.) *War & Society: A Yearbook of Military History* (London: Croom Helm, 1977)

Boog, Horst, (ed.) *The Conduct of the Air War in the Second World War: An International Comparison* (New York/Oxford: Berg Publishers, 1992)

Bowyer, Chas, (ed.) *Royal Flying Corps Communiqués, 1917-1918* (London: Grub Street, 1998)

Boyle, Andrew, *Trenchard: Man of Vision* (London: Collins, 1962)

Brement, Marshall, 'Why Didn't The Soviets Take Warsaw?', in *Military History Quarterly*, vol. 6, no. 3 (Spring 1994)

Bridgman, Leonard, with a commentary by Oliver Stewart, *The Clouds Remember: The Aeroplanes of World War I* (London: Arms & Armour Press, 1936; reprint 1972)

Brinkley, Douglas, *Dean Acheson: The Cold War Years, 1953-71* (Yale

University Press, 1993)

Bruce, J.M., 'The RE8', in *Flypast 10: A Selection of International Aircraft from Profile* (Windsor: Profile Publications, 1972)

Buckley, John, *The RAF and Trade Defence, 1919-1945: Constant Endeavour* (Keele University Press, 1995)

Carlton, David, *Anthony Eden: A Biography* (London: Allen Lane, 1981)

Catchpole, B., *The Korean War* (London: Constable, 2000)

Chalmers, W.S., *Max Horton and the Western Approaches* (London: Hodder and Stoughton, 1954)

Chamier, J.A., 'The Use of Air Force for Replacing Military Garrisons', in *RUSI Journal*, vol. 66 (1921) pp. 205-216.

Chapman, Guy, *Why France Collapsed* (London: Cassell, 1968)

Christie, Carl A. with Fred Hatch, *Ocean Bridge: The History of RAF Ferry Command* (Leicester: Midland Publishing, 1995)

Churchill, Winston S., *The Second World War: Volume 5, Closing the Ring* (London: Reprint Society, 1954)

Claasen, Adam R.A., *Hitler's Northern War: The Luftwaffe's Ill-Fated Campaign, 1940-1945* (Lawrence, Kansas: University Press of Kansas, 2001)

Close, David H., (ed.) *The Greek Civil War, 1943-1950* (London: Routledge, 1993)

Clouston, A.E., *Dangerous Skies* (London: Cassell, 1954)

Cole, Christopher, and E. F. Cheesman, *The Air Defence of Britain, 1914-1918* (London: Putnam, 1984)

Conyers Nesbit, Roy, *The Strike Wings: Special Anti-Shipping Squadrons, 1942-45* (London: Kimber, 1984)

Craven, W.F. & J.L. Cate (eds.) *The Army Air Forces in World War II* (Chicago University Press, 1951)

Cross, Kenneth & Vincent Orange, *Straight and Level* (London: Grub Street, 1993)

Danchev, A., and D. Todman (eds.) *War Diaries, 1939-1945: Field Marshal Lord Alanbrooke* (London: Weidenfeld & Nicolson, 2001)

Davies, Norman, *Rising '44: The Battle for Warsaw* (London: Macmillan, 2003)

Dean, Maurice, *The Royal Air Force and Two World Wars* (London: Cassell, 1979)

Dear, I.C.B., & M.R.D. Foot (eds.) *The Oxford Companion to the Second World War* (Oxford University Press, 1995)

Douhet, Giulio, *The Command of the Air*, translated by Dino Ferrari (1942)

English, Allan D., 'The RAF Staff College and the Evolution of British Strategic Bombing Policy, 1922-1929', in *Journal of Strategic Studies*, vol. 16, no. 3 (September 1993)

Farrar-Hockley, A., *The British Part in the Korean War, vol. l: A Distant*

Obligation (London: HMSO, l990)

Farrell, Brian & Sandy Hunter (eds.) *Sixty Years On: The Fall of Singapore Revisited* (Singapore: Eastern Universities Press, 2002)

Fitzsimons, B., (ed.), *Illustrated Encyclopedia of Weapons & Warfare* (London: Purnell, 1971)

Forrest, Ian, 'Nato's Punch', in *Royal Air Force Flying Review*, vol. xvii, no. 3 (December 1961)

Francillon, René J., *Lockheed Aircraft Since 1913* (London: Putnam, 1987)

Frankland, Noble, *History at War: The Campaigns of an Historian* (London: Giles de la Mare, 1998)

Fredette, Raymond H., *The First Battle of Britain, 1917-1918, and the Birth of the Royal Air Force* (London: Cassell, 1966); re-titled *The Sky on Fire* (Washington DC: Smithsonian Institution Press, 1976)

Gilbert, Martin, *Winston S. Churchill* (London: Heinemann, 1976)

Goulter, Christina J.M., *A Forgotten Offensive: Royal Air Force Coastal Command's Anti-Shipping Campaign, 1940-1945* (London: Frank Cass, 1995)

Gray Peter W., and Sebastian Cox (eds.) *Airpower Leadership: Theory and Practice* (London: HMSO, 2002)

Greenwood, Sean, '"Caligula's Horse" Revisited: Sir Thomas Inskip as Minister for the Co-ordination of Defence, 1936-1939', in *Journal of Strategic Studies*, vol. 17, no. 2 (June 1994)

Gunston, Bill, *The Encyclopedia of the World's Combat Aircraft* (London: Hamlyn, 1976)

Gunston, Bill, et al., *The Illustrated Encyclopedia of Aircraft* (London: Orbis, 1981)

Harris, K., *Attlee* (London: Weidenfeld & Nicolson, 1982)

Hastings, M., *The Korean War* (London: Michael Joseph, 1987)

Healey, Denis, *The Time of My Life* (London: Michael Joseph, 1989)

Henshaw, Trevor, *The Sky Their Battlefield: Air Fighting and the Complete List of Allied Air Casualties from Enemy Action in the First War: British, Commonwealth, and United States Air Services, 1914 to 1918* (London: Grub Street, 1995)

Hinsley, F.H. et al., *British Intelligence in the Second World War* (London: HMSO, 1979)

Hobson, Chris, *Airmen Died in the Great War, 1914-1918* (Suffolk: J. B. Hayward & Son, 1995)

Howard, Michael, 'Sir John Slessor and the Prevention of War', in *Royal Air Force Historical Journal*, no. l9 (1999)

Howarth, Stephen and Derek Law (eds.) *The Battle of the Atlantic, 1939-1945* (London: Greenhill Books, 1994)

Irving, David, *The Rise and Fall of the Luftwaffe: The Life of Luftwaffe Marshal Erhard Milch* (London: Futura Publications, 1976)

Jackson, William & Field Marshal Lord Bramall, *The Chiefs: The Story of the United Kingdom Chiefs of Staff* (London: Brassey's, 1992)

Jackson, William, with Group Captain T. P. Gleave and C.J.C. Molony, *The Mediterranean and Middle East* (London: HMSO, 1987)

Johnston, Andrew M., 'Mr Slessor Goes to Washington: The Influence of the British Global Strategy Paper on the Eisenhower New Look', in *Diplomatic History*, vol. 22, no. 2 (Summer 1998)

Jones, Matthew, *Britain, The United States and the Mediterranean War, 1942-44* (London: Macmillan, 1996)

Jones, Neville, *The Beginnings of Strategic Air Power: A History of the British Bomber Force, 1923-1939* (London: Frank Cass, 1987)

Kingston-McCloughry, E.J., *Global Strategy* (London: Cape, 1957)

Kingston-McCloughry, E.J., *The Direction of War: A Critique of the Political Direction and High Command in War* (London: Cape, 1955)

Kingston-McCloughry, E.J., 'The Gordon-Shephard Memorial Prize Essay for 1933' in *Royal Air Force Quarterly Review*

Kyle, Keith, *Suez* (London: Weidenfeld & Nicolson, 1991)

Latham, H.B., 'The Destruction of Zeppelin L.15: An Early AA Success', in *RUSI Journal*, vol. xxv (August 1950)

Leutze, James, (ed.) *The London Observer: The Journal of General Raymond E. Lee, 1940-1941* (London: Hutchinson, 1972)

Levine, Alan J., 'Was World War II a Near-run Thing?' in *Journal of Strategic Studies*, vol. 8 (March 1985)

Lewin, Ronald, *Slim the Standard Bearer* (London: Leo Cooper, 1976)

Lewis, Peter, *The British Bomber Since 1914: Sixty-five Years of Design and Development* (London: Putnam, 1980)

Lucas, L., (ed) *Thanks for the Memory: Unforgettable Characters in Air Warfare, 1939-45* (London: Grub Street, 1998)

Lukas, Richard C., 'The Big Three and the Warsaw Uprising', in *Military Affairs*, vol. 39, no. 3 (October 1975)

Maclean, Fitzroy, *Eastern Approaches* (London: Cape, 1949)

Macmillan, Harold, *War Diaries: Politics and War in the Mediterranean, January 1943-May 1945* (London: Macmillan, 1984)

Mason, Tony, *Air Power: A Centennial Appraisal* (London: Brassey's, 1994)

May, Ernest R., (ed.) *Knowing One's Enemies: Intelligence Assessment before the Two World Wars* (New Jersey: Princeton University Press, 1984)

Meilinger, Phillip S., *Airwar: Theory and Practice* (London: Cass, 2003)

Meilinger, Phillip S., 'The Historiography of Airpower: Theory and Doctrine', in *Journal of Military History*, vol. 64 (April 2000)

Murray, Williamson, 'Appeasement and Intelligence' in *Intelligence and National Security*, vol. 2, no. 4 (October 1987)

Meilinger, Phillip S., (ed.) *The Paths of Heaven: The Evolution of Airpower Theory* (Alabama: Air University Press, 1997)

Merrick, K.A., *Flights of the Forgotten: Special Duties Operations in*

World War Two (London: Arms and Armour Press, 1989)

Middlebrook, Martin & Chris Everitt, *The Bomber Command War Diaries: An Operational Reference Book, 1939-1945* (London: Viking, 1985)

Moran, Winston Churchill: *The Struggle for Survival, 1940-1965* (London: Constable, 1966)

Moyle, Harry, *The Hampden File* (Tonbridge: Air-Britain Publications, 1989)

Navias, Martin S., 'Terminating Conscription? The British National Service Controversy, 1955-56', in *Journal of Contemporary History*, vol. 24 (1989)

Norris, Geoffrey, 'The Night the Fuel Ran Out', in *Royal Air Force Flying Review*, vol. xiv, no. 3 (December 1958)

Norris, Geoffrey, *The Royal Flying Corps: A History* (London: Frederick Muller, 1965)

North, John, (ed.) *The Alexander Memoirs, 1940-1945* (London: Cassell, 1962)

Omissi, D., *Air Power and Colonial Control: The Royal Air Force, 1919-1939* (Manchester University Press, 1991)

Orange, Vincent, *Ensor's Endeavour* (London: Grub Street, 1994)

Orange, Vincent, *Tedder: Quietly in Command* (London: Frank Cass, 2004)

Orange, Vincent, *Park* (London: Grub Street, 2001)

Orpen, Neil, *Airlift to Warsaw: The Rising of 1944* (Norman: University of Oklahoma Press, 1984)

Oughton, James D., 'Coastal Command Aircraft, 1942-1992', in *RAF Coastal Command Yearbook* (RAF Fairford, Gloucester: IAT Publishing, 1992)

Oxford Dictionary of National Biography

Parton, James, *'Air Force Spoken Here': General Ira Eaker and The Command of the Air* (Bethesda, Maryland: Adler & Adler, 1986)

Parton, James, 'General Eaker, Creator of the Eighth Air Force', in *Air Power History* (Fall, 1992)

Parton, James, *History of Mediterranean Allied Air Forces* (unpublished)

Plowman, Jeffrey, 'The Battle for Florence', in *After The Battle*, no. 129 (2005)

Pope, Rex, 'British Demobilization after the Second World War', in *Journal of Contemporary History*, vol. 30 (1995)

Portal, C.F.A., 'Air Force Co-operation in Policing the Empire', in *RUSI Journal*, vol. 82, no. 526 (May 1937)

Price, Alfred, *Aircraft versus Submarine: The Evolution of the Anti-Submarine Aircraft, 1912 to 1972* (London: Kimber, 1973)

Probert, Henry, *Bomber Harris: His Life and Times* (London: Greenhill Books, 2001)

Probert, Henry, *High Commanders of the Royal Air Force* (London: HMSO, 1991)

Rawlings, John D.R., (ed.) *The History of the Royal Air Force* (London: Temple Press, 1984)

Raleigh, Walter & H. A. Jones, *The War in the Air* (Oxford: Clarendon, 1922)

Report by the Supreme Allied Commander Mediterranean to the Combined Chiefs of Staff on Greece, December 12th 1944 to May 9th 1945 (London: HMSO, 1949)

Ritchie, Sebastian, *Industry and Air Power: The Expansion of British Aircraft Production, 1935-1941* (London: Frank Cass, 1997)

Ritchie, Sebastian, 'A Political Intrigue against the CAS: The Downfall of ACM Sir Cyril Newall', in *War and Peace*, vol. 16, no. 1 (May 1998)

Roberts, J.M., *A History of Europe* (Oxford: Helicon Publishing, 1996)

Roman, P.J., 'Curtis LeMay and the Origins of NATO Atomic Targeting', in *Journal of Strategic Studies*, vol. 16, no. 1 (March 1993)

Roman, P.J., 'Strategic Bombers over the Missile Horizon, 1957-1963', in *Journal of Strategic Studies*, vol. 18, no. 1 (March 1995)

Roskill, S.W., *The War at Sea, 1939-1945* (London: HMSO, 1956)

Schnabel, J.F., & R. J. Watson, *The Joint Chiefs of Staff and National Policy, vol. iii, 1950-1: The Korean War, Part One* (Washington DC: Office of the Chairman of the Joint Chiefs of Staff, 1998)

Slessor, John, *Integration of the Services within the new Defence Organization*, unpublished paper, August 4th 1964

Slessor, John. 'Recollections of the Air Ministry, 1923 to 1953', in *Air Ministry Society Journal*, February 21st 1964

Slessor, John, *Strategy for the West* (London: Cassell, 1954)

Slessor, John, *The Central Blue: Recollections and Reflections* (London: Cassell, 1956)

Slessor, John, *The Great Deterrent* (London: Cassell, 1957)

Slessor, John, Rear-Admiral Sir Anthony Buzzard and Richard Lowenthal, 'The H-Bomb: Massive Retaliation or Graduated Deterrence?' in *International Affairs*, vol. 32, no. 2 (April 1956)

Slessor, John, *These Remain: A Personal Anthology: Memories of Flying, Fighting and Field Sports* (London: Michael Joseph, 1969)

Slessor, John, 'Trenchard and the Birth of the Royal Air Force, 1918', *RUSI Journal*, August 1942

Slessor, John, *Weather and War*, address to the Royal Meteorological Society in London, October 17th 1951

Slessor, John, *What Price Co-existence? A Policy for the Western Alliance* (London: Cassell, 1962)

Slessor, John 'When Soldiering Was Really Soldiering: Aldershot, 1925-1928', in *Time & Tide*, 1956

Smart, C.D., 'The Diary of Lieut. C. D. Smart, No. 5 Sqdn., RFC', *Journal of the Society of World War 1 Aero Historians*, vol. 10, no. 1 (Spring 1969)

Smith, C., *Dive Bomber!* (Annapolis, Maryland: Naval Institute Press, 1982)

Smith, Malcolm, 'The Royal Air Force, Air Power and British Foreign Policy, 1932-37', in *Journal of Contemporary History*, vol. 12 (1977)

Smith, R. Harris, *OSS: The Secret History of America's First Central Intelligence Agency* (Los Angeles: University of California Press, 1972)

Sterne Randall, Willard, 'The Other D-Day', in *Military History Quarterly*, vol. 6, no. 3 (Spring 1994)

Sutton, H.T., *Raiders Approach!: The Fighting Tradition of Royal Air Force Station Hornchurch and Sutton's Farm* (Aldershot: Gale & Polson, 1956)

Taylor, H.A., 'Flying the Consolidated Liberator', in *Air Enthusiast* (February 1972)

Taylor, John W.R., 'The Crow and the Mole', in *RAF Quarterly*, vol. xx (January 1949)

Tedder, Arthur, *With Prejudice: The War Memoirs of Marshal of the Royal Air Force Lord Tedder, GCB* (London: Cassell, 1966)

Terraine, John, *Business in Great Waters: The U-boat Wars, 1916-1945* (London: Leo Cooper, 1989)

Terraine, John, 'Lessons of Air Warfare', in *RUSI Journal*, vol. 137, no. 4 (August 1992)

Terraine, John, *The Right of the Line: The Royal Air Force in the European War, 1939-1945* (London: Hodder & Stoughton, l985)

Wark, Wesley K., 'British Intelligence and Small Wars in the 1930s', in *Intelligence and National Security*, vol. 2, no. 4 (October 1987)

Wark, Wesley K., 'British Intelligence on the German Air Force and Aircraft Industry, 1933-1939', in *Historical Journal*, vol. 25, no. 3 (1982)

Wark, Wesley K., *The Ultimate Enemy: British Intelligence and Nazi Germany, 1933-1939* (London: I. B. Tauris, 1985)

Weinberg, Gerhard L., *A World at Arms: A Global History of World War II* (Cambridge University Press, 1994)

Whitehill, Walter Muir, *Dictionary of American Biography: Supplement 6, 1956-1960* (New York: Charles Scribner's Sons, 1980)

Whittam, J.R., 'Drawing the Line: Britain and the Emergence of the Trieste Question, January 1941-May 1945', in *English Historical Review* (April 1991)

Wilson, A.N., *After the Victorians: 1901-1953* (London: Hutchinson, 2005)

Wingate, Reginald, 'Despatch to the Secretary of State for War': *Second Supplement to the London Gazette*, London, October 24th 1916, pp. 10370, 10371.

Winterbotham, F.W., *The Nazi Connection* (London: Weidenfeld & Nicolson, 1978)

Wright, Peter, 'Khaki and Blue: The Eight Years' Service of Charles J. Beeks, DFM', *Cross & Cockade*, vol. 8, no. 1 (Spring, 1977)

Newspapers and Magazines

The Times, October 15th 1850
The Times, June 11th 1884
The Times, March 3rd 1900
The London Gazette, January 1st 1917
The Times, March 25th 1925
The Times, July 5th 1926
Flight, July 8th 1926
The Times, October 17th 1931
The Times, October 22nd 1931
The Times, June 3rd 1935
The Times, October 16th 1936
Flight, December 17th 1936
The Times, March 25th 1939
The Times, September 14th 1939
The Times, August 21st 1943
Flight, November 1st 1945
The Times, August 28th 1946
Flight, July 3rd 1947
The Times, October 1st 1947
Flight, January 29th 1948
The Times, June 9th 1948
The Times, June 18th 1948
Flight, July 15th 1948
The Times, September 12th 1949
The Times, February 10th 1950
The Times, April 28th 1950
The Times, July 8th 1950
The Times, July 21st 1950
The Times, August 12th 1950
The Times, October 25th 1950
The Times, December 13th 1950
The Times, December 14th 1950
The Times, December 18th 1950
The Times, April 5th 1951
The Times, April 19th 1951
The Times, April 20th 1951
The Times, May 1st 1951
The Times, June 1st 1951
The Times, June 8th 1951

The Times. June 12th 1951
The Times, July 27th 1951
The Times, August 7th 1951
The Times, August 22nd 1951
The Times, September 10th 1951
The Times, October 15th 1951
Flight, October 26th 1951
The Times, November 19th 1951
The Times, February 13th 1952
The Times, March 14th 1952
The Times, March 24th 1952
The Times, April 28th 1952
The Times, May 23rd 1952
The Times, June 9th 1952
The Times, June 19th 1952
The Times, July 10th 1952
The Times, July 14th 1952
The Times, September 13th 1952
The Times, November 13th 1952
The Times, December 18th 1952
The Times, January 7th 1953
The Times, February 12th 1953
The Times, March 2nd 1953
The Times, March 7th 1953
The Times, May 26th 1953
The Times, June 8th 1953
The Times, July 4th 1953
The Times, July 8th 1953
The Times, July 20th 1953
The Times, August 26th 1953
The Times, September 30th 1953
The Times, October 5th 1953
The Times, October 9th 1953
Flight, October 23rd 1953
The Times, February 15th 1954
Flight, June 4th 1954
The Times, June 10th 1954
The Times, August 6th 1954
The Times, October 25th 1954
The Times, November 12th 1954
Aeroplane, January 28th 1955
The Times, January 29th 1955
The Times, July 13th 1955
The Times, September 20th 1955
The Times, January 18th 1956

The Times, February 11th 1956
The Times, April 15th 1956
The Times, May 17th 1956
The Times, August 1st 1956
The Times, August 11th 1956
The Times, October 15th 1956
The Times, November 1st 1956
The Times, November 10th 1956
The Times, December 11th 1956
The Times, April 11th 1957
The Times, April 20th 1957
The Times, April 23rd 1957
The Times, April 30th 1957
The Times, August 24th 1957
The Times, September 19th 1957
The Times, April 21st 1959
The Times, August 29th 1959
The Times, September 3rd 1959
The Times, September 9th 1959
The Times, February 1st 1960
The Times, May 23rd 1960
The Times, February 22nd 1962
The Times, June 2nd 1962
The Times, June 28th 1962
The Times, February 6th 1963
The Times Supplement on British Aviation, June 6th 1963
The Times, September 18th 1963
The Times, May 15th 1964
The Times, November 6th 1964
The Times, June 10th 1965
The Sunday Times, October 31st 1965
The Times, November 1st 1965
The Times, February 26th 1966
The Times, March 2nd 1966
The Times, March 3rd 1966
The Times, March 8th 1966
Punch, March 13th 1968
Flight International, May 22nd 1969
The Times, September 16th 1970
The Times, October 13th 1970
The Times, October 14th 1970
The Times, November 27th 1971
The Times, February 9th 1974
The Times, July 18th 1974
The Times, September 15th 1976

The Times, December 20th 1977
The Times, November 19th 1979
The Times, April 2nd 1993
The Times, April 3rd 1993
The Times, April 6th 1993
Times Literary Supplement, February 23rd 2001
The Daily Telegraph, March 17th 2004
International Herald Tribune, August 7th-8th 2004

Papers

AIR 2/3222	AIR 75/26	AIR 75/61
AIR 8/1701	AIR 75/34	AIR 75/62
AIR 9/84	AIR 75/40	AIR 75/66
AIR 19/185	AIR 75/43	AIR 75/67
AIR 64/67	AIR 75/44	AIR 75/68
AIR 75/5	AIR 75/45	AIR 75/69
AIR 75/10	AIR 75/46	AIR 75/71
AIR 75/11	AIR 75/47	AIR 75/74
AIR 75/12	AIR 75/48	AIR 75/82
AIR 75/14	AIR 75/52	AIR 75/85
AIR 75/17	AIR 75/53	AIR 75/93
AIR 75/19	AIR 75/54	AIR 75/100
AIR 75/20	AIR 75/55	AIR 75/104
AIR 75/23	AIR 75/58	AIR 75/106
AIR 75/24	AIR 75/59	
AIR 75/25	AIR 75/60	

Beaverbrook Papers, House of Lords Record Office, London
Douglas Papers, Imperial War Museum, London
Eaker Papers, Library of Congress, Washington DC
Montgomery Papers, Imperial War Museum, London
Portal Papers, August 9th 1944, Box D, Folder 111
Portal Papers, September 12th 1944, Box D, File 6
Portal Papers, November 26th 1944, Box D, Folder 5, Item 19
Portal Papers, June 20th 1945, Box D, File 6

PREM documents are held in the British National Archives, Kew, London, formerly the Public Record Office.

PREM 3/14/3	PREM 3/246/4
PREM 3/15	PREM 3/475/6
PREM 3/212/4	PREM 3/483/1

Slessor Family Papers kindly made available to me by Sir John's son, Group Captain John Slessor.

INDEX

284

Cromwell's Ironsides, 60
Cunningham, Adm Lord (Andrew), 154
Cunningham Adm Sir John, 167, 169
Cyprus, 264
Czechs/Czechoslovakia, 54, 63, 84, 122,
    231

D
Dakar, 133
Dalmatian coast, 37, 152
Damaskinos, Archbishop, 169
Danube river, 150, 153
Darfur, 11-12, 19
Dartmouth, 253
Daughters of the Revolution, 132
Davidson, Sir Alexander, 205
Davies, Norman, 160n, 163, 165
Deakin, Sir William, 152
Dean, Sir Maurice, 99, 123
De Gaulle, President Charles, 256, 259-60,
    270
Delaney, Rose, 30
Delhi, 13, 42, 236
De L'Isle & Dudley, Lord, VC, 210, 216
Delville Wood, 269
Denikin, LG Anton Ivanovich, 24
Denmark, 69-70, 223
Dervishes, 12
Desert Air Force, 151, 155
D'Este, Carlo, 139, 145
Dewey, Thomas, 215
Diadem Operation, 147-9
Dickson, Sir Pierson, 213, 245
Dickson, MRAF Sir William, 178, 193,
    216, 242, 245-6, 248, 253
Dieppe, 96
Dill, FM Sir John, 35, 96
Dinar, Sultan Ali, 11-12
Dinaric Alps, 154
Doenitz, Grand Adm Karl, 103-4, 111-2,
    116-7, 121-2, 180
Donovan, BG William J., 73, 76, 79, 138,
    153
Douglas, James, 240
Douglas, MRAF Lord (Sholto), 28, 65,
    101-2, 123
Douhet, Giulio, 29, 131
Dowding, ACM Lord, 63-6, 77
Dragoon Operation, *see* Anvil Operation
Druid's Lodge, 24
Drvar, 154
Dulles, John Foster, 212, 215, 222, 240,
    242-5
Dundas, GC Hugh, 216
Dunkirk evacuation, 71-2, 97
Durston, AM Sir Albert, 102, 104, 113
Durston, WC Cecil, 30
Dutch, *see* Netherlands

E
E-boats, 107, 110, 118
Eaker, Gen Ira C., 75, 95, 123, 129-31,
    133-4, 136-42, 144-9, 153-4, 171,
    173; post-
WW2, 198, 208, 219, 224, 250, 270-1
East Africa, 131
Edelsten, R/Adm J. H., 110
Eden, Sir Anthony, 158, 164, 167, 169,
    211, 239-48, 251
EDES, Greece, 167
Edinburgh, 111, 212, 223
Edward VIII, King, 43
Egypt/Egyptians, 19, 174, 179, 211, 225-6,
    240-7, 249
Eire, 62
Eisenhower, Gen Dwight D., 92, 115, 122,
    124-6, 134, 142, 149-50; as
    President, 194-5, 201-6, 212-3, 215,
    224, 232, 239-47, 254
El Alamein, battle of, 122, 201
ELAS/EAM, Greece, 166-70
Elbe estuary, 88
Elgar, Sir Edward, 15
Eliot, George Fielding, 200, 240
Elizabeth II, Queen, 125
Ellington, MRAF Sir Edward, 32, 63-4,
    127, 208
Elliot, ACM Sir William, 140, 154-7, 159,
    182, 194, 197-8, 245
Ellwood, AM Sir Aubrey, 110, 117
Elmhirst, AM Sir Thomas, 27
Elworthy, MRAF Lord, 263-4, 266
Embry, ACM Sir Basil, 86, 195, 218, 223
English Electric, 261
Enigma machine, *see* Bletchley Park
Ensor, WC Mick, 102-5, 107, 211
Epirus, 171
Epsom Downs, 39, 44
Eton, headmaster of, 197
European Union, 163
European Youth Conference, 223
Everest, Mount, 222-3
Evill, Sir Douglas (Strath), 28, 59, 91, 135
Expansion schemes, 52-4

F
Falklands War, 212
Far East Air Force, 210
Farnborough, 18, 29, 37, 201, 269
Farouk, King of Egypt, 234
Fasher, El, 11
Fedden, Sir Roy, 53
Feisal, King of Iraq, 153, 245
Fellowes, Maj Cuthbert, 30
Fellowes, R/Adm Sir Thomas, 30
Ferris, John, 27
Finer, Herbert, 239
Finland, 68, 149
Firth of Forth, 110

N

NAAFI (Navy, Army & Air Force Institute), 186

Naples, 131, 167, 169, 233

Napoleonic Wars, 249

Nash, Frank, 240

Nasser, Gamal Abdul, 234, 239, 241-4, 246-7, 249, 261-2

Nassau, 260, 262-3

National Service, 182-3, 199, 202, 212, 252

NATO (North Atlantic Treaty Organization), 12, 194, 196, 201-3, 205, 208, 210, 212-3, 215, 217-8, 222-3, 225-6, 228, 231-4, 238, 243, 252, 256-9, 263-4, 270

Navies:
Argentine, 212
Canadian, 110-4, 123
German, 70, 89, 100, 103, 111, 117-8, 127, 179-80; post-WW2, 225
Italian, 127
Royal, 61, 72, 77, 88-9, 92, 96, 99-100, 108-9, 111, 116, 118-9, 124-6, 134, 167, 178-80; post-WW2, 198, 211, 214, 224-5, 227, 229, 234, 236, 252-4, 260, 263-4, 266, 269
Soviet, 234
US, 112-4, 116, 123-5, 128, 180, 190; post-WW2, 198, 201, 233-4

Navy League, 222, 229

Neguib, Gen Mohamed, 240-1

Nelson, Adm Lord, 227

Nesbit, Roy Conyers, 120

Netheravon, 25

Netherlands, 72, 93, 110, 119, 197, 202, 222

Netherlands West Indies, 112

New York, 56, 74, 76, 113, 200, 215, 238, 244-5, 250, 252

New Zealand/ers, 67, 122

Newall, MRAF Lord, 27-8, 43, 52-3, 55-7, 59, 63-8, 73, 100, 194

Newfoundland, 110

Newspapers/journals:
Daily Express, 216
Daily Mirror (New York), 133
Daily Telegraph, 12, 132
Evening Standard, 168
Flight, 30
Flight International, 268
Foreign Affairs, 252
Fortune, 76
International Affairs, 223
Les Ailes, 217
New York Times, 244
Punch, 267-8
Reporter (New York), 231
Royal Artillery Journal, 22

Saturday Evening Post, 217

The Times, 12, 14, 30, 39, 42, 47, 132, 143, 162, 171, 198, 202, 206, 211-2, 216, 219, 222-3, 227, 239, 242-3, 247, 255, 259-61, 270

Nieuport, 71

Nile river, 241

Nixon, President Richard M., 255

Noel-Baker, Lord, 126, 185, 187, 258

Nore Command, 119

Normandy, *see* Overlord Operation

Norstad, Gen Lauris, 132, 142, 203-5, 216-7, 223, 233

North, Maj John, 140

Northolt, 19, 243

Northwood, 101-2, 104-5, 108, 114, 116, 123, 129

North Africa, 83, 134, 136-7, 151, 179

North Sea, 117, 120, 233

North-West African Air Forces, 133

North-West Frontier (India), 15, 25-6, 34-5, 41, 237

Norway/Norwegians, 68-70, 89, 93, 110, 117-8, 122, 223, 233

Nottingham, 82

Nuclear weapons, 47, 118, 188-9, 194-5, 197-8, 200, 206, 211-6, 223, 226-9, 231-4, 236, 247-8, 251-2, 255-7, 260

Nuffield, Lord, 14, 17

Nuri-es-Said, PM of Iraq, 245

O

OECD (Organization for Economic Co-operation and Development), 270

Okinawa, 265

Old Sarum, 48, 188, 211

Olivier, Laurence, 77

Omissi, David, 35

Orme, John, 74, 225

ORS (Operational Research Section), 105, 116, 119-20, 123

Osler, Revere, 16

Osler, Sir William, 16n

OSS (Office of Strategic Services), *see* CIA (Central Intelligence Agency)

Ostend, 71

Ottawa, 114, 202

Overlord Operation, 43, 52, 94, 97-8, 121-4, 129, 142-3, 149, 174, 187, 190, 203

Overy, Richard, 49

Owen, Roderic, 72

Owen, Sidney, 15

Oxford, 13-15, 30, 230; Christ Church, 13-14, 128; Dragon School, 14; Magdalen, 14; University College, 13; Chichele Chair, 174

P

Pace, Frank, 250, 252